Beyond Capitalist Realism
The politics, energetics, and aesthetics of degrowth

Samuel Alexander

Beyond Capitalist Realism:
The politics, energetics, and aesthetics of degrowth

Published by the Simplicity Institute, Melbourne,

www.simplicityinstitute.org

Cover image Cover image, detail of 'Roots for Seduction 2' by Maria Peña (www.maria-pena.com). Oil painting on canvas. 2020. 150 cm x 150 cm. Instagram: mariapena_art.

Typesetting and cover design by Sharon France (Looking Glass Press).

Typeset by in Hammersmith One and Stone Sans

ISBN: 978-0-6488405-3-4 (paperback)
ISBN: 978-0-6488405-4-1 (ebook)

Acknowledgments

I'd like to begin by thanking Professor Brendan Gleeson and the Melbourne Sustainable Society Institute, University of Melbourne, for supporting my research and writing over the last seven years. It's been an immense privilege and an honour.

I'd also like to thank Antoinette Wilson for proofreading this book and Sharon France for typesetting it and designing the cover. It has been a delight to work with you both over so many projects. I owe special thanks to Maria Peña for generously allowing me to use a detail of her painting 'Roots for Seduction 2' on the cover (www.maria-pena.com).

This is a new collection of scholarly journal articles, book chapters, and essays that have been previously published in various forums. I gratefully acknowledge the original publications below and welcome this opportunity to republish them in this anthology. Some of these chapters were co-authored, as acknowledged below, and I'd like to thank my various collaborators for the shared intellectual journeys as these writing projects took form. I am a deeper and more refined thinker because of these collaborations.

Chapter One, originally published as 'Everything is thinkable, so what is to be done?' in *Arena Quarterly* no. 2 (Winter) 2020, pp 12–21, co-authored with Brendan Gleeson.

Chapter Two, originally published as 'Energy descent futures' in Richard Slaughter and Andy Hines (eds) *Knowledge Base of Future Studies 2020*, Chapter 29, pp 453–470, published by the Association of Professional Futurists and Foresight International, co-authored with Joshua Floyd.

Chapter Three, originally published as 'Post-capitalism by design not disaster' in *Ecological Citizen* 3 Sup. B, pp 13–21.

Chapter Four, a version to be published as 'Urban social movements and the degrowth transition: toward a grassroots theory of change' in the *Journal of Australian Political Economy* (in press), co-authored with Brendan Gleeson.

Chapter Five, originally published as 'The rebellion hypothesis: crisis, inaction, and the question of civil disobedience', revised postscript in Rupert Read and Samuel Alexander, *Extinction Rebellion: Insights from the Inside*, 2020, pp 162–186, Simplicity Institute, Melbourne.

Chapter Six, originally published as 'The political economy of deep decarbonization: tradeable energy quotas for energy descent futures' in *Energies* 13(17) 4304, 2020, co-authored with Joshua Floyd. DOI: 10.3390/en13174304

Chapter Seven, originally published as 'MMT, post-growth economics, and avoiding collapse' in Haydn Washington (ed.) *Ecological Economics: Solutions: for the Future*, 2020, Chapter 7, pp 139–162, co-authored with Stephen Williams.

Chapter Eight, originally published as 'Neighbourhoods that Work and the Walden Wage: how access to land plus a participation income could change the world' in Haydn Washington (ed.) *Ecological Economics: Solutions: for the Future*, Chapter 8, pp 163–188, co-authored with Alex Baumann.

Chapter Nine, originally published as 'The Simpler Way: envisioning a sustainable society in an age of limits' in *Real-World Economics Review* 87, pp 247–260, co-authored with Ted Trainer.

Chapter Ten, originally published as 'The search for freedom, sustainability, and economic security: Henry David Thoreau as tiny house pioneer' *Ethical Perspectives* 26(4), 2019, pp 559–582, co-authored with Heather Shearer.

Chapter Eleven, originally published as 'Bumps along the road of the Tiny House Movement: practitioner notes with critical reflections' in *Australian Planner* 2019, co-authored with Brendan Gleeson, Tom Coupe, Nick Matyevich, Rob Scott, and Fred Schultz DOI: 10.1080/07293682.2019.1634111

Chapter Twelve, originally published as 'What would a sufficiency economy look like?' in Matthew Ingleby and Samuel Randalls (eds) *Just Enough: The History, Culture and Politics of Sufficiency*, 2018, Ch 8, pp 117–134, Palgrave Macmillan, London.

Acknowledgements

Chapter Thirteen, originally published as 'Suburban practices of energy descent' *American Journal of Economics and Sociology* 79(3), pp 907–940, co-authored with Brendan Gleeson. This article was based on Chapter 5 of our book Degrowth in the Suburbs: A Radical Urban Imaginary, 2019, Palgrave, Singapore.

Chapter Fourteen, originally published as 'Degrowth as an "aesthetics of existence"', being the introduction to Samuel Alexander, *Art Against Empire: Toward an Aesthetics of Degrowth*, 2017, pp 1–33, Simplicity Institute, Melbourne. It was also published as Research Monograph with the Melbourne Sustainable Society Institute, 2017.

iii

Contents

Introduction

'Capitalist realism' is a term popularised by the late political theorist Mark Fisher in a provocative and unsettling book by that name (Fisher, 2009). The term implies that, ever since the fall of Soviet Communism in 1989, capitalism has been the only game in town; the only *realistic* system of production and distribution to structure globalised human society. Everything else is sheer utopianism in the pejorative sense – naïve dreaming of what can never be.

A phrase that has almost become a cliché, capitalist realism points to a failure of imagination, suggesting that it is now easier to imagine the end of the world than the end of capitalism. As one looks around the world today, the case for capitalist realism is, admittedly, disturbingly persuasive – as Fisher himself was the first to admit, even as he resisted it. It can tempt one to despair, for it often seems that there is in fact no realistic alternative to what we know today.

I confess, however, that I have never subscribed to capitalist realism, even though it is clear that capitalist realism is real. To say that it is real is to acknowledge the zeitgeist of the twenty-first century, one shared not only by neoliberal conservatives but also by most on the green-left who, despite a 'progressive' self-image, remain insidiously entrenched in capitalism's growth paradigm. In Fisher's words, there is 'a widespread sense that not only is capitalism the only viable political and economic system, but also that it is now impossible even to *imagine* a coherent alternative to it' (Fisher, 2009: 2). He describes this consciousness as a 'pervasive atmosphere' that conditions 'not only the production of culture but also the regulation of work and education, and acting as a kind of invisible barrier constraining thought and action' (Fisher, 2009: 16).

But here is the disturbing paradox of capitalist realism: just as the dominant cultural imagination has contracted into a singularity of vision – there is no alternative to capitalism! – the very system to which there is apparently no alternative shows itself to be in the process of self-destructing, like a cancer cell growing itself to death, killing its host.

In other words, capitalist realism is unrealistic, non-viable, a dead end – literally. The system is full of internal contradictions that the system cannot resolve, most notably the myth that through market mechanisms we can purchase and consume our way to sustainability. At the very hour when modern humanity has arrived at a self-aggrandising pinnacle of triumph – a global market economy promising riches for all – the skies have been darkened by the terrible spectres of ecological degradation and social decline and polarisation. The climate emergency is only one of these storm clouds, but this alone has the potential to lay waste to our species, as well as most others.

At the same time, vast oceans of debilitating poverty surround small oceans of unfathomable plenty, exposing the violent betrayal of the capitalist growth agenda, euphemistically (or just deceptively) known in public discourse as 'sustainable development'. This is a race leading towards an abyss, both enabled and entrenched by a sterility of imagination called capitalist realism. Fortunately – if that is the right word – capitalist realism 'can only be threatened if it is shown to be in some way inconsistent or untenable; if, that is to say, capitalism's ostensible "realism" turns out to be nothing of the sort' (Fisher, 2009: 16).

Of course, as history relates, capitalism is a dexterous beast, always shifting and changing with the times to exploit new opportunities for profit and in response to new challenges to its legitimacy. Nevertheless, the overlapping range of ecological, social, financial, and health crises indicate that, one way or another, coming years and decades will see growing pressure on the global capitalist system and the emergence of new political and economic forms and imaginaries. As crises intensify, a rupture of some form lies ahead, with overlapping ecological, technological, and social realties destined to disrupt (are already disrupting) the status quo. The pandemic is just one more nail in the coffin of late-stage capitalism. The human challenge is to ensure that the post-capitalist era emerges as far as possible through design rather than disaster, acknowledging all the while that self-determination is a luxury not available to everyone, particularly those facing the violence of and on capitalism's new frontiers.

This book – indeed, all my work – situates itself beyond capitalist realism. I reject capitalist realism as unrealistic, as an artefact of false consciousness; as false consciousness itself, blind to its ecocidal nature. Technology cannot save necro-capitalism from its cannibalistic nature nor will the so-called 'trickle down' effect resolve the deep injustices of its colonial and patriarchal past and present. And no Green New Deal will contribute much to a 'just transition' if it remains hooked onto an extractivist economics of growth which a finite planet evidently cannot bear.

Thinking and acting 'beyond capitalism' is not easy in a one-dimensional world that is increasingly homogenised, commodified, and standardised. Yet, breaking through the cracks of capitalism to *think* otherwise and *be* otherwise is more essential now than ever. In the words of Herman Hesse: 'Nothing is harder, yet nothing is more necessary, than to speak of certain things whose existence is neither demonstrable nor probable. The very fact that serious and conscientious people treat them as existing things brings them a step closer to existence and to the possibility of being born' (Hesse, 1980).

In that spirit I defend and explore an alternative 'degrowth' imaginary throughout this book. I do this as an act of defiant opposition to capitalist realism. In some small way, I hope that this might contribute to a growing sense of *capitalist unrealism* – to a conviction that viable and desirable alternatives to capitalism exist, alternatives that are in the process of being lived into existence by the collective rumbling of social movements that are bubbling everywhere under the surface of the existing order. What is clear is that humanity has not arrived at the 'end of history', as Francis Fukuyama famously declared – for history is always and everywhere just beginning.

◆ ◆ ◆

This is my fourth book of collected essays, each of which explores the same fundamental degrowth paradigm from a range of interdisciplinary or transdisciplinary angles. Put simply, degrowth means planned and equitable contraction of the energy and resource demands of the most 'developed' and overgrown economies. Given the magnitude of contraction needed to operate fairly within the sustainable carrying capacity of the planet, the degrowth movement recognises that this new paradigm of political economy is incompatible with ongoing GDP growth and thus incompatible with the growth imperatives inherent to the capitalist system. That is, the rich world cannot just embrace 'green growth' and hope to decouple economic growth sufficiently to achieve an ecological economy (Hickel and Kallis, 2019). Technology cannot save capitalism from itself. Efficiency without sufficiency is lost. Accordingly, if humanity makes it through the twenty-first century and is able to create a tolerably just and sustainable civilisation, our species will have been through a process of degrowth to a 'simpler way' economy.

Just because degrowth advocates reject the 'green growth' model of progress, this does not mean that degrowth can be defined simply as 'reduced GDP'. Everyone knows that GDP is a very poor measure of societal progress. That metric counts many environmental and social 'bads' as economic 'goods', and says nothing at all about many important societal goals and values, like equitable distribution, sustainability, or meaningful work. The degrowth movement certainly does not define its vision of a just and sustainable world according to the crude GDP accounting system, and it is unfortunate that simple-minded or confused commentators sometimes muddy the definition of degrowth by defining it incorrectly as reduced GDP. That may be a *consequence* of degrowth, but degrowth should never be *defined* in relation to a metric that is so badly flawed and misleading.

After all, *unplanned* economic contraction is already understood as recession, depression, or collapse, and nobody advocates for this because of all the well-known pernicious social effects that flow from it. Those effects include spiralling unemployment, economic insecurity and instability, and increased poverty. But if the energy and resource foundations of an economy are grossly in breach of humanity's safe operating space on this planet, and the decoupling strategy is failing to resolve the problems of ecological overshoot, then the only coherent response is to *plan* for the contraction or degrowth of those environmental demands and impacts. Thus degrowth is first and foremost a biophysical concept, with deep social, economic, and political implications.

From a social perspective, the degrowth paradigm holds that this phase of contraction, to be legitimate, must ensure that all people around the world – indeed, all species – have access to the things needed to flourish in harmony with Earth's biospheric limits. So there is an essential distributive element to the degrowth paradigm (both within nations and between them), not just an ecological one. Indeed, the distributive element is why degrowth is often described as involving a 'decolonisation of the imagination'. If this means anything it means the Global North allowing the nations of the Global South to develop or 'post-develop' according to their own conceptions of flourishing, not forced or coerced onto the industrial path by the dictates of capital. In short, degrowth means rejecting the rule and logics of capital and manifesting a heterogeneous economics of sufficiency. Further definitional content of degrowth is given throughout this book.

My first two volumes of collected essays, *Prosperous Descent* and *Sufficiency Economy*, were published in 2015, and the third volume, *Wild Democracy*, was published in 2017. I'm happy to be preparing this fourth volume in late 2020, which fills in some of the gaps and restates and updates some of the key perspectives. If this book whets your appetite for the theory and practice of degrowth, then please see the earlier volumes of collected essays too. Alternatively (or also), see my book *Degrowth in the Suburbs: A Radical Urban Imaginary*, co-authored with Brendan Gleeson. Readers will also find most of my work freely available online, with much of it posted at samuelalexander.info.

Rather than extend this introduction longer than necessary, let me now provide short overviews of the chapters that follow. As well as providing an insight into the themes of this anthology, the following summaries should allow readers to jump around the book according to interest, although the chapters have been ordered deliberately such that readers would be advised to read from front to back. There is some minimal (and deliberate) repetition of key perspectives in some chapters to ensure they can be read as 'stand-alone' chapters, although I hope this occasional restatement of ideas is useful, given that we live in an age of capitalist realism. As I have said, thinking beyond capitalist realism can be difficult, but I hope reading this book helps in that necessary endeavour as much as writing it did. I also acknowledge that this book is published in the midst of a global pandemic that has shaken capitalism to its core. In one sense this instability opens the imagination in new ways, so this moment is especially fertile for alternative, post-capitalist visions of progress and prosperity.

1. **Everything is thinkable, so what is to be done?** – This opening chapter is the only one written during the COVID-19 pandemic, so it serves as a suitable introduction to this collection by contextualising the book in the midst of this great disruption. Tragic though the pandemic is – and its impacts no doubt will endure for years – we need to remember that COVID-19 is a crisis within a broader ecological and humanitarian crisis. The social, economic, and political trauma caused by the pandemic, however, raises the prospect of an exit from capitalism.

This chapter reflects on this historic rupture, considers what a new degrowth mode of political economy might look like, while also acknowledging that the dominant powers seem primarily concerned about 'bouncing back' to business as usual. For so long we have been told that economies just cannot produce less, only more; that the type of economic contraction we have seen in response to the pandemic was not possible. And yet here it is, in real life. As French philosopher Bruno Latour recently commented: 'Next time, when ecologists are ridiculed because "the economy cannot be slowed down", they should remember that it can grind to a halt in a matter of weeks worldwide when it is urgent enough.'

2. **Energy descent futures** – This chapter examines the growth paradigm through the lens of energy. What might become of our carbon civilisation as finite fossil fuels deplete or as we voluntarily give them up in response to climate change? What would a post-carbon civilisation look like? The dominant energy narrative today tends to acknowledge the need to transition away from fossil fuels but assumes that alternative energy sources, such as renewables or nuclear power, will be able to replace the energy foundations of carbon civilisation without fundamentally reshaping the form of life we have become accustomed to in the most developed regions of the world. More specifically, it is assumed that post-carbon energy sources are consistent with a complex, globalised economy that is structurally designed or required to grow without limits. In short, it is widely assumed that energy will be even more abundant in the future than it is today.

In contrast to that cornucopian vision, the alternative energy narrative outlined in this chapter maintains that we should be preparing for futures not of energy abundance, but rather of reduced energy availability – futures in which viable ways of life are characterised by *energy sufficiency*. With respect to the most energy intensive societies, this means planning for what permaculture theorist and practitioner David Holmgren calls 'energy descent'. While acknowledging a range of uncertainties about how humanity's energy futures will unfold, the plausibility and even the likelihood of energy descent implies that planning and preparing for such futures is the most prudent course of action. This chapter presents an introduction to this marginalised energy narrative.

3. **Post-capitalism by design not disaster** – This chapter examines how we can proactively design the end of capitalism rather than simply wait for its collapse. Capitalism is unable to resolve its emerging crises, for capitalism cannot function without economic growth, yet for ecological reasons economic growth cannot continue. However, there is a coherent alternative political economy – the degrowth paradigm of planned economic contraction. Furthermore, various grassroots alternatives, suitably scaled up, could help to form this post-capitalist economy 'from below'. I am the first to admit that the dominant culture is not yet ready to embrace degrowth, given that consumer affluence and techno-optimism still lie at the heart of mainstream conceptions of the 'good life'. Nonetheless, it is important to keep alive radical ideas of what an eco-centric, post-capitalist economy could look like, for in a crisis, what today seems impossible or implausible can suddenly become possible and even probable. As an old book intones, 'Where there is no vision, the people perish.'

4. **Urban social movements and the degrowth transition: Toward a grassroots theory of change** – It is one thing to be convinced of the desirability of an alternative mode of economy; creating it, of course, is a different question. This chapter examines degrowth from the perspective of transition theory and practice. Much has been written on the 'why' and 'what' of degrowth; this analysis focuses more on the strategic question of 'how'. The specific interest lies in understanding which levers of power in society (e.g., the state, technology, capital, social movements, etc.) may be needed or available to drive a degrowth transition, and how those levers may reshape society, and in what ways, to initiate a degrowth process of planned economic contraction.

While addressing questions of transition and transformation, the further point of departure in this chapter is to look at degrowth through the lens of urban studies – and conversely, to look at urbanity through the lens of degrowth. It is argued that urban social movements will have to be primary organising forces of a degrowth transition, if it is to occur. After defending this grassroots theory of change, the analysis concludes by examining various urban social movements and explaining how they represent what, tentatively, could be considered the birth of a 'degrowth urbanity'.

5. **The rebellion hypothesis: Crisis, inaction, and the question of civil disobedience** – Social and political progress has always involved social movements opposing the existing system and other social movements building the new world(s) within the existing system. In this chapter I focus on Extinction Rebellion, the prominent activist mobilisation that erupted in the UK in 2018 and which was quickly globalised. Although the pandemic has functioned to keep most (but not all) mass mobilisations off the streets, we can expect Extinction Rebellion to burst back onto the scene as soon as the pandemic permits safe mobilisation. (Or is the greater danger *not* mobilising at once?)

    The defining feature of Extinction Rebellion is how it explicitly and unapologetically adopts practices of non-violent civil disobedience as a means of societal change. In adopting this method of peaceful resistance, Extinction Rebellion situates itself in esteemed traditions of social action, including the civil rights movement, the suffragette's movement, and Ghandi's Indian independence movement. This chapter examines civil disobedience in terms of legal and political philosophy and considers how and why Extinction Rebellion activists feel driven to practice grassroots politics in this way.

    In this chapter I also present what I call the 'rebellion hypothesis', which maintains that environmental activism is likely to expand in coming years and decades as the effects of climate change and environmental degradation are personally experienced by more and more people. As the costs of inaction rise, my hypothesis is that more people will experience psychological tipping points and become engaged in social movements, including movements like Extinction Rebellion. Given that one of the demands of Extinction Rebellion is swift decarbonisation of our economies, the question of how that might be achieved is considered in the next chapter.

6. **The political economy of deep decarbonisation: Tradeable Energy Quotas for energy descent futures** – This chapter reviews and analyses a decarbonisation policy called the Tradable Energy Quotas system (TEQs) developed by David Fleming. The TEQs system involves rationing fossil fuel energy use for a nation on the basis of either a contracting carbon emission budget or scarce fuel availability – or both simultaneously – distributing budgets equitably amongst energy-users. Entitlements can be traded to

incentivise demand reduction and to maximise efficient use of the limited entitlements.

This chapter situates this analysis in the context of Joseph Tainter's theory about the development and collapse of complex societies. Tainter argues that societies become more socio-politically and technologically 'complex' as they solve the problems they face – and that such complexification drives increased energy use. For a society to sustain itself, therefore, it must secure the energy needed to solve the range of societal problems that emerge. But what if, as a result of deep decarbonisation, there is less energy available in the future, not more? TEQs offers a practical means of managing energy descent futures. The policy can facilitate controlled reduction of socio-political complexity via processes of 'voluntary simplification' (the result being 'degrowth' or controlled contraction in the scale of the physical economy).

7. **Modern Monetary Theory, post-growth economics, and avoiding collapse** – One major reason preventing degrowth or post-growth economic policies from being embraced is the dominant macroeconomic paradigm that informs policy choices. Since at least the 1970s, the dominant paradigm has been neoclassical economics, which replaced Keynesianism. This chapter outlines a fast-emerging alternative macroeconomics called Modern Monetary Theory (MMT). Given that MMT attempts to describe how monetary systems work, rather than being a policy platform, it is neither inherently pro-growth nor post-growth, as they are policy positions for individual nations depending on their ideology and the size of their economies. However, in this chapter it is argued that MMT is the most accurate description available of the interplay of macroeconomic forces, and it should therefore be used in the formulation of policies, rather than the conventional, but flawed, neoclassical model.

The global crisis initiated by the COVID-19 pandemic has brought the currency-issuing capacity of governments into sharp focus, accelerating interest in MMT. When MMT is understood, post-growth policy options expand dramatically and become more viable, while the dominant neoclassical model is seen to be a kind of ideological straitjacket. Accordingly, MMT should be of interest to everyone concerned with sustainability – including degrowth and steady-state economists, who have, as a group, mostly neglected MMT. While this chapter may raise as many questions as it answers, the hope is that this brief overview provokes a broader discussion about MMT and the policies it can engender.

8. **'Neighbourhoods that Work' and the Walden Wage: How access to land and a participation income could change the world** – Although the degrowth and steady-state schools have no singular vision of the 'good society' or singular theory of transition, many argue that the transition to a just and sustainable world will have to be driven into existence primarily from the grassroots up, with individuals, households, and communities coming together to 'prefigure' a new post-growth society within the shell of the old. According to this broad theory of change, such prefigurative action, which is based on participatory democracy, is projected to filter upwards over time to change social, economic, and political structures in recognition of the systemic nature of the problems. From this perspective, social movements need to create the cultural conditions for structural change, and that structural change can then be a further driver for social change, representing a dynamic mode of society's transformation that relies on multiple movements, innovations, and policies for change (see Chapter Four).

    The privileging of grassroots or community-led action is mainly due to the widely shared belief that the ability or willingness of politicians or businesses to lead a degrowth transition in a neoliberal age is scarce to non-existent. The logic here is that there are just too many 'growth imperatives' built into the economy for us to expect political leaders, corporations, or existing institutions to initiate or facilitate a degrowth transition to a steady-state economy. Nevertheless, despite the coherency of these doubts about 'top down' political change and 'green businesses' leading the way, similar doubts can be levelled against any hope for a degrowth transition rising up from a socio-cultural groundswell.

    This chapter emphasises that this apparent paralysis in degrowth transition theory is owing, in part, to the growth imperatives of the dominant politico-economic order of global capitalism *specifically relating to land*, where ordinary people who are expected to lead the transition 'from below' are typically locked into a very long market commitment in order to buy or rent housing and keep a roof over their head. This structural obstacle to degrowth suggests that deep economic changes relating to land access and governance are needed to help facilitate a degrowth transition to a steady-state economy and empower true democratic agency for those who would subscribe to such a transition.

9. **The Simpler Way: Envisioning a sustainable society in an age of limits** – Although it is widely understood that the global economy is currently unsustainable, few people seem to understand how far beyond sustainable limits it is. Fewer still seem to grasp what it would take for the global population to live equitably within the sustainable carrying capacity of the planet. In this chapter it will be argued that these interconnected social and ecological problems cannot be solved unless we move toward an economics of sufficiency, which means, among other things, that rates of production, consumption, and resource use in rich countries must be dramatically reduced, probably by 80–90 per cent or more. These reductions cannot be achieved merely by 'greening production' through piecemeal efficiency improvements or technological innovation, and they cannot be achieved in a society that is governed by market forces or driven by the insatiable quest for material affluence or the limitless increase in GDP. In other words, a sustainable economy must be a post-growth and post-capitalist economy. But what does that actually mean?

In this chapter it is argued that the only way sustainability can be achieved is through a radical degrowth transition to a 'Simpler Way' society, which would be defined by low but sufficient material living standards, renewable energy, highly localised or 'bioregional' production, egalitarian approaches to wealth distribution, participatory democratic practices of self-governance, and major degrowth to a zero-growth economy. The argument is not that this transition is likely, just that it signifies the only way for human civilisation to operate viably on our finite planet. Fortunately, there are many social and ecological reasons to believe that this transition is in the interests of humanity, both rich and poor, but this requires reimagining the good life beyond consumer culture and embracing ways of living that are outwardly simple, but inwardly rich. This chapter seeks to provide more detail on this vision of a just and sustainable society and briefly highlight the implications this perspective has on questions of transition strategy.

10. **The search for freedom, sustainability, and economic security: Henry David Thoreau as tiny house pioneer** – In 1845, the pioneering environmentalist Henry David Thoreau left his hometown of Concord, Massachusetts, and went to live alone in the woods on the shores of Walden Pond. There he built himself a small cabin and thus initiated his two-year experiment in simple living, which he recorded in his masterpiece *Walden*. This chapter returns to Thoreau's celebrated story and examines the ethical and economic reasons that drove him to live as he did, with a particular focus on his philosophy and practice of housing.

    Drawing primarily from his own words in *Walden*, it will be shown that Thoreau built himself a tiny house as a practical response to grappling with questions of freedom, sustainability, and economic security. Furthermore, it will be argued that a strong case can be made that the contemporary tiny house movement – which purportedly had its genesis in the Pacific northwest of the USA in the late 1990s – is a modern reflection of Thoreauvian struggles, questions, motivations, and ideals, even as the world has changed dramatically. Based on quantitative and qualitative research, as well as reviewing other literature on tiny houses, it will be seen that the struggle for freedom, sustainability, and economic security lies at the heart of the tiny house movement today.

11. **Bumps along the road of the Tiny House Movement: Practitioner notes with critical reflections** – This chapter begins by sharing practical insights and learnings from tiny house builders, highlighting some promising approaches to construction, as well as some challenges faced by the emerging tiny house movement. The analysis also offers a conceptually driven appraisal of this potentially important new housing form that raises serious questions about planning and urban policy. The aim is to present a grounded review of the tiny house movement, and its wider policy resonances, rooted in an empirical review of current practice.

    After the empirical practice notes are presented, the article concludes by going beyond building, construction, and regulatory issues and offers some critical reflections on the promise and limitations of the tiny house movement. These intricacies and potential difficulties include frictions with wider housing and urban policies in Australia, especially those that have favoured transition to higher residential densities and which are themselves fraught with challenges, especially around social equity. In offering a sympathetic critique of tiny houses and asking some hard questions, this review and analysis seeks to present a richer and fuller understanding of the tiny house movement in a way that helps the movement progress and avoid unnecessary pitfalls.

12. **What would a sufficiency economy look like?** – After briefly summarising the 'limits to growth' position (which can be skipped if the reader is sufficiently familiar with it), this chapter highlights the radical implications of that critique by describing a 'sufficiency economy'. This alternative 'post-growth' economic model aims for a world in which everyone's basic material needs are modestly but sufficiently met, in an ecologically sustainable, highly localised, and socially equitable manner. It could be considered the end state of a successful degrowth transition. Once basic needs are met, a sufficiency economy would focus on promoting non-materialistic sources of wellbeing rather than endlessly pursuing material affluence. In other words, a sufficiency economy is one that is structured to promote and support what is often called 'simple living', 'voluntary simplicity', or 'the simpler way'. In a world of almost eight billion people, it is argued that a sufficiency economy is the only way humanity can flourish sustainably within the carrying capacity of Earth.

13. **Suburban practices of energy descent** – This chapter is predicated on the assumption that the cost of energy will rise in coming years and decades as the age of fossil energy abundance comes to an end. Given the close connection between energy and economic activity, it is also assumed that declining energy availability and affordability will lead to economic contraction and reduced material affluence. In overconsuming and overdeveloped nations, such resource and energy 'degrowth' is desirable and necessary from a sustainability perspective, provided it is planned for and managed in ways consistent with basic principles of distributive equity.

Working within that degrowth paradigm, this chapter examines how scarcer and more expensive energy may impact the suburban way of life and how households might prepare for this very plausible, but challenging, energy descent future. Energy demand management in suburbia is examined, so too is the question of how the limited energy needed to provide for essential household services can best be secured in an era of expensive energy and climate instability. After reviewing various energy practices, the need for an ethos of sufficiency, moderation, and radical frugality is highlighted, which is essential for building resilience in the face of forthcoming energy challenges and a harsher climate.

14. **Degrowth as an 'aesthetics of existence'** – In recent decades the 'limits to growth' position has received a great deal of attention, mostly from economic and ecological perspectives. More recently, the degrowth movement has begun contributing an important range of new political and sociological analyses, offering deeper insight into the alternative paradigm, evaluating transition strategies, policies, and obstacles, while also continuing to update and refine the ecological critique of growth economics in response to those who continue to fetishise growth. The purpose of this final chapter, however, is neither to review these existing literatures nor offer another ecological critique of growth, but to extend and deepen the understanding of degrowth by examining the concept and the movement from a perspective that has yet to receive any sustained attention – namely, aesthetics.

I highlight and examine the aesthetic dimensions of degrowth, in the hope that this reveals new and worthwhile insights about the meaning and potential of this emerging sustainability movement. Might the degrowth imperative demand not just a radical political and economic engagement with the structures and goals of our growth-orientated civilisation, but also an engagement and transformation of our aesthetic sensibilities, capacities, and practices? And what is the relationship between the aesthetic dimensions of degrowth and the various ecological, economic, political, and cultural dimensions? These questions motivate and shape this closing analysis, but they also shape the subtext of the whole book.

References

Fisher, M. 2009. *Capitalist Realism: Is There No Alternative?* Winchester: Zero Books.
Hesse, H. 1980. *Magister Ludi: The Glass Bead Game.* New York: Bantam Books.
Hickel, J. and Kallis, G. 2019. 'Is Green Growth Possible?'. *New Political Economy.*
    DOI: 10.1080/13563467.2019.1598964.

Chapter I

Everything is thinkable, so what is to be done?[1]

There is no way to begin this essay, at this time, other than by acknowledging the remarkable, mind-bending moment in which we write these words. It is a time of pandemic, one destined to shape the future of human civilisation for years, if not decades ahead. In Australia, the economy has all but shut down, with little open for business besides medical centres and hospitals, supermarkets and food outlets, and a very select number of other essential services. Against every ideological bone in its body, our conservative government has announced unprecedented stimulus packages, to avoid masses of people in our affluent nation from falling into destitution. The Coalition's 'jobs and growth' mantra now seems terribly outdated in these post-normal times, a quaint reminder of when the economic engine was turning.

Because so many people have lost their livelihoods, banks have had to freeze mortgage repayments for six months and rental evictions are currently prohibited. The national and state borders have been closed, and public gatherings of more than two people are banned. Someone in New South Wales recently was fined for eating a kebab on a park bench. All of this was unthinkable a few months ago. Today the curtailment of individual liberties is the new normal. Citizens endure home detention, consumers face rationing, workers accept state subsidies. Homo economicus is frozen like a bug in amber. Next we'll be queuing for cabbages.

This is the stuff typically reserved for dystopian fiction, not real life, but many other nations around the world are in a similar position to Australia, with more destined to follow as the COVID-19 virus continues its extraordinary disruption. As we write, the date on the computer says 1 April, usually a time for jokes and pranks. We hesitate for a moment: is this for real? Surely someone is playing us for fools. But this is no joke. We are at what seems to be the beginning of a turbulent period whose duration is impossible to forecast. We certainly won't pretend to fully understand what is happening,

---

1 Originally published in *Arena Quarterly* No. 2 (Winter) 2020, pp. 12–21, co-authored with Brendan Gleeson.

and none of us can foresee how this crisis will unfold and what changes it will bring to the world, including its political economy, which for decades has been firmly framed by the diktat of neoliberal globalisation.

For all we know we are writing from within a relative calm that could yet prove to be the eye of an even more transformative hurricane. What if the virus mutates and comes back with a vengeance? What yet lies in store for the so-called 'developing world'? Will the 'old world' (the pre-crisis order already seems strangely distant) simply 'snap back', as willed by one of its chief spruikers, Prime Minister Scott Morrison? It is a time of promise and potential, but also great risk. Apparently, workers and businesses will have to accept the cessation of state support in six months, and the clock's already ticking. Good political luck with that! The point is, though, that this is already looking like a time of radical opening in thought and action. Even the neoliberals are shifting ground and rhetoric. For now, all we can do is nod approvingly at the words degrowth scholar Jason Hickel recently cast out into the Twitterverse: 'Capitalist realism is over. Everything is thinkable.' Indeed it is.

A crisis within a crisis

Utterly tragic though the pandemic is – and it is not over yet – we need to remember that COVID-19 is a crisis within a broader ecological and humanitarian crisis. In short, it is a crisis of the political economic order and all that depends on it (and endures and suffers from it). An insouciant Promethean neoliberalism has been made to suffer what Engels memorably described as the revenge of nature, in this case the terrible furies of a virus that, despite all crypto-racist urgings about its Chinese origins, can only be regarded as a reminder that humans are inseparable from a wider ecology that supports them and gives them life. It is a lesson in humility, a reminder that there are many things we cannot control, try as we might to force nature to bend to our will.

And what a visiting season nature has imposed on us in recent times. It was only months ago that Australia was ablaze, suffering a devastating fire season, drawing international attention, owing to conditions that were exacerbated by global heating. It is estimated that over one billion animals perished in the furnaces – one billion! Who has the emotional capacity to understand that statistic? And what does next summer portend for our shared Anthropocene?

In the sudden new COVID order, mourners are restricted in number at funerals. This extends by analogy to the many other environmental deaths under way, attention to which has been smothered by the latest crisis. Who is currently permitted by the global media and political priority to mourn the grinding loss of planetary ecology? As we write, the Barrier Reef is suffering yet another seemingly terminal bleaching event. The last great earthly forests in Siberia and Brazil are being remorselessly hacked away toward some kind of deathly tipping point. Increasingly there is talk of a Sixth Mass Extinction, while we recall the haunting phrase from James Lovelock that the face of Gaia is vanishing. The 'COVID erasure' of the many dying planetary and regional ecologies speaks a great deal about the current historical political economy that locks us into the treadmill of the present, refusing all consideration of consequence and legacy. And here we are again, with nature visiting revenge in a manner that commands the attention of the dumb beast of neoliberalism by attacking its innards: free trade, consumer sovereignty, land rent and – let's call it out – the ability of capitalism to extract surplus value, always an embodied treasure, from disease-threatened populations.

If there is one thing the coronavirus shows, it is that collective entities – in this historical moment, neoliberal states and their civil societies – really can act as if the house is on fire when we feel it is urgent enough. Therein, however, lies the catch: when we feel it is urgent enough. And, of course, the limits of action are now asserted in the rhetoric of the 'snap back' or 'bounce back'. Contemporary states, recently assayed and reframed by conservative populism (certainly in the Anglophone world), continue to refuse to acknowledge that climate change, species extinction, topsoil erosion, deforestation, pollution, resource depletion, population, poverty, and inequality are real problems of equal or greater urgency.

The morbid political economy of late capitalism, not scientific uncertainty, is to blame for this great caesura in human consciousness. The world knew enough about the science of climate change in 1988 to establish the Intergovernmental Panel on Climate Change (IPCC). And yet last year, over thirty years after this scientific body was established to warn and guide us, carbon emissions continued to rise. But the growth machine and its vassals, notably the Murdoch-dominated Anglophone media, continued to ignore the science and in recent years to actively attack it. Australia's increasingly plagued ecology – unprecedented droughts and bushfires and now the pandemic – have shaken the ramparts of denial, but the forces of reaction, by their very name, are always primed to restore the cause of Promethean capitalism. For now, however, they cannot eschew the widely felt sense that something epochal is under way.

The end of Capitalism – or merely its suspension?

The social, economic, and political trauma caused by the pandemic raises the prospect of an exit from capitalism, about which, to be sure, there has been prolonged speculation and dispute, but which may finally be under way, or is at least prefigured in the current disruptions the virus has invited onto the global stage. The crises of care that this pandemic manifests – both of people and planet – are not new, but they have been highlighted by it, the contradictions deepening and increasingly resistant to resolution within the existing order. There will be no vaccines for these maladies of accumulation that invite death and renewal, no healing of the sickened beast.

This consideration coincides with the dawn of the global urban age and rapid, hypertrophic urbanisation in many parts of the world. Certainly the increasing densification of urban life offers a breeding ground for viruses such as COVID-19 – not itself a knockdown case against urban densification, but a further word of warning against any casual celebration of the 'compact city'. The seemingly paradoxical intersection between these two simultaneous trends – massive system disintegration and vast physical agglomeration – is worth thoughtful consideration.

The prospects for this grand exit are being debated at the levels of meta-theory and observation: Slavoj Žižek in philosophy, Wolfgang Streeck in political economy, Rebecca Solnit and Terry Eagleton in cultural studies and, closer to disciplinary home, David Harvey and J.K. Gibson-Graham. All such castings insist upon a mortal, if perhaps not yet morbid, capitalism – they face the behemoths of conventional wisdom that avow faith in system immortality. Capitalism has shown time and time again that it is a dexterous creature, able to twist and turn in hope of avoiding any fatal attacks on its legitimacy and longevity. Indeed, it may not be done quite yet, although its condition is terminal. But the evidence of capitalism's chronic instability and unsustainability is provided in the natural and social sciences (with the dishonourable exception of mainstream economics), and the humanities, all of which document a series of interlocking deadlocks and defaults at rising spatial scales that manifest as planetary crisis.

Even many on the Left who have traditionally taken the mortal not morbid view of contemporary capitalism – for example, David Harvey – are now persuaded that the system faces seemingly insurmountable contradictions that will force its retrenchment. Similarly, Streeck in his recent writings, notably *Buying Time* and *How Will Capitalism End?*, essays 'five worsening disorders for which no cure is at hand: declining growth, oligarchy, starvation of the public sphere, corruption and international anarchy'. Although political ecology doesn't feature strongly in Streeck's work, he acknowledges that global warming and biospheric collapse are certain to intensify these terminal disorders. He believes the post-Second World War 'shotgun marriage of capitalism and democracy' is heading for divorce and on very bad terms for the latter. In this time of virus management a creeping authoritarianism is certainly evident – a dangerous but perhaps necessary intervention that must be retracted the moment its expediency has passed. But neither Streeck nor Harvey offers even a sketch outline for what dispensation is likely to replace capitalism as it continues its catabolic collapse.

What can we expect during the period of system retrenchment? Streeck writes: 'On the basis of capitalism's recent historical record...a long and painful period of cumulative decay: of intensifying frictions, of fragility and uncertainty, and of a steady succession of "normal accidents"'. In short, a period of intensifying and transformative violence.

Now the planetary force of urbanisation itself is a central circuit of accumulation, generating vast new forms of wealth and debt, as well as driving new patterns of urban inequity and vulnerability. Thus, on closer inspection, we might say that colossal urbanisation, hailed in the mainstream as a new engine of human (and capitalistic) prospect, betrays many of the crises, perturbations and failings observed at the system scale. Of real interest is how the hollowed-out state can manage these mighty, sputtering machines that are said to be central to human prospect. We disagree with the cheerful interpretations of this by popular urbanists. The Australian urbanist Elizabeth Farrelly, for example, in her 2008 book *Blubberland*, intoned that 'Manhattan – or something like it – is the greenest city on earth'. We doubt that this soaring palace of globally mined wealth should ever be described this way. But not even green urbanism can save the metropolitan citadels from the virus: their poorer inhabitants are bearing the brunt of the rampage. And the question of density, of humans and buildings, is raised, if not answered, by the crisis. Some dense cities – not New York, not London – have managed well so far. We fear, however, for the consequences of Australia's market-driven vertical urban sprawl of recent decades, whole swathes of our cities remade to the meanest of specifications, with little space for healthy living.

Such new conditions manifest in rapidly evolving political and material crises in shelter, circulation, health, and ecology that vex and threaten state capacity, hollowed out by decades of neoliberal rescoping and withdrawal. The current situation of the United States is a stark warning to all other nations that, before the virus, were diving ever more deeply into neoliberal ideology and practice. Today the United States is the richest nation on the planet...and at the same time is accumulating the highest death count from COVID-19. On the one hand the virus is the great leveller, reminding us that rich nations and world leaders are as susceptible to the laws of biology as the rest. On the other hand, as always, it will be the poor who suffer more and whose interests will be subjugated to others' whenever necessary in order to advance the interests of elites and maintain the system that serves them for a while longer yet.

Clearly, the long grey night of disorder that the 'morticians' believe we have already entered, and which seems more and more apparent as liberal democracy dims everywhere, will not be a simple or swift slide into chaos. Authority will surely emerge to stem social and natural disorders and restabilise the political economy. As noted above, we can see this playing out now as governments intervene and manage the economy in unprecedented ways, not to begin building a new world but to do everything possible, it seems, to resuscitate the old one. Further, the urban resilience project, freighted with instincts to enclose and defend, may prove to be a 'practice swing' by cities and concerned corporates at what may evolve into a new state securitisation of increasingly unmanageable cities. The 'climate emergency' alone has the power to overwhelm existing capacities to manage urban systems in any setting we can think of. There are insufficient capacities in the withered liberal-democratic state to counter, let alone prevent, heat stress, resource disruption and collapse, new disease pathologies, sudden panicked intrusions and extrusions of populations driven by ever more intense and frequent calamities... The list continues and may have no end.

In any case, these disruptions call forth new diagnoses and treatments that were not developed as modern state capacities. The rousing of authority and force for new state action, especially in cities, is in part already manifest. We may discern in these stirrings a new state form, that of pure corporate authority, which could represent another, perhaps final, attempt to 'buy time' (Streeck) in the face of system collapse.

Can we equitably contract the economy for environmental reasons?

The question that emerges, then, is: if capitalism is feeding off itself, like a snake eating its own tail, what comes next? This is no tired retreat into old conversations about state socialism or the 'third way'. A range of ecological, social, and financial contradictions indicate that, one way or another, coming months and years will see growing pressure on the global capitalist system and the emergence of new political and economic forms and imaginaries. As crises deepen and intensify, a further descent of some form is under way, with new ecological, technological, and social realities destined to disrupt (are already disrupting) the status quo. The human challenge is to ensure that the post-capitalist era emerges as far as possible through design rather than disaster, acknowledging all the while that self-determination is a luxury not available to everyone, particularly those facing the violence of and on capitalism's new frontiers.

In the midst of the current pandemic, which is causing so much human suffering, it is clear that shutting down the aviation industry and much of consumer culture is allowing a moment for the planet to take pause from the onslaught of global industrialism. For so long we have been told that we just cannot produce less, only more; that the type of economic contraction we see today was not possible. And yet here it is, albeit by disaster, not design. As French philosopher Bruno Latour recently commented: 'Next time, when ecologists are ridiculed because "the economy cannot be slowed down", they should remember that it can grind to a halt in a matter of weeks worldwide when it is urgent enough.'

Decades of green censure have done little or nothing to reset the path of growth fetishism, extractivism, and consumerism, and yet suddenly, almost overnight, this pandemic has disrupted the status quo, forcing a massive suspension of capitalism. This invites reflection on whether this new crisis could be a prelude, for better or for worse, to a new economic, political, and social imaginary. Global society has entered a chrysalis era, insecure but with latent potential. Nothing is ordained, and it is the task of politics, or collective action more broadly, to choose the next world. Still, if public discourse is anything to go by, it seems that the primary goal of politics in this time of disruption is to facilitate a 'bounce back' to where we were before the pandemic. Of course, all the evidence suggests that bouncing back would be no solution at all. We must not bounce back. We must bounce otherwise and elsewhere. The key issue then is: bounce to where and how? At this time, can we contemplate a crisis-driven exit from capitalism?

In the prehistory of the present crisis, we explored (in our book *Degrowth in the Suburbs*) the prospects for a systemic transition away from capitalism via degrowth – planned, managed, or imposed. In the radical and surprising opening of thinking and possibility afforded by this historical moment, we offer here some further thoughts on post-capitalist futures and, specifically, how the degrowth thesis itself might be developed, extended, or revised.

What is degrowth?

Degrowth is a movement that sees the goal of limitless economic growth as being dangerously incompatible with a finite planet. From this perspective, the notion of 'green growth' – where it is heralded that economies will grow but in sustainable ways – is a myth. Despite decades of extraordinary technological advance and deep faith in market mechanisms to bring environmental salvation, the so-called greening of capitalism has only produced ever-greater devastation. How long must we wait? With faith in green growth lost, what is needed is a degrowth process that downshifts global material and energy demands to sustainable levels. The growth imperatives of capitalism, however, will not accept this, which is why sustainability implies a post-capitalist world.

Environmental concerns, of course, cannot be isolated from social justice concerns, and the growthists always push back, arguing that the only path to poverty alleviation is via the strategy of GDP growth, on the assumption that 'a rising tide will lift all boats'. Given that a degrowth economy deliberately seeks a non-growing economy – on the assumption that a rising tide will sink all boats – poverty alleviation must be achieved more directly, via redistribution of wealth and power, both nationally and internationally. In other words (and to change the metaphor), a degrowth economy would seek to eliminate poverty and achieve distributive equity not by baking an ever-larger pie but by slicing it differently.

The lens of the 'sharing economy' (at least its more progressive formulations) can also highlight how more value can be acquired from the same 'slice' of the economic output. By sharing more between households – facilitated by the internet or by traditional community engagement – less energy- and resource-intensive production must occur to meet society's needs. Indeed, even in a contracting economy (whether that contraction is by design or by crisis) households can still secure the tools and other things they need, provided that a deeper culture of sharing emerges to replace acquisitive individualism. This soft-sounding notion of sharing entails a bold reinterpretation of 'efficiency' implicit in the degrowth paradigm: produce less, share more. Communities will manage a contracting economy more easily if they share the resources they have.

So, people might ask, is the current economic downturn what degrowth looks like in reality? First of all, let's be clear: degrowth means planned economic contraction. Nothing about the existing economic shutdown in response to COVID-19 was part of the plan for Australia or the world. Indeed, a couple of weeks ago it was almost unthinkable. The plan was economic growth, and then more economic growth. When an economy contracts involuntarily, we know that as a recession or, if it lasts long enough, a depression. Nobody advocates such unplanned economic contraction, because it has all sorts of negative social effects, including rising unemployment, stress, and poverty. So degrowth must never be confused with recession.

In terms of sustainability, the risk is that everything will bounce back to 'normal' levels of growth and consumption as soon as this pandemic passes. History shows that emissions go down during recessions or depressions but tend to rise again as soon as the growth engine restarts. The question is whether we can manage this pandemic in a way that stops the virus from getting out of control and avoids the 'bounce back' to high-impact, carbon-intensive living, while also ensuring that all people feel economically secure in a downshifted economy. The radical challenge this raises becomes especially stark as we read the early estimates from climate scientists suggesting that the current economic shutdown, extensive though it is, may only produce a 5-per-cent drop in global emissions for 2020. What, then, would 50-per-cent emissions reductions look like, let alone a net-zero-emissions economy?

The deep decarbonisation and degrowth required for such contraction would clearly require significant shifts in the ways our economies are structured, including exploring innovative new ways to govern access to land and housing, and having difficult but compassionate conversations about things such as redistribution and population growth. And, if the response to COVID-19 shows us anything, it is that governments can mobilise extraordinary amounts of money when there is political will. This is good news for funding a transition to renewable energy, if we can develop the political will.

A degrowth transition would also mean a cultural recognition that high-consumption lifestyles are unsustainable and that only lifestyles of material sufficiency, moderation, and frugality are consistent with social and ecological justice. This challenges us to reimagine the good life beyond consumer culture, thereby sowing the seeds of a politics and economics of sufficiency. Social movements will be needed to help create the support for these structural and cultural shifts. These might include post-consumerist movements that are prefiguring degrowth cultures of consumption by embracing material simplicity as a path to freedom, happiness, and reduced ecological burdens; community-led resistance and renewal movements; transgressive and creative forms of the sharing economy as means of thriving even in a contracting biophysical economy; and other social movements and strategies that are seeking to develop new (or renewed) informal economies 'beyond the market'.

So, while the pandemic continues to unfold, as a society we need to consider whether our ambition is merely to return to business as usual. Alternatively, shaken awake by this disruption, do we aspire to a radical and final break from neoliberal globalisation and aim to transition to a social form that prioritises human wellbeing and ecology over material accumulation?

What now for degrowth? A cautionary tale

There is no reason to believe that the current season of forced degrowth represents a permanent and final dislocation of the growth-machine ambitions of neoliberalism. The relatively recent experience of the 2008–09 Global Financial Crisis (GFC) and its aftermath is a worrying precedent. There was much joyous banging of cymbals and song from progressive interests as Keynesian desiderata were rediscovered and reapplied, especially and successfully by the Rudd government in

Australia. The revealed downside of this reinstatement of 'progress' was a failure to grasp that Keynes' theories predated political ecology and were intended to rescue, not transform, industrial capitalism. Hence, the way out of the GFC was a massive re-stimulation of consumption and all the ecological destruction that goes with it. After a major dip, carbon emissions were quickly restored and, after some mild disturbance, the planet was set back on its path to climate destruction. The shadow of Keynes lay heavy on the re-firing smokestack economies of the world.

We fear this replay for the current crisis, our anxieties deepened by the observation earlier that neoliberalism is a particularly historically insentient beast. The forces willing snap back are immense and omnipresent throughout the Global North. It's easy to highlight, not to say pillory, the 'let's reopen for business' cant of President Trump, but, as Streeck reminds us, the European Union is a deeply neoliberal institution, essentially a free-trade bloc, that is equally committed in the current historical moment to the earliest possible resumption of the growth machine. The centre-left and green parties typically operate within the same growth paradigm, too often committed to little more than a limp 'third way' that talks of 'greening capitalism' or giving it a human face. That is merely going down the wrong road more slowly.

But caution is advised. The cloak of pessimism is too often the disguise of determinism, a tendency that we reject as bad science and politics. Both defeats and victories are snatched from the jaws of historical crises and it's far too early now to say what will come from the current degrowth moment which we, with the support of Scott Morrison, can type as lockdown. We write, in April 2020, in the steaming mists of the volcanic eruption of the economy and of everyday life. New (or are some old?) social shadows and shapes are discernible: people (often harshly) freed from the neoliberal work frame and finding their way under a closely scripted regime of movement – and, critically, of consumption – laid down by a newly assertive state.

A dialectical play of possibilities is evident, and they are certainly too many to try to list now. But we cannot fail to see on the one progressive hand the radical reassertion of the state and of its care infrastructure, as well as the freeing of households from the treadmill of the neoliberal work order (and all the fractured and gendered coping reflexes that went with it). Equally, we discern and recoil from the authoritarian possibilities unleashed by new state arrogation, especially in Anglophone nations, where populist conservatives reign. Who knows what will emerge from this historical clash of possibilities? Our bleakest vision is the emergence of authoritarian states that will 'lock down the snap back' – that is, reanimate the Earth-eating monster and drive us harder and faster to the graveside of capitalism.

On better days, we hope-think for transition, however messy it might be, to a different social order that finally accepts new ideas of growth and progress. And what mature human being doesn't desire a life marked by growth and self-realisation, a promise-idea seeded most wondrously by the Enlightenment? The simple point of degrowth, and of most radical thought traditions under capitalism, is that this journey mustn't consume the social and ecological substrates that sustain us.

Will crisis play a consciousness-raising role?

It may be that ever-deepening crisis in the existing system of capitalism is the most likely spark for a paradigm shift in both the political economy of growth and its cultural underpinnings. To say this, however, is not to romanticise crisis like dreamy-eyed optimists. In fact, our view of change is based on a deep pessimism about the prospects of smoother and less disruptive modes of societal transformation. As the pandemic deepens or exacerbates the range of pre-existing crises, it seems that our collective task now is to ensure that these destabilised conditions are used to advance progressive humanitarian and ecological ends, rather than exploited to further entrench the austerity politics of neoliberalism.

How to ground this great and terrible opportunity in everyday life? For those who recognise the potential in this moment to think and act differently, our basic function is to keep hopes of a radically different and more humane form of society alive. The encounter with crisis can play an essential consciousness-raising role, if it triggers a desire for and motivation toward learning about the structural underpinnings of the calamity itself.

We believe that social movements should be preparing themselves to play that educational role, and in fact it is heartening to see this already unfolding in the many inspiring social responses to this tragic time. Among many examples of this, we highlight but one: David Holmgren and the permaculture movement, who are mobilising as we write for the creative renewal of our cities and suburbs. Holmgren's relaunch of his brilliant *RetroSuburbia: The Downshifter's Guide to a Resilient Future* during the pandemic exemplifies this vision and faith in grassroots activity. And, importantly, under its warm messaging about restoration of natural ecology and human values lies a serious prosecution of accumulative capitalism.

In the midst of this pandemic, our challenge is to come together and set sail for newer, safer shores and resist the sirens of destruction that would woo us back to the sinking Atlantis of capitalism. This is not a time of species affirmation; it is the hour of gravest peril. It is also a reopening of human possibility. To liberate human prospect, we must cast down, not defend, the burning bridges of a dying capitalist order and be brave enough to entertain the possibility of a permanent and planned economics beyond growth. This pandemic is an ambivalent invitation, even an incitement, to humanity to confront this turning point in the human story with all the creativity, wisdom, and compassion we can muster.

Chapter 2

Energy descent futures[1]

Introduction

It is not necessary to resort to energy determinism or crude reductionism to insist on the fundamental role energy has played, and continues to play, in shaping the rise (and demise) of human civilisations. Energy is not just another resource or commodity: it is the key that unlocks access to all other resources and commodities, thereby giving shape to the physical boundaries within which human societies must take form. In other words, a society's energetic foundations delimit the socio-economic forms that it may take. This is simply to concede that a particular form of society cannot emerge without sufficient energy supplies, in the appropriate forms, to support it. And further, that a society must be able to meet its *ongoing* energy demands if its specific socio-economic form is to persist. If it cannot, the society will transform or be transformed, voluntarily or otherwise (Smil, 2017).

Today we live in a world fundamentally shaped and enabled by access to the energy-dense fossil fuels: coal, oil, and gas. We could call this mode of life carbon civilisation – defined further below – and in its globalised form it is historically unrivalled in its degree of societal complexity. Never have human societies had such advanced technologies, such diversity in social roles, or so many administrative and bureaucratic institutions governing the flow of information, money, and commodities – all of which depend to varying degrees on the energy surpluses provided by fossil fuels (Tainter and Patzek, 2012).

One of the central questions of our age, then, is what might become of carbon civilisation as these finite fossil fuels deplete or as we voluntarily give them up in response to climate change. What would a post-carbon civilisation look like? The dominant energy narrative tends to acknowledge the need to transition away from fossil fuels but assumes

---

1 Originally published in Richard Slaughter and Andy Hines (eds), *Knowledge Base of Future Studies 2020*, Ch. 29, co-authored with Joshua Floyd.

that alternative energy sources, such as renewables or nuclear power, will be able to replace the energy foundations of carbon civilisation without fundamentally reshaping the form of life we have become accustomed to in the most developed regions of the world. More specifically, it is assumed that post-carbon energy sources are consistent with a complex, globalised economy that is structurally designed or required to grow without limits. In short, it is widely assumed that energy will be even more abundant in the future than it is today.

In contrast, the alternative energy narrative we outline in this chapter maintains that we should be preparing for futures not of energy abundance, but rather of reduced energy availability, futures in which viable ways of life are characterised by energy sufficiency (Alexander and Floyd, 2018; see also Floyd, 2012: 21–32). With respect to the most energy intensive societies, this means planning for what permaculture theorist and practitioner David Holmgren calls 'energy descent'. While acknowledging a range of uncertainties about how humanity's energy futures will unfold, we argue that the plausibility and even the likelihood of energy descent futures implies that planning and preparing for such futures is the most prudent course of action.

The implications of this alternative narrative are profound, yet rarely addressed in the dominant discourses around energy. Our goal presently is to broaden the discourse on energy futures. Although we cannot provide comprehensive answers in the space available, we hope at least to provoke thought about new questions, with the aim of unsettling some assumptions about energy futures that we feel are widely held with undue confidence. Such an act of unsettling can prepare the way for developing perspectives on energy futures that better equip humanity to find viable pathways amongst the landscape of emerging global challenges.

What is carbon civilisation?

Just as the bird's nest, the badger's lodge and the bees' hive require investments of energy for their construction and maintenance, so too with human settlements. Taken to the extremes of scale and intricacy, settlements in the form of cities constitute humanity's most energy-intensive creations. In fact, cities might be viewed as meta-creations that enable the emergence and development of other expressions of human creativity, and this creativity, as with all life, depends on energy, in requisite forms and quantities, for its sustenance and development.

A hunger for energy is woven particularly deeply into the nature and condition of modern humanity. We fell the forests and mine the landscapes to construct our dwellings and build our roads. In much of the world, heating of houses and water relies on combustion of wood, gas, oil or coal. Electricity, like a god, gives us light and it powers our abundance of convenient appliances and machines. Oil takes us where we desire to be and back again without effort. The expansion of energy harvesting and use that allows large-scale societies to grow inevitably generates new problems that these societies must then deal with. In turn, responses to such problems typically drive further energy demand. The processes by which large-scale societies take form and evolve are both enabled and constrained by their energetic foundations.

Consider the image of a metropolis at night, as seen from an aeroplane window, to highlight the practical implications of the energy surpluses provided by fossil fuels. The aircraft itself is entirely dependent on the unique power density of oil, not simply to provide the fuel, but also to make viable the range of complex background activities on which modern aircraft depend: the mining of materials and the production of plastics; the laying of roads and runways; the development and production of computers and communications technologies that coordinate the tens of thousands of daily flights; to say nothing of the broader investment in education required to train the engineers, computer scientists, pilots, and so forth.

In this web of dependencies it is not long before one arrives at the combine harvester that plays a key role in feeding much of the population. These machines, also powered by oil, take the Neolithic innovation of freeing up human labour for 'non-food specialisation' and amplify its effects through the industrialisation of agriculture. If in the past essentially all members of hunter-gatherer societies were required to be 'food specialists', in some industrially advanced societies today the proportion of the population required to be farmers has dropped to as low as 2 per cent. During this demographic transition people were displaced from the land by machines and into the factories and offices of the built environment. It is this image of mass migration that perhaps most vividly illustrates the tight interrelationship between intensification of socio-political complexity and the urbanisation of modern life in the industrialised world.

Beneath the aircraft lie the sprawling, glowing suburbs – the defining manifestation of carbon civilisation on the ground. No previous form of human settlement has ever been more energy intensive to produce or to maintain. Again, think through the long and diverse chains of extraction and production on which suburbia depends, not only for its creation but also to support the high-consumption ways of life widely practised there: the underlying energy infrastructure like oil and gas pipelines and the electricity grid; the mining and transport activities that siphon resources from the global periphery to the urban and suburban landscapes; and the final consumer commodities shipped and trucked to the shopping malls, via a vast and complex network of global trade routes and practices; the manufacture of vehicles to transport people to and from work, leisure, and tourist activities; the production of houses, kitchen gadgets, plastics, computers, pharmaceuticals, appliances, and clothing; refrigeration of food; water heating, and space heating and cooling; and, thanks to hydrocarbon-derived fertilisers, the abundant provision of food from all around the world, no matter the season, free from blemishes due to the liberal use of hydrocarbon-derived pesticides and herbicides.

The list really has no end, because in our increasingly globalised and interconnected world-spanning economy everything seems dependent on everything else. Nothing, though, is more fundamental than the fossil fuels that make other physical transformation possible. Just look around the space in which you are reading: it may not always be obvious, but essentially every artefact you see will have a history saturated with fossil energy, especially oil. This is carbon civilisation (Moriarty and Honnery, 2011).

Assumptions of ongoing energy abundance

Throughout history the *over*-use of energy has not been a prevailing problem – more often, the existential challenges that humans have faced can be viewed in terms of energy *scarcity*. Had ready access to new energy sources been available, many past societies may have overcome (or at least delayed) crises that precipitated their demise.

Even so, the provision and use of energy in previous eras caused problems too. Deforestation is not a purely modern phenomenon. The harm caused by airborne particulates from burning wood and coal has a long history. As horses became a dominant mode of urban transport, their manure in the streets became a hazard. That human exploitation of energy resources should drive environmental change is not new. This is as old as the mastery of fire, and our energy use always has and always will have consequences beyond the benefits it brings.

Nevertheless, it seems that we have now entered an age in which problems that can be characterised in terms of the *under*-use of energy are being eclipsed by dilemmas in which *over*-use is central. Granted, humans enjoy vastly disparate access to energy, with billions still living in conditions of energy poverty. Collectively though, we now face dual energy crises that are distinct but intimately connected: first, fossil energy depletion, and secondly, the major contribution that combustion of these same energy sources makes to climate change. Both arise from the vastly increased scale of humanity's energy use during the industrial age. As humanity's demand for energy expands, the problems attending satisfaction of this demand intensify. To the extent that conventional responses to this situation themselves stand to further increase energy demand – including the default reliance on 'technological fixes' – the dual crises perpetuate themselves. This is the energy paradox that is coming to define our age: we expect to solve the dual energy crises with approaches that themselves demand more overall energy use.

Energy forecasting conducted within the auspices of conventional institutions typically reinforces the orthodox assumption that humanity (or the portion living in the rich world, at least) will always be able to satisfy ongoing energy demand in a timely and affordable fashion. This is not necessarily a conscious assumption. Rather, it is a consequence of the ways in which large-scale societies are constituted that the association between institutional responses to collective problems and increased demand for energy is rarely apparent. As citizens of societies organised by industrial economies and market capitalism, we have simply become accustomed to overcoming (or at least displacing) any immediate problem that arises and, simultaneously, to satisfying the aggregate growth in energy demand. In mainstream energy discourse the fact that fossil fuels are finite and being depleted at pace is generally dismissed as a distant concern that will be solved before it arrives. Even if such a view is by no means universal, media narratives both reflect and propagate the widespread and popular assumption that renewable energy or nuclear power will be able to replace current fossil fuel use without significant social or economic disruption, as well as match growing global energy demand into the distant future.

In support of this energy optimism, analysts point to promising advances in technology. Sure, they say, new energy demands will arise, but a clever and resourceful humanity will be able to meet them. Markets and price signals will provide the right incentives. According to this narrative, industrial capitalism will soon be global – a transition almost complete – and efficiency gains and new energy sources and conversion technologies will mean we can avoid the worst oil depletion and climate change scenarios. Just look to history and you will see that in recent periods, humans have always managed to satisfy growing energy demand. The future will be the same, won't it?

Peak oil, climate change, and the limits of alternative energy sources

We seek to challenge that dominant energy narrative from a range of angles and offer an alternative perspective on humanity's energy futures. First, we remind the reader that fossil fuels – currently comprising about 85 per cent of global primary energy use – are finite, and therefore carbon civilisation, one way or another, has a time limit. Our one-off fossil energy inheritance is but a brief anomaly in the evolution of the human story, a momentary energy spike from the perspective of deep time.

Although the timing and trajectory of fossil energy depletion is subject to many uncertainties and controversies, the fact that fossil fuels are finite and subject to depletion is an undeniable geological reality. This is a matter of particular significance in relation to oil, given its role in enabling industrial agriculture, and global transport systems and supply chains. With each passing day, as the low-hanging fruit is picked, it becomes harder to increase or even maintain current net energy supply. In recent years, the large growth in United States oil production due to shale oil developments using hydraulic fracturing ('fracking') techniques has encouraged some commentators to proclaim 'the death of peak oil'.

Our assessment of the evidence suggests that such pronouncements are greatly exaggerated (see Mohr et al., 2015: 120–135; Millar and Sorrell, 2014; Höök et al., 2014; Alexander and Floyd, 2018: Ch. 3). Eventually – perhaps sooner than most think – the rate of oil production will enter a phase of net energy decline, with new discoveries unable to offset the flagging fortunes of existing assets. And while oil has commanded the vast majority of attention to date in public discourse about fossil energy resource depletion, the timelines for gas and coal may not be anywhere near as protracted as is typically assumed. Alongside this, exponential growth trends (both energetic and economic) that have defined dominant conceptions of human development since the industrial revolution can be expected to end, and even reverse. This raises questions not only about what a post-carbon civilisation will look like, but, perhaps more pressingly, how we should best manage the inevitable and foreseeable contraction of fossil energy source production in coming years and decades (Holmgren, 2009; Fleming, 2016).

Secondly, and perhaps most prominently, there is the climate crisis, no longer of the future but the present (Spratt and Dunlop, 2017). What was only a few years ago thought to be a sufficiently distant concern to be deferred or ignored, is now upon us. Compounding the challenge of maintaining energy supply in the face of fossil energy depletion, climate science overwhelmingly concludes that the burning of fossil fuels is a leading cause of anthropogenic climate change. Any adequate response to this potentially existential threat is going to require, among other things, a swift and committed transition beyond fossil energy sources.

The best available science tells us that to keep the impacts of climate change within the range of human adaptation, we need to limit the consumption of fossil fuels even before limits are geologically enforced – that we must leave them before they leave us. The question is whether we are able to muster the wisdom to do this, and what the resultant societies might look like if we succeed. If we fail, then it seems that we will burn – and already things are heating up. According to NASA, seventeen of the eighteen hottest years in recorded history have occurred since 2001, to say nothing of the increasing regularity and severity of extreme weather events. And yet we wait.

In light of the urgent imperative to reduce carbon-based fuel combustion to mitigate climate change, it may be tempting to see the prospect of fossil energy depletion as a red herring. If fossil fuel use is incompatible with maintaining a habitable climate anyway, then why be concerned about geophysical supply constraints? Surely these must, if they come into play in time, only help with the climate imperative for decarbonising economies.

While that perspective makes sense if current fossil energy reliance is viewed in very abstract terms, it oversimplifies the complex relationship between climate change and energy resource depletion. The arrival of peak oil, if planned for, will unfold very differently than if it arrives without any or much preparation. So an assumption that peak oil will necessarily be good for climate change mitigation is by no means self-evident. Furthermore, in our more pessimistic moods, the sluggish political and cultural responses to climate change to date make it plausible that peak oil will transform (or disrupt) the global economy before any serious climate response does. Accordingly, it is not enough to say we *need* to decarbonise the global economy to mitigate climate change. That may be true, but if, in fact, the world fails to mobilise adequately in that regard – which, again, strikes us as a plausible scenario – then peak oil may be the energy challenge the world is *forced* to deal with.

The cursory review of humanity's situation through the overlapping contextual lenses of fossil energy resource depletion and climate disruption sets the scene for a third context of inquiry. This concerns the extent to which alternative energy sources – specifically renewable and/or nuclear energy – will be able to replace the fossil energy sources of carbon civilisation (Moriarty and Honnery, 2016: 3–7). Can this be achieved without significant disruption or fundamental change to its industrial, energy-intensive, extractivist, and expansionary nature? We acknowledge a range of promising technological and economic advances in the energy domain, and categorically support the planned transition to a post-carbon society. At the same time, critical questions must be raised about whether alternative sources can seamlessly substitute for incumbent energy systems, without transformation of the wider social and cultural contexts within which they are deployed.

Unfortunately, this is an area of scholarly debate in which competing schools of thought – 'renewable advocates' vs. 'nuclear advocates' – hold what often seem to be commitments of an almost religious nature to their particular energy solution (see Valentine, Sovacool, and Brown, 2017: 623–630). While we cannot review the intricacies of this debate here, we approach the issues with more circumspection, knowing that the current knowledge basis for energy transitions is uncertain – that reasonable people can disagree. But we maintain that this very uncertainty about the viability of fully replacing fossil fuels with alternative sources, and the knowledge humility this uncertainty demands (Jassanof, 2018: 11–14), ends up supporting the case for energy descent preparation and planning. That is, if we are not sure renewable energy or nuclear power will be up to the task of fully replacing the energy supply from fossil fuels, then we should not assume existing energy supply – and the societal complexity it enables – will be able to be maintained in a post-carbon world. In short, it would be prudent to prepare for an energy descent future, whether one is motivated by peak oil, climate change, or uncertainty about the prospects of alternative energy sources replacing fossil fuels (or all those reasons).

Adding further to the scope of the decarbonisation challenge is the perennial question of 'who benefits?' We must ask distributive questions about how the energy humanity manages to harness should be shared amongst the growing global human population, currently at 7.7 billion and, according to the United Nations, trending toward eleven billion or more by the end of the century. This is the ethical dimension that energy transition inquiries too often marginalise or simply ignore altogether, in favour of technological and market-driven solutions.

In other publications we have provided the evidential foundations for energy descent in much more detail (see Alexander and Floyd, 2018; Floyd et al., 2020). For present purposes, however, our contention is that there are various reasons to think that the future may be shaped by energy descent not energy abundance. Fossil fuels are finite and being depleted at pace; climate change mitigation cannot be solved merely by 'greening' energy supply but also requires choosing radical energy demand reductions; nuclear and renewables cannot fully or directly replace the nature and magnitude of fossil energy surpluses; and finally, distributive concerns suggest that energy-intensive societies should be reducing their energy use in order to share global energy access more broadly. Any one of these energy challenges justifies taking energy descent futures seriously. Considered together, we contend that an energy descent future is more likely than not.

Navigation notes for energy descent futures

So far we have not attempted to describe the range of preparatory or adaptive strategies that are available for dealing with energy descent; nor have we discussed in any detail what a post-carbon civilisation might look like. Our goal has been diagnostic rather than prescriptive. That said, we believe the diagnosis supports the case for, and adaptive potential of, engaging intentionally with energy descent processes.

Drawing attention to this perspective is important because until the plausibility of such energy futures is understood and taken seriously, individuals, communities and political processes will not be mobilised to prepare for their eventuality. A range of looming energy shocks may well arrive and societies will be unprepared for them, which is likely to bring unnecessary suffering, harm, and instability. At the extreme, it potentially precipitates civilisational collapse (Tainter, 1988). In light of this, we will now say a few words on the cultural and socio-economic implications of energy descent, and the variety of responses available. The brief overview we present can only anticipate the much more extensive discussion that the subject both requires and deserves (Alexander, 2015a; 2015b).

We have discussed how energy surpluses are used by societies to solve the problems they encounter and feed growing and evolving material desires. We showed that as societies acquire and invest energy to solve problems and feed desires, they become more socio-politically complex (in the social scientific sense, of increasing social role differentiation and specialisation, with attendant expansion of the means for coordinating these roles; this tends also to be accompanied by expanded suites of technologies and related institutions). This in turn drives the need for further complexification, and hence increased energy use. Because existential problems are in fact being solved, it is widely inferred that such a trajectory of change represents a general progressive improvement in life conditions within a complexifying society – for the time being at least (Tainter, 1988).

As an aside, we stress here that we do not subscribe to the view that increasing socio-political complexification constitutes a trajectory of general progress or improvement. We distinguish this idea of general progress from the ongoing possibility – which we do subscribe to – of localised performance improvement in specific contexts, as measured by appropriately defined and context-specific criteria. Human history is not in our interpretation characterised by a unidirectional, largely deterministic and hence predictable pattern of change from less to more socially desirable states. We just point out that this is an interpretation that is widely held and that is a highly influential cultural characteristic of modernity (Wright, 2005).

Economic growth is one prominent area of performance from which a general trajectory of progress is often inferred. Money and other financial assets – the instruments that mediate economic activity – can be viewed as claims on the product of surplus energy. Societies allocate money to initiatives intended to solve their problems, and the expansion of physical economic activity that this stimulates and incentivises entails increased rates of energy use. This energy-economy relationship is evidenced historically by the close correlation between economic activity measured in terms of GDP and total primary energy use (Alexander and Floyd, 2018: Ch. 3). Provided energy surpluses continue to grow, economies have been able to grow in scale and socio-political complexity. On the surface, then, it is quite understandable why more money and energy are overriding goals of most, if not all, contemporary economies: these are apparently required for maintaining the conditions that are interpreted as 'progress', and that, as such, are widely attributed the status of being of ultimate value.

But what happens (or might happen in future) when a society finds itself with less energy to invest in economic growth, and the socio-political complexification growth both brings and requires? There are two broad pathways it may follow: either it tries to maintain the existing, growth-oriented socio-economic form but solve fewer problems due to the declining energy budget (a phenomenon typically characterisable as societal decay, recession or collapse, depending on the speed and extent of decline); or the society rethinks the range and nature of the problems it is willing to solve, and then reprioritises its investment of available energy in order to create new, less energy intensive socio-political and economic forms.

It seems clear enough that rich nations (our focus herein) are in the process of choosing the former strategy – evidenced by their unremitting hunger for more energy, more (and more diverse) technological solutions, and more economic growth. This dominant strategy is selected on the assumption that more energy will be available in the future to fund the attendant increase in socio-political complexity. This is the message relentlessly pushed by mainstream energy analysts and institutions. However, the central implication of our analysis is that it would be prudent to embrace the radical alternative strategies of voluntary simplification (of the socio-political structures for organising human activity) and economic deintensification, given the likelihood of forthcoming energy descent. What, then, might such voluntary simplification look like? We sketch a view here in the broadest possible terms, and we expect to raise as many new questions as we answer (see also Alexander, 2014: 550–556; Floyd, 2014: 586–607).

Given that sufficient rates of energy supply in appropriate forms are required for production activity within a given socio-political-economic complex, it follows that in an energy descent context voluntary simplification would involve less overall production activity in physical terms, which would also mean less material- and energy-intensive consumption. From an engineering perspective, this decline in production activity is a simple consequence of less overall work and heat transfer being carried out by a society's physical plant, equipment, and infrastructure.

Today the outcome of this process of organised economic contraction widely goes by the name 'degrowth' (which for present purposes can be considered a consequence of success in the positive development of voluntarily simplified societies and deintensified economies) (see generally Weiss and Cattaneo, 2017: 220–230). But degrowth does not merely mean less of the same type of economic activity within the same system; it also means less and different, within a new system. Depending on local context: not simply fewer SUVs, but more bikes (or less desire for transit in the first place); not just less deforestation but more reforestation; not fewer meals in the day, but different diets; and so forth, across all domains of life. In other words, not the same narratives of human identity, success, and wellbeing, but new narratives of what it means to be human.

Within such new narratives, if the social justice imperative of meeting the basic wants of all people were to be realised, the reduced material output of economic activity in a degrowth transition would need to be distributed more fairly than it is in most societies today. In other words, the degrowth economies would not be structured to maximise economic growth and hope that wealth 'trickles down'; instead the economies we envisage here should ensure material sufficiency for all more directly, through the creation of new distributive ground rules that do not rely on growth. Here the same social 'problem' is solved, only in alternative, less energy- and resource-intensive ways, which is a key feature of what we mean by voluntary simplification.

This process of shrinking or abandoning many present economic arrangements in organised ways should not be assumed to automatically imply social hardship or deprivation, provided communities negotiate the transition mindfully. And although significant deindustrialisation would ensue, obviously some economic sectors would expand in order to meet real and ongoing human desires in regenerative and equitable ways (notably renewable energy infrastructure). Granted, consumer affluence as we know it today may not be viable for any or many – clearly requiring a fundamental shift in cultures of consumption and conceptions of the 'good life'. But once basic material wants were met and appropriate technologies developed, degrowth societies would have the freedom to turn away from limitless material advancement and instead seek happiness and meaning in life through less consumptive avenues – where, as it happens, pretty much every wisdom and spiritual tradition advises that lasting fulfilment lies.

Members of post-consumerist cultures enabled by voluntary simplification would thus have increased scope to choose the realm of the spirit, not the shopping mall, to satisfy their hunger for contentment. Paradoxically, the shift to less consumptive pursuits might imply not an outright *rejection* of material culture but a 'new materialism', in which post-materialist cultures actually pay more attention to and exercise greater care for the material realm (e.g., building things to last and taking care of them). This might be motivated by highly utilitarian concerns, such as minimising environmental impacts or resource extraction and discarding of waste. But it can also be consistent with what might be termed spiritual motivations, a move to healing or transcending the supposed enmities between 'culture and nature' and 'body and mind'.

The degrowth in production and consumption required by energy descent is one thing. But it is not just the *magnitude* of energy availability that shapes a society. It is also the *nature* of the energy sources, especially their power density. Assuming that a degrowth society is fully or primarily powered by renewable energy, with little or no use of fossil energy and a limited role for nuclear electricity, it follows that such a society would have to adapt to the fundamentally different nature of energy supply, as well as reduced overall availability (Floyd, 2017).

In order to avoid an economically crippling reliance on expensive energy storage, a degrowth society may need to adjust by storing *work*, using energy as far as possible when the sun is shining or the wind is blowing, rather than assuming that energy is always available on demand and without interruption. While modest biofuel volumes could be produced for tasks deemed socially essential (such as limited use of heavy machinery and aviation), a defining feature of a post-carbon society would be the electrification of essential energy-demanding tools and technologies and even a return to human-labour power for more tasks (including farming). Overall, of course, energy demand would have to be significantly reduced compared to rich nations today. Precise levels, though, are subject to the myriad social, political, economic, technological and cultural characteristics of as-yet-unknown viable human futures.

In short, degrowth processes of voluntary simplification, as we envisage them, would seek to meet genuine human wants and essential needs in sustainable ways through socio-economic practices that are far less energy and resource intensive than in industrially advanced societies today. As well as a range of institutional and structural changes (which we won't attempt to review here) (Alexander and Gleeson, 2019: Ch. 7), such degrowth societies would have to be shaped by values of material sufficiency, moderation, and frugality – simply because there would be insufficient surplus energy to meet the energy (or broader environmental) costs of consumer lifestyles (Trainer, 2010).

Central to the changes we see as plausibly enabling this is a decrease in hours spent working in the formal economy. This would free up increased time for participation in the informal economy at the household and community levels. In such a world, repair, recycling, and reuse would be radically embraced and practised, incentivised by the increased value of materials. Clothes might be second-hand, mended, or produced within the household and neighbourhood economies. Cultures based on rapid fashion cycles would very likely wither away and new aesthetics of sufficiency and timeless classic design might emerge. Home energy use would have to be a fraction of typical usage in rich societies, but homes would be retrofitted for energy efficiency and essential functions could be met. Permaculture gardens and food forests would reshape the urban and suburban landscapes. Car culture would enter its terminal phase as oil becomes ever-scarcer, and bicycles and electrified public transport would become primary modes of transit. Regular air travel would become unaffordable, as would consumer lifestyles more generally. Infrastructure that is currently replicated across all households would increasingly be shared at the neighbourhood scale. Food and other commodities would generally be grown, produced, and traded far more locally than at present. Markets local to living places could be expected to proliferate to facilitate this trade.

This rough and incomplete thumbnail sketch seeks simply to highlight how a degrowth process of voluntary simplification points toward non-affluent but sufficient material living standards. By avoiding the energy inputs currently invested in the vast mediating economic structures necessary to support large-scale societies oriented toward continuous and unchecked growth, degrowth societies would thereby still have sufficient energy available to meet wants consistent with human flourishing.

Approached judiciously and with appropriate care, we see it as entirely conceivable that sufficient surplus energy would also be available to allow continued collective problem-solving on a significant scale (Alexander, 2014). But problems would be solved in ways different to those that have become habitual during the industrial age. Different value-systems would even produce different conceptions of the problems faced and, with this, new ways of thinking about the nature of adequate solutions. This is not to deny the necessary role of technology and engineering in navigating viable energy descent pathways, it is only to emphasise that a techno-fix alone will be insufficient if not set within a suitable framework of reappraised values. Technologies are tools, the use of which is inevitably shaped by the cultural contexts in which they are deployed.

How voluntary simplification unfolds in practice could take an essentially infinite number of forms. It defies precise forecasting. Indeed, the shape of a flourishing degrowth society in an energy descent context is limited only by its members' shared imagination. Scarcity begets creativity. Voluntary simplification is based on an essentially *polycultural* vision, as distinct from modernity's *monocultural* vision. This is a vision where the trajectory of change will involve many of infinite possible social forms being enacted simultaneously, in response to local conditions. This diversity will be amplified by the interactions between groups pursuing viable trajectories free of the constraints of uniformity imposed by massive bureaucracies and centralised institutions. In important respects, as David Fleming has pointed out, this 'simplification' in fact entails a drift to greater complexity (Fleming, 2016). Again, this is simplification only in the limited sense of reduction in the formal socio-political complexity – that is, institutionalised social role differentiation and diversification, and attendant means of coordination – that characterises large-scale societies.

Obviously, such 'simplification' of past socio-political complexity will be experienced very differently if it is chaotically imposed upon a society as a consequence of collapse, instead of being creatively and caringly navigated into existence through deliberate intention. Degrowth by way of voluntary simplification and economic deintensification provides not just an alternative to collapse, but also the potential for prosperous descent.

Nevertheless, no matter how well justified degrowth may be as a coherent response to global crises, we acknowledge that it seems unlikely to be widely embraced by governments or civil societies. But this does not undermine the case for degrowth. If, in the face of the evidence, nations continue to pursue economic growth without end, and thereby continue to collide with ecological limits, then we argue that degrowth values and practices remain justified as a means of building resilience to forthcoming shocks. In other words, we should aim for regenerative forms of social organisation that build rather than deplete the foundations on which they rely.

Conclusion

We set out to show through this critical exploration that much mainstream energy discourse is based on a series of highly optimistic assumptions about future energy supply. The improbability of conditions aligning such that all necessary assumptions are born out implies that the energy futures ahead will diverge strongly from those envisaged within this established discourse. This has potentially profound implications. The availability of energy in the right forms at sufficient rates is the lifeblood of any particular form of civilisation. Energy-related factors are fundamental to how we shape our societies and pursue our goals – yet it seems most individuals and societies are making plans based on highly implausible expectations. We've encouraged readers to treat the prospect that these expectations will *not* be realised as, at the very least, a matter of plausibility.

In the event that mainstream expectations are thwarted, the consequences could range from the disruptive to the catastrophic. This is not a case *against* optimism, but rather of channelling it in directions that lie within humanity's scope of influence. Even within the difficult circumstances that our assessment implies, there is still much good that can be achieved. Ample room remains for adjusting expectations to better reflect underlying energy and environmental realities, and to reconstitute societies – and the economies that support them – accordingly.

Our critique focused on three key issues: (1) the likelihood (or unlikelihood) of meeting growing energy demand as fossil fuels continue to deplete; (2) the size of the available carbon budget for a safe climate and the economic implications of keeping within such a budget; and (3) the degree to which alternative energy sources (renewables and/or nuclear) will be able to replace the fossil energy foundations of carbon civilisation, without significant disruption to today's large-scale societies and the dominant political-economic paradigm of global market capitalism.

On our reading of the evidence the peak oil phenomenon is not dead but at most in short term remission. Ongoing fossil energy depletion is likely to cause supply disruptions in coming years and decades and thereby undermine the energy supply needed to maintain economic growth. In any case, the carbon budget for a safe climate is so tight (and in fact is arguably non-existent) that decarbonising at the rate needed is inconsistent with ongoing economic growth. This means we should be choosing to leave fossil fuels even before they leave us. But as we argued, that requires the unthinkable: transcending the growth imperative that is common to all large-scale societies but which is greatly amplified within competitive economies operating under market capitalism.

Finally, we looked beneath the gloss of promising advancements in energy sources and conversion technologies, reminding readers that alternative energy sources differ dramatically in nature from incumbent sources (intermittency, storage issues, low energy density, system cost, etc.). Considered systemically, these differences imply that the alternatives will not directly replace the fossil energy foundations of carbon civilisation. In short, we have explored the possibility that a post-carbon civilisation is most likely to be one with less energy available, not more, and hence with reduced energy *services* in the form of work, heat, lighting, and data manipulation than is currently available in rich nations. The situation is compounded if distributive questions are taken seriously. Ultimately, this means it would be prudent to be planning for energy descent futures.

In closing, we appreciate the psychological drivers for denying these conclusions and trusting instead in a cornucopian or techno-optimistic worldview. It is less confronting to human identities and ways of life to believe that technology and markets can solve social and environmental problems without needing to rethink the underpinning structures that give rise to those problems. We posit that this means of coping with psychological dissonance, perhaps adaptive in other circumstances, is influential in the apparent 'self-censoring' (consciously or unconsciously) by mainstream energy and economic analysts, resulting in the publication only of perspectives consistent with dominant economic and political paradigms. But critical, evidence-based thinking demands that we should not believe something merely because we wish it to be so. In our view, it is preferable to believe and act upon what is most likely to be true following an honest and frank weighing of the evidence. We have argued that this means accepting more modest visions of future access to energy services and creatively preparing for the socio-economic implications of energy descent.

The age of energy abundance is arguably drawing to an end. The human species has created a form of civilisation the energy demands of which cannot be sustainably or fairly maintained. Certainly, this high-consumption, energy-intensive way of life cannot be globalised to the entire, growing population approaching eight billion. As Joseph Tainter maintains: 'a society or other institution can be destroyed by the cost of sustaining itself' (Tainter, 1988). Our message, therefore, is to accept the implied energy descent futures before their consequences overwhelm us. This is likely to be an extremely challenging and uncertain journey. But it also has the potential to offer people renewed prospects for lives of meaning and purpose, provided we learn to collectively see these overlapping crises as opportunities for deep civilisational transformation.

The human opportunity, as always, is to constitute the future rather than be constituted by it. Today that requires seeing through the dubious and even dangerous optimism of energy cornucopianism and developing an appreciation of, and even *desire for*, futures of the kind that energy descent entails. We acknowledge that this prospect will be interpreted by many as carrying associations of deprivation and defeat, and thus seem undesirable. Consider a metaphor though. For a pilot nearing the range limit of their aircraft's fuel supply, making a controlled descent in order to land safely is so natural and expected that the plane passing overhead is barely registered. It is only in the rare instance in which a pilot, in error or incapacitated, acts contrary to their passengers' and their own interests, crashing to the ground with great violence, that such an everyday occurrence as the end of an aircraft's flight suddenly galvanises collective attention. Dystopian interpretations of descent are not inherent in the concept itself. Rather, they are an entailment of cultural priorities formed around the present civilisation's dominant story of progress.

Given that the energy prospects of the old story are beginning to fade, we find ourselves in a sort of limbo, in between stories. What is required today more than anything else is a new story. Or rather, an assemblage of new stories, which together help us break through the thick crust of conventional thinking and being, thus allowing us to think and be otherwise, as pioneering citizens of a post-carbon civilisation, in a world not yet made.

References

Alexander, S. 2014. 'Voluntary Simplification as an Alternative to Collapse'. *Foresight* 16(6): 550–566.

Alexander, S. 2015a. *Prosperous Descent: Crisis as Opportunity in an Age of Limits.* Melbourne: Simplicity Institute.

Alexander, S. 2015b. *Sufficiency Economy: Enough, for Everyone, Forever.* Melbourne: Simplicity Institute.

Alexander, S. and Floyd, J. 2018. *Carbon Civilisation and the Energy Descent Future: Life Beyond this Brief Anomaly.* Melbourne: Simplicity Institute.

Alexander, S. and Gleeson, B. 2019. *Degrowth in the Suburbs: A Radical Urban Imaginary.* Singapore: Palgrave MacMillan.

Fleming, D. (2016). *Lean Logic: A Dictionary for the Future and How to Survive It.* White River Junction, VT: Chelsea Green.

Floyd, J. 2012. 'Responding to the Millennium Project's Energy Challenge: A Futurist's Perspective'. *Journal of Futures Studies* 16(4): 21–32.

Floyd, J. 2014. 'Sense-making and Acting for Descent Futures: Human and Cultural Pathways'. *Foresight* 16(6): 586–607.

Floyd, J. 2017. 'Retrofitting Suburbia for Energy Descent Futures'. *Beyond this Brief Anomaly.* Available at: https://beyondthisbriefanomaly.org/2017/07/20/retrofitting-suburbia-for-energy-descent-futures/ (accessed 25 March 2019).

Floyd, J. et al. 2020. 'Energy Descent as a Post-Carbon Transition Scenario: How "Knowledge Humility" Reshapes Energy Futures for Post-Normal Times'. *Futures*, 122: 102565.

Holmgren, D. 2009. *Future Scenarios: Mapping the Cultural Implications of Peak Oil and Climate Change.* White River Junction, VT: Chelsea Green.

Höök, M. et al. 2014. 'Decline and Depletion Rates of Oil Production: A Comprehensive Investigation'. *Philosophical Transactions of the Royal Society A* 372.

Jassanof, S. 2018. 'Just Transitions: A Humble Approach to Global Energy Futures'. *Energy Research and Social Science* 35: 11–14.

Miller, R.G. and Sorrell, S.R. 2014. 'The Future of Oil Supply'. *Philosophical Transactions of the Royal Society A: Mathematical, Physical and Engineering Sciences* 372.

Mohr, S.H. et al. 2015. 'Projection of World Fossil Fuels by Country'. *Fuel* 141: 120–35.

Moriarty, P. and Honnery, D. 2011. *Rise and Fall of the Carbon Civilisation.* London: Springer.

Moriarty, P. and Honnery, D. 2016. 'Can Renewable Energy Power the Future?' *Energy Policy* 93: 3–7.

Spratt, D. and Dunlop, I. 2017. 'What Lies Beneath: The scientific Understatement of Climate Risks'. Melbourne: Breakthrough Institute. Available at: https://docs.wixstatic.com/ugd/148cb0_a0d7c18a1bf64e698a9c8c8f18a42889.pdf (accessed 25 March 2019).

Smil, V. 2017. *Energy and Civilization.* Cambridge, MA: MIT Press.

Tainter, J. 1988. *The Collapse of Complex Societies.* Cambridge: Cambridge University Press.

Tainter, J.A. and Patzek, T.W. 2012. *Drilling Down: The Gulf Oil Debacle and Our Energy Dilemma.* New York: Copernicus.

Trainer, T. 2010. *Transition to a Sustainable and Just Society.* Sydney: Envirobook.

Valentine, S.V., Sovacool, B.K., and Brown, M.A. 2017. 'Frame Envy in Energy Policy Ideology: A Social Constructivist Framework For Wicked Energy Problems'. *Energy Policy*, 109: 623–30.

Weiss, M. and Cattaneo, C. 2017. 'Degrowth – Taking stock and Reviewing an Emerging Academic Paradigm'. *Ecological Economics*: 137: 220–30.

Wright, R. 2005. *A Short History of Progress.* New York: Carroll and Graf.

Chapter 3

Post-capitalism by design not disaster[1]

Designing the descent

This chapter addresses the subject of post-capitalist political economy. That is quite an intimidating topic, especially since transcending capitalism is proving to be quite difficult. Capitalism certainly isn't going to lie down like a lamb at the polite request of Left-leaning environmentalists. What this means is that sustainability and justice advocates with radical visions of societal futures need to think very carefully about the question of *strategy*. More specifically, we must confront the question of where and how to invest our time, energy, and resources, if we genuinely seek a fundamentally different type of economic system 'beyond capitalism'.[2]

Attempting to save capitalism through 'green growth' is increasingly recognised as little more than neoliberal ideology, the function of which is to entrench the status quo while pretending to change (Smith, 2016; Hickel and Kallis, 2019). And yet hopes for an imminent proletarian uprising that abolishes capitalism and erects an eco-socialist utopia governed by an enlightened centralised state seems equally misconceived. This paucity of hope has led critical theorist Frederic Jameson (2003) to note that it is now easier to imagine the end of the world than the end of capitalism, although perhaps that says more about a sterility of contemporary political imagination than it does about our future. This exploratory analysis will share some thoughts on what might come after capitalism and how we might manage and drive this transition by design rather than disaster.

1 Originally published in *The Ecological Citizen*, 3 Sup. B, 2020, pp 13–21.
2 Without attempting a comprehensive definition, for present purposes the term capitalism simply refers to a political and economic system, based predominantly on private ownership of the means of production, in which most key decisions about production, consumption, and distribution of resources are made through competitive markets. For a range of reasons – including technological innovation and the imperative for firms to maximise profits – capitalist economies must grow, in terms of GDP, to maintain employment and stability. On that basis, a post-capitalist economy would involve increased socialisation of productive assets (without necessarily abolishing private property); greater social control over markets; and systemic restructuring to maintain employment and stability in the absence of economic expansion. It should be clear that these broad definitions mean that various forms of capitalism and post-capitalism are possible. Further definitional content will be provided as the analysis proceeds (see also, Frankel, 2018; Wall, 2015; Mason, 2015; Friedman, 2002).

I say by design not disaster, hinting at a certain optimism, however it will become clear that there is, in fact, an underlying pessimism that shapes my perspective – a pessimism which some readers might share. Or, perhaps rather than pessimism, a better term to describe my orientation might be 'apocaloptimism'. This neologism can be defined as the view that 'everything is going to hell but things might still turn out ok'. While in truth I am neither apocalyptic nor optimistic, this term does evoke something of the grounded but cautious hope that will inform my analysis.

It will be argued that deepening crisis in the current system is probably unavoidable now, for a range of reasons – our time for a smooth transition may have passed. Nevertheless, I certainly won't use that to justify inaction or despair; quite the opposite. Indeed, the instability created by systemic crisis may be one of the prerequisites for deep societal change – unsettling though that is to admit. Our challenge will be to turn deepening crises, as they emerge, into opportunities to create something other than capitalism; a post-capitalist society that better accords with our shared ideals for social justice, ecological viability, and human flourishing.

If capitalism is coming to an end in coming years or decades as it collides with various ecological and financial limits, we can ask ourselves: *how can we proactively design the end of capitalism* rather than wait for its collapse? Or even, if necessary, how can we design the collapse of capitalism in ways that makes the best of a bad situation? These are the questions of an apocaloptimist.

Over the last ten years I've been part of a movement advocating for a 'degrowth' process of planned economic contraction (Alexander, 2009; 2015a; 2015b; Alexander and Gleeson, 2019). In what follows I'm going to use this alternative economic paradigm to frame and analyse the political economy of post-capitalism. I don't expect anyone to *like* the terminology of degrowth – I know very well it is an ugly term – and it may never be the banner under which a social or political movement marches. But as a slogan for justice and sustainability, I maintain that degrowth captures an essential insight: it directly evokes, more clearly than any other term, the need for *planned contraction* of the energy and resource demands of overgrown or 'developed' economies. That is an agenda that mainstream environmental and social discourse refuses to acknowledge, because significant contraction of energy and resource demands is incompatible with ongoing GDP growth (Hickel and Kallis, 2019). This growth fetish must be overcome.

The following sections offer some thoughts on why the degrowth paradigm signifies the most coherent political economy for a post-capitalist society and how such a transition might unfold. I will also highlight the role grassroots social movements and alternative economic experiments may need to play prefiguring degrowth economies and creating the cultural conditions for a politics and macroeconomics of degrowth to emerge.

Prerequisites for a degrowth transition

Recently the Danish political economist Hubert Buch-Hansen (2018) published a paper which outlined a conceptual framework that is useful for thinking about how paradigm shifts in political economy occur. He argued that there are four main prerequisites:

- First, there must be a crisis or series of crises that cannot be resolved within the existing mode of political economy;

- Second, there must be a coherent alternative political project;

- Third, there must be a comprehensive coalition of social forces attempting to produce the alternative paradigm through political struggle and social activism;

- And finally, there must be broad-based cultural consent, even passive consent, for the new paradigm.

I'm going to adopt this framework, add my own analytical flesh to its theoretical bones, and use it to discuss the question of a degrowth transition to a post-capitalist society. I hope this provides a useful and provocative broad-ranging analysis to get this special issue underway, although I'm sure I'll raise more questions than I answer.

Capitalism is not in crisis – Capitalism *is* the crisis

The first prerequisite, then, for a paradigm shift in the existing mode of political economy is crisis – but not just any crisis. It must be a crisis or series of crises in the system that the system itself cannot resolve. There are many reasons to think this prerequisite is met.

Growth economics is sometimes called the 'ideology of the cancer cell', and this provocative metaphor neatly summarises the fatal anomaly in capitalism, namely, that on the one hand, it *must* keep growing for stability, and, on the other hand, for various ecological and financial reasons, it simply *cannot* keep growing. Like a chorus of others, I don't believe capitalism can resolve this fundamental contradiction, which is creating conditions for a new, post-capitalist paradigm to replace it. Today a range of theorists (from radical reformers, to eco-anarchists and eco-socialists) argue that degrowth is a necessary feature of any coherent macroeconomic alternative (Kallis et al., 2018).

The clearest way to understand the multidimensional crisis of capitalism is to grasp the so-called 'limits to growth' predicament, which I'll now review very briefly, and this will also help frame and define the post-capitalist alternative of degrowth.

Limits to growth: A restatement

By all ranges of indicators, the global economy is now exceeding the sustainable carrying capacity of the planet. Climate change is perhaps the most prominent ecological transgression, but there is also biodiversity loss, resource depletion, pollution, deforestation, and a long list of other deeply unsustainable impacts. In the haunting words of James Lovelock (2010), the face of Gaia is vanishing.

It is important to understand the *extent* of ecological overshoot, because responding appropriately to the global predicament depends on a clear understanding of our situation. The ecological footprint analysis indicates that humanity would need 1.7 planets if the existing global economy could be sustained over the long term (Global Footprint Network, 2019). If the United States or Australian way of life were globalised to the world's population, humanity would need four or five planets worth of biocapacity, implying a need to reduce our 'first world' impacts by 75–80 per cent. This is an imperfect metric for ecological accounting, but most critics feel that the metric underestimates our planetary impacts.

Despite the global economy being in this state of ecological overshoot, it is also known that billions of people on the planet are, by any humane standard, under-consuming (Hickel, 2017). If these people are to raise their living standards to some dignified level of material sufficiency, as they have every right to do, it is likely that this will place further burdens on already overburdened ecosystems.

To make matters more challenging still, there are now 7.7 billion people on Earth, increasing by about 200,000 people every day. Recent projections from the United Nations suggest we are heading for around 9.7 billion by mid-century and 11 billion by 2100.

All this calls radically into question the legitimacy of continuous economic expansion and rising material living standards in rich nations. And yet, despite the fact that humanity is already making grossly unsustainable demands on a finite biosphere, all nations on the planet – including or especially the richest nations – are seeking to grow their economies without apparent limit. It is assumed that a larger economy is always better; that ongoing growth is necessary for progress.

One does not have to be a sophisticated thinker to see that this is a recipe for ecological disaster, although alarmingly this point seems to be lost on almost all politicians and most economists.

Capitalism cannot resolve its ecological contradictions

In theory, there are two broad ways to respond to the limits to growth predicament within capitalism. The first is to try to create a form of capitalism that deliberately stops growing and actually voluntarily contracts in order to operate within sustainable limits. The problem here is that there are various growth imperatives built into the structure of capitalism, which makes the notion of 'degrowth capitalism' a contradiction in terms, to be distinguished of course from capitalism in recession, which is unplanned economic contraction.

Therefore, the only other means of resolving the limits to growth predicament within capitalism is to radically decouple economic activity from environmental impact through what is called 'green growth'. The hope here is that technological innovation, market mechanisms, and efficiency improvements will reduce energy and resource demands even as the economies continue to grow in terms of GDP. Nice in theory, perhaps, but what is happening is that the absolute reductions in energy and resource demands needed for sustainability are not occurring – certainly not to sufficient degrees – and as the global economy seeks ongoing growth, absolute decoupling gets harder and harder to achieve (Kallis, 2017; Hickel and Kallis, 2019). Efficiency without sufficiency is lost.

This brings us to the most egregious flaw in growth economics, which is the apparent failure to understand the exponential function and its ecological implications. Post-growth economist Tim Jackson (2009) has shown that if the OECD nations grew their economies by a modest 2 per cent over coming decades and by 2050 a global population of nine billion had achieved similar income per capita, the global economy would be 15 times larger than it is today. It is obvious that ecological limits will not permit that scenario to eventuate – even an economy twice as large as today's economy would surely wreak ecological havoc. The critical point is that the degree of 'decoupling' required to make ongoing growth 'sustainable' is simply too great.

So capitalism wants or needs what it cannot have: that is, limitless growth on a finite planet. This ecological predicament is the defining contradiction of capitalism in the 21st century, insofar as growth is now causing the problems that growth was supposed to be solving. This suggests that the first prerequisite of a paradigm shift in political economy is well and truly met: capitalism is facing a multi-dimensional crisis that capitalism cannot resolve, and therefore, sooner or later, it will come to an end. The question of our time, as stated in my introductory comments, is how to make the transition beyond capitalism by design rather than disaster.

The crisis of ecological overshoot also provides insight into what any alternative must look like. Broadly speaking, the implications here are clear but radical: if the global economy is to operate within the sustainable carrying capacity of the planet, this requires (among other things) the richest nations to initiate a degrowth process of planned economic contraction, on the path to a 'steady state' economy of stable and sustainable biophysical throughput. Obviously, the poorest nations would also need to achieve some 'steady state' in time, but first their economic capacities must be developed in some appropriate form to ensure basic needs for all are met. But the focus presently is on the wealthy capitalist nations.

An alternative political project

The second prerequisite for a paradigm shift in political economy – for a degrowth transition, in particular – is the existence of an alternative political project. This isn't the forum to comprehensively defend this alternative political project, so I'm just going to state it, or one version of it, in order to show that an alternative post-capitalist political project is beginning to take form.

The following political agenda is, in my view, both coherent and attractive, but it will soon become clear to everyone how disconnected it is from political realism in developed nations (or anywhere) today. Of course, I would argue that this is an indictment of mainstream politics, not the theory of degrowth. However, the political and social unpalatability of degrowth is a point to which I will return, because it has implications on the question of strategy. But as an exercise in political imagination, these policies could initiate a transition to a degrowth society:

- **Alternatives to GDP:** First, any political transition beyond capitalism requires transcending the GDP fetish (Hamilton, 2003) and establishing better and more nuanced ways to measure societal progress, such as the Genuine Progress Indicator (see Kubiszewski et al., 2013). Post-growth measures of progress like this open up space for political parties to implement policy and institutional changes – including those which I am about to review – which would genuinely improve social wellbeing and enhance ecological conditions, even if these would not increase and probably even decrease GDP.

- **Diminishing Resource Caps:** If the rich, overgrown economies are serious about moving toward a just and sustainable human inhabitation of Earth, then first, we must acknowledge that we are hugely over-consuming our fair share of global resources, and second, we must institute diminishing resource caps which put strict limits on national resource flows. Fortunately, this would incentivise the efficient use of resources and dis-incentivise waste, and lead to degrowth in ecological impacts. Eco-socialists would argue that reducing societal material and energy flows will require significant nationalisation of key industries for stability during the planned contraction (Smith, 2016) whereas eco-anarchists would argue that a confederation of small self-governing communities would be the better path (Trainer, 2010). This debate is likely to continue (Alexander and Burdon, 2017) and it may be this controversy can only be resolved through practical experimentation not theory.

- **Reduced Working Hours (in Formal Economy):** One obvious implication of diminishing resource caps is that a lot less resource-intensive producing and consuming would take place in a degrowth economy. This would almost certainly lead to reduced GDP. To avoid the unemployment that typically flows from declining GDP, a degrowth economy would reduce work in the formal economy and share available work amongst the working population. Financial security in a contracting economy could also be maintained through policies like a Universal Basic Income, Universal Basic Services, or a job guarantee, as noted in the final bullet point below. (I will return to the question of informal or household economies in the next section.)

- **Rethink Government Spending:** Currently, as a general statement, governments shape their policies and spend their money in order to promote economic growth. Under a degrowth paradigm, it follows that the ways governments spend their funds would need to be fundamentally reconsidered. For example, fewer airports, roads, and tanks; more bike lanes and public transport. How we spend our money is one way to vote for what exists in the world. Rethinking government spending would also need to go hand in hand with transformations in the systemic provision of basic services. For example, Cubans have better health on average than US citizens and yet spend an estimated 90 per cent less on healthcare per capita (Hamblin, 2016). This suggests that there is ample room to provide for basic services in an affordable way while also making more public money available to fund other social projects (like a Universal Basic Income or renewable energy technologies).

- **Renewable Energy Transition:** In anticipation of the foreseeable stagnation and eventual decline of fossil fuel supplies, and recognising the grave dangers presented by climate change, a degrowth economy would divest from fossil fuels and invest in a renewable energy transition with the urgency of 'war time' mobilisation. This will be much more affordable and technically feasible if energy demand across society is greatly reduced, and that is a key feature of a degrowth society (Alexander and Floyd, 2018). The energy transition needed cannot just involve 'greening' the supply of energy, it must also involve greatly reduced demand. This means anticipating and managing what David Holmgren calls 'the energy descent future'.

- **Banking and Finance:** Our systems of banking and finance currently have a growth imperative built into their structures. Any degrowth society would have to create systems that did not require growth for stability. Debt jubilees would probably be required, especially with respect to the poorest nations. These are particularly complex issues and the forces of opposition will be fierce. But the point is that any post-growth transition is going require deep changes to the most fundamental banking, monetary, and financial institutions of capitalism.

- **Population Policies:** This is always controversial territory, especially in an age of Trump, but the environmental logic is compelling. As a population grows, more resources are required to provide for the material conditions of human wellbeing. As Paul Ehrlich once said: 'whatever problem you're interested in, you're not going to solve it unless you also solve the population problem.' I won't pose specific policies. The point is that we need to discuss this topic openly and with all the wisdom and compassion we can muster (see, e.g., Kuhleman, 2018). Population policy must be part of any coherent politics of sustainability in recognition that we live on a 'full Earth'.

- **Distributive Justice:** Last but not least, environmental concerns cannot be isolated from social justice concerns, both nationally and globally. The conventional path to poverty alleviation is via the strategy of GDP growth, on the assumption that a 'rising tide will lift all boats'. A degrowth economy would recognise that a rising tide would sink all boats, and thus poverty alleviation would be achieved much more directly. Rather than growing the economic pie, a politics of degrowth would slice the economic pie differently through redistribution of wealth and power. Prominent policies in this space include the notion of a Universal Basic Income, while others argue for a 'job guarantee' or 'Universal Basic Services' (see Frankel, 2018). These types of policies would go a long way to directly eliminating poverty, with funding supported by a maximum wage, wealth taxes, and land taxes that sought to reduce inequality. Again, eco-socialists would argue that a just distribution of wealth and power would have to involve significant socialisation of property and curtailment of 'the market'. How far socialisation would need to go, and the nature of such a transformation, is obviously open to debate.

These policy platforms – all in need of elaboration and discussion – are coherent political, economic, and social goals if a transition to degrowth society were recognised as necessary. Each of these policies could take various forms, and there is, and should be, debate within the degrowth movement and beyond about various ways to structure a post-capitalist society. But my present point is simply that a relatively coherent and developed alternative politico-economic project is emerging to replace the capitalist paradigm. So, the second prerequisite for a paradigm shift is also arguably present, which is to say: alternative structures exist.

Nevertheless, as implied above, I am the first to admit that this policy platform, coherent though it may be (to my mind), is so unpalatable to the dominant cultural consciousness that it would essentially be political suicide for any political party to try to implement it at present. In other words, what is arguably politically necessary is both socially and politically unthinkable, which is one reason, no doubt, for our current state of despairing political paralysis.

Because of this situation, whereby the politically necessary is unthinkable, I would argue that the policy platform outlined is unlikely to *initiate* a degrowth transition, but will only ever be the *outcome* of social movements; the outcome, that is, of social forces that emerge out of crisis or a series of crises and which actively create the cultural consciousness that see policies for degrowth as both necessary and desirable (Alexander and Gleeson, 2019). It is through crisis that I see the citizenries in affluent societies being shaken awake from the depoliticising effects of affluence. Encountering crises can play, and might have to play, an essential consciousness-raising role, if it triggers a desire to learn about the structural underpinnings of the crisis situation itself.

While I do not deny the need for, and desirability of, deep structural changes in the nature of our economic and political systems, what I am proposing is that a post-capitalist government may only be the outcome, not the driving force, of a transition to a just and sustainable society. In other words, our best hope for inducing a degrowth transition by design is to build a post-capitalist economics 'from below', within the shell of the current system that is currently in the process of deteriorating (Alexander and Burdon, 2017). Waiting for governments would be like waiting for Godot – a tragicomedy in two acts, in which nothing happens, twice.

Support from a comprehensive coalition of social forces

This leads me to the third prerequisite for a degrowth transition, and that is that it must have support from a comprehensive coalition of social forces. Again, space does not permit an in-depth review of these issues, a few comments will be made on examples of post-capitalist grassroots activities that are exploring modes of economy that are transcending the profit-motive for the common good, or simply building new forms of informal or household economies 'beyond the market'. These can easily be seen to be prefiguring aspects of a degrowth economy, even if this terminology is not used. Below I'll just mention four key features of post-capitalism that I see emerging from the grassroots up, features which I feel must scale up for a degrowth economy to emerge:

- First, non-monetary forms of the sharing economy, whereby communities self-organise to share resources in order to save money, partially 'escape the market', and avoid significant amounts of production (Nelson, 2018). Indeed, this is a key feature of why a degrowth economy could still thrive even when contracting: produce much less but share much more. This is part of what efficiency means in a degrowth economy. Societies can create common wealth through sharing.

- Second, a degrowth economy is likely to require a transformation of the household economy, away from merely being a place of consumption and into a place of production and self-provision. On this topic there is no better place to look than the work of permaculturist David Holmgren (2018), whose vision and insights here are utterly indispensable. There are two main reasons why a resurgence of household economies is central to a degrowth paradigm shift (Alexander and Gleeson, 2019): First, by producing more within the household, less time is needed to work in the formal economy, leaving more time outside the market for social activism and community engagement. This strategy is about escaping capitalism in order to erode it, that is, building the new economy within the shell of the old. Secondly, if financial crises deepen in coming years, the household economy may be an essential means of meeting basic needs, so the task is to prepare now for what may well prove to be harder economic times ahead. We should aim for sustainability, but we may have to settle for resilience.

- A third key feature of a degrowth economy involves significant localisation of the economy, moving toward a 'bioregional' economy where local needs are predominantly met with local resources, shortening the chain between production and consumption (Trainer, 2010).

- Finally, I'll just note that any post-capitalist economy is going to require new modes of production, moving away from profit-maximising corporations which are often owned by absentee shareholders, toward an economy where worker cooperatives, community enterprises, and not-for-profit models are the dominant forms of economic organisation, paying people living wages but reinvesting surpluses back into the community (Gibson-Graham, Cameron, and Healy, 2013; Albert, 2004). Again, there are various ways to imagine such alternative economic arrangements. Experimentation may be required as societies pursue the goal of creating economic and social systems in which more wealth and power are held in common, rather than concentrating it in private hands.

It seems to me that these alternative modes of economy, and many more besides, are bubbling everywhere under the surface, which is a hopeful sign. The Transition Towns Movement, for example, is a coherent manifestation of this grassroots approach to building local, community economies. But one must also admit that often these transgressive experiments remain small and marginalised by the dominant modes of economy. So, in terms of the third prerequisite for a post-capitalist transition, we might have to conclude that the social forces are mobilising but have not yet been able to scale up to positively disrupt, or even significantly threaten, the dominant paradigm.

Cultural consent: The sufficiency imperative

The final prerequisite for a post-capitalist degrowth transition is broad-based cultural consent. Passive consent may suffice here, without the majority of people actively seeking degrowth.

This really is a critical element in any planned transition in political economy and one that currently does not exist in terms of degrowth. It seems that the majority of people either do not think degrowth (or what it represents) is necessary or, if they do, they do not like what it means in terms of reduced and transformed consumption and production practices.

I think there are two main reasons why culture is not ready to embrace degrowth. The first reason is a deep-seated techno-optimism that shapes cultural thinking about environmental problems. This view assumes that technology and market mechanisms will be able to resolve the crises of capitalism without system change and without even much in terms of lifestyle change. In other words, the zeitgeist of our times seems to be that consumer affluence is consistent with justice and sustainability, because it is assumed that efficiency improvements in modes of production will be able to produce 'green growth' without having to rethink consumption practices (Hickel and Kallis, 2019).

Although this techno-optimistic blind spot is a major obstacle to degrowth, I hold some uneasy confidence that as capitalism continues to collide with ecological limits in coming years and decades, the case for degrowth will only become clearer to more and more people, which could act as a mobilising force.

However, even if the crises of capitalism deepen and the majority of people come to desire a post-capitalist political economy, it does not follow that a degrowth economy is what they would demand (Buch-Hansen, 2018). This points to a serious cultural obstacle to a degrowth transition: the fact that the dominant conception of the good life under capitalism is based on consumer affluence. It seems to me that there will never be a post-capitalist politics until there is a post-consumerist culture that is prepared to embrace material sufficiency as a desirable way of life (Alexander, 2015b). Herein lies the importance of the voluntary simplicity, simple living, and downshifting movements. Although in need of radicalisation (and organisation for collective action), these movements or subcultures are beginning to create the cultural conditions needed for a politics and economics of degrowth to emerge.

It all depends on the ideas (and practices) that are lying around

When the crises of capitalism deepen – perhaps in the form of a new financial crisis or a Second Great Depression – the task will be to ensure that such destabilised conditions are used to advance progressive humanitarian and ecological ends, rather than exploited to further entrench the austerity politics of neoliberalism. I recognise, of course, that the latter remains a real possibility, as did the arch-capitalist Milton Friedman (2002: xiv), who expressed the point in these terms:

Only a crisis – actual or perceived – produces real change. When that crisis occurs, the actions that are taken depend on the ideas that are lying around. That, I believe, is our basic function: to develop alternatives to existing policies, to keep them alive and available until the politically impossible becomes the politically inevitable.

I'm not often in complete agreement with Milton Friedman, but on this point I am. Our basic function – and I'm talking now to those who recognise the radical implications of living in an age of severe environmental limits – our basic function is to keep hopes of a radically different and more humane form of society alive, until what today seems impossible or implausible becomes, if not inevitable, then at least possible and perhaps even probable. And on those rare occasions when despair lifts and the human spirit shows itself in noble forms, 'the ideas that are lying around' and indeed 'the practices that are lying around', look so strong and convincing that it tempts even this apocaloptimist into considering becoming a plain, old-fashioned optimist. Or, with a nod to Gramsci, at least one is permitted to proceed with a pessimistic intellect and a cautiously optimistic will.

References

Albert, M. 2004. *Parecon: Life After Capitalism*. London: Verso.

Alexander, S. (ed.) 2009. *Voluntary Simplicity: The Poetic Alternative to Consumer Culture*. Whanganui: Stead and Daughters.

Alexander, S. 2015a. *Prosperous Descent: Crisis as Opportunity in an Age of Limits*. Melbourne: Simplicity Institute.

Alexander, S. 2015b. *Sufficiency Economy: Enough, for Everyone, Forever*. Melbourne: Simplicity Institute.

Alexander, S. and Burdon, P. 2017. 'Wild Democracy: A Biodiversity of Resistance and Renewal'. *Ecological Citizen* 1(1): 45–54.

Alexander, S. and Floyd, J. 2018. *Carbon Civilisation and the Energy Descent Future: Life Beyond this Brief Anomaly*. Melbourne: Simplicity Institute.

Alexander, S. and Gleeson, B. 2019. *Degrowth in the Suburbs: A Radical Urban Imaginary*. Singapore: Palgrave.

Buch-Hansen, H. 2018. 'The Prerequisites for a Degrowth Paradigm Shift: Insights from Critical Political Economy'. *Ecological Economics* 146: 157–163.

Frankel, B. 2018. *Fictions of Sustainability: The Politics of Growth and Post-Capitalist Futures*. Melbourne: Greenmeadows.

Friedman, M. (2002.) *Capitalism and Freedom*. Chicago: University of Chicago Press.

Gibson-Graham, J.K., Cameron, J. and Healy, S. 2013. *Take Back the Economy: An Ethical Guide for Transforming Our Communities*. Minneapolis: University of Minnesota Press.

Global Footprint Network 2019. 'Ecological footprint'. Available at: https://www.footprintnetwork.org/our-work/ecological-footprint/ (accessed 10 February 2019).

Hamblin, J. 2016. 'How Cubans Live as Long as Americans at 1/10th the Cost'. *The Atlantic* (29 Nov. 2016).

Hamilton, C. 2003. *Growth Fetish*. Crows Nest: Allen & Unwin.

Hickel, J. 2017. *The Divide: A Brief Guide to Global Inequality and Its Solutions.* Cornerstone: William Heinemann.

Hickel, J. and Kallis, G. 2019. 'Is Green Growth Possible?' *New Political Economy* 25: 469–486.

Holmgren, D. 2018. *RetroSuburbia: The Downshifter's Guide to a Resilient Future.* Hepburn Springs: Melliodora Publishing.

Jackson, T. 2009. *Prosperity Without Growth: Economics for a Finite Planet.* London: Earthscan.

Jameson, F. 2003. 'Future City'. *New Left Review* 21: 65–79.

Kallis, G. 2017. 'Radical Dematerialization and Degrowth'. *Philosophical Transactions of the Royal Society A* 375 (20160383): 1–13.

Kallis, G. et al. 2018. 'Research on Degrowth'. *Annual Review of Environment and Resources* 43: 4.1–4.26.

Kubiszewski, I. et al. 2013. 'Beyond GDP: Measuring and Achieving Global Genuine Progress'. *Ecological Economics* 93: 57–68.

Kuhleman, K. 2018. 'Any Size Population Will Do? The Fallacy of Aiming for Stabilization of Human Numbers'. *Ecological Citizen* 1: 181–91.

Lovelock, J. 2010. *The Vanishing Face of Gaia.* New York: Basic Books.

Mason, P. 2015. *Post-Capitalism: A Guide to Our Future.* London: Allan Lane.

Nelson, A. 2018. *Small is Necessary: Shared Living on a Shared Planet.* London: Pluto Press.

Smith, R. 2016. *Green Capitalism: The God that Failed.* London: College Publications.

Trainer, T. 2010. *Transition to a Sustainable and Just World.* Sydney: Envirobook.

Wall, D. 2015. *Economics after Capitalism: A Guide to the Ruins and a Road to the Future.* London: Pluto Press.

Chapter 4

Urban social movements and the degrowth transition: Toward a grassroots theory of change[1]

Since the 1970s the 'limits to growth' position has received a great deal of attention, mostly from economic and ecological perspectives (Meadows et al., 1972; Bardi, 2011; Turner, 2014). A key position within this movement is that technological advance and efficiency gains in production will be unable to resolve ecological transgressions if such innovations are applied within a growth paradigm of economy (Hickel and Kallis, 2019; Ward et al., 2016). Given that the global economy already seems to be in significant ecological overshoot, any transition to a just and ecological civilisation will require 'degrowth' in the richest and most developed regions of the world, which means planned and equitable contraction of energy and resource demands. The envisioned end state would involve a 'pluriverse' of highly localised and broadly egalitarian economies based on material sufficiency not limitless growth, powered by renewable energy, and operating primarily within bioregions (see D'Alisa, Demaria, and Kallis, 2015).

This chapter seeks to extend and deepen the understanding of degrowth by examining the concept and the movement from a perspective that has received little attention – namely, theories of transition. Much has been written on the 'why' of degrowth; it is time to focus more on the strategic question of 'how'. Our specific interest lies in understanding which levers of power in society (e.g. the state, technology, capital, social movements, etc.) may be needed or available to drive a democratic degrowth transition. How might those levers reshape society, and in what ways, to initiate a degrowth process of planned economic contraction?

While addressing questions of transition and transformation, our further point of departure is to look at degrowth through the lens of urban

---

1 Originally published in the *Journal of Australian Political Economy* (2020/2021, in press), co-authored with Brendan Gleeson.

studies – and conversely, to look at urbanity through the lens of degrowth (Alexander and Gleeson, 2019). Harvey Molotch (1976) long ago described the city as a 'growth machine'. How to mobilise socially and politically to transform that machine on democratic terms is clearly a pressing issue of our time. Can the emerging degrowth literature shed light on this urban challenge? Can urban studies offer insights for the degrowth movement? Literature at the nexus of these issues is scarce (Lietaert, 2010; Xue, 2015; March, 2016; Lehtinen, 2018) and the question of an urban degrowth transition is sorely neglected. But one thing is clear: it will be in cities where most of humanity experiences, and responds to, the deepening crises of the global neoliberal order (Wright, Nyberg, and Rickards, 2018).

Below we explore the role urban social movements might need to play as the principal democratic organising forces of a degrowth transition in cities. Defined further in later sections, urban social movements are 'urban-orientated mobilizations that influence structural social change' (Castells, 1983: 305). The premise is that through 'self-organization of independent actors' urban social movements raise 'radical possibilities for living different urban lives in reconfigured urban economies' (Bulkeley, 2013: 11). Exploring this mode of societal transformation is especially important for those who hold little faith that governments, especially in capitalist societies, would initiate a degrowth process from the 'top down'. It was that pessimism that led us to develop, in the context of degrowth, a grassroots theory of change 'from below'.

The analysis begins by outlining the various 'growth imperatives' that shape capitalist economies, in order to justify our pessimism with respect to leadership on degrowth coming from governments.[2] Upon those foundations a theory of change is presented that we maintain is the most coherent framework for creating, by design rather than disaster, a post-growth (and thus post-capitalist) urbanity. The degrowth literature is utilised to frame our analysis and to argue that, given the various growth imperatives constraining government action under globalised and increasingly urbanised capitalism today, the emergence of a degrowth society will need to be driven into existence from the grassroots up, rather than from the top down. Put otherwise, in a neoliberal order where so-called 'representative governments' are deeply compromised by unsustainable growth imperatives, any degrowth transition will require

---

2 While some of the growth imperatives we discuss apply equally to socialist or communist economies (e.g., China), the transitional challenge 'beyond growth' raises different questions, so our focus herein is on capitalist societies that have grounding in democracy.

engaged citizenries employing radical and participatory democratic practices to induce this paradigmatic shift in political economy. The long historical conspiracy of liberal democracy and consumptive capitalism suggests that the ballot box is a political tool that will not lead the transition to a post-growth dispensation.

After sketching this theory of change the analysis concludes by outlining how early signs are emerging of what, tentatively, could be considered the birth of a 'degrowth urbanity'. This review includes post-consumerist movements that are prefiguring degrowth cultures of consumption by embracing material sufficiency as a path to freedom, meaning, and reduced ecological burdens; community-led urban resistance and renewal movements; transgressive and creative forms of the sharing economy as a means of thriving even in a contracting biophysical economy; as well as other social movements and strategies that are seeking to develop new (or renewed) informal urban economies 'beyond the market'.

Highlighting the importance of urban social movements does not mean there is no need for structural change via state action. Human behaviour inevitably takes place within structures of constraint that often 'lock' people in to high-impact living (Sanne, 2002), while locking many more out of economic security. This is a systemic problem that will ultimately require a systemic response. Nevertheless, our core thesis is that a post-growth or degrowth state will most likely be the outcome, not the driving force, of a just and sustainable post-capitalist society, with significant structural change occurring only *after* grassroots movements initiate new post-capitalist economies and cultures within the shell of capitalist economies. As David Harvey (2013: xvi) contends, reclaiming the democratic city 'cannot occur without the creation of a vigorous anti-capitalist movement that focuses on the transformation of daily urban life as its goal.' Building on that insight, we will argue that there will never be a transformative politics or economics beyond growth until there is a broad culture of sufficiency, solidarity, and participatory democracy that demands it.

The growth imperatives of capitalism

To lay the foundations for our theory of change, it is necessary to outline why the political economy of growth has acquired its hegemony (Purdey, 2010) and why hopes of an enlightened government or state leading a degrowth transition from the top down seem slim to non-existent (Alexander, 2013). These foundational inquiries are important because understanding the extent of capitalism's 'growth imperative' has implications on political, economic and more specifically business strategies for change. If it is accepted that capitalism requires growth for stability and that ongoing growth is unsustainable, then it follows that capitalism has an ecological time limit.

Our starting premise, then, is that a 'degrowth capitalism' (to be distinguished from capitalism in recession) is a contradiction in terms (Foster, 2011; Trainer, 2012). Below, the logic of this observation is outlined by highlighting the various growth imperatives of capitalism. Note that several of these imperatives blur into each other, even as they represent distinct issues. Even one of these structural issues would suffice to establish that capitalism is growth-dependent; together they show the imperative to grow is compelling.

Microeconomic and macroeconomic growth imperatives

Within capitalist economies, corporate firms must seek to maximise profits and productivity or risk being destroyed by more ambitious and ruthless market competitors (Gordon and Rosenthal, 2003; Binswanger, 2009; Harvey, 2008). While human greed plays a role in the pursuit of profit-maximisation, this first point is more fundamental: the nature and systemic logic of capitalist economies require profit-maximisation at the microeconomic level, which functions to give the capitalist macroeconomy a built-in structural tendency toward growth (Smith, 2010; Blauwhof, 2012). From a systems perspective, this growth imperative is an emergent property of the interactions of the microeconomic agents. Thus, the macroeconomic structure of capitalism is organised in a way that requires the microeconomic organisations within capitalism to accord with its golden rule: expand capital (Harvey, 2011).

Debt as a growth imperative

Similarly, there is a related growth imperative created by debt-based monetary systems, especially but not exclusively under capitalism. Currently most money is loaned into existence by private banks as interest-bearing debt, and in order to pay back the debt plus the interest, this implies an expansion of the monetary supply (Trainer, 2011). Banks will generally prefer to lend to people, organisations, or institutions most able to pay back the debts incurred, and those most likely to make the most profit get given credit first. This lending system inherently gives capitalism a pro-growth structure, since money – and the power it brings – is most readily available to the firms most likely to make the most profit. Again, at the macroeconomic level, the same golden rule of capitalism applies: grow the economy or enter crisis.

Power as a growth imperative

Furthermore, the largest corporations and governments that are doing financially well within the capitalist system would not tolerate a deliberate transition to a post-growth or degrowth economy. At least since Marx there has been a line of critical theory that conceptualises the state as merely a tool for securing and advancing the interests of the richest agents or institutions in society (Marx and Engels, 1985). In a market society, money is power; the powerful want to remain powerful; thus, the powerful want more money to secure and advance their interests. The logic is simple but compelling: 'A government is thus to some extent forced to please the economic elite in order to stay in power' (Boillat, Gerber, and Funes-Monzote, 2012: 601). Governments also seek a growing economy because that implies a larger tax base to draw from to implement their range of policies. There is an important geopolitical factor here: governments need growth to maintain or advance their balance of power in a military sense.

Globalisation as a growth imperative

Indeed, even if a government *wanted* to pursue a degrowth agenda, there are global and national economic forces at play which would obstruct such an agenda being rolled out. Call this the problem of 'Empire', a concept developed by post-Marxist political theorists Michael Hardt and Antonio Negri (2000). Not only are nation-states today constrained by numerous international trade agreements and powerful global institutions, but the free flow of capital around the globe has given new power to an imperium of transnational corporations that can now move their financial resources from country to country with unprecedented ease. If governments were to create unattractive financial conditions (e.g., by raising corporate taxes or minimum wages), corporations could threaten 'capital flight', and just knowing that capital flight is possible can insidiously constrain government action through fear, even in the absence of an explicit threat. The globalisation of capital therefore creates another structural growth imperative.

In summary, the possibility of a state-led degrowth transition seems impossibly constrained by the structural imperatives of capitalism. The growth-dependent, heavily indebted market economies we know today would be unable to adjust to the types and speed of the foundational changes required to avert ecological and financial crisis. This inevitably has an urban dimension too, with the city itself being described as a 'growth machine' by Harvey Molotch (1976), a perspective that has provoked an entire tradition of scholarship and analysis (see Cox, 2017). Molotch (1976: 310) argued that 'this growth imperative is the most important constraint upon available options for local initiative in social and economic reform.' In an age when capitalism has attained near complete hegemony, growth-orientated societies just do not know how to deliberately create a macroeconomy or urban form that produces and consumes *less* – and yet, as the limits to growth (Bardi, 2011) and degrowth literatures maintain (Kallis et al., 2018; Weiss and Cattaneo, 2017), that is precisely what seems to be necessary for ecological viability.

Degrowth from below: Toward a grassroots theory of change

If the global economy is to operate within the sustainable carrying capacity of the planet, this requires (among other things) the richest nations to initiate a degrowth process of planned economic contraction, on the path to a 'steady state' economy of stable biophysical throughput (Hickel and Kallis, 2019). Obviously, the poorest nations would also need to achieve some 'steady state' in time, but first their economic capacities must be developed in some form to ensure basic needs for all are met (Escobar, 2015; O'Neill et al., 2018). We do not argue that a voluntary transformation of overgrown economies is likely, only that, by force of reason and evidence, some such transition will be necessary if there is to be any human reconciliation with Nature.

There is much governments could be doing to help produce more just and sustainable societies – and there is no shortage of literature providing stimulating advice – but the central point from the analysis above is that governments, especially under capitalism, have various growth imperatives built into their structures. It follows that attempting to take control of the state may not necessarily be the best way to initiate the transition to a just and sustainable degrowth economy, for even a socialist state may find itself locked into unsustainable growth just as capitalism is (Sarkar, 1999).

Therefore, a post-growth state may only ever be the outcome, not the driving force, of a movement for degrowth (Alexander and Gleeson, 2019).

This raises the key question of what social, political, and economic forces or mechanisms might drive such a transition beyond growth (Demaria et al, 2013). If conventional representative democracy is unable to accommodate the degrowth imperative by virtue of politicians and dominant institutions being locked into the growth paradigm, then it follows that the emergence of degrowth will have to depend on a post-capitalist politics of participatory democracy and grassroots activism (Gibson-Graham, 2006). This means relocalising political power through participatory and collective action, rather than waiting for governments or corporations to solve problems that they are either unable or unwilling to solve. In an urban age, this may well depend on urban social movements creating, within the city boundaries, post-capitalist degrowth economies and cultures from the grassroots up. The remainder of this chapter outlines and explains this theory of change.

Transforming the city without (at first) taking power

In pro-growth political contexts – particularly contemporary cities in the most affluent regions of the world (Molotch, 1976) – it is at the household and community levels where people arguably have most freedom to influence their urban existence in a post-growth direction (Gibson-Graham, Cameron, and Healy, 2013). Thus it is at this grassroots level where we invest hope for change; where the sparks of transformation are going to have to ignite if a degrowth society is to emerge. People may not feel like they have much influence over the decisions of their members of parliament, or the decisions of big business or other global institutions, all of which are manifestly entrenched within the growth paradigm.

This is especially so in a neoliberal age in which the dominant task of urban governance, according to Harvey (1989: 11), is 'to lure highly mobile and flexible production, financial, and consumption flows into its space.' Furthermore, the distributive implications, as economist and urbanist Hugh Stretton (1970: 310) noted long ago, are that cities become devices for 'shifting resources from poorer to richer'. But within the structural constraints of any society or city there nevertheless resides a realm of freedom through which individuals and communities – insofar as they have escaped or resisted the neoliberal worldview – can resist and oppose the existing order and make their influence felt (Holloway, 2002; Trainer, 2010; Holmgren, 2018). Indeed, urban social movements have often arisen in reaction to neoliberal urbanism (Mayer, 2006), and this conflict may be set to deepen.

It is in those cracks which permit a degree of urban autonomy and self-governance where participants in a degrowth movement need to thrust the crowbar of oppositional activity in the hope of leveraging their influence. Through a process of participatory democracy and grassroots action there might be a chance to 'crack capitalism', as political theorist John Holloway (2010) puts it. We say that there might just be a chance in the sense that it is the best and perhaps only hope. This is not to say that the household or community levels are necessarily the ideal spheres of urban transformation (a question we leave open); it is only to acknowledge that if governments will not embrace degrowth, and businesses must grow for viability, then the household and community levels, acting and organising locally (though still with an eye on the 'big picture'), are the most promising spheres of transformative potential.[3] There is deep historical wisdom to draw on here. For Aristotle, 'economy' meant the good management of the household, and for him the household was the foundation of the *polis*. In our age of apparent governmental paralysis and growth fetishism, this Aristotelian perspective might again highlight the necessity of a political strategy that begins with the intentional transformation of urban daily life (as explored further in the next section).

This perspective could be easily misunderstood, so a word of clarification is in order. Strong top-down governance of (urban) economies would in many ways be desirable. Governments, local and national, could do many things to advance the causes of justice and sustainability, and elsewhere we have shared our thoughts on policies for a post-growth economy (Alexander, 2016; Alexander and Gleeson, 2019). We acknowledge, furthermore, that mobilising for degrowth only at the grassroots (or micro-economic) level is problematic, since voluntarily reducing energy and resource consumption in a market society can function to reduce pressure on markets and hence induce price reductions. Those pricing

---

3 While social enterprises, non-profit businesses, or the 'B corporation' movement might also hold some potential for post-capitalist economics (Khmara and Kronenberg, 2018), these alternative practices and institutions inevitably operate within a growth-orientated system and compete with (and tend to be outcompeted by) conventional capitalist firms that are significantly advantaged in the market by externalising environmental and social costs. Thus, in our view, alternative corporate forms are likely to remain marginal and easily accommodated by the existing system.

dynamics can then lead to *increased* consumption by those actors in society who are not attempting to create a degrowth society and who happily exploit the access to cheaper commodities. This 'wicked problem' has lead Blake Alcott (2008) to highlight the legitimate concern that frugality in some sectors of society might lead to a consumption 'rebound effect' elsewhere. Accordingly, in order to affect structural reduction in energy and resource use, there ultimately needs to be some mechanisms to limit aggregate use – and this needs cooperation by formal political and economic institutions.

Nevertheless, our position is that growth fetishism has such a strong hold on the branches of government that efforts directed toward producing strong top-down policy for a degrowth economy will essentially be ignored by policy makers – unable to make it through the filter of capitalist structures and ideology – thus those efforts for progressive top-down change could well be wasted. Marginal anti-capitalist movements like degrowth do not, of course, have a surplus of energy or resources to waste or misdirect, so if it is the case that the zebra of growth capitalism will not change its stripes, it arguably follows that people should not dedicate their efforts toward convincing it to do so, no matter how desirable that top-down change may be. Rather, people should dedicate their efforts toward areas with the greatest leverage – with the greatest potential to effect positive change. With respect to degrowth, the areas that have the greatest leverage lie amongst the grassroots of social movements and culture, not parliament or the courts – at least at this early stage in the transformation (Alexander, 2013; Demaria et al., 2013).

The socio-cultural domain may have special disruptive potential due to the fact that other spheres of transformation can be understood as tools or means, whereas the socio-cultural sphere can be understood to be the source of goals or ends. In much the same way as the tool of 'fire' can have a positive or negative impact on our lives, depending on how it is used and how much of it there is, the tools of technology, business, and politics can advance or inhibit the transition to a degrowth society, depending on the social values and desires that shape their implementation and development. For these reasons, the socio-cultural sphere can be considered fundamental, in the sense that it provides the ends toward which available means are directed. Put otherwise, a revolutionary consciousness (or new 'social imaginary') must precede the revolution.

This is not meant to downplay the undeniable importance of technological, economic, and political innovations on the path to a new, ecologically viable and socially just way of life. A coordinated, multi-faceted and multiscalar approach is both necessary and desirable (Mayer, 2013). But insofar as technology, business, and politics reflect the culture in which they are situated, it would seem that disruptive innovation in the socio-cultural sphere may need to be the prime mover, so to speak, which would then enable or ignite further disruptive innovations in other spheres of life.

This suggests that we must carefully consider not only what societal conditions would best facilitate the urban realisation of a degrowth economy, but also what role social or cultural movements might have to play in producing those conditions. For even if notions of degrowth were to gain widespread acceptance within a culture, it seems highly unlikely that a degrowth economy would emerge unless people had some idea of what needed to be done at the household and community levels to bring about such an economy. In other words, it is not enough merely to offer a critique of existing *structures* of growth capitalism; it is equally important to explore the question of *how one ought to live* in opposition to those structures. If governments will not lead this process, it arguably follows that social movements might have to change the world without (at first) taking state power (Holloway, 2010; Gibson-Graham, Cameron, and Healy, 2013).

The practice of post-capitalist politics and economics

'[W]ithout social movements, no challenge will emerge from civil society able to shake the institutions of the state through which norms are enforced, values preached, and property preserved.'
Manuel Castells, *The City and the Grassroots* (1983)

In the introduction we noted David Harvey's comment that reclaiming the city 'cannot occur without the creation of a vigorous anti-capitalist movement that focuses on the transformation of daily urban life as its goal' (Harvey, 2013: xvi). While a singular or homogenous anti-capitalist movement does not exist, the following brief review indicates that a heterogeneous body of loosely connected urban social movements is emerging that seems to be prefiguring aspects of a degrowth society. The vocabulary of degrowth does not need to be used for a movement to contribute to degrowth's emergence.

The Voluntary Simplicity Movement

The lived experience of degrowth necessarily implies a deep reevaluation of consumer affluence and an embrace of lifestyles of radical material sufficiency. This exploration of post-consumerist ways of living is currently being undertaken within the Voluntary Simplicity Movement (Alexander, 2009), with participants seeking to live more on less (Kasser, 2017). This is an example of social movement resisting capitalist cultures of hyper-consumption and beginning to establish the counter-cultural conditions needed for a degrowth economy to emerge structurally. Some hard-nosed political economists might be inclined to dismiss this as a naive 'lifestyle movement' of little consequence, but in our view that critique masks its own naivety, since the macroeconomic or structural changes that certainly are needed for degrowth will never arrive until there is a material culture of sufficiency that demands them. As Taylor, O'Brien, and O'Keefe (2017: 796) argue: 'modern mass consumption developed in nineteenth century cities as a bottom-up process of acquisitive behavior [and] ... to reverse the now uber-acquisitiveness will also be a bottom-up process.'

Based on the largest empirical examination of this movement, it has been estimated that as many as 200 million people are exploring 'simpler ways' of living in the so-called developed nations (Alexander and Ussher, 2012), even if it must be acknowledged that this will involve a wide spectrum of practices, from modest attempts to reduce consumption to more radical expressions of downshifting. Challenging the popular conception of 'simple living' as being a rural lifestyle, the same study suggested that approximately 80 percent of voluntary simplifiers are actually based in urban centres. Furthermore, the results showed that 68 percent of voluntary simplifiers have come to conceive of themselves as being part of a simple living movement. This is a significant finding, given that historically the Voluntary Simplicity Movement has tended to be apolitical or escapist (Grigsby, 2004). Much social movement theory suggests that the emergence of group consciousness (or a shared 'social imaginary') is an important and necessary phase in the maturation of a social movement into a more potent political force (see McCann, 2006; Taylor, 2004).

The political and economic significance of the voluntary simplicity movement is most apparent in how it can carve out *more time for people to create the new economy*. Building a new economy from the grassroots up will take time, and currently most households are 'time poor', locked into the work-and-spend cycle (Coote and Franklin, 2013). By rethinking consumption levels, embracing frugality, and exchanging superfluous stuff for more free time, voluntary simplicity provides a pathway that can enable the participation in, and organisation of, grassroots activism, while also being directly in line with the sufficiency-oriented values of degrowth.

As well as facilitating and enabling urban activism, a broader uptake of voluntary simplicity could also impact on the organisation of the economy more broadly. By carving out more time beyond the formal economy, new forms of community engagement and self-provision could arise (see next section) as well as increased 'home-based production', all of which could begin to transform the economic landscape 'from below' by creating new economic agents and entities. Furthermore, existing modes of economic organisation and production may wither away as demand for certain high-impact products and lifestyles lose their cultural appeal (e.g., SUVs, 'fast fashion', fossil fuels, etc.), including a shift in workplace culture and organisation as more people choose time over money, reducing working hours in a contracting formal economy. Indeed, degrowth could be defined as the politics (and macroeconomics) of voluntary simplicity.

Nevertheless, it is clear that the Voluntary Simplicity Movement must expand, radicalise and organise if it is ever to become a transformative political and economic force (Trainer, 2010). This implies 'a shift to change the everyday behaviours of billions of people, and, just as important, to change the "development" aspirations of other billions of people to realize such behaviour' (Taylor, O'Brien, and O'Keefe, 2017: 796). Like all the examples discussed below, it is likely that online networking will need to play a key role mobilising urban social movements in the 21st century (see Bennett and Segerberg, 2012), primarily by reducing the transaction costs of organisation, networking, and information sharing.

Transition Initiatives, permaculture, and localisation movements

The Transition Towns Movement (now generally referred to as 'Transition Initiatives') is a recent social experiment that emerged little over a decade ago – first in the UK and now in more than forty countries around the world. It remains bubbling under the surface in many towns and cities (Hopkins, 2008; Hopkins, 2011). Whereas the more-established Ecovillage Movement has generally sought (or been required) to escape the urban context to establish experiments in alternative living, Transition Initiatives, motivated by similar concerns, tends to accept the challenge of transforming city life from *within* the urban boundary. A 600-page practical urban manual has just been published by co-originator of the permaculture concept, David Holmgren (2018), who calls on people to 'retrofit the suburbs for the energy descent future'.

The fundamental aims of Transition Initiatives are to respond to the overlapping challenges of climate change, peak oil, social isolation, and economic instability by decarbonising and relocalising the economy through a community-led model of change based on permaculture design principles. This urban movement has much overlap with the grassroots politics of degrowth outlined above, as well as broader localisation (de Young and Princen, 2012) and permaculture movements (Holmgren, 2002). Holmgren has even applied permaculture to organisational practices, arguing that they apply equally well to business. He is not referring to the conventional sense of business, defined by self-interested accumulation and all that this implies as a framing for the capitalist growth economy. Rather, he is acknowledging that there would still need to be businesses (i.e., modes of production) in a permaculture or degrowth economy, albeit alternative forms, through which production, circulation, and consumption in society would be organised. This is not the place to attempt to develop a detailed institutional framework for an alternative economy, but the 'participatory economics' of Michael Albert (2004) or the 'community economies' of J.K. Gibson-Graham and colleagues (2013) are paving the way.

Rather than waiting for governments to lead, urban communities in the Transition Movement are embracing the 'power of just doing stuff', as it is expressed by the movement's most prominent spokesperson, Rob Hopkins (2013). In doing so, the movement runs counter to the dominant narrative of globalisation, representative democracy, and economic growth, and instead offers a positive, participatory, highly localised but more humble vision of a post-carbon and post-growth future, as well as an evolving roadmap for getting there through grassroots activism. In the words of post-growth economist Tim Jackson, this international grassroots movement is 'the most vital social experiment of our time' (quoted in Hopkins, 2011).

Although still small in the greater scheme of things, and easily accommodated by capitalism at the current scale, something resembling an upscaled and radicalised Transition Movement may be necessary to the emergence of an urban degrowth economy from below. Again, without attempting a detailed sketch of the new economy, an upscaled and diversified Transition Movement would impact on economic practices and organisation through increased localisation of production, with the focus on collective sufficiency not limitless economic expansion. At the same time, any degrowth economy will need to 'develop' certain elements of the economy (e.g., renewable energy, public transport, organic food, etc.), all of which is indicative of new organisational forms and capacities, decoupled from the logic of accumulation for its own sake.

Reactive urban mobilisations: localised resistance to neoliberal urbanism

While the Transition Movement is generally focused on building the new economy, it is worth noting that there are also examples in history and today of urban communities mobilising in a more reactive way to the city as 'growth machine' (Molotch, 1976), opposing neoliberal urbanism rather than building an alternative. In our context of Australia, the 'Save Our Suburbs' coalition is such an example, which is focused on resisting the destructive renewal of urban consolidation and over-development (Lewis, 1999: Ch 10). This movement seeks to mobilise communities with the aim of establishing planning and design policies that maintain or improve neighbourhood amenity; are environmentally sensitive and sustainable; and are genuinely democratic and consultative in nature. The network is often demonised by planners and progressives who advocate market-based compaction. There is also a risk that the movement reflects a class of privileged actors who, far from being motivated by hopes of contributing to the common good, merely seek to maintain the clean and spacious affluence of their own often expensive and thus exclusive suburban contexts.

Nevertheless, this urban social movement (and others like it) may hold the seeds of something more progressive – at least potentially. The problem with current modes of urban development – especially poorly designed in-fill apartments on suburban subdivisions that are all too common in contemporary Australia – is that the outcome often functions to inhibit or render impossible the very modes of urban sufficiency that are implicit in the vision for degrowth. Until urban communities mobilise in the face of capital and reclaim the right to shape their own urban futures, cities are likely to continue being shaped and reshaped by developers who are driven by profit-maximisation (Harvey, 1989; Gleeson, 2014), not the desire to see the urban landscapes transform in ecologically viable and socially convivial ways.

In this context the nascent Extinction Rebellion deserves note, which recently erupted in the UK and elsewhere (Read and Alexander, 2020). Based on well organised and creative strategies of non-violent civil disobedience, it is the most recent example of reactive grassroots political mobilisation manifesting in urban contexts, drawing inspiration from activists and social movements as diverse as Occupy, Gandhi and the Independence Movement, the suffragettes, and the Civil Rights Movement. While it is too early to assess the full potential and impacts of Extinction Rebellion, it has already achieved some of its goals by bringing much renewed media attention to climate change and loss of biodiversity, and has arguably been a contributing factor to the UK being the first nation in the world to declare a state of environment and climate 'emergency'. This is an apt example of how urban mobilisations can move from the streets to the corridors of power in government, emerging in the socio-cultural sphere but inducing, or threatening to induce, political and macroeconomic shifts in societal structures and institutions, which could then facilitate further cultural shifts; and so on, in a dialectical fashion.

An economics of sharing: Access without ownership

The fast-emerging 'sharing economy' is another primarily urban phenomenon and denotes one of the theoretical buzzwords of recent years (Frenken, 2017). The density of populations in urban centres, coupled with internet access, provide fertile grounds for sharing economies to flourish, and it is heartening to see this movement expanding in cities around the world (Nelson, 2018). By sharing more between households – facilitated by the internet or by traditional community engagement – less energy and resource intensive production needs to occur to meet society's needs. Even in a contracting economy (whether contraction is by design or by crisis), households can still secure access to the tools and other things they need, provided a culture of sharing emerges. This is the revolutionary reinterpretation of 'efficiency' implicit in the degrowth paradigm: produce less; share more. Beyond goods and services, theorists are beginning to explore the potential of sharing land and housing as a promising means of overcoming some of the access barriers to this fundamental need (Nelson, 2018). In what has become a slogan of movement, the sharing economy is about 'access without ownership', suggesting that a revision of property relations is underway.

As always, caution must be shown, given that the sharing economy is a broad umbrella, which can include forms that are easily co-opted by conventional economic practices and lose their transgressive force (Frenken, 2017; McLaren and Agyeman, 2017). Air BnB has few environmental credentials if it merely makes long-distance travel more affordable; access to expensive handbags through sharing schemes is not progressive if it merely entrenches consumer culture; and so forth. In contrast, the online organisation 'Streetbank' is one of the most authentic expressions of sharing, where people create accounts and list what they would like to borrow from neighbours and what they are prepared to share, without money ever changing hands.

It is clear that in a degrowth economy, non-monetary sharing of this latter kind provides a key strategy for adapting to and even flourishing in conditions of economic contraction. 'Wealth' is created by sharing, without needing extra (and even reducing) resource or energy intensive production. So the challenge will be to ensure that the new economic organisations that emerge in the 'sharing economy' are not merely exploiting under-utilised assets for private benefit, but are structured cooperatively to permit and create broadly distributed common wealth (see Bauwens and Amos, 2018). Otherwise the sharing economy will merely be a mask for the same old logic of private accumulation and have little transformative force or effect.

Home-based production and the informal 'gift' economy

An urban degrowth movement might also involve turning the household (once again) into a place of production, not merely consumption. On this point, some inspiration can be found in the past. Urbanists Patrick Mullins and Chris Kynaston (2000) assess what they call the 'urban peasant thesis', and their review of the evidence shows that up until the middle of the twentieth century, Australian urban households had operated a highly developed subsistence-based, domestic economy. This included the production of foodstuffs in suburban backyards, but extended to the manufacture of other household goods, including clothes, furniture, and even owner-built housing. Thus the dwelling and the yard were seen primarily in utilitarian, rather than aesthetic, terms. This 'urban peasantry' declined, however, in the post-war boom, as the rise of mass consumer capitalism enabled households to purchase goods previously produced within the household. Any degrowth or post-capitalist transition may well see the re-emergence of an 'urban peasantry' in this sense, albeit one shaped by different times and concerns. If the automation of the workforce leaves more people unemployed, it may be that people have the time (and incentives) to invest in home-based production as a means of self-provision, thus pointing to new (or resurrected) places of work. This shift from formal economy to household economy is also another example of post-capitalist economics, insofar as things are primarily produced for use, rather than exchange (Gibson-Graham, 2006; Gibson-Graham, Cameron, and Healy, 2013).

An urban degrowth economy also implies an incremental re-emergence of the gift economy – to some extent, at least (Eisenstein, 2011). If material living standards are forever expected to rise, long working hours required to support that ongoing material advance will generally leave people 'time poor', making it difficult for people to gift their skills and resources in the spirit of community and neighbourly support. By consuming less and carving out more time for practices outside the formal economy, the practice of voluntary simplicity can also enliven the informal 'gift' economy. In similar ways to sharing practices, this can ensure society's needs are met even in a contracting (formal) economy.

The multitude of (mostly small) examples: Toward a degrowth urbanity

We have highlighted a few key examples of what can tentatively be considered the emergence of a degrowth urbanity. Other examples deserving of note and further attention are the rise of 'DIY' or 'fix it' repair workshops and 'bike kitchens' (Bradley, 2016); the growing tide of climate activism and divestment campaigns; the exploration of local currencies and crypto-currencies; progressive unions; as well as culture jammers and oppositional artists who are exposing the violence of current institutions and telling new narratives of progress and prosperity. Although most of those subcultures and counter-practices do not use the vocabulary of degrowth, each of them can be seen to be working on an aspect of societal change that is consonant with visions of degrowth (Crossley, 2003). 'Green' political parties are also playing a role, by emphasising value-orientations and policy platforms that are (or try to be) less subservient to the neoliberal rule of capital, but due to the various growth imperatives reviewed earlier, they are finding the enactment of a post-capitalist politics a thorny practical challenge. Accordingly, we agree with Taylor, O'Brien, and O'Keefe (2017: 798) when they state that 'at this juncture of capitalism, there is a need to embrace a myriad of radical groups ... rather than a monolithic single national party to provide opposition to capital.'

Nevertheless, one must not exaggerate what remains a notable but marginal confluence of urban social movements for deep change. The world does not appear to be on the brink of a degrowth revolution. The movements for change noted above could easily fail, unable to thrive in the inhospitable context of neoliberal capitalism. But in our view, there are reasons to think that a degrowth urbanity is emerging, even if it is very much in its infancy. The fact that the degrowth movement *must grow* to achieve its aims is an irony not lost on the present authors.

The triggers which will ignite that expansion is a key question that has not been addressed in any detail. Our analysis began with the pessimistic acknowledgement that we see little hope in governments leading the change for degrowth. We close this chapter by pointing to a different and even deeper pessimism: our expectation that any urban social movements for degrowth are unlikely to scale up significantly until (deeper) global crises shake people awake. Crisis can be a mobilising force (Solnit, 2016), and significant societal change may well require the instability that crisis creates. The urban agriculture practices that emerged in Cuba after the collapse of the Soviet Union (greatly reducing Cuba's oil supply) provides an example of how to turn crisis into opportunity (Friedrichs, 2013; Boillat, Gerber, and Funes-Monzote, 2013), even as one must be careful not to gloss over the hardship Cuba's 'special period' entailed. There are also a range of hopeful responses to the economic crises in Greece, which offer insight into ways of dealing positively with challenging and turbulent times (see Kalogeraki, 2018).

Our vision is for a confluence of networked urban social movements to build a new degrowth economy within the shell of a decaying capitalist economy – not because this grassroots approach is necessarily the best way to create a degrowth economy, but because there does not seem to be any mechanism for its emergence other than social movements building it from below, especially in times of crisis. Only *after* this new economy has significantly scaled up will there be any prospect of a significant politicisation of degrowth from the top down, that is, through the mechanisms of government, law, and regulation. In short, a politics of degrowth depends on a culture of collective sufficiency, solidarity, and self-provision that prefigures a degrowth economy and over time demands its reflection in societal structures and institutions. To begin with a 'top down' approach would be to put the cart before the horse.

Conclusion

The theory of change sketched in this chapter has maintained that there will be no realisation of degrowth visions of the economy and society until there is a confluence of engaged and active urban social movements that demand degrowth (or something very like it) and are prepared to drive new worlds into existence from below. Many cities of the Global North are in thrall to neoliberal governance regimes that remain wedded to freewheeling growth and opposed to democratic steering of economies and resources (Harvey, 2013; Swyngedouw, 2009). In such settings, no single observed movement for degrowth is currently capable of inducing the revolutionary changes that degrowth would require.

Nevertheless, there are a variety of existing and emerging urban social actions and coalitions that, while far from representing an organised movement for degrowth, do prefigure aspects of what a transition politics could look like if radicalised and organised over coming years and decades. In his recent book *The Promise of the Political*, Erik Swyngedouw (2018) asserts the power of urban insurgencies – the sorts of radical uprisings seen in global cities in recent years – to reassert urban politics in a quest for sustainable futures. At a time when so-called 'representative democracies' are deeply compromised by various growth imperatives, urban social movements have a significant and necessary role to play in reasserting participatory democratic control over urban futures.

Furthermore, as the dominant growth economies continue to collide with ecological limits in coming years, the case for degrowth should become clearer to more and more people, which could act as a mobilising force. Given the new urban preponderance, which is likely to continue to strengthen through this century, cities will be the foregrounds of human response to global ecological crisis. If, as urbanists insist, they are machines for human ambition, they must clearly be rewired, literally *reorganised*, for a post-growth world.

References

Albert, M. 2004. *Parecon: Life After Capitalism*. London: Verso.
Allcot, B. 2008. 'The Sufficiency Strategy: Would Rich-World Frugality Lower Environmental Impact?' *Ecological Economics* 64: 770–786.
Alexander, S. (ed.). 2009. *Voluntary Simplicity: The Poetic Alternative to Consumer Culture*. Whanganui: Stead and Daughters.
Alexander, S. 2013. 'Voluntary Simplicity and the Social Reconstruction of Law: Degrowth from the Grassroots Up' *Environmental Values* 22(2): 287–308.
Alexander, S. 2016. 'Policies for a Post-Growth Economy'. MSSI Issues Paper, no. 6, April 2018: 1–15.
Alexander, S. and Gleeson, B. 2019. *Degrowth in the Suburbs: A Radical Urban Imaginary*. Singapore: Palgrave Macmillan.

Alexander, S. and Ussher, S. 2012 'The Voluntary Simplicity Movement: A Multi-National Survey in Theoretical Context' *Journal of Consumer Culture* 12(1): 66–88.

Bardi, U. 2011. *The Limits to Growth Revisited*. New York: Springer.

Bauwens, M. and Ramos, J. 2018. 'Re-imagining the Left through an Ecology of the Commons: Towards a Post-Capitalist Commons Transition'. *Global Discourse* 8(2): 325–342.

Bennett, W.L. and Segerberg, A. 2012. 'The Logic of Connective Action: Digital Media and the Personalization of Contentious Politics'. *Information, Communication and Society* 15(5): 739–768.

Blauwhof, F. 2012. 'Overcoming Accumulation: Is a Steady-State Capitalism Possible?' *Ecological Economics* 84: 254–261.

Binswanger, M. 2009. 'Is there a Growth Imperative in Capitalist Economies? A Circular Flow Perspective'. *Journal of Post-Keynesian Economics* 31(4): 707–727.

Boillat, S., Gerber, J.-F., and Funes-Monzote, F. 2012. 'Economic Democracy for Degrowth? Some Comments on the Contribution of Socialist Models and Cuban Agroecology'. *Futures* 44: 600–607.

Bounds, M. 2004. *Urban Social Theory: City, Self, and Society*. Oxford: Oxford University Press.

Bradley, K. 2016. 'Bike Kitchens – Spaces for Convivial Tools'. *Journal of Cleaner Production* 197(2): 1676–1683.

Bulkeley, H. 2013. *Cities and Climate Change* London: Routledge.

Castells, M. 1983. *The City and the Grassroots: A Cross-Cultural Theory of Urban Social Movements*. Berkeley: University of California Press.

Coote, A. and Franklin J. 2013. *Time on Our Side: Why We All Need a Shorter Working Week*. London: New Economics Foundation.

Cox, K.R. 2017. 'Revisiting "The City as a Growth Machine"' *Cambridge Journal of Regions, Economy and Society* 10(3): 391–405.

Crossley, N. 2003. 'Even Newer Social Movements? Anti-corporate Protests, Capitalist Crises, and the Remoralization of Society'. *Organization* 10(2): 287–305.

D'Alisa, G., Demaria, F., and Kallis, G. (eds). 2015. *Degrowth: A Vocabulary for a New Era*. London: Routledge.

Demaria, F. et al. 2013. 'What is Degrowth? From an Activist Slogan to a Social Movement'. *Environmental Values* 22: 191–215.

De Young, R. and Princen, T. (eds). 2012. *The Localization Reader: Adapting to the Coming Downshift*. Cambridge, MA: MIT Press.

Drews, S. and van den Bergh, J. 2016. 'Public Views on Economic Growth, the Environment, and Prosperity: Results of a Questionnaire Survey'. *Global Environmental Change*. 39: 1–14.

Escobar, A. 2015. 'Degrowth, Postdevelopment, and Transitions: A Preliminary Conversation'. 10(3): 451–462.

Eisenstein, C. 2011. *Sacred Economics: Money, Gift, and Society in the Age of Transition*. Berkeley: North Atlantic Books.

Foster, J.B. 2011. 'Capitalism and Degrowth: An Impossibility Theorem'. *Monthly Review* 62(8): np.

Frenken, K. 2017. 'Political Economies and Environmental Futures for the Sharing Economy'. *Phil Trans. Of the Royal Society A. 375: 20160367*

Friedrichs, J. 2013. *The Future is Not What It Used To Be: Climate Change and Energy Scarcity*. Cambridge, MA: MIT Press.

Gibson-Graham, J.K. 2006. *Post-Capitalist Politics*. Minneapolis: University of Minnesota Press.

Gibson-Graham J.K., Cameron, J., and Healy, S. 2013. *Take Back the Economy: An Ethical Guide for Transforming our Communities*. Minneapolis. University of Minnesota Press.

Gleeson, B. 2014. *The Urban Condition*. London: Routledge.

Gordan, M.J. and Rosenthal, J. 2003. 'Capitalism's Growth Imperative'. *Cambridge Journal of Economics* 27(1): 25–48.

Grigsby, M. 2004. *Buying Time and Getting By: The Voluntary Simplicity Movement.* Albany: SUNY Press.

Hardt, M. and Negri, A. 2000. *Empire.* Cambridge: Harvard University Press.

Harvey, D. 1989. 'From Managerialism to Entrepreneurialism: The Transformation in Urban Governance in Late Capitalism'. *Geografiska Annaler* 71(1): 3–17.

Harvey, D. 2008. 'The Right to the City'. *New Left Review* 53: 23–40.

Harvey, D. 2011. *The Enigma of Capital and the Crises of Capitalism.* Oxford: Oxford University Press.

Harvey, D. 2013. *Rebel Cities: From the Right to the City to Urban Revolution.* London: Verso.

Hickel, J. and Kallis, G. 2019. 'Is Green Growth Possible?' *New Political Economy.* DOI: 10.1080/13563467.2019.1598964.

Holloway, J. 2002. *Change the World Without Taking Power.* London: Pluto Press.

Holloway, J. 2010. *Crack Capitalism.* London: Pluto Press.

Holmgren, D. 2002. *Permaculture: Principles and Pathways Beyond Sustainability.* Hepburn: Holmgren Design Services.

Holmgren, D. 2018. *RetroSuburbia: The Downshifter's Guide to a Resilient Future.* Hepburn: Melliodora Publishing.

Hopkins, R. 2008. *The Transition Handbook: From Oil Dependency to Local Resilience.* White River Junction: Chelsea Green Publishing.

Hopkins, R. 2011. *The Transition Companion: Making Your Community More Resilient in Uncertain Times.* White River Junction: Chelsea Green Publishing.

Hopkins, R. 2013. *The Power of Just Doing Stuff: How Local Action Can Change the World.* Cambridge: UTI/Green Books.

Kallis, G. 2017. 'Radical Dematerialization and Degrowth'. *Philosophical Transactions of the Royal Society A.* 375: 20160383: 1–13.

Kallis, G. et al. 2018. 'Research on Degrowth'. *Annual Review of Environment and Resources.* 43:4.1–4.26.

Kalogeraki, S. 2018. 'Socio-political Responses during Recessionary Times in Greece'. *PaCo* 11(1): 1–11.

Khmara, Y. and Kronenberg, J. 2018. 'Degrowth in Business: An Oxymoron or a Viable Business Model for Sustainability'. *Journal of Cleaner Production* 177: 721–731.

Kasser, T. 2017. 'Living both Well and Sustainably: A Review of the Literature, with Some Reflections on Future Research, Interventions and Policy'. *Philosophical Transactions of the Royal Society A.* 375(2095):20160369.

Lefebvre H (2003[1970]) *The Urban Revolution.* London: University of Minnesota Press.

Lehtinen, A. 2018. 'Degrowth in City Planning'. *Fennia* 196(1): 43–57.

Lewis, M. 1999. *Suburban Backlash: The Battle for the World's Most Liveable City.* Melbourne: Bloomings Books.

Lietaert, M. 2010. 'Cohousing's Relevance to Degrowth Theories'. *Journal of Cleaner Production* 18(6): 576–580.

March, H. 2016. 'The Smart City and other ICT-led Techno-Imaginaries: Any Room for Dialogue with Degrowth?' *Journal of Cleaner Production* 197(2): 1694–1703.

Marx, K. and Engels, F. 1985 (1848). *The Communist Manifesto.* Harmonsworth, UK: Penguin.

Mayer, M. 2006. 'Manuel Castells'. *The City and the Grassroots. International Journal of Urban and Regional Research* 30(1): 202–6.

Mayer, M. 2013. 'Multiscalar Mobilization for the Just City: New Spatial Politics of Urban Movements'. In: W. Nicholls, B. Miller and J. Beaumont (eds). *Spaces of Contention: Spatialities and Social Movements.* Ashgate: Aldershot.

McCann, M. 2006. *Law and Social Movements.* Ashgate: Aldershot.

McLaren, D. and Agyeman, J. 2017. *Sharing Cities: A Case for Truly Smart and Sustainable Cities.* Cambridge: MIT Press.

Meadows, D. et al. 1972. *Limits to Growth.* New York: Signet.

Molotch, H. 1976. 'The City as a Growth Machine: Toward a Political Economy of Place' *American Journal of Sociology* 82(2): 309–332.

Mullins, P. and Kynaston, C. 2000. 'The Household Production of Subsistence Goods: The Urban Peasant Thesis Reassessed'. In: Patrick Troy (ed.). *A History of European Housing in Australia*. Cambridge: Cambridge University Press: 142–163.

Nelson, A. 2018. *Small is Necessary: Shared Living on a Shared Planet*. London: Pluto Press.

O'Neill, D. et al. 2018. 'A Good Life for all Within Planetary Boundaries'. *Nature Sustainability* 1: 88–95.

Purdey, S. 2010. *Economic Growth, the Environment, and International Relations: The Growth Paradigm*. New York: Routledge.

Read, R. and Alexander, S. 2020. *Extinction Rebellion: Insights from the Inside*. Melbourne: Simplicity Institute.

Sanne, C. 2002. 'Willing Consumers – or Locked in? Policies for a Sustainable Consumption'. *Ecological Economics* 42(1): 273–287.

Sarkar, S. 1999. *Eco-Socialism or Eco-Capitalism: A Critical Analysis of Humanity's Fundamental Choice*. London: Zed Books.

Smith, R. 2010. 'Beyond Growth or Beyond Capitalism?' *Real World Economics Review* 53: 28–42.

Solnit, R. 2016, 3rd edn. *Hope in the Dark: Untold Histories, Wild Possibilities*. Chicago: Haymarket Books.

Stretton, H. 1970. *Ideas for Australian Cities*. Adelaide: Self-published.

Swyngedouw, E. 2009. 'The Antinomies of the Postpolitical: In Search of a Democratic Politics of Environmental Protection. *International Journal of Urban and Regional Research*. 33 (3): 601–20.

Swyngedouw, E. 2018. *Promises of the Political*. Cambridge, MA: MIT Press.

Taylor, C. 2004. *Modern Social Imaginaries*. London: Duke University Press.

Taylor, P., O'Brien, G. and O'Keefe, P. 2017. 'Anthropogenic Climate Change is Urban not Modern: Towards an Alternative Critical Urban Geography'. *ACME: An International Journal for Critical Geographies* 16(4): 781–803.

Trainer, T. 2010. *The Transition to a Sustainable and Just World*. Sydney: Envirobook.

Trainer, T. 2011. 'The Radical Implications of a Zero-Growth Economy'. *Real World Economics Review* 57: 71–82.

Trainer, T. 2012. 'Degrowth: Do you Realise What it Means?' *Futures* 44: 590–599.

Trainer, T. 2016. 'Another Reason a Steady-state Economy won't be a Capitalist Economy'. *Real World Economics Review* 76: 55–64.

Turner, G. 2014. 'Is Collapse Imminent? An Updated Comparison of the *Limits to Growth* with Historical Data'. *MSSI Research Paper* (No.4, August 2014): 1–21.

Ward, J. et al. 2016. 'Is Decoupling GDP Growth from Environmental Impact Possible?' *PLOS One* 11(10): e0164733. https://doi.org/10.1371/journal.pone.0164733.

Weiss, M. and Cattaneo, C. 2017. 'Degrowth – Taking Stock and Reviewing an Emerging Academic Paradigm'. *Ecological Economics* 137: 220–230.

Wright, C., Nyberg, D., and Rickards, L. 2018. 'Organizing in the Anthropocene'. *Organization* 25(4): 455–471.

Xue, J. 2015. 'Sustainable Housing Development: Decoupling or Degrowth? A Comparative Study of Copenhagen and Hangzhou'. *Environment and Planning C. Politics and Space*. 33(3): 620–639.

Chapter 5

The rebellion hypothesis: Crisis, inaction, and the question of civil disobedience[1]

Extinction Rebellion has emerged as one of the most active and prominent faces of the environmental movement around the world. While a 'protest' on a particular issue may come and go, a 'rebellion' defines itself by the breadth of its opposition and the refusal to fade away, even in the face of slow progress or backlash from the state – or even in the face of a pandemic that prohibits mass mobilisations in the streets. Whether Extinction Rebellion can live up to its name remains to be seen, but the forces of resistance do seem to be on the rise (Read, 2019), even if the pandemic (as I write in mid-2020) has added new obstacles in the path of mass mobilisation.

Extinction Rebellion (or XR) has three principles or demands:

1. Government must tell the truth by declaring a climate and ecological emergency, working with other institutions to communicate the urgency for change;

2. Government must act now to halt biodiversity loss and reduce greenhouse gas emissions to net zero by 2025;

3. Government must create and be led by the decisions of a Citizens' Assembly on climate and ecological justice.

All these principles deserve critical consideration and ongoing debate (see Farrell et al., 2019), and reasonable people can accept them, challenge them, or disagree with aspects of them. Indeed, XR itself views these demands as part of an ongoing process of discussion and refinement, and how the movement and its key issues are framed has not been free from criticism, even by sympathetic voices (see, e.g., *Resilience*, 2019). What is clear is that achieving the goals of XR will raise all sorts of deep complexities

---

1 A version of this chapter was originally published as the postscript in Rupert Read and Samuel Alexander, *Extinction Rebellion: Insights from the Inside*, 2020, Simplicity Institute, pp 162–186.

and thorny challenges, which may only be resolvable – if resolvable at all – through the messy process of lived experience and experimentation.

Nobody has all the answers; a swift decarbonisation of the global economy is an intimidating task, supported by the science but utterly unprecedented in human history; there is no detailed blueprint to tell us how to do it. But there is a clear distinction between XR and most other forms of thinking and practice in the environmental movement today. In the attempt to respond appropriately to climate breakdown and the broader environmental crisis (see Steffen et al., 2015), XR is explicitly holding up nonviolent civil disobedience as an important and perhaps necessary part of the socio-political strategy for achieving a just and sustainable world (Extinction Rebellion, 2019a; Hallam, 2019).

In this essay I will argue that XR and rebellions like it are almost certainly going to grow in coming months and years as more people around the world become politically frustrated, angry, scared, and directly impacted by inaction in the face of today's overlapping ecological and humanitarian crises. I call this anticipated growth in XR and related movements the 'rebellion hypothesis', and I explain and defend the hypothesis below. Although I sympathise with the broad goals of XR, and have participated in many XR events, my argument herein is not that this and related movements *should* grow – a question I leave open for readers to determine for themselves. My argument is that they *will* grow, as behavioural shifts in society (or psychological tipping points) are provoked by the ongoing deterioration of Earth systems and rising existential threats to the community of life (Tollefson, 2019).

Put otherwise, I will defend the proposition that *inaction has diminishing marginal returns*, which makes social mobilisations for change more likely over time, since the real and perceived cost/benefit analysis of the environmental predicament tilts in favour of collective action. Whether this mobilisation occurs in time to avoid worst-case scenarios, however, is unknowable. Although my focus here is specifically on XR, the primary argument is about the rise of environmental activism more generally in coming years and decades, irrespective of whether these uprisings continue to march under the banner of 'Extinction Rebellion'.

I will also assess the unsettling strategy of 'civil disobedience' – the practice of non-violently breaking the law to advance social, political, or environmental causes. Uncomfortable though it can make us feel, it is important for a society to understand the motivations for civil disobedience and evaluate the reasons given for practising this radical and disruptive strategy for societal change. Some commentators will be tempted to dismiss XR activists as mere 'trouble-makers' or even 'criminals', but such reactions, though understandable, risk mischaracterising these ethically motivated actions that are designed to be confronting, inconvenient, and disruptive – for a noble cause.

Even though most of us probably have reservations and concerns about civil disobedience, we must nevertheless appreciate that many of the most significant social and political advances over the last century owe much to social movements that engaged in civil disobedience as a primary strategy (Chenoweth and Stephan, 2010). One might think especially of Gandhi and the Independence Movement from British rule, the Suffragette Movement, and the Civil Rights Movement. It should be noted that the challenges of these movements and the challenges of XR are qualitatively different. Nevertheless, these esteemed traditions raise the disconcerting question: might future advances in society also demand civil disobedience?

Deep history, deep future: An ecological acknowledgement of country

Before looking more closely at XR, some context is required to fully understand this movement. Accordingly, I would like to begin this Australian-based essay, as one often begins a talk, by acknowledging the traditional custodians of the land on which I write – the Wurundjiri people of the Kulin Nation. I pay my respects to the elders, past, present, and emerging. These have always been lands where people have gathered for purposes of conversation, collaboration, and self-governance, and I feel honoured to be participating in that tradition, even though I find myself in the complex situation of occupying land whose sovereignty has never been ceded. I am still learning how to belong.

But what does it mean to acknowledge the traditional custodians of this (or any other colonised) land? It is very easy to say these things; it is much harder to know what it actually means; harder still to apply and live its truth. Let us briefly recall the colonial history in Australia to which I refer. In 1788 the British Crown turned up in Australia as a military force, and despite seeing the diverse cultures of Aboriginal Australians living on this land, the Crown declared *terra nullius*, which Australian readers will know translates as 'empty land' or 'land that belongs to no one'.

It was assumed that this land was empty because there was nothing which the Crown recognised as 'civilised people' living in Australia, despite the fact there was an Aboriginal population of somewhere between 300,000 and one million (Pascoe, 2018). Since the land was 'empty' according to these self-serving colonial assumptions, this gave a thin veneer of legitimacy to the occupation of Australia – an act of interpretive violence that of course soon evolved into acts of violence plain and simple. Indigenous populations do not often or ever freely give up their land or rights of self-governance to invading nations. Therefore, the stronger military powers have to resort to massacre and violence. Australian history is an example of a broader colonial history.

This colonial history, which still resonates in cultural and institutional reality today, is especially troubling in the context of the environment crisis we find ourselves in, so let me briefly dwell on this connection. Recent archeological evidence suggests that indigenous Australians have walked these lands for probably 65,000 years or longer (Pascoe, 2018). At once there is a striking lesson here: Australia's First Peoples did not undermine ecosystems in fatal ways. I do not want to romanticise indigenous culture or suggest that Aboriginal Australians did not have impacts on ecosystems and wildlife. They did. But the fact is that the First Peoples were able to live on this land for tens of thousands of years without degrading the land-base or fundamentally destabilising Earth systems. On the whole, ecosystems were able to regenerate sufficiently to allow for traditional cultures to be maintained over tens of thousands of years. It could be argued that this type of longevity or sustainability is the first and most important feature of any truly civilised culture: viability through deep history and capable of living on into the deep future. And yet, Aboriginal cultures were dismissed as uncivilised and primitive – invisible through the colonial lens adopted by the British Crown.

Compare this, then, with the industrial civilisation which the British Crown brought with it and established, which is merely two or three hundred years old. Over this very short timeframe – a blink of the eye in geological timeframes – human beings have become so destructive that we have become geological forces. So significant has been our impact that Earth scientists now speak of the 'Anthropocene' – the first geological era caused by humans (Steffen et al., 2015). In fact, industrial civilisation is not so much an era as it is an event. Our industrial and extractivist form of life is decimating wildlife populations and driving ever-more species to extinction, deforesting the planet, destroying topsoil, disrupting the climate, emptying the oceans and poisoning waterways, overconsuming renewable resources, and is overly dependent on non-renewable resources. Plastic is contaminating essentially every ecosystem on Earth, from the deepest reaches of our oceans to the most distant corner of Antarctica. In the haunting words of James Lovelock (2010), the face of Gaia is vanishing.

So, we might fairly ask ourselves: which way of life, in the greater scheme of things, is more civilised? Is it the dominant culture and economic system today, which in a matter of a few centuries have degraded this rich ecosystem in ways that are threatening the viability of our species and all other species? Or is it the culture that was sufficiently civilised to live on the Australian continent for 65,000 years without destroying the planet?

I'm not going to suggest simplistically that we should try to return to the Aboriginal way of life, and it's quite possible that the land-base could not support today's Australian population of 25 million living off the land in that way. But I want to pay the most humble respect to the traditional cultures of Australia's First Peoples, for their ability to live for tens of thousands of years on this land, and to suggest that there will be features of indigenous ways of living, in Australia and elsewhere, that we have much to learn from, as we seek to respond appropriately to the range of deep environmental and social problems that modern, growth-orientated, industrial life presents. So it's not about a return to the past so much as it is about honouring the past and learning from it, as we move into a complex and turbulent future (Norberg-Hodge, 2009; Pascoe, 2018).

And a turbulent future it promises to be (Gilding, 2011). Sometimes scientists put bacteria in a Petri dish, on an organic substrate, and watch as the bacteria grow in numbers until the dominant colony has consumed all the available resources or poisoned itself from its own waste. In a sense, the bacteria grow themselves to death, like a cancer cell, by undermining the life support system upon which they depend, killing the host. But suppose we were aliens on Mars with a strong pair of binoculars and we were watching the happenings on Earth over the last couple of centuries. Could not industrial civilisation on Earth resemble the dominant colony of bacteria in the Petri dish? Are we not also at risk of consuming all the available resources and poisoning ourselves from our waste streams? It is a provocative metaphor but a useful one to get the analysis underway. And perhaps the background question that lies in the sub-text of this essay is this: can we, homo sapiens – so-called 'wise humans' – show ourselves to be smarter than common bacteria and avoid their fate?

In later sections of this essay I will reflect on the theory and practice of civil disobedience, both generally and in application to Extinction Rebellion. But first I'm going to ground my primary argument by presenting what I'm calling the 'rebellion hypothesis'.

The rebellion hypothesis: Why a new wave of activism may be coming

It seems to me that there is a collective rumbling in the world today; a growing anger and anxiety about the troubled future that is unfolding day by day, and a growing sense that, if governments are not going to act decisively in response to today's overlapping ecological and social crises, then ordinary people like you and me will have to be the driving force for change. But feeling anger and anxiety about environmental breakdown and the unfolding extinction of species does not automatically translate into collective action. The history of widespread apathy or half-hearted resistance testifies to this truth. I know people who share their sense of dread with me but who have yet to mobilise and connect with activist groups. And I know a huge amount of people who understand that the world is going to hell but who manage to distract themselves with modern engagements (Netflix, social media, etc.) in order to avoid facing the truth of our global predicament. We all see this social phenomenon which serves to entrench the status quo, and at times, I am sure, we all fall back into that default mode of apathy or inaction ourselves. It is easy to become disenchanted with the world and collapse into resignation or even despair (Bendell, 2018).

Why is it so easy to be complicit in ecocide and do little to resist? Even though the world is burning and billions of people are living in conditions of humiliating destitution, life for many of us in developed nations is relatively comfortable. Indeed, Australia is almost on top of the world in terms of prosperity, having more or less ducked the Global Financial Crisis ten years ago, and our fossil-fuelled economy, prior to the COVID-19 disruption, at least, was growing at a robust pace. Although the disruption caused by the pandemic has cast many more people into economic insecurity, many still have discretionary income to spend on a new pair of jeans or shoes, or a new computer or device, and so forth. With important exceptions that must never be downplayed, not many people in the so-called 'first world' go hungry – even if, again, the unsettling impacts of the pandemic must be acknowledged.

And if our summer days reach infernal temperatures, we are generally able to turn on our air-conditioners and temporarily hide ourselves from harsh ecological realities of global heating. The supermarket shelves are generally well stocked, there is petrol at the service stations, and on-demand streaming television is always waiting to sedate us if we need to self-medicate. Never in history has a comfortable and prosperous citizenry ignited a revolution or rebellion. When life is good, people do not mobilise to overthrow the system that seems to give them what they think they want. On what basis, then, do I formulate the rebellion hypothesis? Why should we expect mass mobilisation of people in coming years?

Let me explain by way of a simple allegory. Suppose you are on a boat, with a large cake, and you suddenly notice that the boat has sprung a leak. The leak is slow and you do not panic. Instead, you cut yourself a slice of cake and it is delicious. As you finish the slice, you assess the leak again. A little water has gathered in the bottom of the boat, but nothing too alarming. So you cut yourself another slice of cake. This slice is also delicious, but perhaps not quite as good as the first one. Upon finishing your second slice you notice that your feet are wet, which is a bit unsettling. It seems the leak has gotten worse and yet you wouldn't mind another slice of cake. What do you do? Is it time to panic and act? Or do you have another slice of cake?

The point of this simple story is to highlight how over time the costs of inaction can grow and the rewards of doing the same old thing begin to decline. This shift will eventually influence our behaviour. To borrow the language of economics, we might say that inaction has diminishing marginal returns. At first, inaction doesn't seem to cost much and might even offer rewards. Over time, the costs of inaction rise as the problems get worse. In this example, each piece of cake isn't quite as good as the last, while at the same time, the costs of not addressing the leak are becoming ever more pressing.

At some point – the tipping point – it becomes clear that the costs of inaction outweigh the benefits of more cake. At that point, the person in the boat switches from being passive consumer into an engaged activist (of whatever form). The meaning of their life has become animated by the desire to stop the boat from sinking. They have come to see that their life will be better if they act – and so they act. Cake is no longer as important or as desirable as stopping the leak. So, they substitute one form of life for a different form of life, because the calculus has changed regarding actual or perceived costs and benefits.

Those people already engaging in individual acts of resistance or collective action have passed their tipping points (Extinction Rebellion, 2019a). They have weighed up the costs and benefits of inaction and concluded that inaction now costs too much. At some point the conscious or semi-conscious calculations regarding the question of whether to rebel produced a positive answer – whether that moment was last week, last year, last decade, or, for the more seasoned activists, even last century. Calls for a 'new environmental radicalism' will be heard more loudly (Hamilton, 2011).

The notion of a tipping point is normally used in relation to ecological systems, where small increments in damage can suddenly lead to swift and drastic change, often irreversible. I am using the same idea but applying it to the human psychology of activism. Every day we become more aware that our planet is dying, putting the entire community of life at risk. Whether it is the arctic or the Amazon burning, or a new species that has gone extinct, or a new climate report explaining why breakdown is happening faster than expected: each of these moments of awareness begin to add up, and yet often people don't respond with action or resistance. People can be bombarded with grim information about the ecological catastrophe unfolding, and yet remain locked in the ruts of life, doing today more or less what they did yesterday. Like the person in the boat, it is easier to continue eating or pursuing cake. This path is easily followed most of the time. But as Albert Camus (2000: 19) once wrote, 'one day a "why" arises – and everything begins in the moment of weariness tinged with amazement. "Begins" this is important.' One day a person asks: Are we the people we have been waiting for? If not us, then who? If not now, then when?

Perhaps my argument is getting clearer. I am suggesting that there is a growing 'affect' for resistance and rebellion in the world. When I speak of the rebellion hypothesis, what I am suggesting is that in coming months and years, more and more people will join XR or related movements as the costs of inaction continue to rise and the rewards of being a passive bystander decline. It seems to me that this is more or less inevitable because the costs of environmental damage will inevitably increase and become ever-more personal and immediate as capitalism continues to cannibalise itself and the planet. A new economics of activism is dawning. Currently, so much of the violence being imparted by our industrial civilisation is being externalised to other parts of the world or to others less fortunate or less powerful, including other species. This makes it easier to pretend that everything is fine and that we are not in an emergency. But as climate breakdown continues and the broader environmental crisis intensifies, the impacts will begin to be felt by more and more people, even in rich nations.

For example, when extended drought returns to (or intensifies in) Australia, as it seems destined to do, we will see more farmers joining XR or related movements as their livelihoods are directly threatened by climate change. Their tipping point will pass, and climate inaction as we know it today will be intolerable – a direct existential threat to their way of life (Fookes, 2019). When those droughts lead to increases in food prices, the urban consumer might stop to think: hang on, this had been predicted by the scientists and it has begun to affect me personally – I had better act. Their tipping point will pass. When the icecap disappears in coming years or decades, and the threat of rising seas levels becomes not a theoretical possibility but a practical problem, people living in coastal regions of the world will realise (as many already do) that climate change is not an abstract problem but something that could wash away their homes. Others will be affected by extreme weather events, and their tipping point will pass also. When children realise that they will be inheriting an unstable climate system, or a world without panda bears and the Great Barrier Reef, they will mobilise and agitate, and soon enough they will enter the voting constituency and provoke a profound political shift. Their tipping point will pass. One could go on.

Of course, to some extent this growing resistance is already underway – XR is hardly the first mobilisation in this vein. Think especially of the noble work of the global School Strikes or, in Australia, the anti-Adani activists resisting new coalmines. The list is long, diverse, and esteemed. But my argument is that the costs of inaction are necessarily going to increase, and as the Earth system deteriorates, the benefits of passive by-standing are going to seem less and less rewarding and socially acceptable. In other words, ever more people will experience a tipping point. Your neighbour, your colleague at work, a child or police officer, perhaps eventually more politicians. Each of them has a threshold or tolerance – and their tipping points are approaching. A cultural shift may be underway, even if it remains in its early stages. This cultural shift could eventually filter upwards and have political and macroeconomic effects. (One must also accept that this social energy at times might be misdirected in regressive ways as people look for minority scapegoats to blame for the harder economic times – a complex issue that is noted but deferred for analysis on another occasion.)

We are all in a lifeboat called Earth. In the 1960s and 70s when the modern environmental movement got underway, people noticed a leak in the boat and recognised it to be dangerous (Meadows et al., 1972). They spoke of a crisis in the future. Things continued to get worse, but most people couldn't resist the cake. Not enough people mobilised to plug the leak. Now the boat is leaking disastrously, and water is up to our necks; some people are already drowning. Crisis has arrived. The future is now. And more and more of us are sick of cake. More and more of us have exceeded our threshold. To change the metaphor, the floodgates are threatening to burst and it is not clear that the growing energy of opposition can be contained (Extinction Rebellion, 2019b).

Furthermore, this growing force is going to lead to increasing pressure within society – like steam increasing in a closed system. As the resistance increases and becomes more energised, we can expect backlash from those still benefiting from the existing system (and again, we are seeing this already). But as the defenders of the status quo lash out and oppress the rising tide of resistance, what they will discover is that their actions in fact only mobilise more people, as the social license of the fossil industry, corporate greed, and the politics of denial fade and ultimately disappear. In other words, one day state and corporate blindness or apathy in the face of worsening ecological catastrophes will offend public morality, and perhaps that day is closer than we think.

Based on empirical studies, it has been estimated that only 3.5% of a population needs to mobilise and engage in collective action to induce deep structural and cultural change (Chenoweth, 2017). While such estimations need to be interpreted critically and cautiously – and every context and situation is different – the point is that surprisingly small social mobilisations can have far-reaching impacts. Of course, such deep transformations do not happen overnight, but the history of disruptive social movements shows that things can happen faster than one might at first think. The environmental movement may not need a Martin Luther King or a Gandhi to lead. Perhaps what is needed is a thousand or a million Rosa Parks to get things done.

Due to the momentum of global capitalism today, global environmental problems are almost certainly going to get worse before they get better, and this will only fuel the fire of rebellion. There is an ecological contradiction built into our society, our economy, and our politics: that contradiction is the assumption that limitless economic growth is possible on a finite planet (Hickel and Kallis, 2019). But even the simplest of folks can grasp that when something cannot continue, it stops. We no longer need to ask, 'can we change the world?' – because the world is inevitably going to change and is already changing. The future is not what it used to be. One way or another, change is coming because the status quo simply cannot be maintained (Read and Alexander, 2019). We are in the process of witnessing a self-destructive civilisation collide with environmental limits, and increasingly people are going to suffer under this perverse system, and increasingly people are going to see that better, freer, less impactful, and more compassionate ways of living are available. People will try to live those new worlds into existence. Both of these things – both suffering under the existing system and the prefigurative 'new world' imagination – are mobilising forces.

My prediction or hypothesis, then, is that this collective rumbling – this emerging matrix of global social movements (Read, 2019) – is only going to intensify and amplify. At some point, it may ignite in ways that currently our imaginations cannot even begin to grasp. Or it may fade away into oblivion like other beacons of hope – think Occupy, for example, which rose as quickly as it fell (even if we can still debate whether Occupy induced valuable impacts and conversations that live on). Social movements have a tendency to surprise us. I am not sure whether forthcoming environmental rebellions will be able to *save* the world, but I feel they are destined to *change* the world as the world changes us.

What Is civil disobedience and is it justified?

Let me now spend some time examining a defining feature of XR – that is, an openness to civil disobedience as a strategy for change. What is civil disobedience? And when, if ever, can it be justified?

In essence, civil disobedience can be defined as 'a public, nonviolent and conscientious breach of law undertaken with the aim of bringing about change in laws or government policies' (Brownlee, 2007: np). For present purposes I will assume that for disobedience to be 'civil' it has to be nonviolent, and indeed this accords with the explicit and unconditional commitment XR has to nonviolence (Farrell et al., 2019). In an important aside, empirical studies show that movements committed to nonviolent disobedience tend to be twice as successful in achieving their aims as violent demonstrations (Chenoweth and Stephan, 2012), thus XR's principled commitment to nonviolence is also pragmatic and evidence based. One might add that it is also a diverse strategy – Gene Sharp famously listed 198 ways to practice nonviolent resistance (Sharp, 1973). Before engaging in such acts, however, individuals and groups should ask themselves: can civil disobedience ever be justified in a democracy?

It can be helpful to begin assessing civil disobedience in relation to basic democratic theory. Imperfect though it is, it can be said that we, in Australia, live in a democracy. Many readers, I suspect, will also be living in societies with a democratic self-image. Among other things, this means that citizens and permanent residents get to vote on who will represent them in government, and government includes a legislative branch that creates law and an executive branch that enforces it. (For present purposes I'll leave to one side the judicial branch that interprets law – or rather, creates law through its interpretations.) Since we all have, in theory, an equal opportunity to influence the law-making process through the ballot box, it is generally assumed that we should obey the law because the democratic process is the best way to organise and structure society and develop public policy that serves the common good.

From this perspective, an opponent of civil disobedience might argue as follows: *We can't all break the law every time we disagree with it. Imagine how unstable society would be if that happened. If we don't like what is happening, we can campaign for change like everyone else, and if we succeed, we can vote the existing government out of power through the electoral process and vote in a new government.* In this way, democratic societies are said to have created the institutions and processes needed for their own peaceful improvement. It may not be a perfect political system, but as Winston Churchill is reported to have said: 'It is the worst form of government, except for all the others.'

So, the main objection to civil disobedience is this: *If you disagree with a law or policy, don't break that law or policy; instead, campaign to get it changed through the democratic process. If you are permitted to break the law just because you disagree with it, then why can't anyone break a law they disagree with?* At first instance, perhaps, this objection seems quite powerful. Indeed, the great philosopher Immanuel Kant argued that '[a]ll resistance against the supreme legislative power... is the greatest and most punishable crime in the commonwealth, for it destroys its very foundations' (Kant, 1970: 81). If people only abide by laws they agree with, then the rule of law would break down. To some extent, then, we might all have sympathy with the political assumption that we ought to obey laws – even laws we don't agree with.

But it is one thing to make that broad and pragmatic concession. It is quite another to suggest that all laws, always, ought to be obeyed. If obedience to law were unconditional and absolute by virtue of the democratic process, it would follow that civil disobedience is always unjustified. How might acts of civil disobedience be interpreted within the contested disciplines of legal and political theory?

First of all, one might argue that civil disobedience is potentially justifiable when the mechanisms of democracy are not working properly, such that laws do not represent the will of the people. This can occur when laws and policies are shaped by the undemocratic influence of foreign governments, billionaires, mass media conglomerates, or other corporate lobby groups (e.g., buying a politician's support) (see, e.g., Mayer, 2016; Tham, 2010). In such cases, one might suggest that laws produced by undemocratic processes do not demand our political allegiance since they were not produced through fair, robust, and representative democratic processes.

There is also a second way in which it might be argued that civil disobedience is justified. That is, to recognise that there is a distinction between law and morality; or a distinction between what is law and what is just. Often, we might admit, there is much overlap between law and justice. The more overlap the better. But any thinking person knows that often in history, and no doubt still today, there are times when we see a clear difference between what is 'law' and what is 'just' – even if justice is an essentially contested term. In other words, democracy may be the best form of government, but this does not mean that a democracy always gets things right. Rather, democracy, when it is functioning properly, reflects culture, and there is *no reason to think that cultural norms and expectations are always just*. Put more directly, a functioning democracy can produce unjust laws when a citizenry knowingly and voluntarily votes for policies that are unjust (even if they are not considered unjust by those voting for them).

For example, we know that democracies have historically declared it illegal to engage in same-sex relationships, and today most members of liberal democracies recognise that such laws were and are in breach of basic civil rights. In the past, laws produced in democracies have institutionalised slavery, ratified unjust wars, legally entrenched racial segregation, criminalised homosexuality or particular religious practices, prohibited women and people of colour from voting, and so forth. Again, what is law does not automatically overlap with what is just. Nobody can deny that unless they still believe in the 'Divine Right of Kings' – and I am sure no one thinks that today's world leaders are God's infallible messengers on Earth chosen to lead us to the Promised Land.

At such times when a law or policy is clearly unjust (e.g., recognising ownership of persons as slaves), a case can be made that there is a place for civil disobedience in democratic societies, on the grounds that we must accept that even democratically produced laws sometimes get it wrong – sometimes *really wrong*. There is a rich and revered tradition in legal and political theory that recognises and accepts these broad lines of argument (see review in Brownlee, 2007). In other words, it is widely accepted that there is a proper place for civil disobedience in liberal democratic societies. In fact, as we look back on social movements in history – whether it is Gandhi's campaign for independence, Martin Luther King, Jnr and the Civil Rights Movement, or Emmaline Pankhurst and the suffragettes – some of the greatest leaps forwards in social and political progress have been a *result* of acts of civil disobedience. It would show a gross lack of historical understanding to dismiss civil disobedience as a regressive social practice. The powerful but uncomfortable inference is that future acts of civil disobedience may also be required to advance our state of society.

Civil disobedience and Extinction Rebellion

So how does this apply to Extinction Rebellion? There are, as I have just implied, two main ways to evaluate civil disobedience. On the one hand, an argument could be made that we live in democracies that are at least partially broken, such that the laws and policies that are produced are sometimes undemocratic because of the undue influence corporate interests have had on the legislative process – for example, the fossil fuel industry, the Murdoch media, or other powerful economic forces (see, e.g., Market Forces, 2019; Tham, 2010; Cooke, 2019; Knaus, 2018; Rudd, 2019). This suggests that even if our culture wanted a strong climate response, vested interests would interfere with any such response and ensure that law and policy kept things more or less as they are. To some extent, this may be part of the reason why climate policy around the world is often weak and sometimes non-existent. In cynical words often attributed to Emma Goldman: 'If voting changed anything, it would be made illegal.' One might say in the same vein: if lunatics have taken over the asylum, a case can be made for the citizenry to break their rules and establish new ones.

Perhaps the more powerful argument for civil disobedience, however, is that, overall, dominant cultures today have yet to fully appreciate the magnitude of climate breakdown and the broader environmental crisis (perhaps due to powerful vested interests shaping public consciousness). After all, as noted earlier, it is still quite easy to distance ourselves from the impacts of these crises, and we also know that Australia, for example, has a government that celebrates coal and essentially denies that climate breakdown is a problem deserving of a significant response. For these reasons, among others, the Australian government is each instant losing some of its integrity. And Australia is not alone.

So, we might draw an analogy here with the anti-slavery or civil rights movements in the US. Where once the state sanctioned and supported the moral wrongs of slavery and segregation, today the state sanctions and supports the moral wrong of climate breakdown. Activists who engaged in civil disobedience during the Civil Rights Movement might accept that white people were in fact voting for racist laws and public policy but justify their disobedience on the grounds that racist laws and policies were wrong and deserved to be disobeyed. We cannot say that the anti-slavery activists or civil rights activists were wrong to break the law and engage in nonviolent acts of civil disobedience. Those racist laws were grossly immoral, and they deserved to be disobeyed. Rosa Parks was right not to give up her seat on the bus on that fateful day in 1955 even though it violated the laws and regulations. According to Henry Thoreau (1982), who published his famous essay on civil disobedience in 1849, this strategy is not just a right but at times a duty. It is no surprise, then, that Gandhi, Martin Luther King, Jnr, Emmaline Pankhurst, and countless other social activists have been inspired to engage in such acts and are now revered for their bravery.

Let us ask with Thoreau: are we expected to resign our conscience to the legislator? Why have a conscience, if we are simply expected to uncritically affirm all acts of government? We must be human beings first and subjects of the state afterward. As Thoreau (1982: 111) argued, 'it is not desirable to cultivate a respect for law, so much as for the right', and indeed, he insisted that respect for law can, at times, make us daily agents of injustice. In relation to his own time, Thoreau argued that one could not be associated with the US government without disgrace, for he could not recognise as *his* government what was also the *slave's* government. He argued that if a government's law is of such a nature that it requires you to be the agent of injustice to another, then: break the law. 'Let your life be a counter-friction to stop the machine,' he declared (Thoreau, 1982: 120). 'Cast your whole vote, not a strip of paper merely, but your whole influence' (Thoreau, 1982: 122).

Since its emergence, thousands of XR activists had been arrested for engaging in civil disobedience. While no one should fetishise 'being arrested' as the only way to participate in XR, and the movement should recognise also that people have different 'biographical availabilities' for being arrested (Beyerlein and Bergstrand, 2013), the fact is that all acts of civil disobedience raise the possibility of being arrested and perhaps imprisoned. No doubt acts of civil disobedience will be perceived by many as annoying and inconvenient and unnecessarily disruptive, but that calculus always has to be weighed against the moral wrong that is motivating the disobedience (see Monbiot, 2019). Slavery and segregation were also 'inconvenient' for those who suffered under racist laws.

In that light, the inconvenience caused by 'sit-ins' and bus boycotts pale in comparison. Similarly, when environmentalists engage in acts of civil disobedience to resist ecocide, the extinction of species, and the unfolding climate emergency, some sectors of society will no doubt be appalled and dismiss the activists as common law-breakers or radical anarchists. Civil disobedience may indeed be inconvenient to many people. But to evaluate the legitimacy of the civil disobedience, one has to resist superficial analyses and ask how that inconvenience compares to the future suffering, and indeed the suffering already being caused, by environmental breakdown (Spratt and Dunlop, 2019; Nixon, 2013).

I can now bring the analysis to a head. Just imagine, for example, that in ten years or twenty years or thirty years – it doesn't really matter when – we discover that our high-impact modes of production and consumption have led to even more alarming ecosystemic breakdown, a future that has mountains of scientific support (see, e.g., Steffen et al., 2015; Spratt and Dunlop, 2017). Suppose the climate reaches its tipping point; Australia and other nations enter indeterminate and intensifying drought (just look at New South Wales or the bushfires of 2019/2020); food production drops even as population grows, leading to mass famine and increased geopolitical tension and war; suppose in ten or twenty years the arctic icecap disappears and the methane release from the permafrost induces a swift jump in global temperatures. Suppose any number of such things happen and people begin to die in greater numbers. When we look back on today, we will ask ourselves: Did we do enough? Were we complicit in a broken system? Should we have been so obedient given that we knew our gutless governments were leading us down a dead end?

These questions are not for me to answer – I am still struggling with them myself. I will remain a sympathetic critic and revise my views as new evidence and insight emerges. None of us can condemn or condone the actions of XR in advance of their particular, context-dependent manifestations. One might sympathise with XR in general while disagreeing with specifics, or vice versa. These are very personal questions (with social effects) which we must meditate on with due diligence. But my point is that if the future turns out how the best scientists are predicting it will turn out if business as usual continues (for reviews, see Steffen et al., 2015; Spratt and Dunlop, 2017; Spratt and Dunlop, 2019), then the younger generation might well ask us what we did to resist the foreseeable collapse of ecosystems and the humanitarian catastrophes such breakdowns will induce (and are already inducing).

Conclusion: On the right side of history?

Writing in the 19th century, Karl Marx announced that he had discovered the laws of history. He maintained that it was inevitable that as the contradictions of capitalism became ever more severe and transparent, eventually the working class would rise up and overthrow the capitalist class and establish communism. I have always been suspicious of determinist conceptions of history, knowing that human societies do not follow predetermined laws. I feel that we will be what we make of ourselves and nothing else, as the existentialists argued, even if we are born into a world not of our own making. But when we freely act in ways that undermine the ecosystems that we (and future generations) depend on for freedom and prosperity, then our lives begin to be shaped not so much by human decisions as by ecological realities and geological forces. At least, human freedom is increasingly *contained and influenced* by those worsening realities and forces. We are living in such times today.

What Marx never foresaw was that capitalism would indeed fall, but not by way of revolution, but by way of deterioration and perhaps collapse. As the broad ecological crisis intensifies, and collapse situations become more common, challenging, and disruptive, I have argued that more and more people will face their psychological tipping points and become engaged in collective action. At some point, tolerance of ecocide will become intolerable.

What is the threshold of your neighbour? Your children or parents? Your work colleagues? Our politicians? I don't know, but my sense is that those tipping points are approaching – if not tomorrow, then next month, or next year, or the year after that. The rebellion hypothesis, as presented, is that every day more people are saying to themselves: 'I am an activist; I am a change-maker not a passive consumer; I am responsible for participating in progressive social change; I want to be; I have to be.' The question we must all face, as global citizens on a dying planet, is whether our governments are meeting their fundamental duty to keep us, our children, and the broader community of life, safe.

Rebellion, I am suggesting, has effectively become a law of history due to ecological realities. The climate crisis is already here, to some extent locked in, and certainly threatening to get much worse. Three hundred years of industrial momentum means that it is now too late for any smooth, non-disruptive democratic shift to some ecological civilisation. For better or for worse, turbulence and disruption will define coming decades. Things are likely to get worse before they get better. But as this happens people will inevitably be mobilised as the calculus of apathy and inaction shifts and the activist is born. As Camus declared: 'Everything begins in that moment of weariness tinged with amazement.'

In six months, or two years, or five years, or ten years, I invite you to reflect back on this essay and assess to what extent you think the hypothesis presented has been verified by growing global social movements or falsified by increased apathy. I feel confident, for the reasons I have outlined, that the future will confirm my prediction. If I am wrong, and the status quo endures, then all the worse for us. In short, I feel the logic of rebellion is becoming irresistible to more and more people and that this trend is destined to continue. And one implication of this is that we should not conceive of XR as something already riding the crest of a wave, but rather, XR represents a movement of movements that is still in its infancy. This entails a prospect of something much bigger that is still in the process of being born, even though it may be that the hour is darkest just before dawn. Still, the promise of a new dawn is not needed to justify the rejection of a world immiserated by capital's violent overreach.

In closing, I have invited you herein to ask yourself: what are the costs and benefits of inaction? What are the costs and benefits of resistance and rebellion? What are the rewards of building a new world arm in arm with your neighbour? My argument has been that this calculus is already shifting in favour of resistance, rebellion, and renewal, and that this shift is now unstoppable, whether one sympathises with XR or not. XR is part of this shift but the global movement and energy are broader than any one framing or articulation. The floodgates are holding for the time being, but the laws of physics will win out, as they always do. Participants in XR are early adopters and if warnings of ecological science are to be taken seriously and prove even vaguely accurate, this movement – despite the negative press it will inevitably receive from some sectors in society – is likely, as George Monbiot (2019) argues, to end up on the right side of history.

With a nod to Thoreau, I see Extinction Rebellion as a counter-friction to the machine.

References

Bendell, J. 2018. 'Deep Adaptation: A Map for Navigating Climate Tragedy'. IFLAS Occasional Paper 2 (27 July 2019).

Beyerlein, K. and Bergstrand, K. 2013. 'Biographical Availability'. *The Wiley-Blackwell Encyclopedia of Social and Political Movements*, viewed 5 September 2019, https://onlinelibrary.wiley.com/doi/abs/10.1002/9780470674871.wbespm012

Brownlee, K. 2007. 'Civil Disobedience'. *Stanford Encyclopedia of Philosophy*, viewed 5 September 2019, https://plato.stanford.edu/entries/civil-disobedience/

Brulle, R. 2014. 'Institutionalizing Delay: Foundation Funding and the Creation of US Climate Change Counter-movement Organizations'. *Climate Change*, vol. 122, no. 4: 681–694.

Camus, A. 2000. *The Myth of Sisyphus*. Penguin: London.

5: The rebellion hypothesis: Crisis, inaction, and the question of civil disobedience

Chenoweth, E. 2017. 'It May Only Take 3.5% of the Population to Topple a Dictator – With Civil Resistance'. *The Guardian*, 2 February 2017, viewed 5 September 2019.

Chenoweth, E. and Stephan, M. 2012. *Why Civil Resistance Works: The Strategic Logic of Non-Violent Conflict*. New York: Columbia University Press.

Cooke, R. 2019. 'News Corp: Democracy's Greatest Threat'. *The Monthly* (May 2019).

Extinction Rebellion. 2019a. Official website, viewed 5 September 2019, http://rebellion.earth

Extinction Rebellion. 2019b. 'A Movement of Movements for the October Rebellion'. Viewed 5 September 2019, https://rebellion.earth/2019/08/29/introducing-the-movement-of-movements-for-the-october-rebellion/

Farrell, C. et al. (eds). 2019. *This is Not a Drill: An Extinction Rebellion Handbook*. London: Penguin.

Fookes, T. 2019. 'Fear of Drought, Flood, and Fires Leads Farmers to Plea for Urgent Action on Climate Change'. ABC News, viewed 13 September 2019, https://www.abc.net.au/news/rural/2019-09-13/fear-of-drought-flood-and-fires-leads-farmers-to-plea-for-action/11508834

Gilding, P. 2011. *The Great Disruption: How the Climate Crisis will Transform the Global Economy*. London: Bloomsbury.

Hallam, R. 2019. 'Common Sense for the 21st Century: Only Non-Violent Rebellion Can Now Stop Climate Breakdown and Social Collapse'. Pre-publication working draft, version 0.3.

Hamilton, C. 2011. 'We Need a New Environmental Radicalism'. *Green Left Weekly*, 29 April 2011, issue 878.

Hickel, J. and Kallis, G. 2019. 'Is Green Growth Possible?'. *New Political Economy* (in press). DOI: 10.1080/13563467.2019.1598964

Kant, I. 1970. *Kant's Political Writings* (edited by H. Reiss). Cambridge: Cambridge University Press.

Knaus, C. 2018. 'Australia's Political Parties Got $62m in "Dark Money" Donations Last Year'. *The Guardian* (3 September 2018).

Lovelock, J. 2010. *The Vanishing Face of Gaia*. New York: Basic Books.

Market Forces. 2019. 'Friends in High Places: Fossil Fuel Political Donations'. *Market Forces* (February 2019), viewed 7 September 2019, https://www.marketforces.org.au/politicaldonations2019/

Mayer, J. 2016. *Dark Money: How a Secretive Group of Billionaires is Trying to Buy Political Control in the US*. London: Scribe.

Meadows, D. et al. 1972. *Limits to Growth*. New York: Signet.

Monbiot, G. 2019. 'History Will Be Kind to Heathrow Climate Protesters Who Stop Us Flying'. *The Guardian*, 4 September 2019.

Nixon, R. 2013. *Slow Violence and the Environmentalism of the Poor*. Cambridge: Harvard University Press.

Norberg-Hodge, H. 2009. *Ancient Futures*. San Francisco: Sierra Club.

Pascoe, B. 2018. *Dark Emu: Aboriginal Australia and the Birth of Agriculture*. Broome: Magabala Books.

Resilience. 2019. Articles on Extinction Rebellion, viewed 5 September 2019, https://www.resilience.org/?type=Filter+by&s=%22Extinction+Rebellion%22

Rawls, J. 1971. *A Theory of Justice*. Boston: Belknap Press.

Read, R. 2019. 'How a Movement of Movements Can Win: Taking XR to the Next Level'. *Rupert Read's Website*, 13 August 2019, viewed 5 September 2019, https://rupertread.net/writings/how-movement-movements-can-win-taking-xr-next-level

Read, R. and Alexander, S. 2019. *This Civilisation is Finished: Conversations on the End of Empire and What Lies Beyond*. Melbourne Simplicity: Institute.

Rudd, K. 2019. 'Democracy Overboard: Rupert Murdoch's Long War on Australian Politics'. *The Guardian* (7 September 2019).

Spratt, D. and Dunlop, I. 2017. 'What Lies Beneath: The Scientific Understatement of Climate Risks'. *Breakthrough Institute*, September 2017.

Spratt, D. and Dunlop, I. 2019. 'Australia's Climate Stance is Inflicting Criminal Damage on Humanity'. *The Guardian*, 3 August 2019.

Sharp, G. 1973. '198 Methods of Non-violent Resistance'. Viewed 5 September 2019, https://www.aeinstein.org/wp-content/uploads/2014/12/198-Methods.pdf

Steffen, W. et al. 2015. 'The Trajectory of the Anthropocene: The Great Acceleration'. *The Anthropocene Review*, vol. 2, no. 1: 81–98.

Tham, J-C. 2010. *Money and Politics: The Democracy We Can't Afford*. Sydney: UNSW Press.

Thoreau, H., 1982[1849] 'Civil Disobedience'. In Bode, C. (ed.). *The Portable Thoreau*. New York: Penguin: 109–137.

Tollefson, J. 2019. 'Humans are Driving One Million Species to Extinction'. *Nature*, vol. 569: 171.

Chapter 6

The political economy of deep decarbonisation: Tradable Energy Quotas for energy descent futures[1]

Introduction

In this paper we offer a new analysis of the policy of Tradable Energy Quotas (TEQs), developed by David Fleming (Fleming, 2016). The TEQs system involves rationing fossil fuel energy use for a nation on the basis of either a contracting carbon emission budget or scarce fuel availability, or both simultaneously, distributing budgets equitably amongst energy-users. The goal is to equitably meet climate change mitigation targets (IPCC, 2018) and/or fossil energy depletion realities (Mohr et al., 2015; Bentley, Mushalik, and Wang, 2020) within a nationally-agreed and cooperative framework, in a manner 'green growth' strategies seem unable to achieve (Hickel and Kallis, 2019).

While the TEQs system is designed to manage the contraction of fossil fuel energy use, the system itself is agnostic with respect to the availability of energy from other sources, namely renewables and nuclear. Given the dependence of all economic activity on having sufficient energy available, and the tight correlation between energy use and Gross Domestic Product (GDP) (Hickel and Kallis, 2019), the implementation of a TEQs system would be expected to incentivise reduced energy demand and/or increased demand for energy from lower carbon sources. All else being equal, the desired rate of increase in energy from alternative sources might be expected to correspond with the rate of decrease in fossil energy use that the TEQs system is intended to deliver. The relationship between demand for lower carbon sources and the means for satisfying this demand is, however, mediated by factors outside the TEQs framework itself. A TEQs system would meet its design objective if fossil fuel energy use was reduced by the intended amount, regardless of the portfolio of energy source substitution and demand reduction measures collectively adopted to achieve this.

---

1 Originally published in *Energies* 13(17): 4304, 2020: https://doi.org/10.3390/en13174304, co-authored with Joshua Floyd.

The extent to which alternative lower carbon sources can meet energy expectations formed in the context of fossil fuels is subject to major uncertainties. It is highly plausible though that such sources will not be able to fully replace the range and scale of energy services currently available (Floyd et al., 2020). Such a view provides essential context for the present analysis. We note the original design of the TEQs system was informed by a similar outlook, and in this respect our analysis can be considered consistent with the system's underlying ethos (Fleming, 2016). Considering this deeper background, TEQs can be seen not only as a system for managing fossil fuel energy contraction, but as a framework for navigating overall 'energy descent'. Such energy descent would not, however, be a consequence of managing the reduction in fossil fuel energy use via a TEQs system specifically, but a general consequence of transitioning away from fossil fuels by any means, under circumstances in which energy supply from other sources is constrained in its capacity to deliver energy services at an equivalent rate.

Given the plausibility of supply-constrained energy descent as a consequence of the transition away from fossil fuels – a premise we unpack in greater detail below – any implementation of TEQs needs to be considered alongside the economic and socio-political implications of contracting overall energy availability. Even in the event, though, that non-fossil fuel energy supply does not constrain the rates at which energy services are available to future societies, the relevance of considering energy descent is not invalidated. While climate change and fossil fuel resource depletion delimit the scope for energy services enabled by fossil fuels, these are only the two most prominent dimensions of the three-pronged energy dilemma faced by human societies. Alongside these two issues is the broader suite of impacts on biospheric integrity resulting from the scale of physical power presently exercised by humans (Steffen et al., 2015; Rockström et al., 2009). All such exercise of power entails the transformation and transport of matter, resulting in impacts on processes essential to biospheric functions. The complexity of these processes means that control over the consequences of the physical power that humans wield is limited. Human activity throughout history and pre-history has had unintended consequences, whether directly related to intended effects, or as a result of second-order co-effects. These unintended consequences are amplified in proportion to the physical power that directs human activity. If lower-carbon energy sources do in fact support ongoing growth in aggregate energy services, then the scale of impacts on the biosphere will also grow, with limits other than those related to atmospheric greenhouse gas concentration coming into play. With the global material footprint of human societies already greatly exceeding what some investigators consider to be sustainable (Bringezu, 2019), the implication is that not only must the rate of fossil fuel use be reduced, but so must the total rate at which energy services affect changes in the biosphere, regardless of the primary energy source.

On this basis, we situate our analysis in relation to Joseph Tainter's theory about the development and the collapse of complex societies (Tainter, 1988). Tainter's theory is predicated on the observation that societies become more socio-politically and technologically 'complex' as they solve the problems they face and that such complexification necessitates increased energy use. For a society to sustain itself, therefore, it must secure the energy needed to solve the range of societal problems that emerge. Since problems continually arise, however, there is persistent pressure for growth in complexity (Tainter, 2011a). Both historically and today, such 'problems' might include securing enough food, adjusting to demographic, climatic, or other environmental changes, dealing with aggression within or between societies, organising society and managing institutions, pandemics(!), and so on. Indeed, the challenges any society might face are, for practical purposes, 'endless in number and infinite in variety' (Tainter, 2011b, p. 91), and responding to problems generally requires increased use of energy and other resources. Tainter describes this development in human organisation and behaviour as a process of socio-political complexification.

Tainter argues that, due to the diminishing returns on complexity, there comes a point when societies may no longer be able to secure sufficient energy or other key resources to solve the range of problems faced. Accordingly, without corresponding advances in resource-use efficiency, such societies may be unable to maintain arrangements corresponding with their peaks of complexity. Put more directly, large-scale societies can collapse (i.e., undergo rapid involuntary reduction in socio-political complexity) when the costs of sustaining their complexity become energetically unaffordable (Homer-Dixon et al., 2015). As outlined below, this is the essential dynamic that Tainter argues 'can explain collapse as no other theory has been able to do' (Tainter, 1995, p. 400). Not only is Tainter's theory of historical interest, we maintain it can offer insight into the evolving nature and dynamics of globalised industrial civilisation, today and in the future (Bardi, 2020; Turner, 2019).

We will argue that TEQs offers a practical and effective means of managing contraction in the use of energy derived from fossil fuels. Furthermore, the system offers an important policy tool to help navigate the overall trajectory of energy descent that will plausibly follow from such contraction. TEQs could therefore act as a vital support for the controlled reduction of socio-political complexity via processes of 'voluntary simplification' and economic 'deintensification' (the result of these processes being 'degrowth' or controlled contraction in the scale of the physical economy (Alexander et al., 2019; Weiss and Cattaneo, 2017). We therefore distinguish voluntary simplification from the similar term 'voluntary simplicity', with the latter generally referring to individuals consuming less within existing structures, and the former referring to a reconfiguration of systems and structures to manage, or actively induce, reduced socio-economic complexity (Alexander, 2014). Structural voluntary simplification, in this sense, would likely require cultural voluntary simplicity, but the converse need not be true.

Under conditions where current levels of socio-political complexity cannot be extended or even maintained, acknowledging the systemic and cultural need for such controlled reduction is, we argue, far preferable to allowing collapse to unfold haphazardly and chaotically, but making this case requires a nuanced engagement with Tainter's theory. For present purposes, we will treat voluntary simplification and economic deintensification as aspects of a general process leading to degrowth of formal economies and socio-political matrices, although to emphasise Tainter's conceptual framework we will generally refer to this process via the term 'voluntary simplification'. Defined further below, this refers to a process of planned contraction of a society's energy and resource demands, with corresponding reductions in socio-political complexity (Alexander et al., 2019; Weiss and Cattaneo, 2017).

Structure and overview

Our substantive analysis begins in the next section by reviewing the literature on renewable energy (RE) transitions. We seek to understand the scope for RE to replace the extent and nature of energy services provided by fossil fuels, a question of urgency for existing economic systems due to both climate change and the finitude of fossil fuels. We proceed from a position of epistemic humility (Floyd et al., 2020) –that is, from an appreciation of deep uncertainties surrounding energy futures, and therefore of what knowledge claims relating to this area of investigation can reasonably be made in the present. These uncertainties imply the need to hold serious doubts about whether RE (or nuclear) can fully replace what it is that human societies do at present via fossil fuels. While we fully endorse the goal of transitioning to RE, we contend it is plausible that a full transition would entail 'energy descent' relative to the availability of energy services in developed regions of the world today (Moriarty and Honnery, 2008; 2011a; 2011b; 2011c; 2016). Given that the degree of socio-political complexity, in Tainter's sense, that can be maintained by a society is dependent on available resources, reduced energy availability is likely to drive significant deintensification of economies, and with this, reduction in socio-political complexity, whether enforced through circumstances that overwhelm human agency, or voluntarily embraced (Alexander, 2014; Floyd, 2014). As discussed in the introduction, even if energy services are not supply-constrained, other biosphere impacts resulting from continued exercise of physical power at the current historically extreme level must at some point force a confrontation with the need for contraction in human energy conversions, and hence with the prospect of reducing socio-political complexity. The term 'deintensification' implies changes that generally result in closer proximity between producers and consumers of goods and services, both geographically and socially. This will typically involve the emergence or reemergence of informal economies at the bio-regional, neighbourhood, and household scales, where mostly local resources are used to provide for mostly local needs, at the expense of formal economic transactions and arrangements where global supply chains coalesce in complex and often energy-intensive ways (Fleming, 2016).

Given the epistemic grounds on which anticipation of energy futures rests, energy descent is no less plausible (and a sound case can be made that it is more so) than alternatives. Individuals, households, nations, and indeed the global community should therefore plan for such an outcome, even if this conflicts with dominant expectations of continued economic growth and corresponding assumptions about the need or desire for ongoing increases in socio-political complexity (Anderson, 2015). Later in the analysis we explore the implications of energy descent informed by Tainter's theory of complexity and collapse. Although we sympathise with much of Tainter's analysis, we seek to show that energy descent pathways involving voluntary simplification and economic deintensification are potentially more viable than is suggested if the historical record is taken as the necessary benchmark. That is, we suggest that pathways may be available differing sufficiently from those attempted previously to make economic deintensification a legitimate policy option for decision makers. In that vein, we outline how a society embracing voluntary simplification could manage energy descent in ways consistent with human and ecological flourishing, although we argue this means deep transformations in societal structures, cultures, and institutions (Alexander et al., 2019; Alexander and Rutherford, 2020), not merely attempting to 'green' today's globalised carbon civilisation (Hickel and Kallis, 2019).

To anticipate later discussions, energy descent futures shaped by voluntary simplification would involve more localised agency in relation to governance and organisation (i.e., more context-specific, context-sensitive, and hence more diverse social forms and structures across bio-regions and cultures); it would require planned contraction of energy and material demands (i.e., degrowth); it would necessitate a more equitable distribution of wealth; and it would involve embracing cultures of consumption that reflect ethics favouring sufficiency, moderation, and frugality. While the likelihood of voluntary simplification, economic deintensification, and consequent degrowth receiving population-wide embrace may not be high, we argue these strategies deserve critical attention, especially since we contend that they are the best, and perhaps the only, means of resolving the overlapping crises facing humanity today (Homer-Dixon et al., 2015; Turner, 2019; Ripple et al., 2017; 2019).

In the last part of the analysis we outline TEQs as a policy tool with practical potential to manage society-wide processes of energy descent in viable and equitable ways. We conclude with brief reflections on obstacles and challenges that lie in the way of TEQs (and other strategies for managing energy descent) being adopted.

Energy descent as a post-carbon transition scenario

In mainstream energy discourse (IEA, 2019a; 2019b) the fact that fossil fuels are finite and being depleted at pace is generally treated as a future concern that will be solved before it arrives – put simply, demand will peak before supply. Climate change, on the other hand, is increasingly recognised as a serious threat, but again the prevailing view seems to be that mitigating and adapting to climate change via deep decarbonisation (supported by negative emissions technologies) will be difficult but manageable. In support of this energy and climate optimism, analysts point to promising advances in technology (e.g., solar photovoltaic (PV), wind turbines, batteries, electric vehicles, etc.) and efficiency improvements (i.e., 'cleaner production'). Furthermore, in an age governed by neoliberal rationality (Harvey, 2005), the dominant policy response is to maintain that markets and price signals will provide the right incentives to drive an optimal energy transition beyond fossil fuels without facing energy shocks or dangerous climate change. 'Optimal transition', in this sense, means minimum impact on GDP relative to conventional growth expectations in the absence of climate change mitigation efforts. From this techno-optimistic view, the growth paradigm of global capitalism is up to the task and system change is not necessary.

Even if such techno-optimistic and pro-market views are by no means universal, media and political narratives both reflect and propagate the widespread and popular assumption that renewable energy (or nuclear power) will be able to replace current fossil fuel use and mitigate climate change without significant social or economic disruption, as well as match growing global energy demand into the distant future. More specifically, there seems to be a widespread assumption that post-carbon energy sources are consistent with a socio-politically complex, globalised economy that is structurally designed or required to grow without limits (Hatfield-Dodds et al., 2015). Moreover, the fact that continued expansion in the scale of energy services will almost certainly be attended by increasing biospheric disruption and damage receives essentially no attention within orthodox energy and economic futures discourse.

Foundational in this view is the assumption that low-cost final energy carriers will be even more abundant in the future than today (IEA, 2019a; 2019b; EIA, 2019). This is not always a conscious assumption. Rather, in large-scale, complex societies, the association between institutional responses to collective problems and increased energy demand is rarely apparent. Citizens of societies organised by industrial economies and market capitalism have simply become accustomed to overcoming (or at least displacing) any immediate problem that arises, and, simultaneously, to satisfying the aggregate growth in energy demand.

In contrast, the alternative energy narrative we outline in this section maintains that we should be preparing for futures not of energy abundance, but rather of reduced energy availability. With respect to the most energy intensive societies, this means planning for 'energy descent', a term we borrow from permaculture theorist and practitioner, David Holmgren (Holmgren, 2009). While acknowledging a range of uncertainties about how humanity's energy futures will unfold, our review of the literature (Floyd et al., 2020; Alexander and Floyd, 2018) supports the view that energy descent is not only highly plausible, but that there is no epistemically sound basis for treating this as simply a 'high-impact but relatively low probability' outcome of the transition away from fossil fuels (see also, Moriarty and Honnery, 2008/2011a/2011b/2011c/2016). This implies that planning and preparing for such futures should be given far greater weight in energy transition praxis than is presently the case.

Fossil fuel depletion, climate change mitigation and preservation of biosphere function as drivers of energy descent futures

The dominant narrative of energy abundance can be questioned from three principal angles. First, we could begin by acknowledging that fossil fuels – currently comprising about 84 per cent of global commercial primary energy use (Floyd et al., 2020; Backhaus, Gausling, and Hildebrand, 2015; Dudley, 2019) – are finite, and therefore today's carbon-based civilisation, one way or another, has a time limit (Moriarty and Honnery, 2011c). Humanity's one-off fossil energy inheritance is but a brief anomaly in the evolution of the human story, a momentary energy spike when considered in context of our species' deep history (Smil, 2017).

Although analysis aimed at anticipating the timing and trajectory of fossil energy depletion is subject to numerous sources of uncertainty, the fact that fossil fuels are finite and subject to depletion is an undeniable geological reality. This is a matter of particular significance in relation to oil (Miller and Sorrell, 2014), given its role in enabling industrial agriculture, and global transport systems and supply chains. As the low-hanging fruit is picked, it becomes harder to increase or even maintain current net energy supply (Murphy, 2014).

In recent years, the large growth in United States oil production due to shale oil developments using hydraulic fracturing techniques has encouraged some commentators to proclaim 'the death of peak oil'. More careful analysis of the evidence suggests that such pronouncements are greatly exaggerated. Eventually, perhaps sooner than most think (Mohr et al., 2015), the rate of oil production will enter a phase of net energy decline, with new discoveries unable to offset the flagging fortunes of existing assets (Fustier, 2016). Despite large oil resources remaining relative to historical production, the economically recoverable proportion of the overall resource is subject to headwinds including increasing production costs and price volatility, as low prices impact the viability of commercial producers (Michaux, 2019).

While oil has commanded the majority of attention to date in public discourse about fossil energy resource depletion, the timelines for gas and coal may not be nearly as protracted as is typically assumed (Mohr et al., 2015). Alongside this, exponential growth trends (both energetic and economic) that have defined dominant conceptions of human development throughout the industrial era can be expected to end, and even reverse. Without attempting a comprehensive review here, in our other work (Alexander and Floyd, 2018) we have analysed the oil situation and provided an evidential case for the ongoing relevance of 'peak oil' dynamics based on the following ten points (see also Mohr et al., 2015; Bentley, Mushalik, and Wang, 2020):

- Excluding the US and Canada, the rest of the world has had flat oil production since 2005.

- There are deep uncertainties over the economic viability of US shale production (especially given unstable oil markets and low prices as a consequence of the COVID-19 pandemic)

- Oil discoveries are at record low and production decline rates are increasing

- Energy-return-on-investment is in terminal decline

- The oil industry is facing major financial challenges, which will be compounded as the emerging climate change response renders as 'stranded assets' much of the fossil fuel production, processing and distribution infrastructure currently in place

- Lack of oil investment due to low prices

- Oil exports (from the remaining oil exporting nations) seem to have peaked, meaning the oil importers should not expect to maintain or grow their share of oil supply

- Failed states and geopolitical disruptions are an ever-present threat to oil supply

- A robust climate response means we should be 'choosing' peak oil now (see carbon budget analysis below)

- Current oil consumption patterns are incompatible with fair distribution of remaining fossil fuels in a global economy characterised by extreme wealth inequality.

Challenges of such nature raise questions not only about what a post-carbon world will look like, but, perhaps more pressingly, how we should best manage the inevitable and foreseeable contraction of fossil fuel production in coming years and decades.

Compounding this challenge of maintaining energy supply in the face of fossil energy depletion, climate science overwhelmingly concludes that the burning of fossil fuels is a leading cause of anthropogenic climate change (IPCC, 2018). Any adequate response to this potentially existential threat is going to require, among other things, a swift and committed transition beyond fossil energy sources (i.e., deep decarbonisation).

The best available science confirms that to keep the impacts of climate change within the range of human adaptation, consumption of fossil fuels must be limited even before limits are geologically enforced. A recent United Nations report (Emissions Gap Report, 2019) concludes that to keep global temperature rise within 1.5°C of the pre-industrial baseline, globally humanity needs to decarbonise by 7.6 per cent p.a. between 2020 and 2030. More challengingly still, Anderson, Broderick, and Stoddard (2020) argue that the most developed nations need to decarbonise by 14 per cent p.a, starting now, to achieve pathways compliant with the Paris Agreement. In 2019, global emissions crept upwards again, and it appears that even a global economic crisis triggered by a pandemic will force only modest emission reductions. At time of writing in mid-2020, the International Energy Agency (IEA) projects that the economic shutdown in response to COVID-19 might reduce emissions by 'merely' 8 per cent in 2020 (Gabbattis, 2020).

Even ignoring fossil fuel depletion then, the socio-economic challenge of decarbonising by between 7–14 per cent p.a. (depending on assumptions and focus) is profound. Some of the decarbonisation needed will be achievable through efficiency gains, but to think that the developed nations can decarbonise by 14 per cent p.a. through efficiency increases for years on end, while also maintaining economic growth, is a dangerous fantasy (Hickel and Kallis, 2019; Floyd et al., 2020; Ward et al., 2016). While efficiency gains must be pursued, staying within carbon budget targets requires that socio-economic structures be adjusted in ways that use less energy. Energy descent, whether a consequence of fossil fuel depletion, climate change mitigation, or both, should now be treated as an uncontroversial feature of the plausible futures envisaged by decision makers in orthodox institutions everywhere. An important task now for communities is to construct images of preferred futures in which energy descent is accepted as a basic contextual feature. Here, energy efficiency becomes a subordinate concern to energy sufficiency as an orienting value (Alexander, 2015).

Finally, continued exercise of physical power at the extreme rates associated with current global energy service provision must ultimately intersect with limits associated with the disruption or damage to essential biosphere functions. All energy conversions entail environmental impacts. The impacts scale with the aggregate global rate of energy conversion (Moriarty and Honnery, 2011c; Ripple et al., 2017). Even in the absence of further climate impacts resulting from greenhouse gas emissions, energy use enabled by natural environmental energy flows that on human timescales can be considered inexhaustible will eventually, if not already, encounter limits associated with the biosphere's capacity to absorb or tolerate impacts imposed on it (Röckstrum et al., 2009; Bringezu, 2019; Homer-Dixon et al., 2015; Turner, 2019; Ripple et al., 2017).

Differentiating fossil fuels and post-carbon energy sources: Epistemic humility regarding energy transition supports energy descent planning

This brief review of humanity's situation through the overlapping contextual lenses of fossil energy resource depletion, carbon budget analysis, and biosphere functionality sets the scene for a further context of inquiry. This concerns the extent to which alternative energy sources and conversion technologies – specifically RE and nuclear power – will be able to replace the energy foundations of today's globalised, fossil fuel-based civilisation.

Contemporary energy transition studies is an area of scholarly debate in which competing schools of thought, e.g., 'renewable advocates' vs. 'nuclear advocates', hold what can seem to be commitments of an almost religious nature to particular energy solutions (Valentine, Sovacool, and Brown, 2017). While we cannot review the intricacies of this debate here (see Floyd et al., 2020; Moriarty and Honnery, 2008; 2011a; 2011b; 2011c; 2016), we approach the issues with circumspection, knowing that the current knowledge basis for energy transitions is uncertain; that reasonable, evidence-based analysis can support divergent views on the best path forward. However, we maintain that this very uncertainty about the viability of fully replacing fossil fuels with alternative sources, and the epistemic humility this uncertainty demands, ends up supporting the case for energy descent preparation and planning. That is, if thoughtful, critical analysis supports contradictory views about whether renewable energy or nuclear power will be up to the task of fully replacing the energy services provided via fossil fuels, broader society should not assume existing energy supply – and the societal complexity it enables – can be maintained in a post-carbon world.

Even for energy analysis with a techno-optimistic orientation that leads to high confidence in the ability of RE to fully replace the energy services provided by fossil fuels, it remains the case that the greater the demand for energy services, the lower the likelihood that RE can meet that demand. As demand expectations decrease, the likelihood increases. The fundamental practical point, with respect to energy-intensive societies, is that it would be better to organise and prepare for reduced energy demand, because the less energy needed, the more readily any transition to 100 per cent RE will be realised.

The case for epistemic humility can only be emphasised further when one looks at the real world to see how slowly the renewable energy transition has advanced in recent decades. The world knew enough about fossil fuels and climate change in 1988 to establish the IPCC, but in the last thirty years, very modest progress has been made on the post-carbon transition. Wind, solar, and geothermal together provided merely between 1.7 per cent (IEA, 2018) and 4.1 per cent (Dudley, 2019) of global primary energy supply in 2019, depending on energy accounting convention. A transition to 100 per cent RE is likely going to be more difficult, slower and almost certainly more expensive than is typically thought to be the case. It follows that it would be prudent to prepare for energy descent futures.

Adding further to the scope of the decarbonisation challenge is the perennial question of 'who benefits?' This involves making distributive assessments or evaluations about how the energy humanity manages to harness should be shared amongst the growing global human population, currently at 7.8 billion and trending toward 11 billion or more by the end of the century (UN DESA, 2019). This is the ethical dimension that energy transition inquiries too often marginalise or simply ignore altogether, in favour of technological and market-driven solutions. In short, if usable energy is scarce, then energy-intensive societies especially need to ask whether they can justify their high demands if that means poorer societies are left in varying degrees of energy poverty.

Elsewhere we have provided an evidential case for energy descent in much more detail (Floyd et al., 2020; Alexander and Floyd, 2018). For present purposes, our contention is simply that there are various reasons to think that the future may be shaped by energy descent not energy abundance. Fossil fuels are finite and being depleted at pace; climate change mitigation cannot be solved merely by 'greening' energy supply but also requires choosing radical energy demand reductions; nuclear and renewables probably cannot fully or directly replace the nature and magnitude of fossil energy surpluses; the earth's biosphere has finite capacity to absorb or tolerate the impacts of the physical power exercised by human societies, and finally, distributive concerns suggest that energy-intensive societies should be reducing their energy use in order to share global energy access more broadly. Any one of these energy challenges justifies taking energy descent futures seriously. Considered together, we contend that energy descent futures are more likely than not. While this statement is subject to the same circumspection that we argue should apply to contrary findings, we contend that energy descent futures, which are presently marginalised (Laugs and Moll, 2017), should be elevated from a peripheral concern to one that actively shapes the ways in which actors engage in energy transition praxis.

The space available here precludes comprehensive treatment of this case. Our aim instead is to unsettle some assumptions about energy futures that today seem to be widely held with undue confidence. Such an act of unsettling can prepare the way for developing perspectives on energy futures that better equip humanity to find viable pathways amongst the landscape of emerging global challenges.

Tainter's theory of societal complexification: Exploring voluntary simplification as an alternative to collapse

It is not necessary to resort to energy determinism or crude reductionism to insist on the fundamental role energy has played, and continues to play, in shaping the rise (and demise) of large-scale societies (Smil, 2017). Energy is not just another resource or commodity: it is the key that unlocks access to all other resources and commodities, thereby giving shape to the physical boundaries within which human societies must take form. In other words, a society's energetic foundations delimit the socio-economic forms that it may take. This is simply to concede that a particular form of society cannot emerge without sufficient energy supplies, in the appropriate forms, to support it, and further, that a society must be able to meet its ongoing energy demands if its specific socio-economic form is to persist. If it cannot, the society will transform or be transformed, voluntarily or otherwise.

In this section we analyse the role of energy in large-scale societies through the lens of Tainter's theory of socio-political complexification and collapse (Tainter, 1988), focusing especially on what energy descent futures could mean for the current growth-orientated and globalised industrial civilisation. We begin with a brief account of the theory, then critically assess the prospects that it leaves open for managing energy descent via the strategy of voluntary simplification.

Overview of Tainter's theory of complexity

In his seminal work, *The Collapse of Complex Societies*, Tainter presents an original theory of social complexification and its maintenance that he offers as the best explanation for the collapse of human societies throughout history (Tainter, 1988). Tainter defines social complexity in terms such as the number of distinct roles that a society incorporates in coordinated ways so that the roles cooperate as a functioning whole (Tainter, 1988, p. 23). According to Tainter, societies increase in complexity in order to solve collective problems that arise as a consequence of present ways of organising their affairs and producing the goods and services on which they rely. For example, solutions to problems might involve developing technical abilities, establishing new institutions, diversifying social, economic, and political roles, as well as increasing production and information flows, all of which requires increasing energy and resource use.

Tainter's central thesis is that while increasing social complexity initially provides a net benefit to a society, eventually the benefits derived from further complexity diminish and the relative costs begin to increase. The diminishing returns on complexity arise from the fact that, when trying to solve societal problems, 'inexpensive solutions are adopted before more complex and expensive ones' (Tainter, 2011b, p. 26), meaning that over time the energy and resource costs of problem-solving tend to increase and the relative benefits decrease. As the overall pool of opportunities available for increasing the productivity of systems is exploited, the remaining scope for further increase diminishes, and a given increment of increase becomes more costly. As the marginal returns on investment in complexity continue to diminish for some area of activity, there comes a point at which these returns become negative, and further investment leads to declines in the overall return that the activity produces. When all the energy and resources available to a society are required just to maintain the society, further problems that arise cannot be solved and the society then enters a phase of decline, or even rapid collapse. That is, societies can be destroyed when the costs of sustaining their complexity become unaffordable in terms of resources in general, and energy resources especially.

One of the most challenging aspects of Tainter's theory is how it reframes – one might even say revolutionises – sustainability discourse (Allen, Tainter, and Hoekstra, 2003; Tainter, 2006). Tainter argues that sustainability is about problem solving and that problem solving increases social complexity. However, he also argues that social complexity requires energy and resources, and this implies that solving problems, including ecological problems, can actually require increases in energy and other resource consumption, not reductions. Indeed, Tainter maintains that sustainability is 'not a passive consequence of having fewer human beings who consume more limited resources' (Tainter, 2006, p. 93), as many argue it is. In fact he suggests that 'voluntary simplification' – which refers to the pursuit of forms of social organisation that remain viable with reduced resource use – may no longer be an option for industrial civilisation (Tainter, 2011b). Instead, Tainter's primary conception of sustainability involves subsidising ever-increasing complexity with more energy and resources in order to solve ongoing problems. We say 'primary conception' because there are subtleties in Tainter's position that leave open theoretical space for alternative conclusions and pathways.

Here we critically examine Tainter's contention that voluntary simplification is not a viable path to sustainability. In fact, given the plausibility of future energy descent, we argue that voluntary simplification is by far the best strategy to implement, even if the chance of adoption in the current political and cultural climate – a climate which promotes growth in consumption, material affluence, and technological advance as pre-eminent societal values – does not provide grounds for much optimism.

Part of the theoretical tension between our position and Tainter's critique of voluntary simplification turns on differing notions of 'sustainability'. Whereas in Tainter's sense sustainability infers sustaining existing forms of socio-political organisation, we extend this to changing the forms of organisation through voluntary simplification, insofar as that is required for humanity to operate within the carrying capacity of the planet (Alexander and Gleeson, 2019). Furthermore, even if attempting to sustain existing forms of organising through ever-increasing complexity continues to be humanity's dominant approach to solving societal problems, we maintain the alternative path of voluntary simplification remains the most effective means of building 'resilience' (i.e., the ability of an individual or community to withstand societal or ecological shocks), and better yet, can lay the foundations for societies to develop the 'antifragile' characteristic of living systems that strengthen in response to stress (Taleb, 2012). This is significant because it justifies the practice and promotion of voluntary simplification, irrespective of the likelihood of it ever being broadly accepted. That is, if an end to industrial civilisation's trajectory of increased socio-political complexity is coming one way or another due to energy descent, then it would be better to accept this energetic trajectory and prepare for it, rather than wait for it to arrive through crisis and collapse.

While we accept that problem solving generally implies an increase in social complexity of the nature Tainter describes, the position we present below is that there comes a point when such complexity itself becomes a problem. At this point voluntary simplification, not further complexity, is the most appropriate response. Not only does industrial civilisation seem to be at such a point today (Homer-Dixon, 2006; Slaughter, 2010; Bardi, 2017), or well beyond it, we hope to show, albeit in a preliminary way, that voluntary simplification presents a viable and desirable option for responding to today's converging social, economic, and ecological problems. This goes against Tainter's primary conception of sustainability, while accepting much of his background theoretical framework. After unpacking our theoretical position, we bring the analysis to a head by discussing Tradable Energy Quotas as a policy tool eminently suited to initiating and managing the voluntary simplification strategy.

Critically analysing voluntary simplification as an energy descent strategy

The conditions characterised by Tainter under the term 'complexity' typically entail homogenisation and standardisation of production and management practices, and exercise of control through centralised governance mechanisms. Fleming points out that in important respects such conditions are better characterised as simple rather than complex (Fleming, 2016). In order to appreciate the potential for the approach that we term voluntary simplification to function as an energy descent strategy, some further nuances associated with the concept therefore require unpacking. The relationships discussed below are summarised in Figure 1.

Where the general problem-solving strategy identified by Tainter implies uniting increasingly large territories and polities under common coordination and control mechanisms, voluntary simplification implies decentralisation of governance and disaggregation of production systems. This in turn supports developing locally adaptive responses to perennial social challenges, and hence leads to diverse forms of organisation, with corresponding increase in redundancy. The outcome of locally initiated and managed voluntary simplification as a means of deintensifying economic systems from the 'bottom up' can in this respect be viewed as leading to an increase in complexity from a macro-scale, external observer perspective. This macro-perspective complexity is a consequence of many local initiatives developing in parallel, according to the differing circumstances of those enacting them. That this is framed in terms of 'simplification' reflects desires of individuals, families, and communities struggling to cope with the demands on their time and attention attending the conditions that Tainter characterises in terms of increased complexity. Therefore, 'voluntary simplification', rather than being a social-scientific description of the macro societal-level outcome from the processes gathered under its banner, is a descriptor for the collective desire that might unite people within a social movement that could respond in a viable way to the dilemma that Tainter's theory presents.

Uniting within a social movement aimed toward greater local autonomy is different, though, from uniting under a uniform means of social organisation. Voluntary simplification requires creation of increased space for local organisation and distributed community-level governance of economic processes, consistent with the general principle of subsidiarity. Realising the benefits of subsidiarity would require that its exercise be allowed via bottom-up civil society organisation, rather than formally mandated from the top down by governments. This implies removing policies, laws, and regulations that impede the development of informal economies at the household, neighbourhood, community, and bio-regional scales. It also means winding back subsidies and policy

	Tainter	This paper
Possible trajectories for civic societies under resource-constrained conditions	**Tainter:** Societies subject to decreasing marginal return on investment in socio-political complexity as problems are solved.	**This paper:** Voluntary simplification enables problem solving with reducing socio-political overheads, and hence without necessitating increased resource use.
Characteristics	Proliferation in social roles and technologies to solve problems, requiring increased coordination effort and new governance institutions. Coordination of increasingly specialised roles accounts for a growing proportion of overall resource use. Sustaining established social structures and organisation entails ever-expanding resource use.	Increasing proximity between producers and consumers of goods and services. Increasing production of goods and services by informal economic arrangements at scales from households to bio-regions. Sustaining viable communities by developing social structures and forms of organisation with lower formal governance and administration overheads.
Inside participant perspective	**'Complex':** Demands for ever-increasing labour productivity with diminishing marginal returns on effort, proliferating rules and regulations, and necessity of engaging with increasingly diverse services result in time pressure and fragmentation of attention for individuals, families, civil society organisations, and work groups. Balancing ever-increasing competing demands leads to the experience of life as increasingly complex.	**'Simple':** Production processes for goods and services, along with functionality of the goods and services produced, will be increasingly transparent from the inside participant viewpoint. While individuals may participate in an increased range of roles and activities, motivation for this will be based to a greater degree on interest, capacity, and capability, and regulated via individual sovereignty rather than formal institutional demands and external authority exercised from a distance.
Outside observer perspective	**'Simple':** Centralised control and coordination of increasingly specialised social and economic functions requires high levels of standardisation and bureaucratic regulation. While role descriptions proliferate, work practices involve increasing uniformity. An outside observer considering a society as a coordinated whole will see a narrow range of repeated patterns. Homogenisation between societies will also be apparent.	**'Complex':** Locally adaptive responses to existential challenges resulting in greater diversity of organisational forms across societies, and even between communities collectively comprising larger civic societies. Governance structures adapted to specific contexts, employing standardised systems and practices where doing so provides the most adaptive fit with local circumstances, rather than 'standardisation by default'.

Figure 1. How the experience of different forms of social organisation as 'complex' or 'simple' varies between participant and external observer perspectives.

supports that favour formal economic arrangements, where informal arrangements are sufficient.

A consequence of this is closer or more direct contact between producers and consumers, including greatly increased production of goods and services by the end-consumers themselves (Holmgren, 2018). For instance, walking and cycling entail self-production of transport, while greatly reducing the scale of the intermediate economy necessary to provide the services (traffic policing, insurance, infrastructure maintenance, health care) required by personal automobile transport. Even an increase in use of electric cargo bikes can have a major impact here. A more diverse transport system based on better matching modes to specific needs is implied, and can be viewed from the macro-perspective as more rather than less complex, while from the micro-perspective of participants it is experienced as simplification. Similar patterns of deintensification through voluntary simplification can be envisaged in areas including food and fibre production, manufacture of clothing and housing, and maintenance and repair of tools and equipment (Fleming, 2016; Alexander and Rutherford, 2020).

These shifts are occurring already in many locations, but are limited in scope by incentive structures that treat employment in the formal economy as vastly more socially legitimate than work in informal economies. Barriers to greater self-production of transport such as proximity of housing to employment opportunities in the formal economy, norms around working hours, and social conventions relating to motor vehicle ownership and access are all amenable to change in concert with moves that give greater status to participation in informal economies. An increase in hours spent working in informal economies at household and neighbourhood scale would involve simpler webs of economic production, in the sense of being far more locally bounded than at present (Norberg-Hodge, 2019; Gibson-Graham, Cameron, and Healy, 2013). This would lead though to increased diversity in patterns of social interaction viewed from the macro-perspective. Whereas the typical trajectory of socio-political complexification that Tainter's model describes leads in the direction of social 'monocultures', economic deintensification through voluntary simplification points toward the emergence of social and economic 'polycultures'. Alongside these changes, overall reductions in resource use could be anticipated (Alexander and Gleeson, 2019).

The question remains though of how locally-initiated economic deintensification through voluntary simplification could possibly emerge across societies that are currently configured on lines diametrically opposed to such trajectories. Under what circumstances could voluntary simplification appear sufficiently attractive as a strategy for achieving life satisfaction, for a sufficient number of people, that it might emerge as a major social movement with scope to shift human societies onto sustainable paths? It is with this question in mind that we now turn attention to TEQs.

Tradable Energy Quotas: A policy tool for deep decarbonisation

Overview of Tradable Energy Quotas

Equitable and just transition to post-fossil fuel societies will entail engaging all sectors of society, and in fact every citizen, in the transition challenge. At the political level, this requires policy instruments that support and influence such a level of engagement, and that enable people to work together toward a common goal. The Tradable Energy Quotas (TEQs) system devised by David Fleming is designed specifically to close the gap that currently exists between the physical reality of energy-use impact on climate, and the political reality of social lock-in to the existing economic system (Fleming, 2016). TEQs is intended to engage every member of society in the task of reducing dependence on fossil fuels, on an equal footing.

TEQs would achieve such equitable engagement by putting a hard cap on a nation's emissions from energy use (Chamberlain et al., 2014). At the centre of the TEQs system is a national emission budget that sets the quantity of carbon emissions permitted in any year. In the event that supply scarcity constrains fossil fuel availability more tightly than would be the case via the national emission budget, the annual budget would be adjusted accordingly so that the TEQs system adapts seamlessly to the new circumstances.

An equal share, or quota, of the national budget is then freely issued to every adult, collectively covering the share of national emissions accounted for by household energy use. Anyone wishing to use more than their free share must purchase additional units from those using less than theirs, in a market set up for that purpose. All non-household energy users (businesses, service providers, government entities at all levels) purchase their emission quota units by tender in a weekly auction.

A year's supply of TEQ units is issued on the first day of operation. This is topped up on a weekly basis, so that a rolling one-year supply of credits is maintained in participants' accounts. Each TEQ unit represents 1 kilogramme CO_2 emitted. Fuels and electricity are rated in terms of the quantity of carbon dioxide emitted per metered unit, over each energy unit's full life cycle. TEQ units equivalent to the corresponding emissions are then surrendered whenever fuel or electricity is purchased. The system's designers envisage unit transactions being handled automatically via integration with the existing credit- and debit-card systems for financial transactions (Fleming, 2016; Chamberlain et al., 2014), thereby avoiding the need for a separate 'carbon card'.

Why Tradable Energy Quotas can manage energy descent in optimal and equitable ways

Voluntary simplification, we contend, offers a viable strategy for bridging the gulf between current large-scale societies reliant on levels of per-capita resource use so extreme that they undermine their own future prospects, and forms of society that could enable large populations to enjoy decent and rewarding lives while allowing their descendants similar opportunity. At the same time, we recognise that sound reasoning and enthusiastic advocacy have little prospect of moving this beyond a fringe view, while cultural narratives of wellbeing are built around ongoing growth in aggregate resource consumption. This places civic leaders, especially in liberal democracies, in an invidious position. Even if the implications of increasing resource consumption for the integrity of the biosphere and continued functioning of human systems are fully appreciated, moves to address this by forcing a shift away from reliance on finite and dangerously polluting resources implies curtailing established and expected freedoms. While the freedoms to use depleting and polluting resources remain unchecked at the population scale, voluntary simplification, which requires self-imposed limits on these freedoms, is even less tenable.

In order for voluntary simplification to become desirable and attractive at population scale, it first needs to be perceived as a pathway to, rather than a constraint on, greater freedoms than are otherwise available. This means that collective mechanisms for limiting the use of depleting and polluting resources must first be in place for voluntary simplification to be effective. Such limits could be either institutionally self-imposed via formal statutes and regulations (as is the case with laws to control pollution), or imposed by biophysical constraints. The latter is evident, for example, in situations where water shortages are imposed on populations through drought, and hence where political-economic power differentials determine relative access to finite water resources. In such cases, power differentials can be ameliorated via statutory or regulatory means.

The TEQs system is of particular interest in this light. Its basic design allows it to function both as a means of institutionally limiting fossil fuel pollution, and as an institutional response to mitigating inequities in access to supply-constrained fossil fuels. Moreover, the system is designed only to limit collectively-agreed social ills (reducing aggregate greenhouse gas pollution within an agreed emission budget, or reducing societal dependence on a supply-constrained essential resource, while in both cases ensuring equitable distribution of the costs). It is non-prescriptive with respect to the alternative social and economic pathways enacted in order to adapt to these limits. As such, it establishes an institutional context within which voluntary simplification has the opportunity to emerge as a viable alternative, without mandating that it be adopted. If it does emerge as a broad social movement, then this will be by collective choice, resulting from its recognition as a viable means of pursuing preferred futures.

The prospect of energy descent, provides the backdrop against which we see the emergence of broader support for voluntary simplification as plausible. Indeed, in the absence of energy descent – if access to energy services continues instead to expand – then we concede that pursuit of 'sustainability' will continue in line with Tainter's model of problem-solving via socio-political complexification. At least, that is, until non-energetic constraints such as ecological collapse or supply-side limits for other critical resources take over. TEQs establishes an institutional context in which the question of energy abundance or sufficiency will be resolved.

From the viewpoint of orthodox policy and economic analysis, the expectation is that restricting the burning of fossil fuels will drive substitution of the associated energy from other sources, principally wind and solar PV, but also nuclear, and smaller shares from other renewables. However, if the collective will is established to self-limit the burning of fossil fuels, then TEQs provides the limiting mechanism and incentive structure for doing so, while remaining silent on what will substitute in its place. Effective functioning of TEQs is measured in terms of reduced fossil fuel use, regardless of the roles played by various supply- and demand-side responses in the substitution task. Under TEQs, fossil fuel consumers are in this sense free to proceed according to whatever non-fossil fuel alternative best meets their expectations for life satisfaction or organisational success. They are equally free to pursue alternative expectations of life satisfaction, for instance, through voluntary simplification, as they are to pursue alternative energy sources in support of their existing expectations.

The question that remains, however, is why has TEQs received such meagre attention and support? This is not the forum to present a 'theory of change' (Alexander and Gleeson, 2019; Buch-Hansen, 2018) or review the range of social, economic, and political obstacles that lie in the way of TEQs being implemented. Nevertheless, we do acknowledge two primary obstacles. First, public recognition of the gravity of the overlapping challenges of fossil energy depletion, climate change, and degradation of ecosystems remains poor. These issues are being discussed to varying degrees, of course, but the magnitude of the energetic predicament underlying a post-carbon transition is still marginalised and understated in mainstream discourse. This is partly due to a prevailing techno-optimism, which broadly assumes that technology, innovation, market mechanisms, and better product design will resolve environmental problems (via 'green growth') without much in the way of reconfiguration of existing societal structures and cultural values (Hickel and Kallis, 2019). If the prospect of energy descent or societal collapse is not clearly seen or its gravity appreciated, then there is little socio-cultural impetus to develop and implement coherent policy responses, such as TEQs. Promisingly, as this paper was under review, 100 prominent economists published an open letter in a mainstream newspaper calling for governments to actively phase out the fossil fuel industry (Sachs et al., 2020). Is TEQs an idea whose time might soon come? This is ultimately governed by political decision-making, and hence indeterminate. It does seem though that the ground is currently being laid for more widespread public discussion in which TEQs might be given serious consideration.

The second reason TEQs may be struggling to lay down roots in a policy context is a simple political reality: the 'powers that be' – especially corporations, their lobby groups, mass media, and the nations and institutions doing well under the growth paradigm – have little incentive to transform a mode of societal organisation that is (for the time being at least) offering them great rewards in terms of wealth and power. If TEQs is inconsistent with the interests of the dominant powers in the existing, globalised economic system, then perhaps it is no surprise that politicians and corporations, and even those enamoured with consumption-oriented ways of life, have little drive to deliberately induce, via TEQs, a paradigm shift in political economy in the direction of voluntary simplification. In short, despite the coherency of TEQs as a tool for managing energy descent, its implementation would depend on both a successful public relations campaign, and sustained socio-political will amongst advocates. However, none of that is likely to occur until energy descent is seen as a plausible future, and TEQs is seen as a coherent and even attractive policy for managing energy descent. It is that preliminary work to which this paper is intended to contribute.

Conclusions: Navigating energy descent pathways

In this paper we contended that there are three primary and overlapping reasons for TEQs to be regarded as a policy mechanism highly suited to reducing fossil fuel dependency in a managed, timely, and equitable way: (1) Fossil fuels are finite and have declining energy return on investment (EROI), thus in the foreseeable future humanity will be forced to manage with reduced net energy availability from fossil energy sources; (2) Tight carbon budget targets strongly indicate that humanity must leave fossil fuels even before their depletion enforces a post-carbon transition and (3) Human energy use drives the transformation of the physical world that is degrading planetary ecosystems, suggesting that sustainable modes of production and consumption may involve creating very different forms of societal organisation that are far less energy dependent. These three issues were discussed in relation to a further context of inquiry: the limits to non-carbon energy sources (RE in particular) delivering the range and scale of energy services upon which current societies depend. We outlined a case for why, when assessed with due epistemic humility, it is unlikely that RE sources will be able to fully replace the energy services provided by fossil fuels. All these reasons suggest that energy descent may lead to human futures shaped by energy sufficiency rather than energy abundance. We have presented TEQs as the most coherent policy for managing this turning point in globalised, industrial civilisation.

Our novel contribution in this paper was to analyse TEQs in relation to Tainter's theory of societal complexity and collapse. As we have seen, Tainter argued that societies become more complex as they solve the range of problems they face, and that solving those problems demands increasing energy and other resources. When societies are unable to secure the resources needed to solve their problems, Tainter argues that they tend to undergo a process of involuntary simplification. In ordinary parlance, involuntary simplification means societal deterioration or even collapse, as more problems are faced that cannot be solved with a declining energy budget within existing modes of societal organisation. Our approach was to theorise an alternative to collapse. Defending energy descent as a plausible energy future, we explored how, within Tainter's theory, a society could manage this energetic turning point without facing a collapse scenario. By analysing the notion of voluntary simplification, we sought to show why an energy descent future need not imply societal collapse, although we did outline various ways in which managing energy descent would result in deep and diverse reconfigurations of fundamental modes of socio-political and economic organisation. We employed the terms economic deintensification and degrowth as supplementary concepts to help explain what voluntary simplification would look like (Fleming, 2016; Alexander and Gleeson, 2019). Our argument was that TEQs would help manage an energy descent future and that voluntary simplification and economic deintensification, leading to economic degrowth, would be required to avoid the collapse scenario otherwise inherent to Tainter's conceptual framework.

Much mainstream energy and sustainability discourse is based on a series of highly optimistic assumptions about future energy supply in a carbon-constrained world. The improbability of conditions aligning such that all necessary assumptions are borne out implies that the energy futures ahead will likely diverge significantly from those envisaged within this established discourse. This has potentially profound implications. The availability of energy in the right forms at sufficient rates is the lifeblood of any particular form of social organisation. Energy-related factors are fundamental to how we shape our societies and pursue our goals, yet it seems most individuals and societies are making plans based on precarious expectations. One of the goals of the present analysis is to encourage readers to treat the prospect that these expectations will not be realised as, at the very least, a matter of plausibility.

In the event that mainstream expectations are thwarted, the consequences could range from the disruptive to the catastrophic. This is not a case against optimism, but rather of channelling it in directions that lie within humanity's scope of influence. Even within the difficult circumstances that our assessment implies, there is still much good that can be achieved. Ample room remains for adjusting expectations to better reflect underlying energy and environmental realities, and to reconstitute societies – and the economies that support them – accordingly. Dystopian interpretations of descent are not inherent in the concept itself; rather, they are an entailment of cultural priorities favouring continuous material and energetic expansion.

In closing, we appreciate the psychological drivers for denying the prospect of energy descent and trusting instead in a cornucopian or techno-optimistic worldview. It is less confronting to human identities and ways of life to believe that technology and markets can solve social and environmental problems without needing to rethink the underpinning structures that give rise to those problems. We posit that this means of coping with psychological dissonance, perhaps adaptive in other circumstances, is influential in the apparent 'self-censoring' (consciously or unconsciously) by mainstream energy and economic analysts, resulting in perspectives inconsistent with dominant economic and political paradigms being marginalised (Anderson, 2015). It would be preferable to believe and act upon what is most likely to be true following an honest and frank weighing of the evidence, supported by a robust public engagement campaign (Shaw et al., 2018)). We have argued that this means coming to terms with the prospect of futures characterised by reduced access to energy services and creatively preparing for the socio-economic implications of energy descent by actively pursuing paths to deintensify economies, via strategies such as voluntary simplification.

All human societies exist interdependently with natural systems that are ultimately beyond human control. It is far preferable, we contend, that societies retain the greatest degree of agency possible in getting to grips with the dilemma of fossil fuel dependence. The alternative is to have our futures dictated to us by breakdown in natural systems that are beyond our capacity to control. The TEQs system offers a means for societies to manage the reduction in fossil fuel use in an orderly and coordinated way, so that citizens retain as much scope as possible for choosing the forms that their post-carbon futures might take.

References

Alexander, S. 2014. 'Voluntary Simplification as an Alternative to Collapse'. *Foresight* 16, 550–566.

Alexander, S. 2015. *Sufficiency Economy: Enough, For Everyone, Forever.* Melbourne: Simplicity Institute.

Alexander, S. and Floyd, J. 2018. *Carbon Civilisation and the Energy Descent Future: Life beyond this Brief Anomaly.* Melbourne: Simplicity Institute.

Alexander, S. and Gleeson, B. 2019. *Degrowth in the Suburbs: A Radical Urban Imaginary.* London: Palgrave Macmillan.

Alexander, S. and Rutherford, J. (eds). 2020. *The Simpler Way: Collected Writings of Ted Trainer.* Melbourne: Simplicity Institute.

Allen, T.F.H., Tainter, J.A., and Hoekstra, T.W. 2003. 'Supply-Side Sustainability'. New York: Columbia University Press.

Anderson, K. 2015. 'Duality in Climate Science'. *Nature Geoscience* 8, 898–900.

Anderson, K., Broderick, J.F., and Stoddard, I. 2020. 'A Factor of Two: How the Mitigation Plans of "Climate Progressive" Nations Fall Far Short of Paris-Compliant Pathways'. *Climate Policy*: 1–15. Available online: https://www.tandfonline.com/ doi/pdf/10.1080/14693062.2020.1728209?needAccess=true (accessed on 15 August 2020).

Backhaus, K., Gausling, P., and Hildebrand, L. 2015. 'Comparing the Incomparable: Lessons to be Learned from Models Evaluating the Feasibility of Desertec'. *Energy* 82: 905–913.

Bardi, U. 2017. 'The Seneca Effect: Why Growth is Slow but Collapse is Rapid'. A Report to the Club of Rome. Singapore: Springer.

Bardi, U. 2020. *Before the Collapse: A Guide to the Other Side of Growth.* Singapore: Springer.

Bentley, R.W., Mushalik, M., and Wang, J. 2020. 'The Resource-Limited Plateau In Global Conventional Oil Production: Analysis and Consequences'. *Biophysical Economics and Sustainability* 5: 10.

Bringezu, S. 2019. 'Toward Science-Based and Knowledge-Based Targets for Global Sustainable Resource Use'. *Resources* 8: 140.

Buch-Hansen, H. 2018. 'The Prerequisites for a Degrowth Paradigm Shift: Insights from Critical Political Economy'. *Ecological Economics* 146: 157–163.

Chamberlin, S., Maxey, L., and Hurth, V. 2014. 'Reconciling Scientific Reality with Realpolitik: Moving Beyond Carbon Pricing to Teqs – An Integrated, Economy-Wide Emissions Cap'. *Carbon Management* 5: 411–427.

Dudley, B. 2019. 'BP statistical Review of World Energy 2019'. London: BP.

Emissions Gap Report 2019. 2019. 'Global Progress Report on Climate Action'. Nairobi: UN Environment Programme.

Energy Information Administration (EIA). 2019. 'International Energy Outlook'. Washington, DC.

Fleming, D. 2016. *Lean Logic: A Dictionary for the Future and How to Survive It.* Edited by S. Chamberlin. White River Junction, VT: Chelsea Green Publishing.

Floyd, J. 2014. 'Sense-making and acting for descent futures: Human and cultural pathways'. *Foresight* 16, 587–607.

Floyd, J. et al. 2020. 'Energy Descent as a Post-Carbon Transition Scenario: How "Knowledge Humility" Reshapes Energy Futures for Post-Normal Times'. *Futures*, 122: 102565.

Fustier, K. 2016. 'Global Oil Supply: Will Mature Field Declines Drive the Next Supply Crunch?'. HBSC Global Research Report. Available online: https://www.ourenergypolicy.org/wp-content/uploads/2017/01/526500-1.pdf (accessed on 15 August 2020).

Gabbattis, J. 2020. 'IEA: Coronavirus Impact on CO_2 Emissions Six Times Larger than 2008 Financial Crisis'. Available online: https://www.carbonbrief.org/iea-coronavirus-impact-on-co2-emissions-six-times-larger-than-financial-crisis (accessed on 7 July 2020).

Gibson-Graham, J.K., Cameron, J., and Healy, S. 2013. *Take Back the Economy: An Ethical Guide for Transforming our Communities*. Minneapolis: University of Minnesota Press.

Harvey, D. 2005. *A Brief History of Neoliberalism*. Oxford: Oxford University Press.

Hatfield-Dodds, S. et al. 2015. 'Australia is "Free to Choose" Economic Growth and Falling Environmental Pressures'. *Nature* 527: 49–53. Available online: http://www.nature.com/nature/journal/v527/n7576/abs/nature16065.html#supplementary-information (accessed on 15 August 2020).

Hickel, J. and Kallis, G. 2019. 'Is Green Growth Possible?' *New Political Economy* 25: 469–486.

Holmgren, D. 2009. *Future Scenarios: How Communities Can Respond to Peak Oil and Climate Change*. White River Jct, VT: Chelsea Green Publishing.

Holmgren, D. 2018. *RetroSuburbia: The Downshifter's Guide to a Resilient Future*; Hepburn Springs: Melliodora Publishing.

Homer-Dixon, T. 2006. *The Upside of Down: Catastrophe, Conflict and the Renewal of Civilization*. Toronto, ON: Alfred A Knopf.

Homer-Dixon, T. et al. 2015. 'Synchronous Failure: The Emerging Causal Architecture of Global Crisis'. *Ecology and Society* 20.

Intergovernmental Panel on Climate Change (IPCC). 2018. 'Summary for Policymakers'. In 'Global Warming of 1.5 °C: An IPCC Special Report on the Impacts of Global Warming of 1.5 °C above Pre-Industrial Levels and Related Global Greenhouse Gas Emission Pathways, in the Context of Strengthening the Global Response to the Threat of Climate Change, Sustainable Development, and Efforts to Eradicate Poverty'. Geneva: SR 1.5.

International Energy Agency (IEA). 2018. 'Key World Energy Statistics 2018'. Paris.

International Energy Agency (IEA). 2019a. 'World Energy Outlook'. Paris.

International Energy Agency (IEA). 2019b. 'Key World Energy Statistics'. Paris.

Laugs, G.A.H. and Moll, H.C. 2017. 'A Review of the Bandwidth and Environmental Discourses of Future Energy Scenarios: Shades of Green and Gray'. *Renewable and Sustainable Energy Reviews* 67: 520–530.

Michaux, S. 2019. 'Oil from a Critical Raw Material Perspective; Report 70/2019; Geological Survey of Finland. Available online: http://tupa.gtk.fi/raportti/arkisto/70_2019.pdf (accessed on 15 August 2020).

Miller, R.G. and Sorrell, S.R. 2014. 'The Future of Oil Supply'. *Philosophical Transactions of the Royal Society A: Mathematical, Physical and Engineering Sciences*: 372.

Mohr, S.H. et al. 2015. 'Projection of World Fossil Fuels By Country'. *Fuel* 141: 120–135.

Moriarty, P. and Honnery, D. 2008. 'Low-mobility: The Future of Transport'. *Futures* 40: 865–872.

Moriarty, P. and Honnery, D. 2011a. 'The Transition to Renewable Energy: Make Haste Slowly'. *Environmental Science and Technology* 45: 2527–2528.

Moriarty, P. and Honnery, D. 2011b. 'Is there an Optimum Level for Renewable Energy?' *Energy Policy* 39: 2748–2753.

Moriarty, P. and Honnery, D. 2011c. 'Rise and Fall of the Carbon Civilisation: Resolving Global Environmental and Resource Problems'. London: Springer.

Moriarty, P. and Honnery, D. 2016. 'Can Renewable Energy Power the Future?' *Energy Policy* 93: 3–7.

Murphy, D.J. 2014. 'The Implications of the Declining Energy Return on Investment of Oil Production'. *Philosophical Transactions of the Royal Society A: Mathematical, Physical and Engineering Sciences*: 372.

Nordberg-Hodge, H. 2019. *Local is Our Future: Steps to an Economics of Happiness.* Local Futures. Available online: https://www.localfutures.org/publications/local-is-our-future-book-helena-norberg-hodge/ (accessed on 15 August 2020).

Ripple, W.J. et al. 2017. 'World Scientists' Warning to Humanity: A Second Notice'. *BioScience* 67: 1026–1028.

Ripple, W.J. et al. 2019. 'World scientists' Warning of a Climate Emergency'. *BioScience* 70: 8–12.

Rockström, J. et al. 2009. 'A Safe Operating Space for Humanity'. *Nature*, 461: 472–475.

Sachs, J. et al., 4 August 2020. 'Letter from Economists: To Rebuild Our World, We Must End the Carbon Economy'; London: *The Guardian*.

Shaw, C. et al. 2018. 'Intermediaries' Perspectives on the Public's Role in the Energy Transitions Needed to Deliver UK Climate Change Policy Goals'. *Energy Policy* 116: 267–276.

Slaughter, R.A. 2010. *The Biggest Wake Up Call in History*. Indooroopilly, Australia: Foresight International.

Smil, V (ed.). 2017. *Energy and Civilization: A History*. Revised edition of: *Energy in world history*. Cambridge, MA: The MIT Press.

Steffen, W. et al. 2015. 'Planetary Boundaries: Guiding Human Development on a Changing Planet'. *Science* 347, 1259855.

Tainter, J.A. 1988. *The Collapse of Complex Societies*. Cambridge, UK: Cambridge University Press.

Tainter, J.A. 1995. 'Sustainability of Complex Societies'. *Futures* 27: 397–407.

Tainter, J.A. 2006. 'Social Complexity and Sustainability'. *Ecol. Complex.* 3: 91–103.

Tainter, J.A. 2011a. 'Energy, Complexity, and Sustainability: A Historical Perspective'. *Environmental Innovation Societal Transitions* 1: 89–95.

Tainter, J.A. 2011b. 'Resources and Cultural Complexity: Implications for Sustainability'. *Critical Reviews in Plant Sciences* 30: 24–34.

Taleb, N.N. 2012. 'Antifragile: Things that Gain from Disorder'. New York: Random House.

Turner, G.M. 2019. 'Is a Sustainable Future Possible?' *Journal and Proceedings of the Royal Society of New South Wales* 152: 47–65.

United Nations Department of Social and Economic Affairs (UN DESA). 2019. 'In World Population Prospects 2019: Highlights'. New York: United Nations.

Valentine, S.V., Sovacool, B.K., and Brown, M.A. 2017. 'Frame Envy In Energy Policy Ideology: A Social Constructivist Framework for Wicked Energy Problems'. *Energy Policy* 109: 623–630.

Ward, J.D. et al. 2016. 'Is Decoupling GDP Growth from Environmental Impact Possible?' *PLoS ONE* 11: e0164733.

Weiss, M. and Cattaneo, C. 2017. 'Degrowth: Taking Stock and Reviewing an Emerging Academic Paradigm'. *Ecological Economics* 137: 220–230.

Chapter 7

Modern Monetary Theory, post-growth economics, and avoiding collapse[1]

Introduction

The ever-expanding global economy has crossed safe planetary boundaries and is in dangerous ecological overshoot, creating fragile conditions that raise the prospect of civilisational collapse this century (Turner, 2019; Ripple et al., 2017; 2020). In recent decades robust and diverse 'post-growth' literatures have emerged which have recognised the existential threat posed by limitless growth on a finite planet (Daly, 1997; 2014; Meadows, Meadows, and Randers, 2004; Lawn, 2016; Kallis, 2017). At its broadest, this heterodox group of economic thinkers call for planned contraction or 'degrowth' of the energy and resource demands of overdeveloped economies, with the aim of creating 'steady state' or 'zero-growth' economies that operate within the sustainable carrying capacity of the planet. With humanity as a whole already in ecological overshoot by about 75 per cent, with no sign of a voluntary plateau on the horizon, the case for rapid but controlled degrowth in many countries seems obvious if incalculable human suffering is to be avoided – not to mention the ongoing suffering and destruction of other species and ecosystems (Steffen et al., 2015; Ripple et al., 2017). Nevertheless, in societies that celebrate increases in gross domestic product (GDP) as the primary indicator of economic and social progress, it is clear that any transition 'beyond growth' would involve profound economic, cultural, and political transformations.

Even as the evidential case for a post-growth economy continues to strengthen, the profound but necessary changes needed to create such an economy have been, and will continue to be, resisted. As a species, we may have evolved over millennia in cooperative and supportive groups, but that does not guarantee the necessary critical thinking skills for long-term projections and accurate risk analysis. Instead, we seem to be

---

1 Originally published in Haydn Washington (ed) *Ecological Economics: Solutions for the Future*, 2020, CASSE NSW, Ch 7, co-authored with Stephen Williams.

hampered by our less noble character traits: greed, ignorance, denialism, wilful blindness, and no doubt other human frailties that frustrate calls for change. Some would even argue that the capitalist economic system itself has various 'growth imperatives' built into its structure (e.g., Binswanger, 2009), which may or may not be true depending on the version of capitalism being discussed (Lawn, 2011; Blauworf, 2012).

However, another major reason preventing post-growth economic policies from being embraced is the dominant macroeconomic paradigm that informs policy choices. Since at least the 1970s, the dominant paradigm has been neoclassical economics, which replaced Keynesianism. This is the macroeconomics still taught in most universities, with Gregory Mankiw's *Macroeconomics* (2018) textbook being the exemplar. In this chapter we outline a fast-emerging alternative macroeconomics called Modern Monetary Theory (MMT) that we believe is superior and will come to replace the current theory. Prominent advocates offer a preliminary definition in the following terms:

> MMT provides an analysis of fiscal and monetary policy applicable to national governments with sovereign, non-convertible currencies. It concludes that the sovereign currency issuer: i) does not face a 'budget constraint' (as conventionally defined); ii) cannot 'run out of money'; iii) meets its obligations by paying in its own currency; iv) can set the interest rate on any obligations it issues (Nersisyan and Wray, 2019).

Given that MMT attempts to describe how monetary systems work, rather than being a policy platform, it is neither inherently pro-growth nor post-growth, as they are policy positions for individual nations depending on their ideology and the size of their economies. However, we argue that MMT is the most accurate description available of the interplay of macroeconomic forces, and it should therefore be used in the formulation of policies, rather than the conventional, but flawed, neoclassical model. The global crisis initiated by the COVID-19 pandemic has brought the currency-issuing capacity of governments into sharp focus, accelerating interest in MMT (e.g. Kohler, 2020; Von Drehle, 2020).

We contend that when MMT is understood, post-growth policy options expand dramatically and become more viable, while the dominant neoclassical model is seen to be a kind of ideological straitjacket. Accordingly, MMT should be of interest to everyone concerned with sustainability – including degrowth and steady-state economists – who have, as a group, mostly neglected MMT (but see Lawn, 2017). While we may raise as many questions as we answer, we hope this brief overview provokes a broader discussion about MMT and the policies it can engender.

What is macroeconomics?

Macroeconomics is the study of the cause-and-effect relationships between aggregate economic data relating to inflation, the labour market, wages, output, productivity, income, savings, taxation, debt, and so on. Ideally, it should also explain the nature of money, the role of treasuries and central banks, and the limits to government spending. If accurate, it should produce models that are highly predictive. It should not be a set of policies or an ideology, but should facilitate accurate predictions about likely outcomes if certain policies are adopted – for example, the likely inflation rate if the government tried to reduce unemployment. In the real world there is likely to be some overlap between pure macroeconomic theory, on the one hand, and policy positions, on the other, such as we see between neoclassical economics and neoliberal policies (Quiggin, 2012: 3).

If macroeconomics is an attempt to correctly describe the interplay of various economic aggregates, then we must search for the most accurate theory, regardless of whether we aspire to growth or non-growth. At the same time, we acknowledge that no theory can claim to be entirely value-free if it has political, economic, or social implications (Washington, 2018a). Contrary to some post-growth advocates, however, we cannot simply choose between competing macroeconomic theories based on a supposition that one will more likely produce post-growth outcomes rather than another (Svartzman, Dron, and Espagne, 2019). Instead, we must choose the theory that most closely represents how economies actually function, mostly by empirical analysis (factual information) and buttressed by its predictive record. Growth, steady state, or degrowth then come through policy choices, political ideology, and biophysical limits, informed by the best macroeconomic theory.

In practice, overturning failing paradigms turns out to be extremely difficult, not least because of the resistance exerted by those who benefit from maintaining the status quo (Cahill, 2011). Even so, there are strong indications that neoclassical economics is increasingly on life support, demonstrated, before the pandemic of 2020, by central bankers increasingly calling on governments to use fiscal policy to achieve economic targets; and government intervention as the pandemic spread.[2]

We argue that the rising star of macroeconomics – MMT – is profoundly different to the failing orthodoxy (see Appendix 1 for a comparison table). In particular, it recognises national governments' massive power to shape and control their economies: either to expand them, maintain them in a steady state, or shrink them. In so doing, such a government can also better control such things as wealth distribution and environmental management. No longer would there be a need for 'money-starved' national governments to continually pacify multinational corporations, financial markets, or credit-ratings agencies, as if the governments were beholden to them. They are not beholden, because the currency-issuing government does not need their money for revenue. Fears of all-powerful economic actors who might, for instance, withdraw financial capital from a territory, are shown to be largely the invention of those who benefited from the fear. We will not argue that a more accurate macroeconomics like MMT is a sufficient condition for a post-growth or sustainable economy, since those outcomes would arise from policy choices, not MMT itself. But, as we will seek to show, MMT enables those policy choices in a way that mainstream macroeconomics does not.

Mainstream growth assumptions are predicated on the belief that we would inevitably be faced with decreased wellbeing, mass unemployment, and even a severe depression if we were to invite permanent recessions by not continuing with exponential expansion (Jackson, 2009: 49). This would appear to force a difficult choice between two evils – either business as usual leading to socio-ecological collapse, or unplanned and chaotic economic contraction with the well-known range of problems that emerge when growth-dependent economies involuntarily enter a contraction. Among mainstream economists, the dominant response to this tension is to claim that there is an elegant solution: pursue 'green growth' (e.g., OECD, 2019; CSIRO, 2019) achieved by decoupling economic growth from environmental harm through efficiency gains and technological advancement (as discussed by Jackson, 2009: 67; Victor and Jackson, 2015).

---

2 For instance, in 2019, the outgoing president of the European Central Bank, Mario Draghi, said new ideas like MMT needed to be looked at: https://www.bloomberg.com/news/articles/2019-09-23/draghi-says-ecb-should-examine-new-ideas-like-mmt

The problem is that evidence on decoupling overwhelmingly shows that green growth is a myth (see Victor and Jackson, 2015; Hickel and Kallis, 2019). The best solution for economies in overshoot is *controlled* biophysical contraction (degrowth to a steady-state), achievable, we argue, through the insights of MMT that show monetary-sovereign governments can exert fine control over their economies to minimise harm, such as mass unemployment, leading to the ultimate goal of a steady-state system. This can only be done by a macroeconomic theory based in reality – including biophysical reality (Washington, 2018a) – rather than myth. We now turn to that macroeconomic theory, which focuses on real-resource constraints rather than perceived fiscal constraints.[3]

Introduction to MMT

MMT developed out of an academic post-Keynesian internet discussion group in the mid-1990s.[4] It is a macroeconomic theory profound enough in its implications to usher in a new societal paradigm (Mitchell, 2017). It is now seriously challenging the dominant theory, with the latter usually called neoclassical (or neoKeynesian). For convenience, MMT can be summarised into a set of principles that we will outline, although readers seeking more detail should seek out the MMT undergraduate textbook (Mitchell, Wray, and Watts, 2019). This new body of knowledge draws on many ideas from the past, while marrying them with more recent experience, especially the post-gold-standard era from the early 1970s onwards, when US president Nixon abandoned the Bretton-Woods system. Again, it is essential to understand that MMT is not a set of policy prescriptions, but is a description of how economies function today, regardless of whether they are growth or post-growth economies, and regardless of whether governments are aware of MMT or not.

MMT begins by separating nations into those that are monetary sovereign and those that are not. To be a monetary sovereign, a nation needs four things: (1) its own currency; (2) a floating exchange rate; (3) no significant government borrowings in foreign currencies; and (4) a central bank setting interest rates.

---

3 In 2005, even US Federal Reserve chairman Alan Greenspan admitted under oath that the US government could create unlimited money, and that the main issue was real resources: https://www.youtube.com/watch?v=DNCZHAQnfGU

4 A collection of scholarly papers on MMT is at http://www.levyinstitute.org/topics/modern-money-theory-mmt. A primer for the general reader is at https://neweconomicperspectives.org/modern-monetary-theory-primer.html. Journalistic articles are at https://wecanhavenicethings.com/about/. An expert blog is at http://bilbo.economicoutlook.net/blog/.

By being a monetary sovereign – as Australia, the USA, Japan, Canada, and the UK are – a nation's government will have maximum policy space to advance whatever programmes it thinks desirable. This is largely because such a government can never be forced to become insolvent: it can always pay any liabilities when they fall due (and social security payments) simply by crediting the relevant bank accounts. It can never legitimately say it does not have the money for this or that policy – such as creating a net-zero-emissions economy – since it creates the funds by spending them into existence. Note that monetary sovereignty is distinct from political sovereignty.[5]

Most nations, including many in Africa, South America, and Europe, are non-monetary-sovereign in the MMT sense, and so they do not have the policy options open to countries like Australia. Not surprisingly, many experts in the MMT community are actively encouraging these countries to become monetary sovereigns – or in the case of European countries that use the euro, to regain their sovereignty. Once a country achieves monetary sovereignty, the following principles apply to its national government.

The government creates new money whenever it spends, usually by electronically crediting bank accounts in the private sector. Note that it is not spending tax receipts.[6] Every dollar the government spends is a new dollar created at the time of spending. Spending must come first, and taxation comes second.

Federal taxes are best understood as merely offsetting government spending, rather than funding it. Using the metaphor of a bathtub to represent the economy, federal spending is equivalent to water entering the bath via the tap. Taxation is money draining from the bath via the plug hole, so that the tub does not overflow. If the government spends too much, or taxes too little, too much inflation will occur (overflow). Taxes are also important to penalise undesirable activities (smoking, pollution) and to limit wealth inequality (through progressive taxation).

The national budget (better described as the fiscal balance) is merely an accounting outcome that shows the difference between government spending and taxation. There is no reason to favour a surplus over a deficit since the government is not equivalent to a household or a

---

5 We will use the words currency and money interchangeably, since this chapter is pitched at an introductory level.
6 This was understood by US Federal Reserve chairman Beardsley Ruml in the 1940s (see Ruml, 1946).

business. Indeed, a federal deficit in any period is exactly equal to the non-government surplus because the two sectors must sum to zero (Mitchell, 2019a: 86). When the government runs a deficit, it does not need to borrow funds from the non-government sector, so there is no absolute need for government 'debt'. When the government voluntarily sells bonds to match its deficit, idle money (reserves) in one account is transferred into another account with better interest. Under current arrangements, this 'soaking up' of reserves helps the central bank achieve its target interest rate (Mitchell, 2019a: 326). The government can always pay the interest, or buy the bonds back, but such bond sales are largely unnecessary anyway and can be seen as a carry-over from the gold-standard days.

Monetary policy, which is the adjustment of interest rates by the central bank, has limited effect on the economy, since there are winners and losers from every adjustment. Fiscal policy – government spending and taxation – is the primary lever of economic control. The central bank is not independent, as mainstream theory claims, but is always under the stewardship of the government that gives effect to its operations.

With respect to the labour market, policymakers only have two choices: to use a buffer stock of unemployed to control inflation (as the mainstream prefers) or use a buffer stock of employed workers via a 'job guarantee' programme to control inflation. MMT prefers the latter on both moral and efficiency grounds (Hail, 2018: 219). In the job guarantee, workers not employed in either the private or regular public sector, are offered a job in their local community at the minimum wage, complete with holidays, sick leave, and so on. This job should be useful work – for instance environmental restoration – that the private sector usually will not do. Besides offering a liveable wage, it is designed to maintain the skills and dignity of the worker until they can be re-employed in the regular economy. The job guarantee sets the minimum standards for work that the private sector has to at least match. Importantly, the government could set fulltime working hours at any level via the job guarantee to help create a non-growth economy (Tcherneva, 2018).

Most importantly, MMT – through what we believe is a correct understanding of money and its creation (Mitchell, Wray, and Watts, 2019: 137) – places an emphasis on available real resources in the determination of wealth, health, and sustainability, with money merely being a kind of point score of who has a claim to what resources. As such, it makes little sense to encourage foreign financial capital into a country like Australia, as if there is a shortage of money. Similarly, it makes little sense to maximise the export of real resources (wealth) in exchange for money, as if the latter were the more desirable item. While trade is a complex subject, MMT basically sees exports as a cost and imports as a benefit.

In sum, government spending, like all spending, is limited by inflation, which in turn is governed by the amount of real resources that can be sustainably put to productive use – creating output and then consumption (Mitchell, Wray, and Watts, 2019: 520). As ecological economists, however, we particularly emphasise that this 'throughput' should be scientifically assessed and kept within sustainable ecological limits, and ideally well within those limits, to avoid *un*economic growth (Daly, 2014).

The implications of this understanding of macroeconomics are profound. So-called federal government debt is not really debt in the normal sense, so increasing GDP (growth) to reduce the debt as a percentage of GDP is non-sensical. Second, a national government budget outcome – either surplus or deficit – is not improved in any meaningful sense by increasing tax receipts relative to government spending, so running an immigration programme to achieve a net increase in taxation is pointless. Third, the federal government can eliminate involuntary unemployment and underemployment whenever it chooses by offering meaningful paid work to all through a job guarantee (Mitchell, Wray, and Watts, 2019: 301). It follows that a technical recession need not result in mass unemployment, a mortgage-default crisis, and a positive feedback into an ever-deeper recession. Thus, three major reasons for forever expanding the size of an economy are shown to be flawed.

MMT also puts into doubt the following, just to name a few:

- the need for universal superannuation

- the need to increase the age when people can claim the age pension

- government support for the private health insurance system

- the need to privatise government assets to 'improve' budget outcomes

- the need to encourage foreign investment

- the need to promote exports, including encouraging foreign students to enrol in universities

- the need for private education and training organisations

- the need for private employment agencies

- the need to rely on the private sector to build and run essential services like electricity generation, communications, ports, roads, and banking

- the need for governments to sell bonds or other securities (so-called government debt).

After considering some criticisms of MMT in the next section, we proceed to explain how an acceptance of MMT could facilitate a degrowth transition to a steady-state economy, and conclude with a list of policy options that are more defendable and achievable through an understanding of MMT.

Criticisms of MMT

Prominent critics of MMT include well-known economists such as Paul Krugman, Olivier Blanchard, Lawrence Summers, Greg Mankiw, Kenneth Rogoff, and Ann Pettifor (Mitchell, 2019a; Harvey, 2019). Invariably, the critics do not correctly define what MMT is (see generally, Tymoigne and Wary, 2013; Mitchell, 2019a). The most common criticisms include the following.

If introduced, MMT would lead to high inflation, or even hyperinflation

MMT is not something that can be introduced; it is a macroeconomic theory that seeks to explain what already exists. Policies based on an understanding of MMT could be inflationary or deflationary, depending on the policies. MMT makes it clear that all spending is potentially inflationary, regardless of whether the spending is public or private. Inflation occurs when demand rises relative to the productive capacity of the economy (demand-pull inflation), not because governments run budget deficits (Mitchell, Wray, and Watts, 2019: 254). Cost-push inflation is also possible, if the cost of production increases, but that is not inherently a government spending issue.

MMT only applies to the USA because it issues the world's reserve currency

This false argument is repeated by Naomi Klein (2019: 283) in a reference to US Congresswoman Alexandria Ocasio Cortez's plan to pay for a Green New Deal. But MMT theory applies to all countries, including countries in the European Union that have lost monetary sovereignty by adopting the euro. MMT shows how countries without their own currency have a budget constraint, unlike monetary sovereigns like Australia.

MMT is nothing new: We've known it all along

This tends to be said by people wanting to defend their reputations, or the reputation of the mainstream in general, by claiming that MMT is not a genuinely new macroeconomics that could disrupt the dominant paradigm (see Mitchell, 2019b). It is true that MMT builds on the work of Hyman Minsky, Michal Kalecki, Abba Lerner, Wynne Godley (and others), but it is more than a rehash of old ideas (Hail, 2018: 141). As with most criticisms of MMT, the critic will usually not have an adequate grasp of the theory. What's more, questioning the originality of MMT's claims tells us little about its veracity.

MMT says budget deficits don't matter

A federal budget deficit (or surplus) does matter in the sense that either outcome could be too big or too small, depending on other factors in the economy. More correctly, MMT says countries like Australia should never aim for a particular budget outcome, but should let the outcome rise and fall to achieve desirable ends like ecologically sustainable full employment and increased wellbeing. Since budget deficits do not need to be funded by borrowing money or selling assets, there is no accumulating debt burden for future generations (Mitchell, Wray, and Watts, 2019: 333). In short, it serves no useful purpose to balance the budget over some arbitrary economic cycle.

MMT is 'printing money' which everyone knows is highly inflationary

In mainstream economics, it is thought that a federal government mostly spends tax receipts. If it wants to spend beyond that, it either has to borrow money through bond sales or sell assets (Mitchell, Wray, and Watts, 2019: 333). As a last resort it might 'print money', which usually means creating new money without borrowing. This is thought by mainstream economists to be highly inflationary and addictive for imprudent governments. But MMT proponents claim all of the above is false, and the government only spends one way – namely, every dollar the national government spends is a new dollar (literally spent into existence), whether that is acknowledged or not. According to this logic there can be no special case of money printing when 'revenue' runs out.

Our country has laws that would prevent MMT-type spending

As discussed by Mitchell (2018), critics sometimes claim that certain laws in certain countries – such as government debt ceilings and budget appropriation laws – would prevent some governments from engaging in the type of spending necessary to build renewable-energy infrastructure, offer free tertiary education, free healthcare, and so on. However, as the MMT position emphasises, such laws are voluntary restraints that can be removed if the legislature decides that the spending would increase social and ecological wellbeing (Mitchell, Wray, and Watts, 2019: 337). In 2020, in response to the pandemic, we are now seeing these voluntary restraints removed as governments spend large amounts to counteract the loss of private spending. Once policy-makers realise that fiscal and budget outcomes are not the limiting factor, but that sustainable resource use is, misconceived laws with an austerity bias (such as debt ceilings) are more likely to be repealed. Even constitutions can be amended if there is enough support for the change.

MMT is ideologically biased toward growth

Finally, some in the sustainability movement dislike MMT because (a) they see it as an optional policy platform instead of macroeconomic principles attempting to describe reality; and (b) they think, if it were widely accepted, it would result in an acceleration of the ever-increasing money supply that they (quite rightly in our view) associate with perpetual economic expansion (Mitchell, 2012). With respect to (a), we have explained that it is not a policy platform, but is descriptive rather than prescriptive. We are all forced to choose, consciously or unconsciously, between competing macroeconomic theories, and the failed neoclassical paradigm, besides not explaining actual outcomes (such as Japan's high government debt and low inflation), has no inherent benefit for post-growth policies. In respect to (b), it is policy choices allowed by the macroeconomic paradigm that determine the size of the economy, such as the policy of allowing private banks to increase the money supply through their lending. MMT insights provide maximum control by maximum policy choice – to either expand an economy or to shrink it. It is essential not to confuse pro-growth policies offered by many MMT advocates with MMT itself.

How MMT could facilitate post-growth economics

If we are to stop or reverse the expansion of economies in the overdeveloped world, we must address the main reasons for their growth. These reasons include: 1) concerns about national government debt; 2) concerns about national government budget balances; 3) concerns about recessions and resulting unemployment; and 4) concerns that financial markets will punish a government that does not meet market expectations. From the perspective of MMT, these concerns are largely wrongheaded, so the growth imperative is greatly diminished.

Government debt. A key reason for continually increasing a country's GDP is that it reduces the government debt as a per centage of GDP (assuming the debt does not increase as much as GDP), where government debt reduction is assumed to be a good thing. However, advocates of MMT argue (Mitchell, Wray, and Watts, 2019: 326) that monetary-sovereign nations never need to borrow: selling government securities (so-called debt) to match a budget deficit is stated as being unnecessary, (although it helps the central bank meet its interest-rate target by soaking up reserves). But even if the securities are sold (they are actually auctioned in the first instance) there is no great imperative to buy them back or grow the economy to make the debt seem relatively smaller. The simplest thing is for the national government to stop selling these risk-free investments that amount to corporate welfare.

Budget outcome. Increasing a country's population via migration will not only increase its GDP but is believed by the mainstream to 'improve' federal budget outcomes: because of their relative youth, migrants will pay more in taxes compared with their welfare claims (Australian Treasury and Department of Home Affairs, 2018: 35). Former Australian prime minister Tony Abbott's then chief of staff, Peta Credlin, explained how immigrant numbers were ramped up in chaotic pre-budget meetings to get the 'right' budget projection, with zero thought to sustainability (van Onselen, 2018). Yet MMT shows that aiming for any particular budget outcome is foolish, meaning one of the core assumptions driving Australia's high migration policy is foolish. Ultimately, the government has limited control of the budget outcome anyway, since it cannot accurately forecast tax receipts, welfare payments, or the non-government sector's desire to net save rather than spend. This leads to the MMT position that governments should try to balance the economy, not the budget.

Recessions. Continually increasing GDP avoids technical recessions and associated increases in labour underutilisation (unemployment and underemployment). But according to MMT, a national government can achieve full employment (1–2 per cent unemployment and zero underemployment) via a government job guarantee scheme. It follows that the government could largely ameliorate the otherwise destabilising effects of economic recessions by making sure that wealth and income was distributed more fairly, just as it could when transitioning from a fossil-fuel economy to a renewable-energy economy.

Financial markets. The main fears here are that bond 'vigilantes' will no longer want government securities if the government is seen to be financially reckless (big budget deficits and/or low or no growth). However, this has not been seen in practice, as the case of Japan shows (Mitchell, Wray, and Watts, 2019: 29); and we have previously said that the government does not need to sell securities anyway. Second, and more serious, is the fear that the government's currency will be devalued by speculative currency traders in a non-growth scenario. The MMT response is capital controls, where the government simply blocks the currency transfers (Mitchell, Wray, and Watts, 2019: 398). Ultimately, a government's currency will always be attractive in a democratic nation where the rule of law prevails, corruption is minimised, natural capital is protected, and where health, education, and skill levels are high.

As long as a society uses money as a medium of exchange, it is necessary for policymakers to understand such things as the nature of money, how it is generated, what are the limits to its generation and spending, what is the nature of central bank and commercial bank operations, and what are the implications for money generation at various levels. Since the abandonment of the Bretton-Woods system and the gold standard in the early 1970s, mainstream neoclassical economics has failed to provide an adequate description of these things. Now, with a new financial crisis in 2020 caused by a pandemic, the mainstream is struggling to make sense of government new-found power and largess, while the MMT community simply point to the MMT literature. When policymakers better understand the cause-and-effect relationships in macroeconomics, including currency operations, it is more likely they will accept the possibility of a controlled descent toward a steady-state system, vouchsafed by government fine control. We have briefly outlined how MMT provides that understanding of government control.

We believe that without MMT, policymakers who advocate for things such as a Green New Deal, or even stronger sustainability measures, will be restricted by notions of a government budget constraint; the fear of the necessity to raise taxes to fund government spending; the fear of government debt and insolvency; and a fear of financial markets that might choose to inflict punishment by not buying government debt and/or devaluing a nation's currency. MMT, as a coherent macroeconomics, states that these concerns are largely, or totally, unfounded. If MMT were to be accepted, we maintain that policy options such as the following are more likely.

Policies for a sustainable, post-growth economy

Governments in the neoliberal era have gradually abandoned what we think are their main responsibilities (Murphy, 2020). These responsibilities include ensuring a healthy natural environment; full employment with price stability; and increasing general levels of wellbeing. In short, governments have failed to understand, let alone address, sustainability.[7] Extreme wealth inequality, which they have allowed to run rampant, is not consistent with sustainability (Daly 2013). Ideally, the size of any economy should be reduced to near the optimum (that is, smaller than the maximum ecologically sustainable size) where cost-benefit curves are at their maximum distance from each other (Lawn, 2017).

Without making any claims about the list of policies below being complete or uncontroversial – and due to space constraints, we have stated rather than defended them – here are some bold ideas for facilitating a degrowth transition to a steady-state economy (see also, Daly, 2013; Alexander, 2016) which are supported by an MMT position on macroeconomics:

---

7 For instance, the UN Sustainable Development Goals, which Australia endorses, call for ongoing economic growth.

1. Declare a state of emergency that goes beyond the climate emergency to encompass the unsustainable nature of society as a whole and the risk of collapse. This would mean that all government decisions would need to address the new priority of sustainability (including the social- and ecological-justice dimensions). MMT focuses on the availability of sustainable real resources as the limit to government spending. It also removes the imperative to (a) grow the economy to ameliorate government debt; and (b) increase the number of taxpayers to 'improve' budget outcomes. It should not be surprising, therefore, that MMT is strongly associated with the movement for a Green New Deal, given it acknowledges that resources need to be used sustainably (Nersisyan and Wray, 2019; 2020).

2. Establish a permanent statutory office whose sole task would be to advise government, and the public, on the path to sustainability (Washington, 1991). It would coordinate the work of other bodies, such as climate change, agriculture, and energy authorities. A key task would be facilitating the design and construction of a 100 per cent renewable-energy system. MMT, unlike neoclassical economics, accepts that resources need to be used sustainably. Therefore, if policymakers accepted MMT, they would be more likely to establish such offices, especially when its recommendations (for instance, to reduce economic growth) would be less problematic than under a neoclassical framework.

3. Enact a bill of rights (or charter of rights) that explicitly acknowledges rights to a healthy natural environment. In so doing, enact a plan to reserve at least 50 per cent of terrestrial and aquatic territory for non-human species (Wilson, 2016; Dinerstein, et al., 2017), ensuring all key ecosystems are protected. Pay farmers (or give tax subsidies) if they adopt the best regenerative practices that protect the environment. We have explained above how MMT undercuts the imperative to continually expand an economy. We have also said that MMT emphasises that real resources need to be sustainably managed.

4. Explore a range of wellbeing measurement tools (e.g., Genuine Progress Indicator, see Lawn, 2016) that would become the primary focus of government reporting, especially at budget time, and during election campaigns. MMT acknowledges that 'conventional market-based measures of national income as indicators of well-being are flawed in several ways' (Mitchell, Wray, and Watts, 2019: 520), and most ecological economists see the value in alternatives like the Genuine Progress Indicator.

5. Stabilise the human population as quickly and ethically (in line with accepted human rights) as possible (Engelman, 2016) to ensure the rights of both human and non-human creatures, now and into the future, and plan for a controlled decrease in the human population. Excess accommodation would eventually be bought by government to control real estate prices. We gave the example of how positive net migration policies are flawed insofar as they are based on myths about 'improving' budget outcomes (via more tax receipts) and facilitating economic expansion. With an increasing focus on sustainably managed real resources, population numbers beyond an optimum level will dilute provisioning of these resources, leading to reduced income per capita and/or unacceptable incursions into natural capital.

6. Introduce gradual tax increases over a period of, say, 10 years, so that personal annual income greater than $1 million is taxed at 100 percent (i.e., a maximum income, see Washington, 2018b), together with an otherwise highly progressive tax regime.[8] At the same time, introduce a progressive inheritance tax to remove extreme wealth.

7. Vastly expand the regular public service as government nationalises banking, ports, airports, essential services such as electricity generation and distribution, and natural monopolies. In particular, employ the vast knowledge and experience of the indigenous population to manage protected natural areas (Dinerstein, et al., 2017). Ensure that critical government agencies such as the CSIRO, Australian Bureau of Statistics, Bureau of Meteorology, tax office, federal police and courts, hospitals, and publicly funded media are properly resourced.

8. Introduce a federal job guarantee (Mitchell, Wray, and Watts, 2019: 301) to eliminate involuntary unemployment and underemployment and control inflation. This scheme will set minimum pay and working conditions that the other employment sectors would need to at least match. It will also set normal hours for the working week, which we suggest could be initially four days. This scheme should be seen mostly as a safety net for those workers who are temporarily not wanted by regular employers (public and private), although a minority of people would likely be semi-permanent in the scheme.

9. Gradually decrease the retirement age to 60, while ensuring the age pension meets people's needs, especially those in rental accommodation.

---

8 About 13,000 Australians earn $1 million or more a year (Hutchens 2018).

This will likely mean expanding public and social housing – this will not be difficult as the population stabilises and slowly decreases. Disabled persons should receive similar protections. Stop promoting superannuation and gradually remove all tax concessions associated with it. The age pension should be seen as the normal and adequate retirement income.

10. Do not means-test free services such as education, health care, and so on, but provide them as a citizen's right. This will eliminate much unnecessary bureaucratic checking on the one hand, and the temptation to deceive on the other – not to mention resentment by those who would otherwise miss out on benefits paid to others. If a person has considerable assets or income, tax them at a higher rate (see point 6 above).

11. Increase the range of fee-free services to include childcare, vocational training, and higher education. Cancel all student debt. Add dentistry to Medicare. Like the following policies, the government can pay for this (if there are idle real resources) and tax accordingly to avoid inflation.

12. Increase higher education funding by increasing tenured teaching and research positions while eliminating the need for researchers to rely on industry support. In short, stop politicising higher education. The same can be said of once-great research institutions such as the CSIRO.

13. Establish government-owned and co-operative manufacturing ventures (where the private sector is absent) to reduce reliance on trade – both imports and exports – with the aim of creating a more self-sufficient nation. In so doing, legislate for rethink, repair, re-use, and recycling in manufactured goods (using the waste hierarchy).

14. Increase restrictions on foreign investment in line with the new state of emergency (degrowth to optimum size) and the knowledge that foreign financial capital is not required.

15. Work internationally to cancel unconscionable debt owed by developing nations. Increase foreign aid (especially that which targets women's health and family planning), international cooperation, and the transfer of cleaner technology, so that poorer countries can quickly increase their sustainability and stabilise population.

Again, we make no claims about this list being exhaustive or uncontroversial. In fact, it barely scratches the surface of the restructuring that would be required to initiate and manage a degrowth transition to a steady-state economy. The policy ideas above are merely illustrative of the types of options that open up when the political economy of sustainability is viewed through the lens of MMT.

Conclusion

We believe the discipline of ecological economics provides the best overall framework for understanding the relationship between economic activity and biophysical limits, and should replace the neoliberal framework (Daly, 2014; Kallis, 2017). Its tools will help us determine the optimum size of any economy, recognising that the optimum size could change somewhat with, for example, technological improvements and population levels. But within that framework, and subject to its principles of living within biophysical limits and maximising wellbeing, there is still a need for an accurate macroeconomics.

MMT has been called 'macroeconomics done properly' (Harvey, 2019). Whether a society wants to increase the size of its economy, stabilise it, or reduce it to an optimum size, it will benefit from the most accurate macroeconomic theory to dispel false assumptions and give policymakers predictive confidence. Mainstream macroeconomics has failed to do that.

As we have argued, advocates of MMT outline how and why monetary sovereign states have many more policy options available to them than the mainstream allows. Such nations have massive power compared with the private sector, if only they would use it (as the 2020 pandemic is demonstrating). Rather than set policy to placate the bond markets, currency speculators, and corporate greed in general, the national government can concentrate on maximising human and non-human welfare through a fairer distribution of sustainably-managed resources in the knowledge that business interests will always seek to invest in stable, democratic nations.

Once it is understood that government can have fine control over the economy using the levers of monetary and fiscal policy – but especially the latter – it becomes clear that a just (or green) transition is more easily achievable than currently thought. For rich, overdeveloped nations, that means a degrowth transition of planned economic contraction, leading to, somewhat paradoxically, increased wellbeing. Our view is that MMT

is the best available macroeconomics to facilitate the transformation –
and to avoid collapse.

Appendix I

Comparison of neoclassical theory and MMT as applied to monetary-
sovereign nations (compiled by the authors).

Neoclassical	MMT
Little or no focus on money sovereignty	Essential focus on money sovereignty
Does not prioritise theory of money	Prioritises theory of money
Government is like a household, has budget constraint: 'sound finance'	Government nothing like a household, no budget constraint (except inflation, sustainability): 'functional finance'
Continual budget deficits accumulate and will lead to higher taxes, inflation, possible insolvency	Continual budget deficits do not accumulate; spend up to full employment and no further
Government must fund spending with tax receipts, borrowing, asset sales	Government does not 'fund' its spending, never needs to borrow its own money
Government can 'print' new money in exceptional circumstances	Government spends new money into existence whenever it spends (never prints money)
Government borrowing (bond sales) 'crowds out' private-sector borrowing, investment	No 'crowding out' as banks will lend to any credit-worthy customer by lending money into existence (do not lend deposits)
Government must sell bonds to match deficit, at mercy of bond vigilantes	Bond sales are optional, used to soak up excess reserves so central bank can achieve overnight interest rate target
Government collects taxes, then spends them	Government spends, then collects taxes (as an offset). Taxes are destroyed, not spent
Monetary policy is best tool to control economy	Fiscal policy is best tool to control economy
There is a natural rate of unemployment where inflation is stabilised (NAIRU)	No natural rate of unemployment
Market determines unemployment rate	Government determines unemployment rate

Neoclassical	MMT
Use buffer stock of unemployed to control inflation	Use fiscal policy, buffer stock of employed workers in job guarantee pool (on minimum wage) to control inflation
Central bank is independent of government	Central bank is part of government
Market, central bank sets interest rates	Government can set interest rates at any level, including zero
Usually a need for foreign financial capital	Government and its agents (private banks) can provide all financial capital
Government should respect credit-rating agencies	Government should ignore credit-rating agencies; cannot be forced to default
Government should fear sudden and deep currency depreciation	Government can implement capital controls if speculators dump currency
Little fear of resource depletion due to human ingenuity, substitution	Management of real resource constraint determines wealth, inflation, sustainability
Government is at mercy of international forces, large corporations, financial sector	Citizens, via elected government, are masters of country's destiny

References

Alexander, S. 2016. 'Policies for a Post-Growth Economy'. *MSSI Issues Paper* No. 6. Melbourne: Melbourne Sustainable Society Institute, The University of Melbourne.

Australian Treasury and Department of Home Affairs. 2018. 'Shaping a Nation: Population Growth and Migration Over Time'. Available at: https://research.treasury.gov.au/sites/research.treasury.gov.au/files/2019-08/Shaping-a-Nation-1.pdf (accessed 20 February 2020)

Binswanger, M. 2009. 'Is There a Growth Imperative in Capitalist Economies? A Circular Flow Perspective'. *Journal of Post-Keynesian Economics* 31(4): 707–727.

Blauwhof, F. 2012. 'Overcoming Accumulation: Is a Steady-State Capitalism Possible?' *Ecological Economics* 84: 254–261.

Cahill, D. 2011. 'Why Does Neoclassical Thinking Still Dominate Economics?' *The Conversation* (17 October 2011). Available at: https://theconversation.com/why-does-neoclassical-thinking-still-dominate-economics-3861 (accessed 20 February 2020).

CSIRO. 2019. 'Australian National Outlook 2019'. Available at https://www.csiro.au/en/Showcase/ANO (accessed 9 April 2020).

Daly, H. 1997. *Beyond Growth: The Economics of Sustainable Development*. Boston: Beacon Press.

Daly, H. 2013. 'Top 10 policies for a steady state economy'. CASSE The Daly News. Available at https://steadystate.org/top-10-policies-for-a-steady-state-economy/ (accessed 11 April 2020).

Daly, H. 2014. *From Uneconomic Growth to a Steady-State Economy*. Cheltenham, UK; Northampton, MA: Edward Elgar.

Dinerstein, E. et al. 2017. 'An Ecoregion-Based Approach to Protecting Half the Terrestrial Realm'. *BioScience* 67(6): 534–545.

Engelman, R. 2016. 'Nine Population Strategies to Stop Short of Nine Billion'. In: Washington, H. and Twomey, P. (eds.). *A Future Beyond Growth: Towards a Steady State Economy.* Routledge, London: 32–42.

Hail, S. 2018. *Economics for Sustainable Prosperity.* London: Palgrave Macmillan.

Harvey, J. 2019. 'MMT: Sense or Nonsense?' *Forbes* (5 March 2019). Available at: https://www.forbes.com/sites/johntharvey/2019/03/05/mmt-sense-or-nonsense/#602a54585852 (accessed 20 February 2020).

Hickel, J. and Kallis, G. 2019. 'Is Green Growth Possible?' *New Political Economy.* DOI: 10.1080/13563467.2019.1598964.

Hutchens, G. 2108. 'Number of Australians who Earned More than $1m a Year Yet Paid no Tax Surges 30%'. *The Guardian* (27 April 2018).

Jackson, T. 2009. *Prosperity Without Growth: Economics for a Finite Planet.* London: Earthscan.

Kallis, G. 2017. 'Radical Dematerialization and Degrowth'. *Philosophical Transactions of the Royal Society A.* 375: 20160383: 1–13.

Klein, N. 2019. *On Fire: The (Burning) Case for a Green New Deal.* New York: Simon & Schuster.

Kohler, A. 2020. 'Accepted Wisdom out the Window as Government Takes Control'. *The Australian,* 28 March 2020.

Lawn, P. 2011. 'Is Steady State Capitalism Viable? A Review of the Issues and an Answer in the Affirmative'. *Annals of the New York Academy of Sciences* 1219(2011): 1–25.

Lawn, P. 2016. *Resolving the Climate Change Crisis: The Ecological Economics of Climate Change.* Singapore: Springer.

Lawn, P. 2017. 'MMT and Ecological Sustainability'. Lecture organised by the Binzagr Institute for Sustainable Prosperity. Available at: https://www.youtube.com/watch?v=Cfk418pC54E (accessed 20 February 2020).

Mankiw, N.G. 2018 (10th edn). *Macroeconomics.* New York: Worth Publishers.

Meadows, D., Meadows, D., Randers, J. 2004. *Limits to Growth: 30-Year Update.* White River Junction: Chelsea Green Publishing.

Mitchell, W. 2012. 'MMT and Environmental Sustainability – Part 1'. Available at http://bilbo.economicoutlook.net/blog/?p=22222 (accessed 7 April 2020).

Mitchell, W. 2017. 'Paradigm Shift – Not from the CORE Econ Project – As mainstream as You Will Get'. Available at http://bilbo.economicoutlook.net/blog/?p=36855 (accessed 9 April 2020).

Mitchell, W. and Fazi, T. 2017. *Reclaiming the State: A Progressive Vision of Sovereignty for a Post-Neoliberal World.* London: Pluto Press.

Mitchell, W. 2018. 'Where Do We Get the Funds from to Pay Our Taxes and Buy Government Debt'. Available at http://bilbo.economicoutlook.net/blog/?p=38885 (accessed 7 April 2020).

Mitchell, W., Wray, L.R., and Watts, M. 2019. *Macroeconomics.* London: Red Globe Press.

Mitchell, W. 2019a. 'A Conga Line of MMT Critics – Marching into Oblivion'. Available at http://bilbo.economicoutlook.net/blog/?p=41727 (accessed 7 April 2020).

Mitchell, W. 2019b. 'The Mainstream Old Guard Tell It As It Is – and How Different That Is To MMT'. Available at: http://bilbo.economicoutlook.net/blog/?p=41869

Murphy, R. 2020. 'The Financial Times Has Abandoned Neoliberalism – And They Must Never Be Allowed To Forget This'. Available at https://www.taxresearch.org.uk/Blog/2020/04/04/the-financial-times-has-abandoned-neoliberalism-and-they-must-never-be-allowed-to-forget-this/ (accessed 8 April 2020)

Nersisyan, Y. and Wray, L.R. 2019. 'How to pay for the Green New Deal'. Working Paper No. 931, Levy Economics Institute.

Nersisyan, Y. and Wray, L.R. 2020. 'What MMT Is, and Why We Should Not Wait for the Next Crisis to Live Up to Our Means'. Available at http://multiplier-effect.org/what-mmt-is-and-why-we-should-not-wait-for-the-next-crisis-to-live-up-to-our-means/ (accessed 7 April 2020).

7: Modern Monetary Theory, post growth economics, and avoiding collapse

OECD. 2019. *OECD Work on Green Growth*. OECD.

Quiggin, J. 2012. *Zombie Economics: How Dead Ideas Still Walk Among Us*. Princeton: Princeton University Press.

Ripple, W. et al. 2017. 'World Scientists' Warning to Humanity: A Second Notice'. *BioScience*, 67(12): 1026–28.

Ripple, W. et al. 2020. 'World Scientists' Warning of a Climate Emergency'. *BioScience*, 70, Issue 1: 8–12.

Ruml, B. 1946. 'Taxes for Revenue are Obsolete'. *American Affairs*, Winter Number, VIII(1). Available at https://www.constitution.org/tax/us-ic/cmt/ruml_obsolete.pdf (accessed 10 April 2020)

Steffen, W. et al. 2015. 'The Trajectory of the Anthropocene: The Great Acceleration'. *The Anthropocene Review* 2(1): 81–98.

Svartzman, R., Dron, D., and Espagne, E. 2019. 'From Ecological Macroeconomics to a Theory of Endogenous Money for a Finite Planet'. *Ecological Economics* 162: 108–120.

Tcherneva, P. 2018 'The Job Guarantee: Design, Jobs, and Implementation'. Levy Economics Institute of Bard College. Working Paper No. 902.

Turner, G. 2019. 'Is a Sustainable Future Possible?' *Journal and Proceedings of the Royal Society of NSW* 152(1): 47–65.

Tymoigne, E. and Wary, L. 2013. 'Modern Money Theory 101: A Reply to Critics'. Working Paper No. 778, Levy Economics Institute of Bard College.

van Onselen, L. 2018. 'Credlin Blows Lid on How 'Fraudulent' Migrant Intake is Set'. *MacroBusiness* (13 March 2018). Available at: https://www.macrobusiness.com.au/2018/03/credlin-blows-lid-on-how-fraudulent-migrant-intake-is-set/ (accessed 20 February 2020).

Victor, P. and Jackson, T. 2015. 'Toward an Ecological Macroeconomics'. In: Brown, P. and Timmerman, P. (eds). *Ecological Economics for the Anthropocene*. New York: Columbia University Press.

Von Drehle, D. 2020. 'So Long, Balanced Budgets. Everyone's into Endless Spending Now'. *The Washington Post*, 8 April 2020. Available at https://www.washingtonpost.com/opinions/so-long-balanced-budgets-everyones-into-endless-spending-now/2020/04/07/1e2d49f2-78f5-11ea-9bee-c5bf9d2e3288_story.html (accessed 9 April 2020).

Washington, H. 1991. *Ecosolutions: Environmental Solutions for the World and Australia*. Tea Gardens, NSW: Boobook Publications.

Washington, H. 2018a. 'Harmony – not Theory'. *The Ecological Citizen* 1(2): 203–10.

Washington, H. 2018b. *Positive Steps to a Steady State Economy*. CASSE NSW.

Wilson, E. 2016. *Half-Earth: Our Planet's Fight for Life*. New York: Liveright Publishing.

Chapter 8

'Neighbourhoods that Work' and the Walden Wage: How access to land plus a participation income could change the world[1]

Access to land as a barrier to sustainability: A statement of the problem

Industrial civilisation is facing an alarming barrage of overlapping crises, together presenting an existential threat to life as we know it (Ripple, 2017; Turner, 2019). Climate breakdown is intensifying; human economic activity is decimating natural habitat and wildlife populations; and more generally, our life-support system called Earth is trembling under the weight of overconsumption and the waste streams that flow from it (Steffen et al., 2015). Just as concerning are the social consequences. The global economic system has produced deep, socially corrosive inequalities and poverty around the world is extreme (Hickel, 2017). Furthermore, even those who are 'winning the rat race' so often find that the promises of consumer lifestyles are unfulfilling (Lane, 2000).

In response to these overlapping ecological, economic, and cultural crises, a diverse school of ecological economists has emerged over recent decades calling for the developed, or rather over-developed, regions of the world to initiate a 'degrowth' process of planned and equitable contraction of their energy and resource demands (see generally, D'Alisa, Demaria, and Kallis, 2015; Kallis et al., 2018). The fundamental vision is to move toward a stable, broadly egalitarian, steady-state (or zero-growth) economy that operates within sustainable environmental limits (Daly, 1997; Washington and Twomey, 2016; Frankel, 2018). This radical 'post-development' paradigm of political economy (Escobar, 2015) is generally recognised as being incompatible with the accumulative and profit-maximising logic of capitalist development (Blauwhof, 2012).

---

1 Originally published in Haydn Washington (ed) *Ecological Economics: Solutions for the Future*, 2020, CASSE NSW, Ch 8, co-authored with Alex Baumann.

8. 'Neighbourhoods that Work' and the Walden Wage

Although the degrowth and steady-state schools have no singular vision of the 'good society' or singular theory of transition, many argue (see D'Alisa, Demaria, and Kallis, 2015; Holmgren, 2018) that the transition to a just and sustainable world will have to be driven into existence primarily from the grassroots up, with individuals, households, and communities coming together to 'prefigure' a new post-growth society within the shell of the old. According to this broad theory of change (Buch-Hansen, 2018), such prefigurative action, which is based on participatory democracy, is projected to filter upwards over time to change social, economic, and political structures in recognition of the systemic nature of the problems (Trainer, 2010; Alexander, 2013). From this perspective, social movements need to create the cultural conditions for structural change, and that structural change can then be a further driver for social change, representing a dynamic mode of society's transformation that relies on multiple movements, innovations, and policies for change (Washington, 2018).

The privileging of grassroots or community-led action is mainly due to the widely shared belief that the ability or willingness of politicians or businesses to lead a degrowth transition in a neoliberal age is scarce to non-existent (Alexander and Gleeson, 2019; Kallis et al., 2018; Holmgren, 2018). The logic here is that there are just too many 'growth imperatives' built into the economy for us to expect political leaders, corporations, or existing institutions to initiate or facilitate a degrowth transition to a steady-state economy (Blauwhof, 2012). Nevertheless, despite the coherency of these doubts about 'top down' political change and 'green businesses' leading the way, similar doubts can be levelled against any hope for a degrowth transition rising up from a socio-cultural groundswell (Frankel, 2018).

Indeed, in this chapter we seek to emphasise that this apparent paralysis in degrowth transition theory is owing, in part, to the growth imperatives of the dominant politico-economic order of global capitalism *specifically relating to land*, where ordinary people who are expected to lead the transition 'from below' are typically locked into a very long market commitment in order to buy or rent housing and keep a roof over their head. We will attempt to demonstrate the way in which this very demanding cost of land for housing has significant societal implications, affecting what we do for work, how much we work, and a range of other engagements with consumer society. We will highlight the way that modern capitalist economies have developed in perverse ways, particularly when it comes to land and housing cost. In our view, land – just as with air or water – is not a product of the market but a part of our collective natural heritage and inheritance that must be shared equitably with each other and all other species (OHCHR, 2013, n.d.). Accordingly, we wish to explore whether true political freedom is undermined in light of this lifelong land buy-in and resultant dependence on market opportunity, and whether there are alternative land governance arrangements that could better serve people and planet.

Our reading of this structural obstacle to degrowth suggests that deep economic changes relating to land access and governance are needed to help facilitate a degrowth transition to a steady-state economy and empower true democratic agency for those who would subscribe to such a transition. While the biophysical aspects of the degrowth and steady-state perspectives are critically important, coherent, and by and large compelling – indeed, we accept the validity of the case (Meadows, Randers, and Meadows, 2004; Turner, 2019; Kallis, 2017; Daly, 1997; 2014) – we argue that the broad 'post-growth' movements have given insufficient attention to land (and housing) cost. It is our view that this is a significant barrier in the way of a grassroots-driven degrowth transition, in particular, and genuine democratic participation, more generally, highlighting the deep and complex relationship between cultural and structural drivers for change.

The promise and limitations of the Walden experiment: How the privatisation of land can function to coerce people into consumerism

We would like to highlight the premise of our argument with reference to the great 19th-century philosopher of 'simple living', Henry David Thoreau. Now a canonical figure in the environmental movement (Walls, 2017), Thoreau famously spent two years living on the shores of Walden Pond, where he built himself a small abode, grew his own food, and generally lived an abundant life of voluntary simplicity (see Thoreau, 1982). He had very little by way of material wealth and possessions, but even so, he had enough to 'live deep and suck out all the marrow of life' (Thoreau, 1982: 344). This living experiment at the pond provoked an entire tradition of theory and practice that has sought to explore the prospects of living more on less (Grigsby, 2004; Cafaro, 2006), as 'part and parcel of Nature' (Thoreau, 1982: 592).

While living in the woods, Thoreau wrote his autobiographical manifesto *Walden*, in which he presented a fiery critique of the emerging consumer culture in the United States and a beautiful defence of simple living. Both his example and his words are provocative and inspiring – and, in an age of overconsumption, more important today than ever before (Steffen et al., 2015). To be successful, any sustainability transition will require high-impact societies moving away from consumerist cultures of consumption, and increasingly seeking happiness and purpose in non-materialistic sources (social relations, community engagement, self-governance, and generally privileging more time over more things, etc). Promisingly, the social science on the correlation between income and happiness (reviewed in Kasser, 2017; Alexander, 2012) supports Thoreau's case for sufficiency and moderation as a guiding ethics of consumption. It seems that beyond a relatively modest material threshold, getting richer stops contributing much to wellbeing, and things other than material wealth become increasingly important factors in quality of life (Lane, 2000). In a key passage, Thoreau (1982: 325) writes:

> I am convinced, both by faith and experience, that to maintain one's self on this earth is not a hardship but a pastime, if we will live simply and wisely.

But Thoreau's living experiment at Walden Pond depended on access to land (his friend Ralph Waldo Emerson owned the land and allowed free access), and in this chapter we are suggesting that for most people today, acquiring access to land is a significant barrier to people living simply and sustainably. In other words, it is hard to follow Thoreau's example of sufficiency-based living, even for those of us who want to. As detailed further below, most of us have to work full time in an unsustainable growth economy just to afford somewhere to live. And not many of us have friends like Ralph Waldo Emerson to grant us access to land to live on in the woods on the shores of a beautiful pond.

The critical point is that Thoreau's low-impact lifestyle of 'voluntary simplicity' – necessary though such practices may be to a just and sustainable world (Trainer, 2010) – are generally available only to people who have access to land – a *place* to live simply, grow food, and perhaps even build one's own house. But for most people today, especially in urban contexts, access to land generally means extensive market engagement in an unsustainable economy to pay for somewhere to live. Our concern, then, is that practising voluntary simplicity on expensive land is a compromised example of prefigurative degrowth practices. This is not an argument against voluntary simplicity, of course. The point is that systems of land governance within which we live can make voluntary simplicity very difficult to practice. People are often pressured to conform to high-impact living (Sanne, 2002), primarily because they find themselves needing to work in the existing growth economy to afford a place to live.

To unpack this point, we will now seek to illustrate that the struggle for access to land for housing regularly locks people into sustained but not sustainable market participation. Moreover, by sketching an outline of the tremendous housing cost pressure faced by many Australians, we will attempt to demonstrate how the expense of the mortgage or rent means that people otherwise sympathetic to a degrowth transition to a steady-state economy will often find themselves participating unsustainably in growth-dependent or growth-promoting practices.

The cost of land and housing: Willing consumers or locked in?

Australia's long-running housing crisis has seen house price inflation outstripping income growth since the early 2000s (Wilkins and Lass, 2015). This increase in housing prices relative to incomes also means that housing affordability has declined dramatically, and home ownership has become progressively beyond the reach of many households. According to the Grattan Institute, median Australian house prices have 'increased from around 4 times median incomes in the early 1990s to more than 7 times today (and more than 8 times in Sydney)' (Daley, Coates, and Wiltshire, 2018: 16).

This most recent affordability crisis has often been discussed within the context of 'late neoliberalism', and the financialisation of housing (Aalbers, 2016; Morris, 2018).[2] However, this global trend, to increasingly view land and housing as a means to accumulate capital, represents nothing essentially new. Indeed, land's commodification (and the social exclusion that inevitably results) can be traced all the way through Australia's housing history (Troy, 2000), shaped by early land privatisation. This began in Europe, with the privatisation (enclosure) of commons, and spread through the world through colonisation (Thompson 1991; Miller 2001). Legal commentators such as Blackstone (Blackstone and Sharswood, 1875) and Locke (1980), as well as economic philosophers like Marx (1985[1848]) and Proudhon (1876), recognised enclosing the commons via land privatisation

---

2 'The increasing dominance of financial actors, markets, practices, measurements and narratives, at various scales, resulting in a structural transformation of economies, firms (including financial institutions), states and households' (Aalbers, 2016: 2).

as the instigating structural shift that gave birth to capitalism. On this, Miller (2001: 111) states:

> The emergence of the capitalist world economy also saw the beginning of the first major wave of enclosure. This marked the start of a worldwide process of privatization and commodification of land, ocean and atmosphere. It fundamentally restructured the way people perceived themselves, each other and the land.

While commoner land rights were indeed restricted and far from ideal in feudal times, the extent to which land remained unexploited by the nobility allowed the continuation of ancient subsistence traditions.[3] However, because of exploitative conditions on which feudalism was built, these land rights were ultimately eroded and lost as it became profitable for the nobility to enclose the commons (Thompson, 1991).

Thus ended the era of the agrarian commoner, and any common law notion of rights to land, and began the era of private land and the capitalist market subject, with citizenship rights and responsibilities pivoting on market employment (Wallerstein, 1974; Miller, 2001). From this inception point onward, land commodification resulted in a dispossession from land and a shift to a dependence on the market as a source of income to buy or rent land for housing. This was socially problematic from the start, resulting in widespread peasant riots and hardship.[4]

In terms of this analysis around land commodification and affordability, contemporary housing scholars, such as Pawson, Milligan, and Yates (2020: para 2), recognise that the problem of housing unaffordability is:

---

3 Commoners held joint legal rights over common land which preceded parliament's statute law and was protected under common law (Yandle, 1992). Peasant farmers typically had their own plots of land and could choose what to grow there and keep at least most of what they raised (Yandle, 1992). They were also able to use commons to pasture animals, fish, take sods of turf for fuel, take gravel and sand and take wood. There was also the belief and practice that 'if an Englishman could build a house on common land, raise the roof over their head and have a fire in the hearth between sunrise and sunset, then they could have the right of undisturbed possession' (Harrison, 1989: 135). While this perception and practice was not corroborated in common law, it was not until the Erection of Cottages Act 1588 (an Act against the erecting and maintaining of cottages) which coincided with the emergence of enclosure laws, that the state made a legal stance against landless peasants 'squatting' on commons (Harrison 1989).

4 Angry tenants impatient to reclaim pastures for tillage were illegally destroying enclosures. Revolts swept all over the nation, and other revolts occurred periodically throughout the century (Thomson, 1991: 237).

... fundamentally structural – not cyclical – in nature. Yes, periodic turbulence affects prices and rents. And yes, market conditions vary greatly from place to place. Australia-wide, though, there is an underlying dynamic that – over the medium to long term – is driving housing affordability and rental stress in one general direction only: for the worse.

Surely, if there were a 'structure' we may seek to review in this regard, it would be the structure of the commodification of land, which is not so much a market good and more a social need. Like the housing affordability crises that preceded it, our most recent affordability crisis has placed tremendous pressures on a broad gamut of Australian households, from intensifying rental affordability problems for those with lower incomes, to over indebting and locking out would-be first home buyers (Pawson, Milligan, and Yates, 2020). Essential Research (2018) findings show that these pressures are being felt deeply across Australia, with more than half of all Australians feeling 'stretched' in order to meet their current housing commitments, be they mortgage or rent. Even more concerning, their research also showed that 42 per cent of households fear they could become homeless if their circumstances (e.g., cost of living, health, employment, etc.) were to change for the worse.

For the fast-growing group that we would position as most vulnerable, pre-COVID Australia was already beset with an estimated 1.6 million low-income people struggling to meet their housing costs (Bentley and Baker, 2020). Far from atypical, this housing crisis is consistent with Australia's long trend in high and unaffordable housing prices (Wilkins and Lass, 2015). Indicative of how long this affordability crisis has run, the 2020 Australian Productivity Commission report finds that the number of low-income households struggling to pay their rent had doubled in the past two decades. Bentley and Baker (2020: para 30) now estimate that if 'unemployment in Australia jumps from the pre-COVID level of around 700,000 to 1.7 million, it translates to 2.4 times more people unemployed. In real terms, this means more than 550,000 extra insecurely-housed families'.

So, what does this widely experienced and long-standing housing and land cost pressure mean, in terms of the sort of freedom required to disinvest oneself from the market and embark on a more sustainable 'degrowth' path?

The cost of land and housing creates market dependency

If a household wanted to step out of the cycle of their dependence on consumerism and economic growth, and instead wanted to choose the sort of sufficiency-based lifestyles advocated by the degrowth and steady-state movements, they would first still need to contend with the cost of land and housing. However, as indicated above, access to this most basic need is a serious and often lifelong economic determinant. In short, securing land for housing requires a lot of 'dropping in', before one can conceivably 'drop out' of market engagement.

The central problem here is that this housing cost generally coerces people into specialised and extensive market employment, and, given the housing cost pressures most face, people cannot be too fussy about the sort of market opportunity they take up. Indeed, for all Australians to have the job opportunity they need to service their housing costs within a neoliberal framework, Australia requires ongoing economic growth to accommodate for a growing population and the redundancies that can flow from technological innovation (Purdey, 2010; Pandey, 2019). This apparent lock-in has a broad range of implications, from the economic growth and consumer industries we must depend on for employment opportunity, to things like our need for transportation and the clothes we must buy and wear in our market roles. Our specialised labour also means we have become increasingly time poor, and we are outsourcing more and more of our household responsibilities (Oster et al., 2018), and are thus relying on specialised production and distribution of an ever-increasing range of goods and services.

This brings us to our next point, which is that very few if any livelihoods in market societies can be considered sustainable. Even the wages of post-development academics like us (how the authors pay for their housing) flow from university investments in fossil fuels industries, and overall we are earning an income from an extremely carbon-intensive education sector, with its reliance on student aspiration to secure their market share, international student intake, and generally high levels of academic travel (Miles, 2017).

Those in the degrowth or downshifting movements who have been fortunate enough to afford land and housing may well be in a position to grow their own organic food, put solar panels on their roof, bike to work, and reduce working hours in the formal economy – and these practices may indeed provide some important prefigurative degrowth examples of localised economy, downshifted consumption, and post-carbon energy practices. However, we argue that they provide a fundamentally compromised example of a degrowth pathway, because their path to housing security relies on long and deep market participation for anyone who seeks to follow their lead. For these unwitting followers, who face an even higher cost of housing, they would have to earn wages or profits in an unsustainable economy to afford their rent or mortgage payments.

There is absolutely no way affluent consumption practices of the developed regions of the world can be globalised to all 7.8 billion people on the planet today, let alone the 9.7 billion expected by 2050 (UNDESA, 2011; Trainer and Alexander, 2019). Technology alone cannot solve this ecological contradiction (Hickel and Kallis, 2019). If we are to respond effectively to the overlapping crises of our times, we need (among other things) to empower individuals, households, and communities to transcend consumer culture and embrace a 'simpler way' of life.

In short, the case we seek to make is that, even for those who share the vision of degrowth or a steady-state economy, this underlying land-for-housing 'buy in' requirement creates a significant structural impediment to people engaging in prefigurative degrowth practices that could be more broadly adopted. This barrier makes it very hard for degrowth sympathisers to live in a way that accords with their visions of societal downshifting for sustainability and justice. We argue that this represents a problematic curtailment of political and democratic freedoms, because land privatisation, and how it functions as a significant economic constraint, only permits 'lifestyle options' to emerge within the context of an unsustainable, growth dependent, market economy.

Political implications

With land and housing cost being such an inescapable and overwhelming economic determinant for so many people, we now explore the idea that this pivotal cost also plays a significant role as a determinant related to political orientation. As was reported in Essential Research (2018), job opportunity was one of the only issues that rated higher than housing affordability. Given the direct link between economic opportunity and people's ability to secure their housing, it is little wonder that this is the case, and that 'Jobs and Growth' has become the unyielding political mantra of the major Australian parties. In one sense it is quite understandable why people perceive political parties promising market growth as attractive, given that a growing economy – *from a neoliberal perspective* – is fundamentally needed to allow them to service their rent or mortgage payments. This perceived need for growth is a reality that has become very clear during the COVID-19 economic crisis, as the crashing economy is resulting in a crisis related to people's ability to service their rent and mortgage payments (Ong Vifor, 2020). We also contend that it is because of the economic and political need to deliver jobs and growth that parties like the Greens succumb to promoting industries like tourism, despite the demonstrable unsustainability and carbon privilege involved in such carbon-intensive industries (Miles, 2017; Malik and Sun, 2018).

We also argue that this has undemocratic effects in that it puts significant structural pressure on people struggling to afford access to land and housing to vote for political parties that seek growth and income, thus constraining the political imagination and making it difficult to vote for political parties (if such parties existed) that sought to initiate a degrowth to a steady-state economy. As things presently stand, there is no mainstream political party that campaigns for degrowth or steady-state economy. Even if one is able to vote for some *future* manifestation of a degrowth or steady-state party, people's daily democratic, economic, and lifestyle practices will be fundamentally constrained by their mortgage/rent obligations.

Ecologically, all this entrenches the destructive paradigm of economic growth, in many ways coercing people into market participation and high-impact lifestyles, and inhibiting people from prefiguring local and post-carbon modes of production and consumption. We are not even free to live simply off the land. How, then, can we expect a broader prefigurative degrowth movement to emerge within current structural constraints? Our foundational point is that neoliberalism thwarts the democratic right to pursue genuine sustainability in our lives and politics.

The fundamental implication of this argument is that degrowth, and the broader movement of ecological economics of which it is a part, should give increased attention to land, housing, and property rights as critically important aspects of any degrowth transition to a steady-state economy (Buch-Hansen, 2018). In short, we argue that without non-commodified access to land, the democratic freedoms of citizens will emerge within a market paradigm of growth economics, thus erecting structural constraints that make it difficult to live and vote in opposition to that paradigm. Our policy proposal outlined below seeks to enable low-impact living for more people, by providing access to land (in the form of secure housing) and a 'participation income' (a modest living wage). The goal is to help create a structural context that would allow more people to live lives of voluntary simplicity.

Let us explain how it could work.

A policy proposal

Having demonstrated the way in which access to land is a serious obstacle in the way of a sustainability transition, we'd like to make a positive, constructive intervention by offering a policy proposal that we feel has transformative potential.

Despite the land privatisation that has continued unabated under neoliberalism, many countries around the world maintain a heritage of public housing. In some of these public housing communities, residents self-select to participate in community development programmes (sometimes under the umbrella of tenant participation) such as community food gardens, resources repair/share programmes, housing management, maintenance and, in the UK, even housing construction (Baumann and Alexander, 2019). In this way, public housing provides an (albeit limited) example of publicly owned land for a form of community development that is local, cooperative, and not inherently defined by a dependence on market consumer growth.

At its simplest, our proposal involves further supporting unemployed public residents who self-select into these collaborative programmes by providing them with a basic, living wage – which we will call a Walden Wage in acknowledgement of Henry Thoreau's example of voluntary simplicity. With housing and other basic needs secured, the goal would be to enable these self-selecting public residents to participate in the creation of 'simple living' communities and neighbourhoods that are sustainable, resilient, and consistent with human flourishing and the flourishing of the broader community of life. Put otherwise, we will argue for a strategy we call 'Neighbourhoods that Work', which essentially involves providing people marginalised by capitalism with (1) access to public land and housing; and (2) a 'participation income' (i.e., a modest living wage) for helping build new, relocalised, ecologically viable, and socially just communities and economies on our shared planet.

If successful, our hope is that these initial examples could be scaled up to support those marginalised or cast aside by the existing economic system – an expanding group because of the increasing realities of globalised labour, technological job redundancy (CEDA, 2015; Madgavkar et al., 2019; Thomas and Lambert, 2019), and environmental limits to consumer jobs and growth (Turner, 2019). This alternative housing and productive opportunity could also attract people across the political divide as a foundation for an alternative economy – a viable, sustainable, steady-state economy. Central to this vision is the recognition that land is not a market product but a shared inheritance that ought to be managed democratically to advance the best interests of people, other species, and ecosystems. As we outline this approach and unpack a broader vision for transition, we argue that this strategy could support the prefigurative action called for by many in the degrowth and steady-state movements and, just as importantly, expand the political imagination to make more space for a degrowth transition to a steady-state economy.

Unpacking the vision of 'Neighbourhoods that Work'

In recognition of an inescapable need for inclusivity and degrowth (and therefore land access reform) and the confrontational and unlikely acceptance of such a radical reform in contemporary Western capitalist nations, we will now explore a preliminary land and community development strategy that has the potential to be politically palatable. Indeed, it is a strategy (if framed correctly) that has the potential to provide benefits that could be marketed to economic and social conservatives and the broader politically and economically conservative public – not just ecological economists and degrowth advocates.

First, people must *see* how liberating access to land and housing can be when coupled with collaborative practices of collective sufficiency (e.g., growing food, home-based production, sharing resources, fixing things, etc.). When some limited but practical and real-world examples are seen, it is our hope that the political imagination could be expanded in ways that could deepen the institutional restructuring needed to provide such opportunities to more people. We feel there is potential to use public housing to show that access to land can remove a barrier to sustainability and provide a foundation upon which to escape market imperatives and begin building new forms of local, collaborative, and sharing economies consistent with the degrowth perspective.

At its simplest, the Walden Wage is similar to a 'voluntary-work-for-the-dole' scheme – but with a broader vision that we will share. This scheme is entirely voluntary, as opposed to mandatory programmes like Work for the Dole in Australia or workfare schemes in the UK. The mandatory programmes have shown themselves to be very problematic and would certainly undermine the ethics and participant-driven viability of our proposal. Also, where mandatory work-for-the-dole and workfare represent a situation where the unemployed are used as cheap labour at the bottom end of the labour market, our proposal offers a path of work integrity, community connection, and housing and economic security.

The policy's most important feature is linking a secure but modest income with access to public land and housing. This housing and income option would be offered (at first) to unemployed people who are already in, or on the top of the waiting list for, public housing. These self-selecting public residents would choose to be involved in around 15 hours per week of local community programmes, like growing food, maintaining the neighbourhood, facilitating sharing schemes, or even building new homes.

In other words, the Walden Wage would provide a participation income (Atkinson, 1996) for jobless public residents wanting to engage in the necessary work of creating new forms of sufficiency-based living, enabled by access to land. The 'wage' part of this scheme has some similarity to the notion of a 'universal basic income' (UBI), which is being talked about and analysed a lot these days (Washington, 2018; Frankel, 2018). However, there are some critical differences. The primary difference is that it would be offered, not universally, but only in the context of public housing and localised, community economies – as a minimal and sustainable living wage. This would make it affordable to governments, and since it is linked to access to public land and housing, people receiving the Walden Wage would not find themselves needing to 'top up' their incomes by engaging in an unsustainable growth economy in any significant way.

Interestingly, the fact that this income (through the voluntary-work-for the-dole scheme) is already available (in Australia) for unemployed people who are over 55 demonstrates that it has already been deemed affordable by government. And, unlike the UBI, it would neither be universal (i.e., paid to all citizens) nor promote or depend on a limitless-growth economy to fund it. Indeed, a Walden Wage would function to support the building of sustainable economies (Hopkins, 2011; Gibson-Graham, Cameron, and Healy, 2013), based on a more inclusive and liberating land governance arrangement. If participants over 55 could show a viable pilot, we believe this option could be extended to those under 55 who are unemployed in public housing. Indeed, there could be a pilot experiment available for any keen practitioners of simple living who 'self-select' into the scheme.

Land, we should add, would still be owned by the Commonwealth, and we propose that residents would pay 25 per cent of their income in rent. Without having the expense of private land and housing, the goal is to ensure that a modest participation income would be sufficient to live well and sustainably. If we assume that income is a (very rough) proxy for environmental impact (Wiedmann et al., 2015), we can also say that the Walden Wage would imply roughly an 85 per cent reduction in impacts compared to the national average, on the basis that a Walden Wage at a level of the dole (currently $489.70 per fortnight) would be roughly 15 per cent of the average Australian income.

Given the security of public housing and the many benefits of local collaborative development, this wage could be sufficient and even desirable. If shown to be viable, it's a way of living that represents a massive reduction in market dependence and certainly puts it in the ballpark of global sustainability. In short, we could end up with neighbourhoods that work – the name of our scheme.

The benefits and prospects

The best thing about this seemingly radical idea is that it isn't actually that radical. With the right support, it could begin now – given that the policy settings are already in place to allow public residents who are over 55 to self-select into voluntary-work-for-the-dole programmes. Such a pilot could show that access to land plus a participation income could help build genuinely sustainable forms of economy. If this pilot showed some success, it's not hard to see how one pilot could turn into two, and even be offered to some willing participants who are under 55.

The next phase could be slightly more ambitious. If governments were to provide more land (see Palm, Whitzman, and Raynor, 2018), these public residents could not just develop relocalised, community economies around existing public housing projects, but actually participate in the building of their own homes, in collaboration with others, and under the guidance of experts. This would also reduce pressure on existing public housing, giving others the opportunity to participate in this scheme.

Also, providing these public residents with such an opportunity, coupled with a voluntary-work-for-the-dole scheme (reframed as the Walden Wage), represents a shift many on the political right may want too, in the direction of less passive and more active forms of 'welfare'. In fact, this policy would totally reframe welfare for those who self-select. If such an opportunity could be encouraged, the identity we give to public housing tenants who participate could begin to be uplifted and even celebrated. Their status in society, and how they might conceive of themselves, could move from being regarded as 'social dependants' to 'pioneers of a sustainable economy'.

What if things scaled up?

As more people are cast into unemployment by the automation of jobs, the globalisation of labour, or the phasing-out of high impact industries like fossil fuel power stations, it is highly likely that more and more people will require a new and sustainable housing and community development option like the one being proposed here. We should also remember that the so-called 'Golden Age' of public housing emerged as a result of governments having to deal with post-war economic reconstruction and the Great Depression. If challenging economic times lie ahead for the world again, then governments will *have* to respond as growing portions of the population are made redundant and cast into unemployment, as evidenced by governmental responses to the COVID-19 pandemic. Indeed, governments may *want* to respond, because otherwise there is the likely prospect of escalating poverty, serious security issues, and political instability, since multitudes that cannot afford food or housing are a recipe for serious social unrest and decline. It is important that examples are provided in advance of deepening crises so that governments can see how best to respond when circumstances force them to act.

With the community economies we envision becoming increasingly self-reliant, it is possible that this 'Neighbourhoods that Work' approach, having started with the unemployed in public housing, could expand to include the growing numbers who have found themselves alienated from the market.

This is where things get really interesting, and where our policy may show most promise. Once this local and cooperative sector of the economy begins to flourish, it is possible that the sustainability dream may come to fruition – we can imagine bike lanes weaving their way through food forests, with a few shared electric vehicles available for occasional use; renewable energy micro-grids and large water tanks supporting these new communities on public land; people enriched by the process of participating in the building of their own sustainable homes (e.g., mud-brick) under expert supervision, and in collaboration with others. Soon enough, these pioneers, who have been liberated from a market mortgage or rent, may well be living as free eco-citizens in a thriving, local economy of sufficiency. With this structural economic shift from a market economy (private land and paid work) to a 'commons economy' (Wall, 2014; McGuirk, 2015; Baumann and Alexander, 2019) (public land and collaborative local work), a degrowth transition to a steady-state economy might well be underway.

This work building new sustainable communities would 'earn' or justify the small participation income, providing many benefits – not only to participants, but also to the broader neighbourhood. As noted above, through the participants' 15 hours per week in local sustainable productivity (collaboratively run community gardens, resource share schemes, and repair programmes, etc.), many neighbours could opt to be involved and enjoy collaborative benefits. Neighbours could also enjoy a greater sense of community connectedness. Importantly, all neighbours would also benefit from a much more sustainable future.

Empirical studies show that some simple living communities (Lockyer, 2017) and strategies (Trainer, Malik, and Lenzen, 2019) can reduce ecological impacts by up to 90 per cent or more, which is arguably the scale of downshifting needed to bring developed nations within sustainable limits of the planet (Trainer and Alexander, 2019). Our policy provides an important aid to helping such sustainable communities and neighbourhoods proliferate, namely, by empowering people with access to land and housing (thereby freeing them from the lifelong debt of mortgage/rent and everything that goes along with it).

Over time, as the realities of globalised labour, technological job redundancy, and environmental limits to consumer growth really start to kick in, thousands of these ecovillages could emerge within, and integrating with, existing urban societies. If this happened, we might at last see the planned contraction of energy and resource demands that is so clearly necessary for any degrowth transition to a sustainable, steady-state economy. Let governments be as ambitious as the Senegalese government, which has announced a plan to establish and support 14,000 ecovillages (Olivier, 2015).

As more people recognise the forthcoming dangers presented by the 'limits to growth' predicament (Turner, 2019), we expect that the degrowth and steady-state movements will expand more broadly into the cultural consciousness. This is arguably already underway (Drews and van den Bergh, 2016). When this larger sector of society sympathising broadly with degrowth also realises that governments and businesses will not lead a degrowth transition (given the various growth imperatives), the expanding social movement will be part of the drive to change from the grassroots up. This is a primary alternative strategy for deliberate societal change. More people will endeavour to live materially downshifted, post-carbon lives, only to discover that access to land makes that difficult. Frustrated by this barrier to living their values and exercising their democratic agency, the movement will shift its focus to how land is governed in society, in order to broaden access to land and housing, which would allow greater democratic freedoms to choose a sufficiency-based way of life without such extensive and prolonged market engagement. If such a movement for change were successful, people would no longer be under such constraining financial pressure to meet basic land and housing needs via extended market participation. Sufficiency-based living would be a viable option for more people through new land governance arrangements. This post-consumerist culture may expand the political imagination beyond growth politics and, over time, lead to more extensive institutional and structural changes that could take place in the direction of degrowth to a steady state (Alexander, 2020). We contend that the logic of this theory of change is sound, even if we accept that many social, economic, and political barriers lie in the way of its realisation.

Build a new model

Despite its foundational relationship to consumerism, land privatisation is a subject typically unseen or disregarded by most would-be environmental and social reformers, including, as we have noted, degrowth advocates and ecological economists more broadly. Even in the extremely rare cases where it is acknowledged, it is typically the view that any kind of land reform is extremely threatening to the private property status-quo, that it sits on the extreme Left politically, and so is not politically palatable or pragmatic. There is no denying that both ideologically and economically, Australia – and Western nations more generally – is a society deeply invested in land privatisation. Any mention of land reform is typically met with deep suspicion and deep ideological objection, even from those who might benefit most directly from new frameworks of land governance. Because of this, the most common response to the need for land reform is that it represents unachievable structural change, and that it's simply too big a project, given the limited time we have to address what is clearly a climate emergency (Spratt and Dunlop, 2017).

However, the widely held reform proposition – that we endeavour to 'green' capitalism through a shift to renewables – is simply untenable without a meaningful plan to halt perpetual growth (Hickel and Kallis, 2019). After all, a growth-oriented world running on renewables will still be necessarily wasteful and consumeristic – and will certainly push us beyond environmental limits (Turner, 2019). With countries like China and India now rapidly developing, the global trajectory of growth and consumerism over the next decade simply cannot be made sustainable through renewables alone – not in a way that will adequately address our now overwhelming environmental challenges (for literature reviews examining the promise and limitations of renewables, see Floyd et al., 2020; Alexander and Floyd, 2018). Indeed, while green technological development and the shift from fossil fuels are essential to any sustainability transition, this shift will fail to achieve sustainability if it is not accompanied by a systemic shift toward ending our collective reliance on (and pursuit of) economic growth and high-impact consumer lifestyles (Daly, 1997; Hickel and Kallis, 2019).

However, in this chapter we have argued that without a new land opportunity that would free people from a lifetime of participation in an unsustainable market economy, we are socially, politically, and economically constrained from achieving low-impact lifestyles consistent with planetary limits. We believe that experiments with ways to broaden access to land are indispensable to any degrowth transition, and since degrowth in some form is necessary to the ongoing inhabitability of Earth, we maintain that land access ought to be given far more attention by all those seriously concerned about sustainability, social and ecological justice, and the flourishing of the community of life on Earth.

We believe it is time to experiment with alternative frameworks that can increase access to land for housing. This would empower more people to explore lifestyles of reduced consumption, increased self-sufficiency, and local economic collaboration, thereby enabling a prefigurative degrowth transition to a steady-state economy and reducing pressure on planetary ecosystems. Our vision is that if people are provided with affordable rent through public land and housing opportunities to undertake their own sufficiency-based living experiments, like Henry Thoreau, then many people would do so. Access to land liberates people from market growth and facilitates ways of living consistent with genuine sustainability. At the very least, it makes sense to support all willing pioneers and encourage their skill development and empower them to build new worlds within the shell of the old (Trainer, 2010; Holmgren, 2018).

As Buckminster Fuller (BFI, n.d.) once said: 'You never change things by fighting against the existing reality. To change something, build a new model that makes the old model obsolete.'

References

Aalbers, M.B. 2016. *The Financialisation of Housing: A Political Economy Approach.* Abingdon: Routledge.

Alexander, S. 2012. 'The Optimal Material Threshold: Toward an Economics of Sufficiency'. *Real-World Economics Review* 61: 2–21.

Alexander, S. 2013. 'Voluntary Simplicity and the Social Reconstruction of Law: Degrowth from the Grassroots Up'. *Environmental Values* 22 (2): 287–308.

Alexander, S. 2020. 'Post-capitalism by Design not Disaster'. *The Ecological Citizen* 3 (Suppl B): 13–21.

Alexander, S. and Baumann, A. 2020. 'Towards the Walden Wage'. *The Ecologist* (4 March 2020).

Alexander, S. and Floyd, J. 2018. *Carbon Civilisation and the Energy Descent Future: Life Beyond this Brief Anomaly.* Melbourne: Simplicity Institute.

Alexander S. and Gleeson B. 2019. *Degrowth in the Suburbs: A Radical Urban Imaginary.* Singapore: Palgrave Macmillan.

Atikinson, A. 1996. 'The Case for a Participation Income'. *The Political Quarterly.* 67 (1): 67–70.

Baumann, A. and Alexander, S. 2019. 'Access to Land is a Barrier to Simpler, Sustainable Living. Public Housing Could Offer a Way Forward'. *The Conversation* (22 August 2019).

Bentley R. and Baker E. 2020. 'Australian Homes on the Line'. *The Pursuit* (3 April 2020). Available at: https://pursuit.unimelb.edu.au/articles/australian-homes-on-the-line.amp (accessed 8 April 2020).

Berry, M. 1999. 'Unravelling the Australian Housing Solution: The Post-War Years'. *Housing, Theory and Society*, 16 (3): 106–123.

BFI. (No date.) Quote by Buckminster Fuller. Buckminster Fuller Institute. See: https://www.bfi.org/ideaindex/projects/2015/greenwave

Blackstone, W. and Sharswood, G. 1875. *Commentaries on the Laws of England: In Four Books (Vol. 2).* London: JB Lippincott & Company.

Blauwhof, F. 2012 .'Overcoming Accumulation: Is a Steady-State capitalism Possible?', *Ecological Economics* 84: 254–261.

Buch-Hansen, H. 2018. 'The Prerequisites for a Degrowth Paradigm Shift: Insights from Critical Political Economy'. *Ecological Economics* 146: 157–163.

Cafaro, P. 2006. *Thoreau's Living Ethics: Walden and the Pursuit of Virtue*. Athens: University of Georgia Press.

CEDA. 2015. 'Australia's Future Workforce?'. Committee for Economic Development of Australia. Available at: https://www.ceda.com.au/Research-and-policy/All-CEDA-research/Research-catalogue/Australia-s-future-workforce (accessed 10 May 2020).

Daly, H. 1997. *Beyond Growth: The Economics of Sustainable Development*. Boston: Beacon Press.

Daly, H. 2014. *From Uneconomic Growth to a Steady-State Economy*. Cheltenham, UK; Northampton; MA: Edward Elgar.

Daley, J., Coates, B., and Wiltshire, T. 2018. Housing Affordability: Re-imagining the Australian Dream. Grattan Institute.

D'Alisa, G., Demaria F., and Kallis G. (eds). 2015. *Degrowth: A Vocabulary for a New Era*. London: Routledge.

Drews, S. and van den Bergh, J. 2016. 'Public Views on Economic Growth, the Environment and Prosperity: Results of a Questionnaire Survey'. *Global Environmental Change* 39: 1–14.

Escobar, A. 2015. 'Degrowth, Postdevelopment, and Transitions: A Preliminary Conversation'. *Sustainability Science*. 10 (3): 451–462.

Essential Research. 2018. 'The Essential Report: Homelessness Questions'. Essential Research Report. Available at: http://www.essentialvision.com.au/wp-content/uploads/2018/08/Essential-Report-310718_homelessness.pdf (accessed 10 May 2020).

Floyd, J. et al. 2020. 'Energy Descent as a Post-Carbon Transition Scenario: How "Knowledge Humility" Reshapes Energy Futures for Post-Normal Times'. *Futures* (in press).

Frankel, B. 2018. *Fictions of Sustainability: The Politics of Growth and Post-Capitalist Futures*. Melbourne: Greenmeadows.

Gibson-Graham J.K., Cameron J., and Healy S. 2013. *Take Back the Economy: An Ethical Guide for Transforming our Communities*. Minneapolis: University of Minnesota Press.

Grigsby, M. 2004. *Buying Time and Getting By: The Voluntary Simplicity Movement*. Albany: State University of New York.

Harrison, L.F.C. 1989. *The Common People: A History from the Norman Conquest to the Present*. Glasgow: Fontana.

Hickel, J. 2017. *The Divide: A Brief Guide to Global Inequality and its Solutions*. London: William Heinemann.

Hickel, J. and Kallis, G. 2019. 'Is Green Growth Possible?'. *New Political Economy*. DOI: 10.1080/13563467.2019.1598964.

Henry, K. 2020. 'The Unemployment Rate Doesn't Go Back to Normal After a Recession – There Are Long-term Effects'. *The Guardian* (26 March 2020).

Holmgren, D. 2018. *RetroSuburbia: The Downshifter's Guide to a Resilient Future*. Hepburn Springs: Melliodora Publishing.

Hopkins, R. 2011. *The Transition Companion: Making Your Community More Resilient in Uncertain Times*. White River Junction: Chelsea Green Publishing.

Kallis, G. 2017. 'Radical Dematerialization and Degrowth'. *Philosophical Transactions of the Royal Society A*. 375: 20160383: 1–13.

Kallis, G. et al. 2018. 'Research on Degrowth'. *Annual Review of Environment and Resources*. 43: 4.1–4.26.

Kasser, T. 2017. 'Living Both Well and Sustainably: A Review of the Literature, with Some Reflections on Future Research, Interventions and Policy'. *Philosophical Transactions of the Royal Society A 375*.

Lane, R. 2000. *The Loss of Happiness in Market Democracies*. New Haven, CT: Yale University Press.

Locke, J. 1690/1980. *Second Treatise of Government*. Indianapolis and Cambridge: McPherson, Hackett Publishing Company.

Lockyer, J. 2017. 'Community, Commons, and Degrowth at Dancing Rabbit Ecovillage'. *Journal of Political Ecology*. 24 (1): 519–542.

Malik, A. and Sun, Y. 2018. 'The Carbon Footprint of Tourism Revealed (It's Bigger Than We Thought)'. *The Conversation* (8 May 2018).

Madgavkar, A. et al. 2019. 'The Future of Women at Work: Transitions in the Age of Automation'. McKinsey Global Institute. Available at: https://is.gd/LBb3qy (accessed 10 May 2020).

Marx, K. and Engels, F. 1985(1848). *The Communist Manifesto*. Harmonsworth, UK: Penguin.

McGuirk, J. 2015. 'Urban Commons Have Radical Potential – It's Not Just About Community Gardens', *The Guardian* (16 June 2015).

Meadows, D., Randers, J. and Meadows, D. 2004. *Limits to Growth: The 30-year Update*, Vermont: Chelsea Green.

Miles, J. 2017. 'For the Love of Earth, Stop Traveling'. *Washington Post* (3 November 2017).

Miller, M. 2001. 'Tragedy for the Commons: The Enclosure and Commodification of Knowledge'. In. Stevis, D. and Assetto, V.J. (eds). *The International Political Economy of the Environment*. Boulder: Lynne Rienner: 111–134.

Morris, A. 2018. 'The Financialisation of Housing and the Housing Affordability Crisis in Sydney'. *Housing Finance* 32 (4): 63–69.

OHCHR. (No date.) 'Land and Human Rights'. United Nations High Commission for Human Rights. Available at: https://www.ohchr.org/EN/Issues/LandAndHR/Pages/LandandHumanRightsIndex.aspx (accessed 21 April 2020).

Olivier, T. 2015. 'The Senegalese Ecovillage Network: The Past, Present, and Future'. Available at: https://ecovillage.org/wp-content/uploads/drupal_files/files/5_report_senegalese_ecovillage.pdf (access 20 February 2020).

Ong Vifor, J.R. 2020. 'As Coronavirus Widens the Renter-Owner Divide, Housing Policies Will Have to Change'. *The Conversation* (20 April 2020).

Oster, A. et al. 2018. 'NAB Wellbeing Insight Report Time: How we Use it and Value it' (September 2018). NAB Behavioural & Industry Economics. Available at: https://business.nab.com.au/wp-content/uploads/2018/09/Special-Report-The-Value-of-Our-Time-September-2018.pdf (accessed 10 May 2020).

Palm, M., Whitzman, C., and Raynor, K. 2018. 'Put Unused and "Lazy" Land to Work to Ease the Affordable Housing Crisis'. *The Conversation* (7 September 2018). Available at: https://theconversation.com/put-unused-and-lazy-land-to-work-to-ease-the-affordable-housing-crisis-102720 (accessed 10 May 2020).

Pandey S. 2019. 'Australia's GDP Growth Hits Decade Low, Stimulus Needed to Avoid Recession'. Reuters (5 June 2019). Available at: https://www.reuters.com/article/us-australia-economy-gdp/australias-gdp-growth-hits-decade-low-stimulus-needed-to-avoid-recession-idUSKCN1T606I (accessed 11 May 2020).

Pawson, H., Milligan, V., and Yates, J. 2020. 'Australia's Housing System Needs a Big Shake-Up: Here's How We Can Crack This'. *The Conversation*. Available at: https://theconversation.com/australias-housing-system-needs-a-big-shake-up-heres-how-we-can-crack-this-130291 (accessed 2 April 2020).

Productivity Commission (2020) 'Report on Government Services 2020'. Available at: https://www.pc.gov.au/research/ongoing/report-on-government-services/2020 Accessed 20 April 2020.

Proudhon, P.J. 1876. *What is Property?: An Inquiry into the Principle of Right and of Government* (Vol. 1). Paris: BR Tucker.

Purdey, S. 2010. *Economic Growth, the Environment, and International Relations: The Growth Paradigm*. New York: Routledge.

Ripple, H. et al. 2017. 'World Scientists' Warning to Humanity: A Second Notice'. *Bioscience*, 67 (12): 1026–1028, see: https://science.gu.se/digitalAssets/1671/1671867_world-scientists-warning-to-humanity_-a-second-notice_english.pdf. (accessed 27 March 2019).

Sanne, C. 2002. 'Willing Consumers – or Locked in? Policies for a Sustainable Consumption'. *Ecological Economics* 42 (1): 273–287.

Spratt, D. and Dunlop, I. 2017. 'What Lies Beneath: The Understatement of Existential Climate Risk'. Breakthrough Institute. Available at: https://www.breakthroughonline.org.au/whatliesbeneath (accessed 20 February 2020).

Steffen, W. et al. 2015. 'The Trajectory of the Anthropocene: The Great Acceleration'. *The Anthropocene Review* 2 (1): 81–98.

Thomas, R. and Lambert, J. 2019. 'Technology and the Future of Australian Jobs: What will be the Impact of AI on Workers in Every Sector?'. Available at: https://www.cisco.com/c/dam/m/en_au/cda/cisco-future-of-australian-jobs-report2019.pdf (accessed 10 May 2020).

Thompson, E.P. 1991. *The Making of the English Working Class*. London: Penguin.

Thoreau, H. 1982. *The Portable Thoreau*, edited by Carl Bode. London: Penguin.

Trainer, T. 2010. *Transition to a Sustainable and Just World*. Sydney: Envirobook.

Trainer, T. and Alexander, S. 2019. 'The Simpler Way: Envisioning a Sustainable Society in an Age of Limits'. *Real World Economics Review* 87: 247–260.

Trainer, T., Malik, A., and Lenzen, M. 2019. 'A Comparison Between the Monetary, Resources, and Energy Costs of the Conventional Industrial Supply Path and the "Simpler Way" Path for the Supply of Eggs'. *Biophysical Economics and Resource Quality* 4 (3): 1–7.

Troy, P. (ed.). 2000. *A History of European Housing in Australia*. Cambridge: Cambridge University Press.

Turner, G. 2019. 'Is a Sustainable Future Possible?'. *Journal and Proceedings of the Royal Society of NSW* 152 (1): 47–65.

UNDESA. 2011. 'World Economic and Social Survey 2011: The Great Green Technological Transformation'. New York: United Nations Department of Economic and Social Affairs.

Wall, D. 2014. *The Commons in History: Culture, Conflict, and Ecology*. Cambridge, Mass.: MIT Press.

Wallerstein, I. 1974. *The Modern World-System I: Capitalist Agriculture and the Origins of the European World-Economy in the Sixteenth Century*. New York: Academic Press.

Walls, L.D. 2017. *Henry David Thoreau: A Life*. Chicago: University of Chicago Press.

Washington, H. and Twomey, P. 2016. *A Future Beyond Growth: Towards a Steady-state Economy*. London: Routledge.

Washington, H. (ed.). 2018. *Positive Steps to a Steady-state Economy*. Sydney: CASSE NSW.

Wiedmann T. et al. 2015. 'The Material Footprint of Nations' *Proceedings of the National Academy of Sciences*. 112: 6271–6276.

Wilkins, R. and Lass, I. 2015. 'The Household, Income and Labour Dynamics in Australia Survey: Selected Findings from Waves 1 to 12'. Melbourne: Melbourne Institute of Applied Economic and Social Research, University of Melbourne.

Yandle, B. 1992. 'Escaping Environmental Feudalism'. *Harvard Journal of Law and Public Policy*, 15: 517.

Chapter 9

The Simpler Way: Envisioning a sustainable society in an age of limits[1]

Overview

Although it is widely understood that the global economy is currently unsustainable, few people seem to understand how far beyond sustainable limits it is. Fewer still seem to grasp what it would take for the global population to live within the sustainable carrying capacity of the planet. The most developed regions of the world have greatly exceeded levels of resource use and ecological impact that could be maintained or spread to all people, and as a result we are rapidly moving toward catastrophic planetary breakdown (WWF, 2018; Steffen et al., 2015; Ehrlich and Ehrlich, 2013). The alarming global problems threatening humanity today include climate change; the pollution of air, soils, rivers, and oceans; deforestation and severe biodiversity loss; resource and topsoil depletion; and conflicts over access to scarce resources. From a social perspective, billions of people, mostly in the Third World, still suffer under conditions of deprivation (Hickel, 2017), while quality of life deteriorates even for many living high-impact, consumerist lifestyles in the richest countries (Lane, 2000). The global economic system and the cultures of consumption it celebrates are failing both people and planet.

It will be argued that these interconnected problems cannot be solved unless we move toward an economics of sufficiency, which means, among other things, that rates of production, consumption, and resource use in rich countries must be dramatically reduced, probably by 80–90 per cent or more (see 'Global Predicament' section below). These reductions cannot be achieved merely by 'greening production' through piecemeal efficiency improvements or technological innovation, and they cannot be achieved in a society that is governed by market forces or driven by the insatiable quest for material affluence or the limitless

---

1 Originally published in the *Real-World Economics Review* 87, 2020, pp 247–260, co-authored with Ted Trainer.

increase in GDP. In other words, a sustainable economy must be a post-growth and post-capitalist economy. But what does that actually mean?

We contend that the only way sustainability can be achieved is through a radical transition to a 'Simpler Way' society, which would be defined by low but sufficient material living standards, renewable energy, highly localised or 'bioregional' production, egalitarian approaches to wealth distribution, participatory democratic practices of self-governance, and major degrowth to a zero-growth economy (Trainer, 2010; Alexander, 2015). We do not argue that this transition is likely, just that it signifies the only way for human civilisation to operate viably on our finite planet. Fortunately, there are many social and ecological reasons to believe that this transition is in the interests of humanity, both rich and poor, but this requires reimagining the good life beyond consumer culture and embracing ways of living that are outwardly simple, but inwardly rich. Although we will surely raise more questions than we can answer, this chapter seeks to provide more detail on this vision of a just and sustainable society and briefly highlight the implications this perspective has on questions of transition strategy.

The global predicament

It is important to indicate briefly why the reductions in resource and energy use must be dramatic and far greater than most people appreciate. Only then can an adequate response be formulated. Consider the following outline of the global predicament from a 'limits to growth' perspective.

The commonly cited 'Ecological Footprint' index shows that to provide the average Australian with food, settlement area, water, and energy takes about 7gha of productive land (Global Footprint Network, 2018). If by 2050 the expected 9.8 billion people were to have risen to the present 'living standard' in Australia, and the planet's amount of productive land remains the same as it is today (which is doubtful), then the amount available per capita would be in the order of 1.25 gha. In other words, Australians today are making ecological demands per capita that are about six times what would be possible for all people to make. It follows that the impacts of affluent living standards would need to be reduced by more than 80 per cent to meet the sustainability criteria of the Ecological Footprint analysis.[2]

---

2 Although the Ecological Footprint metric is an imperfect measure of planetary demand, many critics think it understates the levels of impact, so for present purposes it can be considered a conservative measure of ecological impact and overshoot.

Wiedmann, Schandl, and Moran (2015) state an even more striking conclusion: the per person consumption of the ten highest iron ore- and aluminum-consuming nations is around 80 times that of all the rest. On a finite planet facing ecological limits, these disparities in consumption and impacts are plainly unjust and unsustainable, and they begin to indicate the degree of reductions needed to achieve sustainability and distributive equity. Moreover, what if humanity leaves a fair share of the planet for other species? The 'Living Planet Report 2018' (WWF, 2018) concludes that between 1970 and the present, the populations of vertebrate species have declined on average by 60 per cent due to human economic activity, leading some writers to speak of the 'Sixth Great Extinction'.

However, the problem of ecological overshoot is far more disturbing when we consider the fundamental commitment (even by rich nations) to ceaseless *growth* in production, consumption, trade, investment, 'living standards', wealth, and GDP. If the Australian economy continues to grow by 3 per cent p.a. and by 2050 the global population of 9.8 billion people achieved the same levels of GDP per capita, then total world economic output would be around 18 times the present amount. The Global Footprint Network (2018) finds that the *present* global economy already overshoots sustainable impacts by 70 per cent, and yet the dominant economic paradigm is aiming to grow economic output many times over coming years and decades. This is, as Edward Abbey once said, 'the ideology of the cancer cell'.

Rejection of the limits to growth position is usually based on the belief that technical advance will deal with the associated problems by way of 'decoupling'; that is, by enabling continued increase in production and consumption globally while bringing environmental impacts down to sustainable levels (e.g., Breakthrough Institute, 2015). It is not difficult to show the extreme implausibility of this 'technofix' approach. The above figures show the enormity of the reductions that would be required. For the growth economy to operate within the sustainable carrying capacity of the planet and leave a share of the planet for other species, impact rates per unit of GDP would arguably have to be cut by 90 per cent or more by 2050.

What makes the decoupling vision even more implausible is that despite decades of extraordinary technological advance, global energy and resource use continue to rise steadily, not decline as the decoupling theory would imply. A litany of studies on decoupling show that efficiency gains within a globally growing economy have not led to, and will not lead to, reduced overall impacts, let alone reduce them sufficiently to achieve sustainability (Wiedmann et al., 2015; Alexander, 2015; Ward et al., 2016; Trainer, 2016a).

If economists are serious about designing a sustainable economy that could work well for all people (and species), not just for a minority in the highly developed regions of the world, then the severity of this 'limits to growth' perspective must be central in their accounts. It is wrong and indeed dangerous to assume the legitimacy of high-impact modes of living that could not possibly be shared by all people. However, presently ever-rising GDP per capita is the goal to which most people and all nations aspire, puffed up by fantasies of sufficient decoupling. This 'green growth' approach is a recipe for ecological and thus humanitarian disaster. Whether we like it or not, humanity will have to deal with the implications of living in an age of pressing ecological limits.

Thus, the essential conclusion to be drawn from the limits to growth position is that the magnitude of ecological overshoot is so great that a transition to a sustainable society will require significant 'degrowth' in the rich world to levels of per capita resource use that are likely to be in the region of one-tenth of present Australian per capita levels. Across the political spectrum, little attention has been given to the profound implications of this for social, economic, or political theory and practice (Trainer, 2019). Even some prominent figures in the schools of post-growth and steady state economics do not seem to appreciate what this degree of downshifting means in terms of the economics of sustainability, especially when we are talking about timescales needed to avoid dangerous climate change (see Anderson, 2015).

Vision and basic principles of the Simpler Way

The following sections outline in general terms the kind of economy that we argue must be adopted in view of the limits to growth predicament. Few existing proposals for a new economy deal satisfactorily or explicitly, if at all, with the essential themes, principles, and implications deriving from the need to reduce impacts of affluent living standards by 90 per cent or more. Even within the degrowth, eco-socialist, and related movements there is a general failure to grasp the enormity of the consequences that follow if the limits to growth analysis and its implications are accepted.

Achieving the reductions necessary will include huge demand-side reductions (consuming less and differently) as well as significant efficiency gains (cleaner production), but primarily the task is to create a Simpler Way society that transcends the growth paradigm and systemically supports ways of living based on frugal but sufficient material living standards. Sometimes the rejection of growth economics or consumerist lifestyles are broadly stated by those who appreciate the limits to growth predicament, but rarely is the alternative form of economy this implies unpacked in any detail. This is problematic, because without a relatively clear vision of where we need to end up, our theories of transition cannot know *to where* we must transition.

Globalised production and distribution vs. the Simpler Way

In order to begin unpacking our vision of an alternative society, consider a simple example of egg production, from which broader lessons can be derived. A study by Trainer, Malik, and Lenzen (2018) presents an analysis comparing the supply of eggs via the normal industrial / supermarket path with a local cooperative supply path. The dollar and energy costs of the former were found to be in the order of 50 to 200 times larger than those of the latter. Such achievements are due to the smallness of scale, proximity, self-sufficiency, cooperation, and integration of communities, which makes it possible to totally eliminate many costly inputs, to recycle 'wastes', to benefit from 'co-products', and to administer via spontaneous and informal social interaction.

For instance, the typical supermarket egg has vast and complex global supply chains involving distant shipping fleets, agribusiness, trucking and thus roads and petroleum, warehousing, chemicals for disease control, infrastructures, supermarkets, storage, packaging, marketing, legal services, the finance, advertising and insurance industries, waste removal and dumping, computers, a commuting workforce, and expensively trained personnel. It also involves damage to ecosystems, especially via carbon emissions and agribusiness effects including the non-return of nutrients to soils.

However, eggs supplied via worker cooperatives within integrated settlements based on local production can avoid almost all these costs, while enabling immediate use of all 'wastes'. Permaculture design ensures that elements in a system are highly self-maintaining, perform many functions at the same time, and that all 'wastes' become valued resources (Holmgren, 2018). For instance, recycling of kitchen scraps along with free ranging can meet total poultry nutrient needs. Poultry and other animal manures, including human, can be directly fed into nearby methane digesters or compost heaps, thereby eliminating the need for inputs to village food production from the fertiliser industry. Essentially no transport is required, given local production is geared to meeting local needs, using mostly local resources. Poultry perform multiple functions automatically, including providing meat, fertilising orchards, cleaning up garden beds and fruit fly lavae, producing the next generation of chicks, and maintaining fire breaks. Monitoring and maintenance of systems can be totally informal, via spontaneous discussion and action within the community. In addition, cooperative care of poultry and other animals adds to amenity and leisure resources and facilitates community bonding.

This example is indicative of how localised modes of production, supply, and consumption can radically reduce energy and resources demands, while providing various benefits (e.g., healthier food, better treatment of animals, enjoyable production, etc.). The same approach can be applied to most other domains of social and economic life, including other food items, dwelling construction, clothing supply, many services, as well as providing leisure, entertainment, and education. The 'Remaking Settlements' study (Trainer, 2016b) explores the potential when applied to an outer suburb of Sydney, finding that radical restructuring might enable almost all food needs to be met within the suburb while enabling many other material and social benefits. These include eliminating unemployment, avoiding the need for a sewer system, dramatically reducing the need for transport for work and income, and creating thousands of person-hours of community improvement per week via voluntary working bees and committees.

The foregoing discussion has been of theoretical possibilities, but the claims are supported by evidence from actual communities functioning along the lines being advocated. Lockyer's (2017) study of the Dancing Rabbit Eco-village in Missouri found the following per capita use rates compared with national US averages. Car use, 8 per cent; distance driven, 10 per cent; liquid fuel use, 6 per cent; solid waste generated, 18 per cent; proportion of solid waste recycled on site, 34 per cent; electricity use 18 per cent, with three times as much electricity sent to the grid as is used; water use, 23 per cent, with two-thirds of this collected from village roofs. Furthermore, the community's quality of life indicators align with the evidence from other studies of eco-villages; e.g., 81 per cent of respondents rate happiness with life situation at 7/10 or better, and almost all say life had improved since moving to the community. (For similar findings see Grinde et al., 2017; Alexander and Ussher, 2012.) Another way of putting these findings is that it takes remarkably little in the way of monetary or resource expenditure to ensure a highly satisfying lifestyle, if communities accept materially simple ways and are organised to this end. A materially simple life can be a spiritually richer life. (For further supporting argument and evidence, see Trainer 2016b; 2013.) We argue that a just and sustainable society cannot be achieved unless these highly communal, localised, self-sufficient, and frugal ways become the norm.

Implications for specific aspects of the Simpler Way economy

The following sub-sections briefly sketch various ways that sectors of an integrated Simpler Way economy could function to yield high levels of sustainability, economic justice, and quality of life. It focuses primarily on aspects of the neighbourhood and town levels. Implications for the national and international levels are briefly considered later.

The local geography of the economy

Dealing adequately with the dual challenges of climate change and fossil energy depletion implies significantly reducing energy demand compared to current levels in the rich nations and meeting that reduced demand with renewables (Alexander and Floyd, 2018). Given the close connection between energy and economy, an energy descent future implies moving away from the energy-intensive modes of globalised production and distribution and toward highly local production, using mostly local resources.

Given the commitment to materially simple lifestyles and to simplified local supply systems, far less would need to be produced than at present (in rich nations) and most of the goods and services one would need in everyday life would come from within at most a few kilometres of where one lived. Most people could get to work on foot or on a bicycle, although a few would need to travel further, mostly in buses or trains powered by electricity or biofuels (the greatly reduced distances and regularity of travel would make these modes financially and ecologically affordable). Community vehicles might be available for occasional use when needed (e.g., moving bricks or timber to a construction site). Every household owning a private automobile, even if electric, has no place in a sustainable economy (Alexander and Gleeson, 2019). Because very little transport would be needed, many roads and car parks could be dug up or converted to different uses, significantly increasing space in cities for local gardens, orchards, forests or woodlots, animal pens, or fish ponds. Very little air travel would be needed.

Economic self-sufficiency (or rather collective sufficiency) should be seen in terms of concentric circles. In the centre will be the most important economic and social unit of all, the highly productive and highly self-sufficient household (see Holmgren, 2018; Trainer, 2016b). Even in the present economy more than half the work done takes place there, although most of it is unpaid. The household would be embedded within the neighbourhood economy, involving free goods from commons, sharing/gifting surpluses, mutual assistance, cooperatives, swapping and bartering, working bees and committees, and including many small enterprises, co-operatives, and household hobby production.

The next circles out would include the suburb, and then the town or city (Alexander and Gleeson, 2019). Ideally the area surrounding the settlement would contain its dairy, timber plantation, grain and grazing lands. Several towns might be found within a region, maybe 10 km across, including a few factories producing items such as fridges, bicycles, and radios for local use and for export to the wider economy. As noted further below, few resources or commodities would need to come from the state and national economic sectors, and very little from overseas, perhaps only items such as high tech medical or computer equipment or resources needed for essential energy infrastructure (e.g., solar panels). There would need to be no reduction in research and development of appropriate technology in a Simpler Way society, since so many resources would be saved by avoiding wasteful consumption and production. For example, there would be little need for marketing expenditure in a Simpler Way society, so the trillion dollars per annum currently spent on advertising (WARC, 2016) could be redirected to better uses, such as funding the transition to renewable energy. No effort would be made to persuade people to purchase and consume.

Sectors of the new economy

One of the (overlapping) sectors of the new economy would still use money. It could include a large domain in which market forces were allowed to operate (although in the long-term future we might decide we do not need the market.) One sector would be fully planned and under participatory social control (e.g., for provision of water, energy, housing, and health care). One would involve non-profit community cooperatives. One large sector would not involve money. It would include household production, barter arrangements, mutual aid, working bees, cooperatives, the gifting of surpluses, and free goods from the commons.

The commons would be extensive, including the public fruit and nut orchards, clay pits, fish ponds, herb patches, woodlots, and various supply systems, for instance via poultry, honey, and fish farming cooperatives. Many buildings or constructions such as community centres, craft rooms, store sheds, and windmills, and especially neighbourhood workshops, would be constructed and managed as community property. As many of these as needed would be crammed into space created by the elimination of most roads and car parks, and also located just outside settled areas.

Probably the largest sector would be made up of small privately-owned firms and farms. These would best be thought of as the tools which people use to make their social contribution and draw a stable, sufficient income via a secure livelihood. They would not be capitalist enterprises. They would not involve investment of capital by profit-seeking individuals or organisations. Their value would be in giving many families and small groups the freedom to enjoy owning their venture and exercising their skills, and running it in the way they wished. Privately owned firms would be required to keep within socially determined guidelines monitored by the town assembly.

The zero-growth economy we are describing would automatically eliminate almost all the financial sector, primarily because, as few realise, interest could no longer be charged on loans. If a loan is to be repaid plus interest the borrower must create more 'value' than was borrowed, meaning there will be economic growth. Without interest-bearing loans rich people could no longer receive large incomes from 'investments', and without having to do any work for them. Banks would therefore do little more than hold savings and lend some of them out for an administrative fee. A corollary is that banks would no longer create money via the fractional reserve system. In a zero-growth economy no new money needs to be created and put into circulation.

It should therefore come as no surprise that the economy being described is one in which there is no aggregate growth, and all important functions are decided by rational social decisions. Cooperation not competition is the supreme principle, there is no interest paid, and little is left to market forces. In short, a degrowth transition to a Simpler Way society is not compatible with a capitalist economy.

The craft economy

Many goods would be produced in households and very small firms by artisan producers. The main reason for this is that artisan or craft production is enjoyable; producing in factories is not. Given that the volume of production in a frugal degrowth economy would be far lower than it is now, people who delight in making pottery, furniture, clothing, toys etc. might provide most of the goods the community needs.

Production of most of these goods would only need to replace breakages and wear, meaning production would not need to meet the shifting needs of fashion. It would make sense for some items to be mass-produced in factories, such as work shoes and boots. Automated corporations can produce much more 'cheaply', but the required scale necessitates long-distance transport of inputs and finished goods, and provides little or no satisfaction for workers. Living simply and obtaining many things without the need for money makes it more likely that we would be happy to pay more for well-made and durable goods.

Social control of the economy

There cannot be a satisfactory economy unless there is the collective power to make sure that the things produced are those that should be produced, so that all people have their needs met, social cohesion and morale are kept in good condition, the environment is cared for, and development is socially desirable. A free enterprise or capitalist economy will not do these things. Markets ignore need, justice, morality, social benefit, and ecological values. They can do no other because they allocate scarce things according to 'effective demand', i.e., those who offer to pay more money for an item get it. Millions of people die every year not due to scarcity of resources but because the provision of food and water is determined by what will maximise the profits of those who supply them. Markets therefore are incapable of doing anything other than allocating scarce resources to the rich and developing the most profitable industries as distinct from those that are most needed.

Polanyi (1944) was among those who have stressed this fundamental mistake in the economy. In ancient and in medieval times all one's behaviour was expected to be governed by a general moral code, which for instance prohibited taking advantage of another person's misfortune. But Polanyi and others have pointed out that with the advent of capitalism the rules governing economic behaviour became separated from the general code, enabling entrepreneurs to ruin their competitors or pounce on a fire sale, and to concern themselves only with whether or not monetary benefits to themselves could be secured. Damage caused to others or to society or to ecosystems need no longer be considered. Polanyi pointed out that unless 'market forces' were kept under social control, society and the environment would eventually be destroyed. That explains most of what is wrong with the world today.

Therefore, especially in a context of very scarce resources, desirable outcomes will not be possible unless the main economic functions are under social control, that is, determined by careful discussion and deliberate, rational decision making and collectively defined regulation. However, it will be emphasised below that this must be carried out by participatory democratic means, not by centralised bureaucracies.

The town or suburb, through informal deliberations and committees, and ultimately its local assemblies, must be in control of shaping the local economy. The citizens will be clearly aware that their fate depends on whether or not their settlement works well and has established the arrangements that enable it to provide basic necessities. If some needs are not being met then the town will realise that it must take action, for instance set up a cooperative to plug the gap. If private enterprise and the market can meet the need then the town would be relieved not to have to deal with the problem. Thus, although the town council or committee would have a lot to attend to, it would be wise to take a minimalist approach, dealing with and fixing only those things that need attention.

The over-riding concerns would be to maximise town self-sufficiency and thus resilience, and to ensure that many essential needs are provided for as locally as possible, using local resources. Thus the town must work out how to make sure that everybody has a livelihood, a way of making a valued contribution through enjoyable productive activity. There is no excuse for unemployment; that is only found in deeply flawed societies. There is much to do and many cooperatives and working bees needing people. Indeed, the main form of tax payment would be giving time to the working bees building and maintaining local infrastructures, harvesting from the commons, and providing many services. Only a little tax in the form of money would be needed to pay for maintenance of town systems and for national government revenue.

Significant monetary inequality would cease to be an issue. It would be of no consequence whether or not one had a high income or great monetary wealth, and there would be little or no point in seeking these. One's 'wealth' – the richness of one's life – would depend primarily on one's community resources and all would have equal access to these.

Only if the town has control over its own fate can decisions take into account all the relevant considerations and prevent outcomes being determined solely by what will maximise monetary returns to those with money to spend or invest. Often it will be obvious that considerations such as equity, environment, aesthetics, and the public good should outweigh those that a market system would focus on.

How will the control be exercised?

Few if any would want the social control and regulation of the economy to be exercised by large, authoritarian, centralised state bureaucracies, but in the economy under discussion that is not only avoidable, it is impossible. In a world of very limited resources, a sustainable society will have to be made up mostly of many small and highly self-sufficient and self-governing community economies. These will have to be run as participatory democracies – they cannot be run effectively any other way. They will not make viable decisions unless people familiar with the situation make those decisions. There will be few paid bureaucrats or councils, because in a world of scarce resources not much paid government will be affordable. Therefore, most policy formation and management of 'public works' will have to be carried out by local citizens, by committees and town assemblies, and by voluntary working bees. The right decisions for the town will not be made or implemented unless arrived at and supported by conscientious citizens. Fortunately the small and simplified economies which do not grow and are largely cooperative will make it easier for the social control to be exercised via participatory democratic processes; that is, by spontaneous informal discussion leading to decisions by town assemblies.

Many and possibly most of the economic activities would not need any formal control. Informal discussion would sort out whether too many tomatoes were planted last year. In addition, the many committees would study and advise on issues such as the best apple varieties to plant when the parking lot is dug up. Adjustments, repairs, and research would primarily be carried out spontaneously by citizens who knew their fate depended on good maintenance of systems and who enjoyed keeping their town in good shape. These are the kinds of 'administrative' practices that make many eco-villages function well without paid politicians or bureaucrats.

If it became clear that, for instance, there were more bakeries than was sensible, the community would have to work out the best solution for all concerned. This might include helping some people to transfer to other necessary activities. No firm would be allowed to go bankrupt; the town needs to look after all its members and make good use of all its resources. It would have its own bank and 'business incubator', i.e., a panel of experienced advisers, and its working bees would help firms to set up or modify premises. All would understand that their town could not thrive unless all take collective responsibility for making sure that it does, and unless it looks after everyone. Thus, there would be a profoundly different ethos compared with today; it would be seen as 'our economy' – ours to keep in good shape and to provide for the community.

Obviously there would be a need to think carefully about desirable limits to social control, and to minimise interference with freedoms. Ideally the concern would be to take remedial action only where social needs were not being met. This would mostly be a matter of plugging gaps rather than blocking or coercing. Two factors would make the control task easier: firstly, the economy would not be complex; and secondly, it would be driven not by profit or market forces but by citizens who prioritised the common good.

Work

The corollary of radical economic degrowth is that far less work and production would take place, especially in the formal economy, and many of the things that were needed would be produced in far less resource-expensive ways. For example, food supply would require little work to produce trucks to bring food to towns. As has been explained, there would be no involuntary unemployment. The town would make sure that all who wanted work had a share of the work that needed doing.

Because the amount of work to be done for money would be dramatically reduced, most people might only need to do work one or two days per week, although much of their time would be going into productive use within the household, commons, and working bees and committees. Some people, such as professionals, could choose to work full time for money, perhaps paying more montetary tax than those who paid by working bee contributions.

Consumer-capitalist society has destroyed work. For most it is more or less a burden that has to be endured. It is hardly fulfilling or a source of anything valuable aside from the pay packet. In the new economy, alienation as Marx described it would be largely eliminated. Indeed, it could be argued that 'work' as such could easily be totally eliminated in a Simpler Way society. In eco-villages, members generally produce via their enjoyable small farm or craft activities and contributions to working bees, which are usually experienced as forms of leisure activity. Potters see their products benefiting and being appreciated by others. Working bees can turn work that would be boring or otherwise unpleasant in capitalist society into enjoyable and socially bonding festivals. Thus the distinction between work and play might completely disappear. People would generally be more active in their working lives, contributing to fitness and health and therefore minimising need for expensive healthcare. It is notable that Cubans have better health than citizens of the US, despite spending around one tenth on healthcare (O'Hanlon and Harvey, 2017).

The economy beyond the town or suburb

The foregoing discussion has focused on the local economy, arguing that in a resource-scare world this must be the new basic economic unit if per capita impacts are to be reduced to sustainable levels. National and international economies will have a necessary role but they will be far smaller than at present and of much less significance. Their main function will be to enable the local economies to thrive, by providing those relatively few things they need but cannot conveniently produce in their local bioregion.

Despite the productive power of the local economy there will always be a relatively small number of important items the towns cannot produce for themselves, and some of these will have to come from large industries far away. How then might economic systems beyond the town level be organised? The basic concept must be the location within or close to towns of some small capacity to produce items for export to other towns within the national economy. For instance, it is not feasible for each town to produce its own refrigerators, so a few towns would specialise in the production of these or of components, making them available for purchase by other towns, thereby earning the export income needed to purchase similar items from the national economy.

The main economic role of the (remnant, small) 'state' will be to organise the distribution and functioning of these industries, to ensure that all towns have the capacity to earn sufficient income from their exports into the national economy to pay for their purchases from it. It is unlikely that it would make sense for these exporting firms to be other than town cooperatives. The state and national governments would also have to attend to provision of infrastructures and systems enabling these supply chains, such as roads and railway networks, and finance, insurance, and legal systems.

Some firms at this level would be large, such as those producing steel, cement, and railway equipment. In a zero-growth economy with a very small GDP it is not clear why it would make sense for these firms to be privately owned. This would mean that issues to do with investment, innovation, efficiency, restructuring etc. would have to be dealt with via public ownership and management; i.e., some form of socialism.

What role for the state in the transition?

If enough communities manage to establish commitment to taking control of increasingly self-sufficient and self-managed local economies, then before long their dependence on the national economy for those few but crucial inputs will force them to demand and then initiate radical change in that economy. They will insist that governments focus their attention on restructuring the national economy so that its primary role is to make sure the towns and settlements can get the basic inputs they must have but can't produce for themselves. If financial crises resurface in coming years, as is likely, national governments will be faced with the task of urgently enabling devastated workers and towns to grope toward local self-sufficiency, given that the industries they used to work in would have collapsed and could not be restored. Thus national governments will be forced to gear available national productive capacity to building the required alternative local structures and systems, including especially the training and demonstration facilities.

Central governments would quickly realise that they cannot implement the required changes. They could not construct or run viable local economies. The right decisions can only be made and implemented by people who understand their specific conditions and have the necessary ideas, attitudes, social cohesion, and morale.

Before long this pressure is likely to shift from submitting requests to the state to making demands on it, and then to taking increasing control of it. There will be increasing insistence that frivolous industries must be phased out so that scarce resources can be devoted to meeting fundamental town and regional needs. Meanwhile towns will be driven by necessity to bypass the centre and take initiatives such as setting up their own farms, energy supplies, and factories, thus taking various functions out of the hands of the state. It will be increasingly recognised that the local level is the only one where the right decisions for highly self-sufficient communities can be made. As communities become familiar with taking control of their own fate, they will be less inclined to allow the centre to continue calling the shots.

The final step would be the grass roots pushing their way into the centre; that is, taking direct control over the remaining state functions through the classic anarchist mechanisms whereby federations and delegations thrash out policy proposals which are brought back down to the town assembly level for endorsement. The increasing interest now in Citizen Initiated Referenda indicates how this is feasible. Some city budgets are now worked out by the CIR process. One of its merits is that decisions are not made, handed down, and enforced from the top, so they are more likely to be widely accepted. The ultimate goal is to make sure that endorsement is carried out at the level of the town assemblies, and thus that representative government is replaced by direct participatory government.

Accordingly, a Simpler Way society would not be an eco-socialist economy, if that means a centrally planned society governed by a strong centralised state. As has been detailed, a Simpler Way society would have to involve thoroughly participatory democratic decision making, spontaneity, subsidiarity, and rejection of hierarchy and professional rulers. Issues beyond the town level would be handled by sending delegates to meetings within federations. And the basic transitional strategy would be 'prefiguring' the new world within the shell of the old. This economy can therefore be described as eco-anarchist.

Is all this too unrealistic?

The common response to this vision is that it is far too utopian; that it fails to recognise that humans are not capable of making such an alternative society work. This response reveals a serious misunderstanding. The argument has not been that this economy is going to be achieved, or that it is likely to be achieved. It is quite unlikely to be achieved. The argument has been that we had better try very hard to achieve it, because whether we like it or not, there is no other way to defuse the major global problems now threatening to destroy us.

Clearly the ways of living outlined in this chapter would not work in mainstream society today, because they require quite different attitudes and values to those predominant now. In consumer-capitalist society most people are out to maximise their self-interest, see nothing wrong with competitive systems in which they might be one of the winners while many end up with less than enough, and would oppose the enlightened social regulation and restraint needed to ensure satisfactory outcomes for all. It is essential to realise that a satisfactory society cannot be designed for such people. Most make the mistaken assumption that we can have a peaceful, sustainable, and just world while we all go on living affluently and competitively and continually striving to increase our 'living standards' and GDP without limit. However, these are the core behaviours and goals that are causing global problems.

But are these dispositions too deeply entrenched to alter? An important feature of The Simpler Way is that while it *requires* values like moderation, frugality, sharing, and cooperation, it also *rewards* them. A satisfactory life in a thriving community will not be possible unless there is cooperation and willing contribution and concern for the common good, but it will also be a situation in which those values and practices will be enjoyable. If the new ways can be established they will tend to be self-reinforcing. This suggests that, for those people who accept the general vision outlined in this paper, one of the primary goals is to help develop the social consciousness and understandings required for a sustainable economy to emerge. Until that consciousness emerges, the necessary system change to a Simpler Way society will not emerge. Thus what is required is essentially a cultural revolution, which would create the conditions needed to drive the necessary economic and political revolutions.

Conclusion

There has been insufficient recognition of the way all the major global problems derive primarily from having exceeded the sustainable limits to growth. For instance, the damage being inflicted on ecosystems can only increase unless we move to lifestyles and systems involving far lower per capita consumption than we are familiar with in the rich world. The soon to be 7+ billion people living in poorer countries can only receive a fair share of the planet's resources if those living in the rich countries reduce their consumption dramatically. Most armed conflict is to do with fierce competition to secure scarce resources and markets, meaning that if we insist on remaining affluent we will need to remain heavily armed. And the social cohesion and quality of life even in the richest countries will continue to deteriorate. These problems cannot be defused unless simper lifestyles and systems are willingly embraced.

Several analysts have stressed the fragile house-of-cards nature of the global economy in our age of financial and ecological limits (see, for e.g., Korowicz, 2012; Morgan, 2013; Greer, 2008). Above all is its dependence on debt, now in excess of $250 trillion, three or more times global GDP and far higher than before the GFC. These considerations align with Marx's fundamental insight regarding the self-destructive contradictions built into the foundations of capitalism, even though he did not clearly envisage its resource limits.

In an oil dependent economy, it is highly likely that if the yield from shale oil production falters in the next decade or so a global debt crash of unprecedented proportions will suddenly impact. It might not be the final GFC; some envisage partial recovery initiating a 'bumpy road down' or a slow 'catabolic collapse' (Greer, 2008). But others foresee the end of civilisation and the die-off of billions. What is to be hoped for is a 'Goldilocks depression' that falls short of catastrophic breakdown but is serious enough to jolt large numbers into recognising that the growth and greed system is not going to provide for them.

From the Simpler Way perspective little can be done to influence that trajectory. Strategically it is doubtful whether striving to reform consumer-capitalist society is a good investment of time and resources. It is locked on a suicidal path that its institutions and culture are incapable of recognising let alone altering. What is to be done instead is to work to prepare for the building of sensible systems as the existing system continues its deterioration. This involves what the anarchists call 'prefiguring' – that is, building here-and-now the kinds of local lifestyles and systems sketched in the earlier sections of this paper. Many are striving to develop those ways within the voluntary simplicity, eco-village, permaculture, and Transition Towns movements. A smooth or successful transition is very unlikely, but these movements currently embody the most coherent strategy for working toward a resilient landing.

References

Alexander, S. 2015. *Prosperous Descent: Crisis as Opportunity in an Age of Limits*. Melbourne: Simplicity Institute.

Alexander, S. and Floyd, J. 2018. *Carbon Civilisation and the Energy Descent Future: Life Beyond this Brief Anomaly*. Melbourne: Simplicity Institute.

Alexander, S. and Gleeson, B. 2019. *Degrowth in the Suburbs: A Radical Urban Imaginary*. Singapore: Palgrave Macmillan.

Alexander, S. and Ussher, S. 2012. 'The Voluntary Simplicity Movement: A Multi-National Survey Analysis in Theoretical Context'. *Journal of Consumer Culture* 12(1): 66–88.

Anderson, K. 2015. 'Duality in Climate Science'. *Nature Geoscience* 9: 898–90.

Breakthrough Institute. 2015. *An Ecomodernist Manifesto*. Available at: http://www.ecomodernism.org/ (accessed 10 February 2019).

Ehrlich, P. and Ehrlich, A. 2013. 'Can Collapse of Global Civilization be avoided?' *Proceedings of the Royal Society B*. 280(1754). Available at: https://royalsocietypublishing.org/doi/full/10.1098/rspb.2012.2845 (accessed 10 February 2019).

Global Footprint Network. 2018. 'National Footprint Accounts 2018'. Available at: http://data.footprintnetwork.org/#/ (10 February 2019).

Greer, J.M. 2008. *The Long Descent: A User's Guide to the End of Industrial Civilisation*. Gabriola Island: New Society Publishers.

Grinde, B. et al. 2017. 'Quality of Life in Intentional Communities'. *Social Indicators Research* 137(2): 625–640.

Hickel, J. 2017. *The Great Divide: A Brief Guide to Global Inequality and its Solutions*. London: William Heinemann.

Holmgren, D. 2018. *RetroSuburbia: The Downshifter's Guide to a Resilient Future*. Hepburn Springs: Melliodora Publishing.

Korowicz, D. 2012. 'Trade Off: Financial System Supply-Chain Cross Contagion – A Study in Global Systemic Collapse'. *Feasta* (30 June, 2012). Available at: http://www.feasta.org/wp-content/uploads/2012/10/Trade_Off_Korowicz.pdf (accessed 10 February 2019).

Lane, R. 2000. *The Loss of Happiness in Market Democracies*. New Haven, CT: Yale University Press.

Lockyer, J. 2017. 'Community, Commons, and Degrowth at Dancing Rabbit Ecovillage'. *Journal of Political Ecology*, 24(1): 519–542.

9. The Simpler Way: Envisioning a sustainable society in an age of limits

Morgan, T. 2013. *Perfect Storm: Energy, Finance, and the End of Growth.* Tullet Prebon Report, Strategy Insights (Issue 9). Available at: https://ftalphaville-cdn.ft.com/wp-content/uploads/2013/01/Perfect-Storm-LR.pdf (accessed 10 February 2019).

O'Hanlon, C. and Harvey, M. 2017. 'Doing More with Less: Lessons from Cuba's Health Care System'. *Georgetown Journal of International Affairs* (2 October 2017). Available at: https://www.georgetownjournalofinternationalaffairs.org/online-edition/2017/10/2/doing-more-with-less-lessons-from-cubas-healthcare-system (accessed 10 February 2019).

Polanyi, K. 1944. *The Great Transformation.* New York: Farrer and Rinehart.

Steffen, W. et al. 2015. 'The Trajectory of the Anthropocene: The Great Acceleration'. *The Anthropocene Review* 2(1): 81–98.

Trainer, T. 2010. *Transition to a Sustainable and Just Society.* Sydney: Envirobook.

Trainer, T. 2013. 'Your Delightful Day: The Benefits of Life in the Simpler Way'. *Simplicity Institute Report 13b*:1–8.

Trainer, T. 2016a. 'Another Reason Why a Steady-State Economy will not be a Capitalist Economy'. *Real-World Economics Review*, 76: 55–64.

Trainer, T. 2016b. 'Remaking Settlements: The Potential Cost Reductions Enabled by the Simpler Way'. Available at: http://thesimplerway.info/RemakingSettlements.htm (accessed 10 February 2019).

Trainer, T. 2019. 'Entering the Era of Limits and Scarcity: The Radical Implications for Social Theory'. *Journal of Political Ecology*, 26(1): 1–18.

Trainer, T., Malik, A., and Lenzen, M. 2018. 'Comparing the monetary, resource and ecological costs of industrial and Simpler Way local production: Consider egg supply'. Working paper available at: http://thesimplerway.info/Eggs.html (accessed 15 February 2019).

WARC. 2016. 'Global Marketing Spend to Hit $1tr'. Available at: https://www.warc.com/NewsAndOpinion/News/Global_marketing_spend_to_hit_1tr/37178 (accessed 10 February 2019).

Ward, J. et al. 2016. 'Is Decoupling GDP Growth from Environmental Impact Possible?' *PLOS One* 11(10): e0164733. Available at: http://dx.doi.org/10.1371/journal.pone.0164733 (accessed 10 February 2019).

Wiedmann, T., Schandl, H., and Moran, D. 2015. 'The Footprint of Using Metals: New Metrics of Consumption and Productivity'. *Environmental Economics and Policy Studies*, 17(3): 369–388.

Wiedmann, T. et al. 2015. 'The Material Footprint of Nations'. *PNAS* 112(20), pp. 6271–6276.

WWF. 2018. 'Living Planet Report 2018'. Available at: https://wwf.panda.org/knowledge_hub/all_publications/living_planet_report_2018/ (accessed 10 February 2019).

Chapter 10

The search for freedom, sustainability, and economic security: Henry David Thoreau as tiny house pioneer[1]

Introduction

If there is one figure in history who evokes the image of living in a tiny house more than any other, surely it is Henry David Thoreau (1817–1862). A pioneering environmentalist and passionate advocate of self-reliance and voluntary simplicity, Thoreau is well known as a lover of nature and author of the unclassifiable masterpiece *Walden, or, Life in the Woods* (in Bode, 1982). He is also widely recognised as inspiring Gandhi, Martin Luther King, Jr., and indeed an entire tradition of civil disobedience, with his landmark essay 'Resistance to Civil Government' (in Bode, 1982). But more than anything else, Thoreau is remembered as the young, romantic poet-philosopher who built himself a small cabin in the woods on the shores of Walden Pond, in which he lived for two years and two months, before returning to his hometown of Concord, Massachusetts, to live out his days as a 'sojourner in civilized life' (Bode, 1982: 258).[2]

In this chapter we wish to return to Thoreau and re-examine his life and writings, in order to excavate the historical foundations of the contemporary Tiny House Movement. What was Thoreau's philosophy of life? How did he see the world? What drove him to exit his society and build himself a tiny house in the woods? And did his return to Concord after two years mean that his living experiment at Walden Pond was a failure? As we reflect on Thoreau's philosophy and consider the ways in which he justified his life decisions, a strong case can be made that the contemporary Tiny House Movement is a modern reflection of Thoreauvian struggles, questions, motivations, and ideals, even as the world has changed dramatically.

---

1 Originally published in *Ethical Perspectives* 26(4), 2019, pp 559–582, co-authored with Heather Shearer
2 Throughout this chapter, unless otherwise indicated, page numbers next to quotes relate to *The Portable Thoreau* (1982), edited by Carl Bode.

The 'contemporary' Tiny House Movement – which purportedly had its genesis in the Pacific northwest of the USA in the late 1990s – traces its roots back much further, to Thoreau and even earlier movements, such as minimalism and voluntary simplicity (Anson, 2014; Anson, 2017; Kilman, 2016; Mangold & Zschau, 2019). We will argue that at the centre of Thoreau's philosophy of life are the questions of freedom, sustainability, and economic security, and that grappling with these questions was what led Thoreau to build himself a tiny house. Based on personal involvement in the Tiny House Movement in Australia (Alexander, 2016) and ratified by the emerging empirical literature (Shearer and Burton, 2019; Penfold, Waitt, and McGuirk, 2018; Shearer, 2017), we contend that a very similar struggle for freedom, sustainability, and economic security lies at the heart of the Tiny House Movement today. The analysis begins by telling the story of Thoreau's life and reviewing his worldview in the hope of shedding some philosophical light on the historical roots of the contemporary Tiny House Movement. After this substantive statement, we then offer a review of the contemporary Tiny House Movement, drawing on our own quantitative and qualitative research in Australia, and explore the extent to which it can be understood as a reflection of Thoreauvian questions and impulses.

Crisis of vocation

We begin with a brief biographical sketch (see Bode, 1982; Walls, 2017) to highlight some of the pressures and circumstances that led to Thoreau undertaking his tiny house experiment out at Walden Pond.

Graduating from Harvard in 1837, Thoreau found himself facing a crisis of vocation. He had a passion for writing poetry, but his poetry, though often beautiful and inspired, was not a commodity that sold well in the market. Indeed, it did not sell at all. So, upon returning to his hometown of Concord after finishing his studies, the young Thoreau was confronted by those great economic questions all of us must face when trying to establish financial security and independence in a world of scarce resources: *How best to earn a living? How much time should one spend at it? How much does one need to live well and to be free?*

Aside from the fact that his poetry would not sell, there were certain expectations that attached to a Harvard graduate at the time, and being a poet was not one of them. It turned out a teaching vacancy soon arose in Concord, and Thoreau, no doubt swept along by parental and societal expectations, as well as economic need, applied for and was offered a teaching position at the town school. Though he applied himself to this job, within a month he was taken aside by a member of the school committee and reprimanded for not caning disruptive students, which was the school policy and apparently beyond negotiation. In protest to what he considered the absurdity of corporal punishment, Thoreau re-entered the classroom, randomly selected six students, administered to them a caning, then resigned.

With his principles intact (somewhat dubiously, perhaps) but without a job, Thoreau's crisis of vocation deepened. There was some temporary respite when he and his brother established their own Concord Academy, a private school which ran quite successfully for a couple of years. But by March 1941 the project was abandoned and the vocational crisis re-emerged, as he was not particularly drawn to teaching. Over the next few years, lacking any clear direction, Thoreau found himself periodically employed in a variety of miscellaneous roles, including labourer, pencil-maker, gardener and general handyman at the Emerson residence, tutor for Emerson's nephew, occasional lecturer, and editor. We review these details because our forthcoming literature review of the contemporary Tiny House Movement suggests that many people living in a tiny house today, or aspiring to, would sympathise with Thoreau's crisis of vocation, his economic insecurity, and the struggles he endured trying to find meaningful employment in a precarious job market. After all, if well-paid meaningful employment was easy to come by, and decent housing and access to land was affordable, the incentive to explore *alternative* ways of living would not be so pressing (Alexander and Baumann, 2019; Milkman, 2016).

Thus, for Thoreau, the economic problem of how to support himself was not yet solved. How was he to be free to follow his true calling as a poet but still earn a living? It is a question, perhaps, to which we can all relate, in our own way. Feeling that books and his formal education had failed him, Thoreau turned his attention to his contemporaries, the people of Concord, to see whether their lives could provide him with some insight into the art of living well, the art of freedom. His observations, however, far from showing him the way, instead gave rise to one of the most penetrating critiques of materialistic culture that has ever been laid down, one all the more piercing due to the fact that Thoreau was both a ruthless critic and a literary genius. Only by examining this critique can we understand what ultimately drove Thoreau out of his township and into the woods. Again, the relevance of Thoreau's critique to the consumerist cultures of our own day will not be hard to see.

Thoreau on materialistic culture

'Let us consider the way in which we spend our lives,' Thoreau began one of his essays, noting that since time was short he would 'leave out all the flattery, and retain all the criticism', (632) as was his way. 'What is it to be born free and not to live free?' (650) he asked his fellow citizens. 'Is it a freedom to be slaves, or a freedom to be free, of which we boast?' (ibid). America may have been free from political tyrants, but it was painfully clear to Thoreau that it was 'still the slave of an economical and moral tyrant' (ibid). A tyrant called Mammon.

This world is a place of 'incessant business', he lamented (632). He felt that 'It would be glorious to see mankind at leisure for once,' but there is 'nothing but work, work, work' (ibid). To be sure, Thoreau was not opposed to labour, industry, or enterprise, as such. His concern, rather, was that the ways by which money is acquired 'almost without exception lead downward' (643). And 'those services which the community will most readily pay for, it is most disagreeable to render' (634). Thus, 'It is not enough to [say] that you worked hard to get your gold. So does the Devil work hard' (640).

For these reasons Thoreau thought that to do anything merely for the sake of acquiring money or material superfluities was to be 'truly idle or worse' (634). The following passage states his position directly:

> If I should sell my forenoons and afternoons to society, as most appear to do, I am sure that for me there would be nothing left worth living for.... I wish to suggest that a man may be very industrious, and yet not spend his time well. There is no more fatal blunderer than he who consumes the greater part of his life getting his living (636).

But Thoreau saw his townsfolk labouring under this very mistake. 'It is a fool's life,' he asserted bluntly, 'as they will find when they get to the end of it, if not before' (261). He had travelled widely in Concord and everywhere, in shops, offices, and fields, the inhabitants seemed to him to be leading lives of 'quiet desperation' and doing penance in a thousand remarkable ways. 'The twelve labors of Hercules were trifling in comparison with those which my neighbors have undertaken; for they were only twelve, and had an end; but I could never see that these men slew or captured any monster or finished any labor' (260). Thoreau likened people's materialistic cravings to the heads of a hydra, noting that 'as soon as one head is crushed, two spring up' (ibid).

In short, Thoreau was telling his contemporaries that they had 'enough' but that they did not know it, and so were poor. Always wanting more luxuries and comforts and never content with less, he felt that they did not understand the meaning of 'economy', did not understand that the 'cost of a thing is the amount of... life which is required to be exchanged for it' (286). 'Most men,' he wrote, 'even in this comparatively free country, through mere ignorance or mistake, are so occupied with factitious cares and superfluously course labors of life that its finer fruits cannot be plucked by them' (261). By a 'seeming fate', there was 'no time to be anything but a machine'(ibid).

And for what? People's lives were being 'ploughed into the soil for compost' (ibid) just to obtain 'splendid houses' and 'finer and more abundant clothing... and the like'. But as Thoreau insisted, 'Superfluous wealth can buy superfluities only' (568). Indeed, he claimed that 'Most of the luxuries, and many of the so-called comforts of life, are not only not indispensable, but positive hindrances to the elevation of mankind' (269). Thoreau was astounded by how 'frivolous' people were with respect to their own lives, more concerned about accumulating nice things or climbing the social ladder than they were about their own destinies. We can imagine Thoreau being equally or even more critical of contemporary housing trends in places like the United States and Australia, where house sizes have grown to unprecedented levels (McKinlay, Baldwin and Stevens, 2019; Wotton, Skates, and Shutter, 2018), locking people into decades of labour to pay for them and demanding ever more resources to build them and fill them with stuff, and requiring ever more energy to heat and cool them due to their extravagant size (Kilman, 2016; Wotton, Skates, and Shutter, 2018). Likewise, Thoreau may well be horrified at the price of houses. Australian (and American) houses are not only some of the largest in the world, but also some of the most unaffordable; for example, Melbourne and Sydney in Australia regularly rank in the top five of the most unaffordable cities in the OECD (Cox and Pavletich, 2018; Pawson, Milligan and Yates, 2020).

Thoreau was living in a time of great economic transformation and for him the railroad was the emblem of industrialisation. He often spoke of it metaphorically, as a representation of the emerging economic system that was fast changing the face of America and indeed the world. 'We do not ride upon the railroad,' he asserted, 'it rides upon us' (345).

It appeared to Thoreau as if his neighbours had fallen into the common mode of living not because they preferred it to any other, but because they honestly thought there was no choice left. 'So thoroughly and sincerely are we compelled to live, reverencing our life, and denying the possibility of change. This is the only way, we say' (266). But Thoreau was not convinced. He was of the view that 'there are as many ways as there can be drawn radii from one center' (ibid). Even 'the life which men praise and regard as successful is but one kind,' and 'why should we exaggerate any one kind at the expense of the others?' (274). Forever the thoughtful non-conformist, Thoreau tended to believe that, 'What old people say you cannot do you try and find that you can,' and on that basis he boldly proposed that there should be, 'Old deeds for old people, and new deeds for new' (264).

It was time for Thoreau to begin his 'tiny house' living experiment at Walden Pond.

The Walden experiment

On Independence Day, 1845, a few days before his twenty-eighth birthday, Henry Thoreau left his town of Concord and went to live alone in the woods, on the shores of Walden Pond, a mile from any neighbour. He there built himself a modest cabin – a tiny house – and for two years and two months earned a simple living by the labour of his own hands. Although Thoreau's example is fairly questioned on the grounds of him being a relatively privileged and educated white man, living on land provided by Ralph Waldo Emerson, and sometimes relying on family and friends while espousing an individualistic philosophy of self-reliance (Solnit, 2013; Bode, 1982), Thoreau's example and writings remain a great inspiration and provocation to many, raising questions and challenges that many face today. While living at the pond Thoreau wrote, among other things, his masterpiece, *Walden*, which gives a philosophical, literary, and autobiographical account of his two-year stay. This is arguably the greatest statement ever made on the living strategy now variously known as 'voluntary simplicity', 'simple living', or 'downshifting'. It is, in a word, a philosophy of 'sufficiency' and we will see his central question can be summarised as: 'How much is enough?'

In the second chapter of *Walden*, entitled 'Where I Lived, and What I Lived For', Thoreau offers us an explanation for his exit from conventional society: 'I went to the woods because I wished to live deliberately, to front only the essential facts of life and see if I could not learn what they had to teach, and not, when I came to die, discover that I had not lived' (343). He 'did not wish to live what was not life,' he tells us, 'living is so dear'; nor did he wish to 'practice resignation, unless it was quite necessary' (ibid).

Elsewhere he said that his purpose in going to Walden Pond was to 'transact some private business with the fewest obstacles' (275). In one sense, this private business was simply to write in solitude, close to nature and away from distractions. In another sense, though closely related to the first, his private business was to solve, or at least better understand, the economic problem of how to be free in a world of scarce resources. Perhaps, Thoreau had decided, the best path was to reduce his material wants and live a simple life. Simplicity of life was to be his means to the elevation of purpose.

Thoreau had come to suspect that if one's trade were with the 'Celestial Empire' (ibid) – by which he meant, 'If your concerns are "higher" than merely getting and spending' – then very little is actually needed to live well and to be free, provided life is approached with the right attitude. 'Simplify, simplify' (344) was to become his refrain. A modest shelter from the elements should be fixture enough. Old clothes will do, will they not? Grow some of your own food and become more self-reliant.

This, in essence, was the method Thoreau put to the test at Walden Pond, by living simply and rejecting the division of labour. As far as possible he secured his own food, by growing beans, peas, corn, turnips, and potatoes, and occasionally fishing in the pond. He cut down some local trees, gathered some second-hand materials, and built himself a house with but one small room, and made some basic furniture. It was not much, but it was enough. And just enough was plenty. He did not wish to be chained to the economy, so he practiced self-reliance; he did not wish to be slave to artificial material desires, so he practiced self-discipline; and he did not wish to live what was not life, so he practiced self-culture.

The economic significance of Thoreau's life in the woods can only be understood if we always keep in mind what he was trying to accomplish there. We have seen that Thoreau, in the eight years between his graduation from Harvard and his excursion to the pond, struggled in vain to find an occupation which would not conflict with the activities that yielded his poems and essays. His options, it seemed, were either to make some compromises and pursue a different vocation – that is, to do something for which there was much more demand in the market – or else somehow find a way to become much less dependent on the market.

Thoreau was clearly terrified of falling into the ruts of tradition and conformity, of compromising his dreams and wasting life in the pursuit of luxuries or fine houses, as he saw so many of his contemporaries doing and which he considered to be 'not so sad as foolish' (275). He knew that he would not be able to pluck life's 'finer fruits' if he devoted too much of his time to the 'coarse labors of life', and so he set about lowering his denominator, reducing his needs. Thoreau's experiment with simple living in the woods, then, was not a renunciation of life, but an affirmation of it. He wanted to live without dead time, and he went to Walden Pond to learn how to achieve this; or, at least, to see if it were possible. Building and living in a tiny house was central to this existential enquiry.

Thoreau's philosophy of housing

We are now in a position to look more closely at Thoreau's philosophy of housing. Thoreau did not deny that shelter is now a necessity of life, though he did make a point of noting that there are instances of human beings, no hardier than ourselves, doing without shelter for long periods in colder countries. Assuming, however, that shelter is indeed a necessity of life, Thoreau proposed that we '[c]onsider first how slight a shelter is absolutely necessary' (283). He had seen Indians in his town living in tents of thin cotton cloth, which in the first instance could be constructed in a day or two, at most, and taken down and put up in a few hours; and every family owned one. He had even seen a large box by the railroad, six feet long by three feet wide, in which the labourers locked their tools up at night, and it suggested to him that anyone who was hard pushed might get such a one for a dollar, and, having bored a few holes in it to admit the air at least, get into it when it rained at night, and hook down the lid, 'and so have freedom in his love, and in his soul be free' (284). This will strike some as a ridiculous proposition, but Thoreau was 'far from jesting' (ibid). An average house in his neighbourhood cost about eight hundred dollars at the time and Thoreau noted that to lay up this sum would take from ten to fifteen years of the labourer's life; add the farm and one would have to spend twenty, thirty, or forty years toiling – more than half of one's life is easily spent. Would the Indians have been wise to give up their tents on these terms?

It is in this context where Thoreau made his alternative economics of housing most explicit, expressing one of his central ideas: 'If it is asserted that civilization is a real advance in the condition of man – and I think it is, though only the wise improve their advantages – it must be shown that it has produced better dwellings without making them more costly; and the cost of a thing is the amount of life which is required to be exchanged for it, immediately or in the long run' (286). On this basis, Thoreau suggested that 'when the farmer has got his house, he may not be the richer but the poorer for it, and it be the house that has got him' (288). What is more, *'if the civilized man's pursuits are no worthier than the savage's, if he is employed the greater part of his life in obtaining gross necessaries and comforts merely, why should he have a better dwelling than the former?'* (289, emphasis in original).

Thoreau wanted to show at what sacrifice our more 'advanced' dwellings were obtained and to suggest that, by living more simply, we may secure all the advantage without suffering any of the disadvantage. With this in mind, he went to Walden Pond with an axe, cut down some trees, and in about three unrushed months had built himself a modest but sturdy cabin. Again exemplifying his alternative mode of economic analysis, Thoreau declared that, 'I intend to build me a house which will surpass any on the main street in Concord in grandeur and luxury, as soon as it pleases me as much and will cost me no more [in terms of life] than the present one' (304).

It appears, then, that Thoreau was perfectly content with his shelter, modest though it was. Did this not make him richer than a king who is dissatisfied with his palace? With a little more wit we could all be richer than kings, Thoreau implied; but, unfortunately: 'Most men appear never to have considered what a house is, and are actually though needlessly poor all their lives because they think that they must have such a one as their neighbors have' (290).

Furthermore, Thoreau thought that there is something important in the experience of providing for oneself, of being self-reliant, that has been lost as a result of so-called 'modern improvements' and capitalism's extreme division of labour. He wondered whether 'if men [sic] constructed their dwellings with their own hands... the poetic faculty would be universally developed, as birds universally sing when they are so engaged?' (300). But, alas, 'we do like cowbirds and cuckoos, which lay their eggs in nests which other birds have built' (ibid).

'Shall we forever resign the pleasure of construction to the carpenter?' (300) he asked, noting that never in all his walks had he come across anyone engaged in so simple and natural an occupation as building their own house. 'Where is [our] division of labor to end? And what object does it finally serve? No doubt another may also think for me; but it is not therefore desirable that he should do so to the exclusion of my thinking for myself' (301). Thoreau had come to believe that his contemporaries were endeavouring to solve the problem of their livelihoods by a formula more complicated than the problem itself. 'To get his shoestrings he speculates in herds of cattle' (288). But Thoreau showed that, if one is prepared to live simply and with more self-reliance, 'the student who wishes for a shelter can obtain one for a lifetime at an expense not greater than the rent which he now pays annually' (304) and 'become richer than the richest are now' (295).

Thoreau's calculus here is simple but profound. Perhaps it would be nice to live in a palace or a mansion or even the nicest house on the block, but it must not be forgotten that the more expensive one's housing is the more of one's life will probably be spent earning the money needed to buy or rent it. So why not keep housing modest and simple? Since housing is the greatest overall expense in most people's lives, this is an area where people should be particularly cognisant of the time / freedom cost of consumption. Perhaps by lowering our material 'standard of living' (measured by consumption in housing) people could actually increase 'quality of life' (measured by subjective wellbeing)? Indeed, Thoreau's suggestion is that by living in modest accommodation people can literally save years if not decades of labour and thereby become 'richer than the richest are now', not in terms of property, of course, but in terms of freedom and contentment. 'If I seem to boast more than is becoming,' he concluded, 'my excuse is that I brag for humanity rather than for myself' (304).

As our analysis of the contemporary Tiny House Movement will soon show, this type of reasoning is a primary motivation for many people living in (or wanting to live in) tiny houses today. Earning a deposit for a house or even paying rent requires a sufficiently high-paying job (Pawson, Milligan and Yates, 2020) – not necessarily a meaningful job, just well paid – and for some people of Thoreauvian inclination that is a compromise not taken lightly. The more expensive housing costs are, the more one will be obligated to accept work just in order to pay those costs. So, rather than accepting the conventional path, people in the Tiny House Movement today – like Thoreau – are asking: How can I avoid the necessity of selling myself (or so much of myself) to the market? As we will see, to some people, at least, living in a tiny house is an answer to this fundamental economic question (Shearer, 2017).

After Walden

On 6 September 1847, Thoreau left his cabin at Walden Pond and again took up residence in Concord, where he remained for the rest of his years, a 'sojourner in civilized life' (258). Though he always lived a life of voluntary simplicity, he came to accept that industrial capitalism was an impersonally dictated social order within which he had to live, however much he despised it. Since his material needs were so few, however, for a long time he found that he barely had to work one month each spring and autumn to support himself (Bode, 1982). At the beginning of life, as at the end, Thoreau was very careful not to be seduced into exchanging his precious time for an insufficient amount of comforts and luxuries. Before proceeding to the contemporary Tiny House Movement, let us conclude the Thoreauvian analysis by inquiring into whether Thoreau's living experiment out at Walden Pond can be deemed a success.

Was Thoreau's experiment a success?

Even though Thoreau is now recognised as one of America's finest and most important writers, the focus of this chapter has been the alternative economics of housing that he practiced during his experiment at Walden Pond, and the question that remains is: Was his experiment a success? The question is a complex one, although perhaps not so complex as it is sometimes made out to be. If, in his experiment at the pond, we attribute to Thoreau the aim of living a life of complete independence and self-sufficiency – like Adam, or Robinson Crusoe, perhaps – a life in which he ate only what he grew and grew only what he ate, neither worked for another nor hired another, and avoided all trade and barter, then we must conclude that his experiment was a failure. Thoreau, after all, lived on Emerson's land; he borrowed an axe and other tools to get himself started; he set himself up in an unproductive corner of Massachusetts as a marginal commercial farmer whose cash crop did not bring in enough money to satisfy all his needs; he therefore hired himself out as a day labourer when he needed to make ends meet, and occasionally hired labour himself; furthermore, he was no stranger in the village, and would sometimes dine comfortably with his family or at the Emerson residence. These are the types of reasons that led critics like James Russel Lowell to allege that '[Thoreau's] shanty life was a mere impossibility, so far as his own conception of it goes, as an entire independency of mankind' (see Mazel, 2001: 32).

But this is to misunderstand the nature of Thoreau's project, and to misjudge it on that account. There is nothing to indicate that Thoreau sought 'an entire independency of mankind'. He did not set out to reject features of civilisation that were of genuine advantage or to live as a hermit. Let us not forget that he lived a mile from society, but only a mile. Our point, here, is that before we are in a position to judge the success of Thoreau's experiment we must have a proper understanding of its nature, and to help us understand this we should look to Thoreau's own carefully crafted words: 'My purpose in going to Walden Pond was neither to live cheaply nor live dearly there, but to transact some private business with the fewest obstacles' (275). In one sense, as noted earlier, this 'private business' was simply to write in privacy. Since we now know that while he was at the pond he wrote *A Week on the Concord and Merrimack Rivers*, the bulk of *Walden*, and probably a draft of his essay 'Resistance to Civil Government' – three texts (especially the latter two) which are now considered among the greatest works of American literature – it would seem that his experiment at the pond must be judged a resounding success. But this is to move too quickly, perhaps, since earlier we saw that his 'private business' also included his struggle with the economic problem of how to live a life of freedom in a world of scarce resources. To what extent can we say that this struggle was a success?

To live freely according to Thoreau essentially involves: (1) providing for one's material needs in a way that is meaningful, fulfilling, and respectful of nature; and (2) having the freedom and independence for one's 'proper pursuits', whatever they may be. On this basis, it would seem equally clear that, in his struggle for freedom, Thoreau met with some real success in his experiment (even though it turned out that the struggle did not so much lead to a destination as much as it was an ongoing creative process). In hewing timber for his cabin on 'pleasant spring days, in which the winter of man's discontent was thawing' (296) he discovered 'the pleasure of construction', he sang as he worked, and 'made no haste in [his] work, but rather made the of most it' (297).

As for his work in the bean field, he tells of how hoeing his rows 'yielded an instant and immeasurable crop' (408) and attached him to the earth in a way that was nourishing. Even when Thoreau felt the need to hire himself out as a labourer – an occupation which he deemed 'the most independent of any' (324) – it was not always time wasted. In one journal entry he wrote: 'Great thoughts hallow any labor. Today I earned seventy-five cents heaving manure out of a pen, and made a good bargain of it' (15). Perhaps the most significant feature of his time at the pond, however, was his discovery that by living simply and generally relying on himself for his needs, he could maintain himself by working about six weeks per year only, leaving him with the whole of his winters, as well as most of his summers, 'free and clear for study' (323), or, more generally, for following the bent of his genius. On top of these successes, there are good reasons for thinking that throughout his time at the pond Thoreau was, quite simply, happy. 'My life was ecstasy,' he wrote in the most successful expression of this feeling.

Nevertheless, before we can conclude that Thoreau's experiment at the pond was largely a success, we must confront the question: 'Why, then, did he leave?' After all, he only stayed for two years and two months, after which time he returned to live in Concord. But if he had secured the freedom, tranquillity, and happiness that he sought, why did he not remain at the pond his whole life? This is sometimes considered a fatal blow, proof that his experiment was an idealised distortion of social and economic reality, one that not even Thoreau could sustain.

We should hesitate, however, before judging his experiment a failure on this account. During his time at the pond Thoreau had learned by experience that very little is actually needed to live well and to be free, if only life is approached with the right attitude. Furthermore, he had cultivated a deep understanding of 'the essential facts of life' and developed a genuine love of simplicity. All this meant that he was able to live with an 'inexpressible confidence' (410) and 'calm trust in the future' (ibid), knowing that if he were ever to lose all his possessions he would be 'nearly as well off as before' (310). Could he not then leave his experiment behind yet take its lessons with him? Was he not correct in his claim that, '[i]t is not the tub that makes Diogenes, the Jove-born, but Diogenes the tub'? We should not dismiss in advance the possibility that those who successfully prosecute an inward voyage might learn to live in acquisitive society and yet above it, liberated from imprisonment within its values.

'I left the woods for as good a reason as I went there' (562), Thoreau tells us near the end of *Walden*. 'Perhaps it seemed to me that I had several more lives to live, and could not spare any more for that one' (ibid). It should not surprise us that there is a measure of uncertainty in this explanation, given that his time at the pond was an enormously positive and creative period in his life. It would surely have been very tempting to stay. Indeed, a journal entry written five years after leaving the pond reads: 'But why I changed– ? Why I left the woods? I do not think I can tell. I have often wished myself back.' In another entry, however, he was less regretful: 'Perhaps I wanted a change.... Perhaps if I lived there much longer I might live there forever – One would think twice before he accepted heaven on such terms.' This last point, we contend, gets to the heart of the matter. Sublime though his experience was at the pond, Thoreau's ethic of self-cultivation and his constant yearning for self-renewal required a stance of openness to new and diverse experiences. Expressing this need to move onward and upward, he wrote: 'I did not wish to take a cabin passage, but rather to go before the mast and on the deck of the world, for there I could best see the moonlight amid the mountains. I do not wish to go below now' (562).

In the end, whether we judge Thoreau's experiment to be a success or a failure is arguably beside the point, since Thoreau cared little for the 'smoke of opinion' (264) and instead chose to think for himself. His own assessment of his time at the pond is perhaps best represented in the following passage (562):

> I learned this, at least, by my experiment: that if one advances confidently in the direction of his dreams, and endeavors to live the life which he has imagined, he will meet with a success unexpected in common hours. He will put some things behind, will pass an invisible boundary; new, universal, and more liberal laws will begin to establish themselves around and within him; or the old laws be expanded, and interpreted in his favor in a more liberal sense, and he will live with the license of a higher order of beings. In proportion as he simplifies his life, the laws of the universe will

appear less complex, and solitude will not be solitude, nor poverty poverty, nor weakness weakness. If you have built castles in the air, your work need not be lost; that is where they should be. Now put the foundations under them.

The contemporary Tiny House Movement: Reflecting Thoreauvian struggles, motivations, and questions

Let us move now to the contemporary Tiny House Movement and consider the extent to which it can be understood as a reflection of Thoreauvian struggles, motivations, and questions. As highlighted in the introduction, the contemporary Tiny House Movement originated around 1998, in the Pacific northwest of the USA (Shearer and Burton, 2019; Anson, 2014; Evans, 2019; Kilman, 2016; Mangold and Zschau, 2019). The movement began largely when some of the creative class – architects, writers, and designers – became dissatisfied with restrictive planning regulations (minimum size houses), affordability, and a search for more sustainable living, and instead built their own houses on to a trailer base (Ford and Gomez-Lanier, 2017; Kilman, 2016). This, in essence, differentiated the tiny house from a standard house and reclassified it as a vehicle. The movement started very small and was largely restricted to the continental US, but around 2010 – subsequent to the Global Financial Crisis (GFC) and the rise in the use of social media – interest in tiny houses grew exponentially and spread to other countries, particularly those characterised by housing affordability issues and larger houses (Penfold, Waitt, and McGuirck, 2018).

Tiny houses can be differentiated into fixed tiny houses (as in Thoreau's case) or mobile tiny houses (Tiny Houses on Wheels or THOW) (Shearer and Burton, 2019). THOW are often considered as the archetypal tiny house, built on a trailer base to counter planning restrictions, as affordable housing and to achieve 'freedom' (Anson, 2014; Weetman, 2018). These are not new forms, however, having their antecedents in earlier tropes as the Gypsy (Romani) Wagon and early 'trailer' homes (Evans, 2019). Fixed tiny houses too have been, arguably, the dominant global housing form for much of human history; it is only since around the 1950s, in some Anglophone ex colonies of Britain such as the US, Australia, Canada, and New Zealand, that housing for 'the average person' has become supersized (McKinlay, Baldwin, and Stevens, 2019; Wiesel, Pinnegar, and Freestone, 2013).

As we indicated in the beginning, there are major similarities between the contemporary Tiny House Movement and Thoreau's philosophical goals of freedom, sustainability, economic security, and self-reliance. Empirical research conducted since 2015 in Australia (see Table 1) found that the main drivers for tiny house living has remained constant over the time, with interest continuing to grow strongly (Shearer, 2017; Boeckermann, Kaczynski, and King, 2019). These most common reasons given for wanting to 'go tiny' are affordability, environmental sustainability, a DIY ethos, and freedom (Shearer et al., 2018; Shearer, 2017).

Table 1: Summary of Research Methods

Method	Date	valid n	Notes
Questionnaire Survey	June 2015	56	80% aged 40+; 57% female; 10/49 tiny house owner
Questionnaire Survey	Sept 2017	369	78% aged 40+; 67% female; 52/369 tiny house owner
Questionnaire Survey (ATHA)	Sept 2019	640	66% aged 40+; 78% female/non-binary; 170/640 tiny house owner
Interviews	Jan 2015–present	12	Mix of genders and ages; younger couples more common, three had young children
Participant Observation	Jan 2015–present	na	Attended and spoke at numerous tiny house gatherings, festivals and meetups

The housing affordability crisis in Australia has prevented many 'ordinary' people from being able to afford even the simplest dwelling, reasonably close to services and employment (Gurran et al., 2018; Pawson, Milligan, and Yates, 2020). Faced with the choice of either buying into a high-rise apartment in the inner city, commuting for hours every day from the outer suburbs, ongoing insecure renting, or living in share houses, it is little wonder that people see tiny houses as a way to achieve economic freedom, without sacrificing decades of their lives, or the opportunity to have a pet or garden. As Thoreau stated, 'There is no more fatal blunderer than he who consumes the greater part of his life getting his living.'

Likewise, tiny house dwellers in Australia felt that buying into conventional housing required them to sacrifice their freedom: 'I don't want to be trapped in mortgage servitude for life and I want to live an environmentally conscious life'; and 'I'm a single woman and I don't need a big house with multiple empty bedrooms, but I'd also like to live somewhere I can have a pet and a veggie garden. A tiny house on its own patch of land would be an excellent compromise. I also worry about renting and potential homelessness if I experience economic insecurity in the future' (Survey respondents, 2017).

Similarly, the Tiny House Movement is replete with references to self-reliance and self-sufficiency, albeit couched in more modern terminology such as DIY (do it yourself), off-grid, and even survivalism: 'I want to be able to be self-sufficient and live on my property in a tiny house. And be able to take my house with me when I travel Australia' (Survey respondent, 2019). The ability to not only build one's own simple house, but to do so without (too much) debt and ongoing cost, and, in doing so, gain economic freedom was deeply reminiscent of Thoreau when he said a person '..can obtain [a shelter] for a lifetime at an expense not greater than the rent'. Another said, the tiny house '...could give me a "home base"...as I don't have enough money to build a full house but...I could at least install a road, water tanks and solar power then start building a hemp/lime masonry house and finish it slowly as funds and labour become available' (Survey respondent, 2019).

Finally, to unpack the most pertinent, yet the most complex of all the themes arising from the study into the contemporary Tiny House Movement, that of freedom. Freedom to Thoreau was multi-faceted – as is the concept in the Tiny House Movement. To him, it meant economic freedom and freedom from the constraints of society (Anson, 2014); and arguably, freedom from regulation – libertarianism. Some even consider Thoreau as the first libertarian (Hamowy, 2008). These interpretations of freedom almost mirror the concerns, dreams, and drivers of the contemporary Tiny House Movement, with the only exception being freedom of movement. As one Survey respondent (2019) said: 'We were financially forced into going down this tiny living road, but along the way have come to realise what a freedom it is to live like this, and are very grateful for it, and feel it's a better way of living.'

This is the crux of the argument; like Thoreau, some feel forced, by external circumstances, into the Tiny House Movement. Thoreau could not make any money as a poet, and the work he could find required him to sacrifice his principles. Nowadays, many people also feel they are 'living lives of quiet desperation' – spending most of their waking lives in jobs they hate, to pay the mortgage on a house too large for their needs. 'Too many people spend money they haven't earned to buy things they don't want to impress people they don't like.'[3] People may go tiny by choice or necessity, but like Thoreau, they find the experience changes them immeasurably. Many also only live temporarily in their tiny houses, but the lessons learned stay with them for the long term – like Thoreau continuing his voluntary simplicity for the remainder of his life, the positive sustainable behaviours of tiny house dwellers continues long after they leave their tiny house (Saxton, 2019).

> Living in a tiny house with kids stretches you and teaches you lessons you'd never know without the experience. It teaches you to be creative with space and play. Our bed doubled as the lounge, change table, and play area. It had its challenges, for sure, but it definitely drew our family together (Megan, ex tiny house dweller).

Conclusion

So ends our examination of the relationship between Thoreau's living experiment at Walden Pond and the contemporary Tiny House Movement. Or does this examination, by its very nature, have no end? After all, living a life of 'simplicity, independence, magnanimity, and trust' involves solving 'some of the problems of life, not only theoretically, but practically also' (270). And this is not so much a destination as it is an ongoing creative process. Our review has left much unsaid, necessarily, and perhaps the discussion has raised more questions than it has answered. But perhaps that is how Thoreau would have wanted it. He was not interested in giving us detailed instructions on how to live a simpler life; nor did he want to save us the trouble of thinking for ourselves. Rather, he wanted to stoke the fire in our souls and inspire us with ideals. 'Don't spend your time in drilling soldiers,' he once wrote, 'who may turn out hirelings after all, but give to the undrilled peasantry a country to fight for' (see Stoller, 1957: 123).

Even as a young man, Thoreau believed that the object of life was 'something else than acquiring property' (Stoller, 1957: 120) and that true success did not consist in 'much money, many houses' but in 'trying to better [our] condition in a higher sense than this' (ibid). He had no desire to succeed in the desperate measure of getting rich or comfortable merely. Thoreau's life is a reminder that dedicated individuals can

---

3 Source unknown, attributed to Will Rogers.

establish a simpler, freer way of life for themselves, by adopting a new frame of mind and acting upon it with creativity and conviction. Doing so may not be easy, of course, since it will involve moving in the opposite direction to where most of humankind is marching. But as Thoreau would say: 'If a man [sic] does not keep pace with his companions, perhaps it is because he hears a different drummer. Let him step to the music which he hears, however measured or far away' (564–5). Thoreau would also advise us not to wait for our politicians or peers to attain enlightenment before we begin our journey toward simplicity, for it might be a long time before they wake up. It seems to us that participants in the Tiny House Movement today are showing Thoreauvian courage.

References

Anson, A. 2014. '"The World is My Backyard": Romanticism, Thoreauvian Rhetoric, and Constructive Confrontation in the Tiny House Movement'. In Holt, W. (ed.), *From Sustainable to Resilient Cities: Global Concerns and Urban Efforts* (Research in Urban Sociology, Volume 14) Emerald Group Publishing: 289–313.

Anson, A. 2017. 'The Patron Saint of Tiny Houses'. In Finley, James (ed.), *Henry David Thoreau in Context*. Cambridge: Cambridge University Press: 331–341.

Alexander, S. 2016. 'A Prosperous Descent: Telling New Stories as the Old Book Closes'. *Griffith Review* 52: 4–24. Available at: https://www.griffithreview.com/wp-content/uploads/GR52_Alexander_Adcock-Ebook.FINAL_.pdf [accessed 10 February 2020].

Alexander, S. and Baumann, A. 2019. 'Access to Land as a Barrier to Simpler, Sustainable Living: Public Housing Could Offer a Way Forward'. *The Conversation* (22 August, 2019). Available at: https://theconversation.com/access-to-land-is-a-barrier-to-simpler-sustainable-living-public-housing-could-offer-a-way-forward-121246 [accessed 10 February 2020].

Boeckermann, L., Kaczynski, A., and King, S. 2019. 'Dreaming Big and Living Small: Examining Motivations and Satisfaction in Tiny House Living'. *Journal of Housing and the Built Environment* 34(1): 61–71.

Cox, W. and Pavletich, H. 2018. '14th Annual Demographia International Housing Affordability Survey'. Available at: London: http://demographia.com/dhi.pdf (accessed 10 February 2020).

Evans, K. 2019. 'Exploring the Relationship between Visual Preferences for Tiny and Small Houses and Land Use Policy in the Southeastern United States'. *Land Use Policy*, 81: 209–218.

Ford, J. and Gomez-Lanier, L. 2017. 'Are Tiny Homes Here to Stay? A Review of Literature on the Tiny House Movement'. *Family and Consumer Sciences Research Journal*, 45(4): 394–405. Available at: https://www.researchgate.net/publication/317769558_Are_Tiny_Homes_Here_to_Stay_A_Review_of_Literature_on_the_Tiny_House_Movement

Gurran, N. et al. 2018. 'Supporting Affordable Housing Supply: Inclusionary Planning in New and Renewing Communities'. *Australian Housing and Urban Research Institute* (April 2018). DOI: 10.18408/ahuri-7313201.

Hamowy, R. 2008. *The Encyclopedia of Libertarianism*. London: Sage Publications.

Kilman, C. 2016. 'Small House, Big Impact: The Effect of Tiny Houses on Community and Environment'. *Undergraduate Journal of Humanistic Studies* 2(Winter 2016): 1–12.

10. The search for freedom, sustainability, and economic security

Mangold, S. and Zschau, T. 2019. 'In Search of the "Good Life": The Appeal of the Tiny House Lifestyle in the USA'. *Social Sciences* 8(1): 26.

Mazel, D. 2001. *A Century of Early Ecocriticism*. London: University of Georgia Press.

McKinlay, A., Baldwin, C., and Stevens, N. 2019. 'Size Matters: Dwelling Size as a Critical Factor for Sustainable Urban Development'. *Urban Policy and Research* 37(2): 135–150.

Milkman A. 2016. 'The Tiny House Fantasy: the tiny house movement embraces individualistic visions of property while ignoring the real causes of housing insecurity'. Jacobin (19 January 2016). Available at: https://www.jacobinmag. com/2016/01/tiny-house-   movement-nation-tumbleweed-environment-consumerism/ (accessed 20 February 2020).

Pawson, H., Milligan, V., and Yates, J. 2020. 'Unpacking Australia's Housing Affordability Problem'. In *Housing Policy in Australia*: 51–85. Singapore: Springer.

Peck, H.D. (ed.). 1993. *A Year in Thoreau's Journal: 1851*. London: Penguin.

Penfold, H., Waitt, G., and McGuirk, P. 2018. 'Portrayals of the Tiny House in Electronic Media: Challenging or Reproducing the Australian Dream Home'. *Australian Planner*, 55(3–4): 164–173.

Saxton, M. 2019. 'The Ecological Footprints of Tiny Home Downsizers: An Exploratory Study'. *Virginia Tech*. Available at: https://vtechworks.lib.vt.edu/ handle/10919/89224 (Accessed 10 February 2020).

Shearer, H. 2017. 'Interest in Tiny Houses is Growing, so Who Wants Them and Why?' *The Conversation* (20 September 2017).

Shearer, H. et al. 2018. 'Planning for tiny houses'. *Australian Planner* 55 (3–4): 147–156.

Shearer, H. and Burton, P. 2019. 'Towards a Typology of Tiny Houses'. *Housing, Theory and Society*, 36(3): 298–318.

Solnit, R. 2013. 'Mysteries of Thoreau Unsolved: On the Dirtiness of Laundry and the Strength of Sisters'. *Orion* May/June: 18–23.

Stoller, L. 1957. *After Walden: Thoreau's Changing Views on Economic Man*. Redwood City: Stanford University Press.

Bode, C. 1982. *The Portable Thoreau*. London: Penguin.

Walls, L.D. 2017. *Henry David Thoreau: A Life*. Chicago: University of Chicago Press.

Weetman, V. 2018. 'Resistance is Fertile: Exploring Tiny House Practices in Australia'. *Australian Planner*, 55(3–4): 232–240.

Wiesel, I., Pinnegar, S., and Freestone, R. 2013. 'Supersized Australian Dream: Investment, Lifestyle and Neighbourhood Perceptions Among "Knockdown-Rebuild" Owners in Sydney'. *Housing, Theory and Society*, 30(3): 312–329.

Wotton, J., Skates, H., and Shutter, L. 2018. 'Tiny House – When Size Matters'. *Australian Planner* 55(3–4): 209–220.

Chapter II

Bumps along the road of the Tiny House Movement: Practitioner notes with critical reflections[1]

Networking in Victoria's Tiny House Movement

In 2016 a documentary was released called *A Simpler Way: Crisis as Opportunity*, which was based on a tiny house demonstration project in Gippsland, Victoria (Alexander, 2016). This film quickly exceeded one million views online, pointing to the cultural fascination with tiny houses in an era of housing insecurity and rising sustainability concerns. Over the last five years, this Gippsland project has erected seven tiny houses of various forms, which were constructed during building workshops. Through this process some of the most active tiny house builders in Victoria were connected, including Tom Coupe, Nick Matyevich, Rob Scott, and Fred Schultz, who are co-authors of this paper. Collectively these builders have led or participated in over 70 tiny house builds – almost all tiny houses on wheels – meaning that these co-authors are amongst the most experienced tiny house builders in Australia. Samuel Alexander and Brendan Gleeson (2019) are urban theorists with the Melbourne Sustainable Society Institute, University of Melbourne. They collated the notes from these builder practitioners and present them below along with critical reflections.

This chapter shares those practical insights and learnings, highlighting some promising approaches to construction, as well as some challenges faced by the emerging Tiny House Movement, focusing primarily on building issues and techniques. Of course, this is a forum neither to provide a comprehensive 'how-to guide' nor provide specialist advice on specific builds or regulations, which are typically context and jurisdiction dependent. Furthermore, this body of authors is not a homogenous group who all think the same thing or practice exactly the same techniques. Nevertheless, the opening sections of this chapter offer some practice-based reflections for tiny house builders and potential inhabitants to consider as they prepare and plan for their building

---

1 A version of this chapter was originally published in *The Australian Planner*, 2019, co-authored with Brendan Gleeson, Tom Coupe, Nick Matyevich, Rob Scott, and Fred Schultz. DOI: 10.1080/07293682.2019.1634111

projects. It is hoped that this practical review is of broader relevance too, including to theorists of tiny houses and the social movements that promote them, by offering insight into various challenges faced as tiny houses are constructed. The Tiny House Movement is a complex contemporary social force, but its materiality also includes the industry and practitioners that realise it. As always, theory is best when informed by practice.

As well as the practice review of tiny houses, the chapter also offers a conceptually driven appraisal of this potentially important new housing form that raises serious questions about planning and urban policy. The aim is to present a grounded review of the Tiny House Movement, and its wider policy resonances, rooted in an empirical review of current practice. After the empirical practice notes are presented, the analysis concludes by going beyond building and construction issues and offers some critical reflections on the promise and limitations of the Tiny House Movement. While we have no desire to throw water on the movement's fire, so to speak, we do wish to question some of the romanticism and at times the apparent naivety surrounding the movement, by offering an insight into the Tiny House Movement's range of complexities, which ought not to be neglected (Anson, 2014). These intricacies and potential difficulties include potential frictions with wider housing and urban policies in Australia, especially those that have favoured transition to higher residential densities and which are themselves fraught with challenges, especially around social equity. The desire for a 'simpler life' may sometimes motivate participants in the Tiny House Movement (Boeckermann, Kaczynski, and King, 2018), but simplicity can be also be the hardest thing to achieve in wider social and policy realities. In offering a sympathetic critique and asking some hard questions, this review and analysis seeks to present a richer and fuller understanding of the Tiny House Movement in a way that helps the movement progress and avoid unnecessary pitfalls.

Practical notes: Things to think about when planning a tiny house build

This section begins with a definitional comment, then briefly considers the regulation of tiny houses, before reviewing a number of practical matters, including: trailers and mobility; the pros and cons of using second-hand materials; water use, capture and water-proofing; and strategies to increase fire resistance of tiny houses. These are not mere epiphenomena for urban theory but constitute real material considerations that point to the underlying complexities and challenges of tiny house promotion and construction for the wider regulation of the built environment. The section concludes by reviewing a range of miscellaneous points.

What is a tiny house?

There is no single form or definition of a 'tiny house' (Shearer and Burton, 2018). The term usually refers to a small timber-framed abode that sits upon a trailer – a 'tiny house on wheels' – typically ranging from 2.5m to 7m in length, 2.5m in width, and under 4.2m in height. Some tiny houses are placed on 'skids' rather than wheels, which allows the abode to be dragged about (including onto a truck), thus avoiding permanent fixture to the land.

These small dwellings are usually under 37 square metres (or 400 square feet) and are often loosely compared to a large caravan or RV (Bares et al., 2017). Some of these abodes have showers, composting toilets, and kitchens. Others primarily serve as a bedroom and living space, without further amenities. For present purposes these simple words of definition will suffice.

Regulatory issues

This section does not attempt to provide a comprehensive or comparative review of the regulatory issues surrounding tiny houses in Victoria or elsewhere (see Bares et al., 2017). Instead, we highlight some of the key things to think about and explore. By way of background, in Australia there is no Federal or State legislation specifically governing tiny houses on wheels, except insofar as a tiny house is treated as a road vehicle. In terms of sitting a tiny house on a property, the key regulations governing tiny houses will generally be specific to each local council. In brief, the best 'rule of thumb' presently is to assume that, for regulatory purposes, a tiny house on wheels will generally be treated by councils as a caravan. The tiny house can thus be seen from the urban studies point of view as part of the wider relocatable dwelling phenomenon that has received attention from Australian scholars (e.g., Mowbray, 1994; Bunce, 2010).

There should be no issue registering a tiny house on wheels as a road vehicle, provided that the trailer is suitably robust for the weight of the house and contents; is within the size limits for road travel; has appropriate clearance lights, etc. Where you can park a tiny house legitimately and live in it raises more problems. The same rules which govern caravans will generally but not always apply to tiny houses. There are cases where councils have treated tiny houses on wheels as a building, not a caravan or road vehicle.

Typically, in areas where living in a caravan is permitted, it would be possible to live in a tiny house. But generally, there are significant council restrictions here, and permits cannot always be acquired. Indeed, permits specific to tiny houses generally do not even exist, so rules governing caravans tend to apply. We hope that in time these regulations are modified and clarified, because currently the uncertainty or strictness of council regulations regarding living in caravans or tiny houses is inhibiting the growth of the Tiny House Movement. There is now a public database where people can research their local regulations regarding tiny houses and upload their findings (see Shultz, 2019).

Of course, the key benefit of building a tiny house *on wheels* is that, even if a permit is not acquired, the house can be moved if a council or neighbours ever object. This seems to be the approach taken by many participants in the movement today. Rather than seek formal council permission, people with a tiny house will often seek some lease or tenancy arrangement with a landowner (usually but not exclusively in a rural context to avoid attention). Given that a tiny house on wheels (or on skids) is not attached to the land, planning permission is generally not required to place a tiny house on land (in much the same way planning permission is not generally required to place a caravan on land). But often the rules governing caravans will prohibit or severely limit people *living* in a caravan on land without a permit, which are not always easily acquired. Depending on jurisdiction, living in a caravan can be entirely prohibited, while other jurisdictions can permit temporary residency of two years or more. Again, this temporary or uncertain status, even when a permit is acquired, often leads to tiny houses operating 'under the radar' of regulations, being placed in secluded places on rural properties to avoid notice by the authorities.

The other approach is to discuss the placement of a tiny house with surrounding neighbours, to ascertain whether there would be any objections in advance. Generally, councils don't have the resources to seek out problems to resolve, but if neighbours complain councils will generally be required to enforce the law. So, one strategy employed is to be upfront with neighbours and establish good relations, trusting that if no one complains, residing in a tiny house will not give rise to any objections or obstruction. That said, this strategy means that there is always an underlying insecurity of tenure for non-permitted tiny house dwellers, knowing that a new neighbour might object or a council worker might one day knock on the door and ask to see a permit. From personal experience living in a tiny house, one co-author of this paper reports that this insecurity can be a cause of 'housing stress' or 'housing anxiety'. Again, councils could develop more accommodating and clearer guidelines about tiny houses to provide more security.

Trailers, roadworthiness, and mobility

This sub-section makes several points regarding trailers, roadworthiness, and mobility. First, builders should ensure that the trailer used for a tiny house is built for this application, since trailers have surprisingly complex engineering aspects to them depending on their purpose. Some trailers are built to accommodate a tonne or more of gravel placed in the centre, or to have a car drive onto it, meaning that the trailer must be able to accommodate its maximum weight allowance concentrated in isolated areas of the trailer. Conversely, the weight of a tiny house is quite broadly distributed over the trailer and static, so this affects how a tiny house trailer would be engineered. A key aspect here is to ensure the trailer has 'load sharing suspension', commonly called 'rocker roller suspension'. Nevertheless, trailers should always have more load over the front than the rear – with 6–8% load on the tow ball – to avoid tail wagging when towing (see Darling, Gao, and Tilley, 2009). Side to side balance is important too, because the height of many tiny houses means the potential to roll is greater.

Some tiny house trailers are created with steel joists built into the design, meaning that one can lay the flooring material directly on the trailer (with appropriate waterproofing and insulation from below). This can save time, since it is not necessary to lay timber floor joists, but this practice can lead to a structurally over-engineered trailer with superfluous steel, which can increase costs. It would generally be cheaper to lay timber joists than have steel joists built into the structure of the trailer, and this might only take an experienced builder a few hours so is probably the most cost effective method, and probably the more environmentally friendly approach since timber (a renewable resource) replaces steel as the joists.

The second point worth emphasising here is that a tiny house on wheels must be securely attached to the trailer. That sounds obvious, but some of the present authors have seen tiny houses insufficiently fastened to their trailers. This can occur even when a tiny house is built by a registered or experienced builder, since attaching a house to trailer is not something many builders have much or any experience in. In this regard it must be remembered that a tiny house is not so much a house as a road vehicle, one that vibrates as it travels down roads that are sometimes bumpy and rough. If a tiny house on wheels ever comes apart on the road and causes damage or injury, this will be highly problematic in itself, and may also have broader implications, potentially creating a hostile regulatory environment and making progressive reforms more difficult. The same goes for construction or environmental practices more broadly – for example, improper grey water or black water disposal or treatment may put the industry (and potential legal status) years back.

The third point is something of a counter-point to the previous point: yes, tiny houses on wheels should be built in ways that make them safe and functional as a road vehicle, but in terms of mobility, a tiny house on wheels has different characteristics and so should not be conceived of as the same as a caravan in this regard. A caravan is designed to be a regular travel vehicle. Even the shape of a caravan is generally aerodynamically designed to minimise wind resistance, making it suitable to move from campsite to campsite every few days. The design of most tiny houses makes regular road travel very fuel-inefficient and they are generally heavier and more difficult to drive around than a caravan. If regular travel is a goal of a mobile home, a caravan may be a better option. If a mobile might only need to be moved once every few years, then a tiny house on wheels may be an appropriate alternative.

Second-hand materials or buy new?

Whether to build a tiny house with second-hand / salvaged or new materials, or what mixture of these is used, is obviously going to be context and household dependent. If a prospective tiny house builder has time to search for materials and space to store them, building materials can generally be found very cheaply or even for free. Tip shops, house demolitions, skips on the side of the road, and trawling through Gumtree postings, can provide a great source of cheap or free materials. But from experience this can take a lot of time and generally requires quick responses, since the culture of salvaging materials seems to be on the rise. That said, when one goes searching one will quickly discover how wasteful industrial societies are. If you seek, generally you will find. Salvage yards also allow for materials to be acquired more cheaply than purchasing brand new, but from experience good second-hand materials from salvage yards are not always much cheaper than buying new.

In short, the primary benefits of using second-hand materials are that they can be cheap or free, and that putting second-hand resources to good use, rather than have them go to landfill, seems consistent with the environmental ethic that drives many tiny house builders (Shearer, 2017; Saxton, 2019). You can also end up with a particularly quirky and unique product, with many salvaging stories to tell.

However, it is also important to bear in mind that at times second-hand materials can be much harder to work with, and extend the time needed for building. For example, house demolitions often allow for old hardwood framing timber to be acquired, but this will generally need to be de-nailed (adding time) and over decades hardwood can become ever-harder, making it much more difficult to work with. Old windows, reclaimed floorboards, or second-hand doors will also need more preparation or fixing before they are ready to be used, and if they aren't high quality, second-hand materials can reduce the longevity of the build. Design can be difficult when it isn't clear what materials you will have available, but this can also be part of the adventure. One also needs to consider the issue of weight: a hardwood frame, for example, will be considerably heavier than a pine frame, and trailers have weight limits, an issue which must be borne in mind. So there are certainly pros and cons with either approach. Salvaging can significantly reduce the costs of a build; but working with new pine is very different to working with 100-year-old hardwood.

Water: Keeping it out, and collecting what one can

Due to restrictions on the width of tiny houses for road travel, the eaves of tiny houses tend to be small or non-existent. This can expose a tiny house to more weather than an ordinary house receives, so be particularly mindful of waterproofing well. This deserves emphasising, especially if the build includes water use indoors, with a kitchen sink, toilet, or shower. Good air flow inside can assist with drying too (e.g., cross ventilation with a low window on one side of the tiny house and a high window on the other), or even a 12v exhaust fan in the shower.

Showers obviously present a high risk of causing water damage if not sealed well. Fibreglass cubicles are useful here, as these minimise 'joins' which can be points of weakness. Priming and painting (marine) ply or thin steel can be used to waterproof the underside of the trailer.

The other aspect to highlight concerns water *capture* (see Bares et al., 2017: 43). In many cases tiny houses seek to be off grid, but remember: the roof of a tiny house has minimal (or very small) roof area. Often rainfall will be insufficient to meet all water needs, especially if there is only a small water tank available or multiple people drawing from it. Therefore, think through this aspect carefully. Options include installing a larger water tank not attached to the tiny house, even if it has to be topped up with external sources occasionally, or being somewhere accessible to mains water. Either way, living in a tiny house is likely to incentivise frugality with water, which is a good thing in an age where the climate is changing and historical rainfall or access to cheap fresh water should not be taken for granted. A flush-less composting loo is a key feature here to minimise water use (see Bares et al., 2017, 43).

Fireproofing tiny houses

Fireproofing tiny houses is one issue that barely gets a mention in the Tiny House Movement, but in bush fire-prone areas of the world, including much of Australia, this matter deserves closer attention. Tom Coupe (co-author of this paper) is a prominent voice in this area, having recently built what may be the first fireproofed tiny house on wheels in the world. He used over 20 fire resistant products and employed over 40 fireproofing building techniques and designs.

Interestingly, and somewhat disturbingly, he has received some resistance from some participants in the movement, as fireproofing may introduce additional regulatory measures as well as increase costs – both of which are generally seen as negatives. But ultimately, if safety of people and property are given due weight, the Tiny House Movement should be mindful of fire safety techniques, practices, and regulations for those houses that may be placed in areas that are at risk of bush fire.

This is not the place to provide a comprehensive guide to increasing the fire-resistance of a tiny house, but some general comments can be made. First, choosing the right materials can improve fire resistance, such as cladding with corrugated iron or hardwood; using fire-resistant paint, gap-filler, and silicon; having gutter guards to keep dry leaves from gathering; and having windows and doors with toughened glass. There are also building techniques that can improve fire resistance, such as fold-down sides to minimise embers catching alight underneath the carriage and protecting tyres; window shutters; flat design where possible to reduce places for embers to catch; steel mesh over vents; filled corrugations in the roof's edge; a steel undercarriage, and so forth. The final issue to bear in mind is placement: keep the tiny house a safe distance from bush and surrounding vegetation, with precise distances being jurisdiction and fire-code specific. We can't provide context specific answers here, but these are important questions for builders and inhabitants of tiny houses to consider. A tiny house cannot be deemed sustainable if it burns down needlessly and requires rebuilding, nor will it provide housing security.

Miscellaneous notes

For present purposes, we will close this practical part of the discussion with some miscellaneous notes on various aspects of tiny house construction and inhabitation:

- Be conscious of the full dimensions of the build, taking into consideration things like gutters, ridge capping, eves, exterior door handles, and window flashing. If these are not taken into account, the structure might end up a few millimeters over the limit and not be able to be registered.

- Again, we won't attempt to list every regulation relevant to tiny house builds, but as an example, Section 22.1 of the Vehicle Standard Bulletin 1 (VSB1) reads: 'A caravan or trailer equipped with cooking facilities or living or sleeping accommodation must have only outward opening or sliding doors. At least one such door must be located on the left-hand side or at the rear.' Not abiding by such regulations can mean your tiny house may not be registerable.

- Insulating a tiny house for heat and cold raises different issues depending on context and climate. Both aspects are extremely important to take into consideration, although generally insulating to retain heat is given more attention than designing the house to avoid overheating (even though the latter may be more important in Australia). With respect to retaining heat, don't have more windows than you need, since even double-glazed windows will lose more heat than a well-insulated wall (and fitting superfluous windows will extend the time needed to build). It is not much good doubling the insulation in the walls and roof if most of the heat is being lost out the windows. Higher windows will lose more heat than lower windows, and skylights will lose the most. Keep them small to minimise heat loss. A basic principle of passive design for winter heating is to have most windows on the northern wall to maximise passive heating in winter.

- On the other hand, most conventional houses have eves which function to minimise summer sun from entering a house. Most tiny houses do not have eves due to width restrictions, but detachable or flip-down eves are possible. North-facing windows without eves are great in winter but can lead to overheating in summer. Ensure good cross ventilation for cooling in warm weather. In Australia, you are more likely to get too hot in a tiny house than too cold. When insulating a house to protect from summer heat, heat-reflective material and an air gap are key.

- It can seem like a nice idea to cook on a potbelly in a tiny house, especially if the aim is to be off grid, but be mindful of the fact that heating the pot belly sufficiently to cook on it might turn the tiny house into a hotbox, especially in warmer months – and even in winter. We know of tiny house inhabitants who need to have the windows open on winter nights when cooking to avoid overheating the space.

- Given that many tiny houses end up on rural properties, insects can be problematic. Ensure that mosquito and fly screens are used on all doors and opening windows.

- Before purchasing your solar array and batteries, do careful calculations in order to match your expectations and avoid under- or over-capacity. Under-capacity can mean you find yourself without energy, say, to keep your fridge on during a cloudy week. Over-capacity can mean you spend thousands of dollars more on your solar system than you need to.

- 12v electricity supply doesn't need to be installed by an electrician; 240v does. Most tiny houses are only wired to 12v but a 240v inverter can mean it is possible to charge a computer, for example. As a participant in a tiny house building workshop once commented: 'Lights plus a computer equals civilisation.'

- Gas plumbing: this will need to be done by a registered plumber to get a certificate of compliance. Without further regulatory guidance from government, one can assume that the same rules that apply to caravans apply also to tiny houses.

- Lofts are a good use of space, but are not ideal for older people / less mobile people, and many staircases found in tiny houses wouldn't get approved if they were in a conventional house. Lofts also function as a very strong mid-stud brace.

Critical reflections: The promise and limitations of tiny houses

Having shared these practitioner notes gleaned from years of building tiny houses, we now wish to step back from these practice issues and share some more theoretical reflections on the movement, where it is going, and its challenges and potential. The discussion so far has outlined and explored both the ethics and the practicalities of tiny houses. It pointed to the socio-technical foundations of the movement – if it can be loosely called that – which is advocating for, constructing, and *living* in these new forms of small dwellings.

We say new forms of what has gone before because of course humans historically inhabited small dwellings – a long, varied chronicle of necessity and in some cases preference. It is true, however, that in western modernity the long-run collective preference has been to elect for larger and more featured dwellings as permitted by wider and personal circumstances, such as household wealth, materials and land availability, market conditions and public policy (Troy 2000; Davison, 2016). This was reflected in the trend toward suburbanisation from the latter half of the 19th century, first by the affluent stratum and later by the 'subordinate classes' of Victorian industrialism. This great social election was especially evident in Australia, which Graeme Davison (1995: 40) regards as the world's 'first suburban nation'. Consequently, average dwelling sizes continued to grow during the 20th century, a trend accelerated after World War Two by household motorisation that permitted suburbanisation to occur at ever-greater social and spatial scales. Nonetheless, even in the context of ever larger houses (and other built forms), the appeal and facility of smaller re-locatable dwellings was maintained and confirmed in the form of caravans that suburbanites mostly deployed for recreation and sometimes also to meet ordinary accommodation needs (e.g., overflow shelter in backyards) (Mowbray, 1994).

With the rise of compact city advocacy and policy from the 1980s, the project of suburbanisation was challenged and in some places slowed or countered. More generally it was confounded as a universal form of urban expansion by structural conditions such as growing resource shortages, including land, changing household size and structure, new housing preferences, and financial and other economic stringencies (Gleeson and Low, 2000). Thus, whilst suburbanisation continues generally apace in Australian cities and regions, it accounts for a much smaller (and in some places rapidly declining) proportion of new housing stock than previously as smaller dwellings in multiunit developments (which vary greatly in scale) have become increasingly common and a necessary choice for many households (Hamnett and Freestone, 2018). At the same time, from the 1990s and through the first decade of the new millennium, average new dwelling sizes continued to rise, often taking the form of large dwellings on small-lot greenfield estates (Gleeson, 2010). There is, however, some evidence that this trend has tapered in recent years. Average new home (houses and apartment) sizes are down 1.6 per cent over the year of 2018 and have fallen to a 22-year low (mainly due to increasing proportion of apartments). That said, new free-standing houses are still amongst the largest in the world at 230.8 square metres over 2017/18, down 0.9 per cent on the year but 30 per cent larger than 30 years ago (CommSec, 2018).

In these historical and contemporary contexts, the advent of the tiny house phenomenon and movement bears some critical reflections for planning. These take both social and policy forms. First, there is the obvious question of whether tiny houses express real underlying social preferences or imposed necessities – i.e., real or constrained choices? In a world of finitude, especially of increasingly pressing ecological limits, constrained choice is not necessarily a bad thing, but it does raise profound equity issues for society and for policy. Recent and contemporary urban compaction in Australia, which in many ways runs counter to the compact city ideal (Forster, 2006; Gleeson, 2017), has introduced a tidal wave of smaller dwellings – usually in the form of large apartment block developments – that has arguably reduced housing choice (both in terms of size and quality) for low and modest income groups. It has further constrained the options for the substantial proportion of smaller households who do not prefer small dwellings; a preference well established by Wulff, Healy, and

Reynolds' (2004) study. In this dynamic context – viz., fast growing cities experiencing rapid social changes – the tiny house model, if generalised, represents a further potential risk to choice and equity, if not carefully matched to social need. An obvious risk is 'industry forcing', where the development sector pressures policymakers to deregulate housing and planning standards and allow the mass production of tiny houses. The fig leaf of 'improved environmental performance' might be deployed to rationalise this shift, even in the face of evidence that asserts no fixed relation between dwelling size and per capita resource usage (Gray, Gleeson, and Burke, 2010). In this case the socially progressive instincts and ambitions of the Tiny House Movement would surely be subverted. Bunce (2010) earlier raised the spectre of long-term caravan dwelling as a 'medieval' tenure form in the contemporary Australian city, and this caution resonates equally in consideration of tiny houses.

Another critical reflection manifests at the planning and housing policy scales and relates to the discussion above. It must be asked: are tiny houses an answer to manifest and increasingly pressing housing affordability and quality problems which could be brought to 'social scale' through well planned (not market driven) supporting policies? This begs the question of the larger 'here and now', including the looming and increasingly pressing problems of resource depletion and climate change. With these threats in mind, which arguably call for enhanced social solidarity and new supporting communal behaviours to cope with expected shocks and stresses, the further division of households into ever smaller and detached cellular structures may be judged problematical and counter to resilience imperatives (see Alexander & Gleeson, 2019 on this). Evidence suggests (e.g., Myors, O'Leary, and Helstroom, 2005) that well designed and carefully planned medium-density residential landscapes are best equipped to mitigate and adapt to such perturbations – both physically and through providing good prospects for (if not the predestination of) enhanced social capital. If new forms of shared and collective living in close but not crowded proximity – including reinhabited (not redeveloped) traditional suburban landscapes – are the best means to societal resilience in an age of threat, then any generalisation of tiny houses in existing urban fabrics would need to be carefully planned. Forms that either strengthen or weaken resilience are imaginable. The former might be well designed tiny houses carefully placed into suburban landscapes in ways that raise densities without compromising amenity and resource self-reliance. The latter could be unplanned scatterings or dense congregations of tiny houses that compromise these resilience values.

A general point to be made from the above reflections is that any social upscaling of tiny housing should be through planned not market driven means. The latter have the demonstrated potential to further deteriorate housing quality and choice and undermine regulatory standards. It is worth bearing in mind the political efforts that have had to be deployed in recent years in states such as NSW and Victoria to restore minimum apartment construction standards in the face of industry tendencies to pursue the lowest common design denominators (e.g., see Dow, 2016; Nicholls, 2012). This was not before the proliferation of much poor-quality multiunit development, especially in Sydney and Melbourne, at great cost to neighbourhood amenity, housing choice, and household wellbeing. It could therefore be agreed that tiny dwellings have a potential role to play in future cities; necessarily, however, as part of a larger public and policy commitment to enhanced comprehensive and careful planning in quest for improved urban sustainability and resilience.

Conclusion

We have presented an unusual or at least atypical essay, which attempts to synthesise consideration of practical built environment considerations with urban theory. An underlying rationale for this synthesis was to highlight the fact that urban theory needs to consider any new housing form, in this case the tiny house, within the panoply of development technologies and practices that are the focus of built environment regulation, including land use planning. We have emphasised that tiny houses and the interests promoting them are a socio-technical phenomenon, and that, necessarily, their technological (i.e., constructed) dimensions are important considerations for urban debate. Our practice reflections have shown that as an innovative technical phenomenon, tiny houses raise questions, and indeed frictions and paradoxes, for existing built environment regulation. Our leitmotiv here was to urge a more discriminatory institutional approach which would not view tiny houses simply as caravans, an historically evolved and specifically regulated form. As we pointed out, blunt regulation neglects the social rationale driving tiny house construction – the desire for innovative, affordable, and usually permanent dwellings – which marks them out from traditional relocatable dwelling forms (though we recognise how the latter in recent decades increasingly became a more permanent dwelling option in many contexts (Bunce, 2010)). Evidence already suggests that inflexible regulation will tend to drive this housing form into the shadowlands of informal and irregular development. This would not serve the public interest because the Tiny House Movement raises important issues – notably affordability, security, equity, and sustainability – that go to the heart of contemporary urban debate and action. As Australia's cities continue to grow and densify, in the context of emergent environmental threats and economic challenges, the public urban interest will be best served if all housing forms, especially the newest and most innovative, are brought explicitly into the discriminatory light of scholarly debate and institutional consideration. We urge this critical consideration of tiny houses by urbanists, practitioners, and theorists.

References

Alexander, S. 2016. 'A Prosperous Descent: Telling New Stories as the Old Book Closes'. *Griffith Review* 52: 4–24. Available at: https://griffithreview.com/wp-content/uploads/GR52_Alexander_Adcock-Ebook.FINAL_.pdf (accessed 10 December 2018).

Alexander, S. and Gleeson, B. 2019. *Degrowth in the Suburbs: A Radical Urban Imaginary*. Singapore: Palgrave Macmillan.

Anson, A. 2014. 'The World is My Backyard: Romanticism, Thoreauvian Rhetoric, and Constructive Confrontation in the Tiny House Movement'. In Holt, W. (ed.) *From Sustainable to Resilient Cities: Global Concerns and Urban Efforts* (Research in Urban Sociology, Volume 14) Emerald Group Publishing: 289–313.

Bares, V. et al. 2017. 'A Place for Tiny Houses. Exploring the possibilities: Tiny House Planning Resource for Australia 2017'. http://www.qshelter.asn.au/elements/2017/06/Tiny-House-Planning-Resource.pdf

Boeckermann, L., Kaczynski, A., and King, S.B. 2018. 'Dreaming Big and Living Small: Examining Motivations and Satisfaction in Tiny House Living'. *Journal of Housing and the Built Environment* 34(1): 61–71.

Bunce, D. 2010. 'Relocatable Homes: Medieval Tenure in the 21st Century?' *Urban Policy & Research* 28(3): 277–92.

CommSec, 2018. 'Economic Insights'. Available at: https://www.commsec.com.au/content/dam/EN/ResearchNews/2018Reports/November/ECO_Insights_191118_CommSec-Home-Size.pdf (accessed 10 December 2018).

Davison, G. 1995. 'Australia: The First Suburban Nation?' *Journal of Urban History* 22(1): 40–74.

Davison, G. 2016. *City Dreamers: The Urban Imagination in Australia*. Sydney: New South.

Darling, J., Gao, B., and Tilley, D.G. 2009. 'An Experimental Investigation of Car-Trailer High-Speed Stability'. *Proceedings of the Institution of Mechanical Engineering Part D.* 223(4): 471–484.

Dow, A. 2016. 'Apartment Rules Overhaul: Still Tiny But at Least They'll Have Windows'. *The Age*, 14 August. Available at: https://www.theage.com.au/national/victoria/new-apartment-standards-for-windows-ceiling-heights-but-not-floor-size-20160813-gqropx.html (accessed 13 December 2018).

Forster, C. 2006. 'The Challenge of Change: Australian Cities and Urban Planning in the New Millennium'. *Geographical Research* 44(2): 173–182.

Gleeson, B. 2010. *Lifeboat Cities*. Sydney: UNSW Press.

Gleeson, B. 2017. 'The Metropolitan Condition', in Hamnett, S. and Freestone, R. (eds). *Planning Metropolitan Australia*. Abingdon, UK: Routledge, 170–186.

Gleeson, B. and Low, N. 2000. *Australian Urban Planning: New Challenges, New Agendas*. Sydney: Allen & Unwin.

Gray, R., Gleeson, B., and Burke, M. 2010. 'Urban Consolidation, Household Greenhouse Emissions, and the Role of Planning'. *Urban Policy and Research*. 28(3): 335–46.

Hamnett, S. and Freestone, R. 2017. 'The Metropolitan Perspective', in Hamnett, S. and Freestone, R (eds). *Planning Metropolitan Australia*. Abingdon, UK: Routledge, 1–25.

Mowbray, M. 1994. 'Wealth, Welfare and the City: Developments in Australian Urban Policy'. *Urban Policy & Research* 12(2): 91–103.

Myors, P., O'Leary, R., and Helstroom, R. 2005. 'Multi Unit Residential Buildings: Energy and Peak Demand Study' (Report, October 2005). Available at: https://www.ausgrid.com.au/-/media/Documents/Reports-and-Research/Energy-use-research/Multi-Unit-Residential-Buildings.pdf?la=en&hash=205EBFE983FCBB5B3545165D5E5C510520FFD18B (accessed 25 March 2019).

Nicholls, S. 2012. 'Architects Push to Keep Design as Key to Overhaul'. *The Sydney Morning Herald*, 14 July. Available at: https://www.smh.com.au/national/nsw/architects-push-to-keep-design-as-key-to-overhaul-20120713-221bx.html (accessed 13 December 2018).

Saxton, M. 2019. 'When People Downsize to Tiny Houses, they Adopt more Environmentally Friendly Lifestyles'. *Resilience* (11 April 2019). Available at: https://www.resilience.org/stories/2019-04-11/when-people-downsize-to-tiny-houses-they-adopt-more-environmentally-friendly-lifestyles/ (accessed 20 May 2019).

Shearer, H. 2017. 'Interest in Tiny Houses is Growing, So Who Wants Them and Why?'. *The Conversation*, 20 September. Available at: https://theconversation.com/interest-in-tiny-houses-is-growing-so-who-wants-them-and-why-83872 (accessed 10 December 2018).

Shearer, H. and Burton, P. 2018. 'Towards a Typology of Tiny Houses'. *Housing, Theory, and Society*. DIO: https://doi.org/10.1080/14036096.2018.1487879

Shultz, F. 2019. 'Council Regulations for Tiny Houses on Wheels'. *Fred's Tiny Houses*. Available at: https://fredstinyhouses.com.au/council-regulation-database-for-tiny-houses-on-wheels/ (accessed 10 March 2019).

Troy, P. 2000. 'Introduction: house and home'. In Troy, P. (ed.). 2000. *A History of European Housing in Australia*. Melbourne: Cambridge University Press, 1–5.

Wulff, M., Healy, E., and Reynolds, M. 2004. 'Why Don't Small Households Live in Small Dwellings? Disentangling a Planning Dilemma'. *People and Place* 12(1): 57–70.

Chapter 12

What would a sufficiency economy look like?[1]

When [we have] obtained those things necessary to life, there is another alternative than to obtain superfluities; and that is, to adventure on life now, [our] vacation from humbler toil having commenced.

– Henry David Thoreau

Introduction

The notion of 'sufficiency' has been defended in wisdom and spiritual traditions throughout history and across the globe. Overlapping perspectives range from the Buddha's 'middle way', to the 'moderation' of Socrates, Plato, Aristotle, and Epicurus, to the 'radical simplicity' of Diogenes or Gandhi. Some practices of sufficiency have taken on social forms, such as the simple living Amish communities or contemporary ecovillages, while others, such as Henry Thoreau, have explored more individualistic forms. The Quakers ground their embrace of simplicity upon religious ideals, whereas a range of thinkers, from William Morris to Benjamin Franklin, recognise the political significance of enlightened material restraint. More recently, the 'hippie' counter-cultures of the 1960s and 70s, as well as the modern Voluntary Simplicity Movement, see lifestyles of sufficiency as a low-impact path to an increased quality of life (see generally, Alexander and McLeod, 2014).

On reflection it is quite remarkable the range and diversity of thinkers and movements that uphold the moral, hedonic, and/or ecological benefits of material sufficiency, not only from across the political spectrum but also from within all the major religions. There must be something to it. At the same time, this rich history of sufficiency thinking and practice has always been marginalised and is certainly not reflected widely in mainstream discourse today. In an age when consumerist cultures are expanding across the globe, talk of sufficiency can seem old-fashioned, austere, or even anti-progress. Furthermore, social theorists have long pointed out that

---

1 Originally in Matthew Ingleby and Samuel Randalls (eds) *Just Enough: The History, Culture and Politics of Sufficiency*, 2018, Palgrave Macmillan, Ch. 8, pp 117–134.

consumption reaches beyond our relationship to the material world and is used to express and create identity and indicate belonging to a social group or class, making calls for reduced consumption problematic (see Douglas, 1976; Miller, 2008). Nevertheless, as I will argue in this chapter, sufficiency is a concept that is more relevant today than ever before, even if it must be reinterpreted and applied in context specific ways.

The purpose of this chapter is to describe a radical vision of sustainability, which I will call a 'sufficiency economy'. This is an economy that has low energy and resource requirements relative to developed economies, but which sufficiently provides for local needs using mostly local resources. In contrast with growth-orientated economies (Purdey, 2010), a sufficiency economy would not be driven to expand continuously by the imperatives of profit-maximisation and consumerist cultures. Instead, the underlying goal would be to universalise a modest but sufficient material standard of living, where everyone has 'enough' to flourish within planetary limits (Princen, 2005; Latouche, 2009; Trainer, 2010; Alexander, 2015a).

The analysis begins by briefly outlining the overlapping problems humanity faces today, not for the purpose of providing a thorough review of the global situation but simply to contextualise the discussion that follows. If we do not have a clear understanding of the magnitude of the problems we face, we are unlikely to formulate an appropriate response. Focusing on the developed nations, the analysis then considers what life would be like if we gave up the limitless pursuit of growth and transitioned to a highly localised 'sufficiency economy' based on far lower resource and energy consumption.

The value of these envisioning exercises lies in their ability to expand the imagination and help people conceive of radically different forms of human flourishing and organisation. Too often when discussing the world's problems with students and colleagues I am faced with nodding heads, only to confront the rejoinder: 'But what's the alternative?' By outlining a sufficiency-based alternative below, I hope to provide at least a partial answer to that important question. After all, if we do not have some relatively detailed vision of where we would like to end up – or may need to end up – it is very difficult to formulate coherent strategies for how to get there. In this sense the following exposition builds upon the history of utopian speculation (de Geus, 1999), for the exposition is designed to provoke thought about the possibility, feasibility, and even the desirability of alternative forms of life based on notions of sufficiency, moderation, and frugality.

The global predicament

Most people, including many environmentalists, seem to believe that affluent lifestyles and the growth economies that support them can be sustained and even globalised, provided the world transitions to systems of renewable energy and produces commodities more cleanly and efficiently. The following review briefly outlines some of the interrelated reasons why this assumption is invalid, providing evidential grounds for radically rethinking the nature of dominant economic structures and goals.

Ecological overshoot and the limits of technology

The ecological footprint of the global economy now exceeds the sustainable carrying capacity of the planet by 70 per cent (Global Footprint Network, 2018). Despite decades of extraordinary technological advance, the overall ecological impacts of economic activity continue to increase (Jackson, 2009: Ch. 4; Wiedmann et al., 2015). To be sure, human beings are getting better at producing commodities more cleanly and efficiently. But we are also producing more commodities due to economic growth, and it turns out that those production increases outweigh the efficiency gains in production, leading to an overall increase in the impacts of economic activity, not a decrease. Efficiency without sufficiency is lost (Alexander, 2015b: Ch. 1).

When we do the arithmetic of growth, the impossibility of a technological fix to environmental problems becomes perfectly clear. If the developed nations were to grow their economies, in terms of GDP, at a modest 2 per cent over coming decades and by 2050 the poorest nations had caught up, then by that stage the global economy, which is already in ecological overshoot, would be almost 15 times larger than it is today (Jackson, 2009: 81). This means, for example, that if we are to meet the emissions targets of the Intergovernmental Panel on Climate Change (IPCC, 2007) then the carbon intensity of global economic output must be 130 times lower than it is today, requiring 11 per cent reductions every year. And yet efficiency improvements over the period 1990–2007 were merely 0.7 per cent per year (Jackson, 2009: 79). These hard numbers ought to shatter the faith of techno-optimists. Technology alone cannot make a growth economy sustainable. The extent of decoupling required is simply too great. As will be argued below, the consumer class also needs to consume less – a lot less.

Poverty amidst plenty

The harsh reality of ecological overshoot is even more challenging when we bear in mind that in the poorest parts of the world today great multitudes are living lives oppressed by extreme poverty. The human community therefore must find a way to *raise* the material standards of living of the world's poorest people – who surely have a right to develop their economic capacities in some form – while at the same time *reducing* humanity's overall ecological footprint (Meadows, Randers, and Meadows, 2004: xv). What is clear is that the current 'trickle down' approach to poverty alleviation is neither working sufficiently well nor ecologically sustainable, as evidenced by a report from the New Economics Foundation (Woodard and Simms, 2006). This study shows that between 1990 and 2001, for every $100 of growth in the world's average income per capita, merely $0.60 contributed to reducing poverty below the '$1 per day' line. This means that to achieve $1 of poverty reduction at that ratio, an extra $166 of global production and consumption is required. Not only do these figures expose global growth as an extremely inefficient means of reducing poverty, it also implies that the amount of growth needed to alleviate poverty would be, without question, environmentally unsupportable.

Overpopulation

Exacerbating these issues further is the fact that global human population is expected to exceed nine billion by mid-century and reach eleven billion by the end of the century (Gerland et al., 2014). Obviously, this will intensify greatly the already intense competition over access to the world's limited natural resources and put further pressure on fragile ecosystems. But even if humanity somehow managed to stabilise population at once and thereby avoid the expected increases, the global economy would nevertheless remain in gross ecological overshoot. This again points to the need to rethink the current economic model based on growth and the pursuit of affluence. Sustainability means globalising sufficiency, not affluence.

Consumer malaise

A final reason to abandon the growth-orientated economy is that high-consumption lifestyles, so often held up as the peak of human development, have actually achieved disappointing results in terms of happiness and life satisfaction (Lane, 2000; Pickett and Wilkinson, 2010). There is a mounting body of sociological and psychological evidence (Alexander, 2015a: Ch. 2; Kasser, 2002) indicating that lives orientated around achieving high levels of consumption often result in such things as time poverty, stress, physical and mental illness, wasteful status competition, loss of community, disconnection from nature, unhappiness, and even a sense of meaninglessness or alienation in life.

Fortunately, however, this evidence raises the tantalising possibility that members of the global consumer class could live more fulfilling and meaningful lives by *reducing* their consumption, perhaps in exchange for more time, while at the same time reducing their ecological footprint and leaving more resources for those in greater need (Jackson, 2005; Brown and Kasser, 2005; Alexander and Ussher, 2012).

Interestingly, the prospect of 'living more on less' has been a line of argument employed by most advocates of sufficiency throughout history. This is a point worthy of emphasis, because calls for sufficiency will surely speak to a broader audience if people come to see that their own lives may actually be enriched by avoiding superfluous consumption and instead seeking the good life in non-materialistic sources of meaning and fulfilment. As the ancient Chinese philosopher Lao-Tzu once said: 'He who knows he has enough is rich', which implies that those who have enough, but who do not know it, are poor.

Envisioning a prosperous descent

For all of the above reasons we must explore alternative ways to flourish beyond consumer culture, and embracing a post-growth economy based on material sufficiency is one means of doing so, and evidently a necessary means. Accordingly, the remainder of this chapter is dedicated to providing some of those details, at least as far as they apply to urban contexts in the developed world. By attempting to envision a sufficiency economy, in something of a utopian spirit, my hope is to advance the debate around what genuine sustainability actually means for daily life. Some readers may find the nature of this economic vision confronting and want to dismiss it in advance as being too frugal and austere. But in a context of gross ecological overshoot and seven billion people, I contend that a 'fair share' ecological footprint would demand changes similar to what is described below (Odum and Odum, 2001; Trainer, 2010).

Water

In most urban contexts the amount of roof space available to collect water would be insufficient to secure the necessary water supplies for such dense populations. What this means is that urban contexts *require* the water mains to exist, at least for the foreseeable future, for if this system failed for more than a few days most people would quickly perish. Accordingly, a sufficiency economy must at least have the energy supply and stability to maintain the water mains at a sufficiently high level of regularity and safety.

Despite a relatively conventional mains system remaining in place, in a sufficiency economy attitudes to water consumption and collection would undergo a revolution. Today, average daily household water consumption in the United States is around 370 litres per person. The United Nations and the World Health Organisation advise that 20 litres per person, per day, is the minimum needed for the most basic subsistence (drinking, cooking, and sanitation). In a sufficiency economy, domestic water consumption would fall to a fraction of average US consumption – perhaps somewhere between 50–70 litres per person, per day – which is enough to live a dignified existence without leaving much room for waste.

In order to reduce water consumption so drastically, various steps would be taken. First of all, every household would maximise its roof water collection via water tanks. People will become proficient in creating and connecting systems of water collection and reuse. Greywater systems, for example, will become the household norm, including the use of tank water to flush the toilet. Similarly, water could be collected in a bucket while showering, to flush the toilet. Eventually, composting toilets could replace the flush toilet, further reducing water consumption (Jenkins, 2005).

In those times when people are required to draw from the mains, frugality and conservation are key. Being conscientious of water consumption when preparing food and cleaning dishes, and never watering (or even having) lawns, are important and easily implemented conservation strategies. Perhaps the largest savings in the domestic sphere can come from how we wash our clothes and ourselves. Clothes could be washed less often and showers could be taken less regularly, as well as reduced to a minute or two. In fact, in a context of extreme water scarcity, cleaning occasionally with a bucket of water and some soap would be perfectly adequate for cleanliness and hygiene.

Food

In a sufficiency economy, food production would be highly localised and produced organically, in order to decarbonise the food system and build resilience (Holmgren, 2002). One of the most significant, but often overlooked, implications of the transition away from industrial food production is the increased labour needed for organic production. The increased labour requirements arise primarily from the absence or great reduction of mechanised (oil-dependent) farm machinery, but organic fertiliser production and pest control are also typically more time intensive than industrialised techniques.

A transition to organic food production, however, will have many benefits, including environmental benefits, reconnecting communities with the local land base upon which they depend for subsistence, and the health benefits associated with moving away from sedentary office or factory work toward the more active and outdoor work of farming. Governments should do everything they can to support localised, organic agriculture, starting by putting a price on carbon. But communities can get to work now without waiting for the state.

A sufficiency economy would aim to maximise organic food production *within* the urban boundary. This would involve digging up lawns and turning them into productive vegetable gardens, and planting fruit trees in all available spaces. Nature strips would be cultivated; parks would be turned into small farms or community gardens; suitable roofs would become productive, herbs would grow on balconies and windowsills, and generally all food producing potential would be realised. Most households in suburbia would keep chickens for eggs, bees for honey, and some might even keep small livestock, such as goats for milk and cheese. Animals are also a great source of manure for compost, and many permaculturists build animals into their organic systems. There is also great potential for building raised beds on driveways, some footpaths or roads, and car parks. Mushrooms could be cultivated on the shady side of the house, and household or neighbourhood aquaculture systems could provide urban centres with some of their fish supply. Cuba provides an inspiring example of what can be achieved in terms of urban agriculture.

Even in a sufficiency economy, however, we can expect our households to 'import' various foods in various forms, if not from around the world, then certainly from rural contexts. This, in fact, would probably be a necessity in most urban contexts, because growing space probably does not permit strict self-sufficiency (MacRae et al., 2010). Even if urban agriculture were enthusiastically embraced, most large urban areas across the world would still need to import a significant portion of its fruit and vegetables, to say nothing of its meat, grains, minerals, and other goods.

The local and organic food production would also drastically change our consumption habits. Food would be eaten 'in season' in order to avoid having to import non-seasonal foods from the other side of the world. Preserving foods would be the most appropriate way to access those foods out of season. Generally, food would be unprocessed and require no disposable packaging. In order to minimise the environmental impact of our diets, demand for meat, fish, and dairy would be greatly reduced. This would open up huge tracts of land for human food production that are currently used to produce grain for animals.

Finally, as well as composting human waste for 'humanure' via composting toilets (Jenkins, 2005), a sufficiency economy would vigilantly compost all its organic food wastes in order to supply the growing need for organic fertilisers and biogas digesters, reducing the amount of so-called 'waste' currently sent to landfill.

Clothing

The primary function of clothing is to keep us warm, and its secondary function, is to cover nakedness. In consumer societies today, however, the purpose of clothing has evolved to become primarily about expressing one's identity or social status. In a sufficiency economy, the fashion industry would be considered a superfluous luxury and accordingly it would be amongst the first industries to disappear. Of course, people will always want to express themselves through what they wear, so 'style' would not disappear so much as evolve. A new aesthetic of sufficiency would develop, and soon enough the social expectation to look fashionable would become a quirk of history, incomprehensible to the new generation.

In a sufficiency economy, we would salvage, swap, and reuse clothing diligently, as well as get very good at sewing and mending. For the next few decades we can do this adequately by simply reusing and recycling the abundance of clothing produced in consumer society. In the future, when new clothing is needed, the primary aims of production would be functionality and sustainability, not profit-maximisation strategies playing on the pernicious desire for ever-changing styles. Fabrics like nylon and polyester would be minimised as they are made from petrochemicals and are non-biodegradable; and cotton requires extensive use of pesticides. Functional, low-impact fabrics would be used instead, such as agricultural hemp and organic wool.

Housing

The issue of housing is particularly difficult and complex. Sometimes well-meaning environmentalists give the impression that we can move directly, in the next few decades to an agrarian village scenario where everyone is living in self-built cob houses or 'Earthships'. The fact is, however, that over the next few critical decades, most people are going to find themselves living in an urban environment that already exists – suburbia. In other words, the houses and apartment blocks that already exist now, in most cases, will remain over coming decades, no matter how inadequate they are from an ecological perspective.

Given this reality, the immediate task is making best use of existing infrastructure (Holmgren, 2012). This might involve things like taking in boarders or putting a caravan in the driveway to help resist further urban sprawl, or putting up thick curtains and sealing gaps in windows and doors to increase energy efficiency. It might involve changing all the light bulbs or going to the expense of getting an energy efficient fridge or another water tank. It would certainly involve refraining from spending large amounts of money renovating for purely aesthetic reasons or extending the house to create a games room. Of course, much of the existing housing stock is poorly designed so there are real limits to what retrofitting can achieve. But much can be done to improve the ecological performance of existing housing. We are hardly going to knock down the suburbs and start again.

In the longer term, the housing stock will need to be replaced, and within a sufficiency economy there would be certain expectations about how to do this. Materials should be sourced as locally as possible and designed for long-term durability and energy efficiency. Straw-bale or mud-brick houses may become common. More people and communities would take part in the construction of their own homes to reduce costs. To limit the resources required, as well as limit the spaces needed to heat and cool, houses would be much smaller and densely inhabited than is typically the case today. But they would be sufficient.

Energy

In terms of energy use, the contrast between a growth economy and a sufficiency economy could hardly be starker. Whereas growth economies seek as much energy as possible at the lowest market price, a sufficiency economy requires only enough energy to provide a modest but sufficient material standard of living for all. This means much lower energy requirements, primarily through renewable sources. Even more important than 'greening' supply is reducing demand, because renewables are unlikely to ever be able to fully replace fossil fuels (Moriarty and Honnery, 2012). Therefore, a sufficiency economy implies an energy descent future (Odum and Odum, 2001; Alexander, 2015a).

Due to the close connection between energy and economy, reductions in energy would inevitably imply significantly reduced production and consumption (Latouche, 2009; Trainer, 2010). This would not necessarily be a problem, however, because as has already been made clear, consumption levels in a sufficiency economy would be considerably lower than in consumer societies today, thus requiring much less energy to support them. As well as economic contraction, efficiency improvements and conservation efforts would also lessen the energy requirements of a sufficiency economy.

Hydro, solar, and wind would provide the bulk of electricity provision, and some limited use of biofuels can be expected for critical transport and machine fuels. Fossil fuels will be phased out, although some limited but ongoing use will be required to assist in the transition to a fully renewable energy system. The use of neighbourhood methane gas digesters could be used to provide some domestic gas for heating and cooking.

Transport

In a sufficiency economy, major reductions in transport energy will be achieved through the relocalisation of economies (Rubin, 2009). To the limited extent that international trade continues, it will probably be conducted in the main by sail, as it was prior to the petroleum age.

Transport savings achieved through relocalisation especially applies to food production. Industrial food systems are highly dependent on oil not only for transport, but also for things like pesticides and plastic packaging. As noted above, a post-industrial food system will mean more localised, organic food production, and therefore vastly reduced energy requirements for transport and production. Some of the food for cities would be imported from rural contexts, mainly by electric trains.

The other major area of energy savings relates to driving cars. In order to decarbonise the economy, people will need to drive much less, or not at all. Electric cars will not be able to escape this imperative, because producing them depends on fossil fuels, and also for most people electric cars are and will remain unaffordable. Just as importantly, it would take many decades or even a century to replace the one billion petroleum-powered vehicles on the roads today with electric vehicles, and we do not have that much time to mitigate the effects of peak oil and climate change. The only solution is driving less (Moriarty and Honnery, 2008).

Various studies have estimated that around half of all car trips are less than 5 kilometres, and around one third are less than 3 kilometres (Ludlum, 2012: 21). In many cases those could be replaced with walking, cycling, or public transport. In order to make these options viable, governments will need to invest heavily in a good system of electricity-powered public transport, such as light trains or trams, as well as networks of bike lanes.[2] Putting a price on carbon will also provide appropriate economic incentives to reduce car dependence and build a post-carbon infrastructure.

In the longer term, however, the most significant reductions in car dependence will result from economic relocalisation. If this transformation were to occur, driving would be unnecessary for many people, as their place of work would be either at home or a short walk down the road. Longer distances would be covered on bicycle or public transport.

Work and production

The most significant changes to work and production, noted immediately above, are that the household would once again become a place of

---

2 There are, however, deeper structural complications underlying the requirement to stop driving as much, which should not be ignored. For many people today, driving is the only way of getting to work, so the injunction to 'get out of your car' may frustrate those people who would love to drive less but cannot, due to a lack of viable alternatives. Suburbia was built on the basis of cheap oil, which meant that 'sprawl' was not seen as much of a problem. But as oil enters the era of scarcity, the long commutes will become increasingly problematic, not only from a cost perspective, but also from an environmental perspective (Alexander, 2015b: Ch 8).

production. Rather than hiring other people to grow all our food, cook our meals, make our clothes, build our furniture, look after our children, maintain our houses, etc., we would generally take care of such things ourselves, so far as it were possible (see Astyk, 2012). Furthermore, households would sometimes produce goods for trade or barter, such as furniture, crockery, clothes, or food, and thereby contribute to the broader local economy. Artisans might also produce speciality goods at the household level, such as musical instruments, paintings, or various tools.

Nevertheless, the sufficiency economy should not be understood to mean strict self-sufficiency at the household level. It would still be desirable for much production to take place beyond the household, but the nature of what would be produced and the values motivating production would be very different. The provision of basic needs – such as food, clothing, shelter, tools, and medicine – would be the primary focus of production, and the motivation would be to produce what was necessary and sufficient for a good life, rather than to produce luxuries or superfluous abundance. While some large factories would probably remain in order to provide certain materials or hi-tech equipment, small private businesses and worker cooperatives would in most cases replace the mega-corporation, with the local grocer and hardware store returning to Mainstreet, and community-owned-and-operated farms providing much of the community's sustenance (Trainer, 2010).

The greatly reduced level of production and consumption in a sufficiency economy would allow for reduced working hours for most people, at least in the formal/cash economy. This would create far more time for leisure and the necessary home production.

Money, markets, and exchange

The question of what role money, markets, and exchange would play in a sufficiency economy is complex and cannot be fully addressed here. Nevertheless, some broad comments can be made on these subjects.

First of all, it is worth noting that throughout history, human beings have exchanged goods and services with each other, either by way of barter, gift, or through the use of money. These practices are going to continue although the nature of money, markets, and exchange will have to evolve greatly, as will our attitudes toward them. There will remain 'markets' for various goods that cannot be produced within the household, and money will likely remain as the most convenient tool for 'keeping accounts', so to speak. But non-monetary forms of exchange, such as gift, barter, and sharing, are likely to become much more prominent modes of economic activity. Since profit-maximisation would not be the aim of market activity in a sufficiency economy, less attention would be given to producing things that fetch the highest price, and more attention would be given to producing what the community most needs.

The fact that markets of some variety would probably still remain in a sufficiency economy implies that some forms of private property are likely to endure, although it is just as likely, and desirable, that more of the economy comes under social control. Although the balance between private and social control of the economy could unfold in an infinite variety of ways – a decision that will rightly be left to the localised democratic communities – a sufficiency economy must be designed so that everyone has enough, and this means taking responsibility for ensuring that the basic needs of all are universally met. This will require a significant degree of social control of the economy, as basic needs would not be adequately met if resource allocation were purely left to market forces. The most important issue would be that everyone had access to land and affordable housing, and communities might have to experiment with how best to ensure this occurred (see, e.g., Alexander, 2011: Chs 2 and 5).

In terms of monetary systems, one of the greatest problems today is that money is loaned into existence as debt that accrues interest. For such systems to function they require economic growth in order for the debts *plus* the interest to be paid back (Trainer, 2011). Interest payments therefore imply an expansion of the money supply. A sufficiency economy could not by definition have a monetary system that required growth, so it follows that interest-bearing loans could not be the primary means of creating money. The alternative may have to look something like Ted Trainer's proposal for community-owned banks that provide zero-interest credit for ventures that have been selected on the basis that they serve community interests (Trainer, 2010).

Technology

In a sufficiency economy, many technological conveniences we know today will largely disappear. Microwaves, vacuum cleaners, electronic kitchen gadgets, mobile phones, etc., may all become relics of history, but without causing much hardship at all. That said, we should also remember that the sufficiency economy may arrive in the wake of industrial civilisation's deterioration (Greer, 2008). This will mean that vast quantities of industrially produced goods, tools, and materials will already be in existence, and for many decades, perhaps centuries, we would be living in what some have called the 'salvage economy' (Greer, 2009). Human beings will doubtless prove to be exceedingly creative in the use and reuse of existing materials. The old ethics of the depression era will return, as people learn to 'use it up, wear it out, make it do, or do without'.

The clothesline will replace the clothes dryer; the bike will largely replace the car; and the television will essentially disappear. I suspect that washing machines and fridges will be the last things we give up, but life would go on even if they became unavailable or unaffordable. Hopefully computers will remain to do some important tasks, although private computers might become much less common. The main thing is for communities to put their mind to the question of what technologies are 'appropriate' (Schumacher, 1973).

Conclusion

There are countless other avenues that this analysis could explore, including: what would become of existing health and education systems, or pension schemes? How would people spend their leisure and what art forms might flourish? How would the sufficiency economy differ in urban centres as opposed to rural settings? And how would sufficiency in the global North affect the global South? These are all issues that deserve further attention, but those discussions must be deferred for another occasion.

The sufficiency economy clearly represents a fundamentally different way of life for most people in consumer societies today. This raises the question of how we would transition to such an economy, a question that is also beyond the scope of this chapter, but something I have addressed elsewhere (see, e.g., Alexander, 2015a: Ch. 10). Could the transition be voted in through the mechanisms of parliamentary democracy? Would it require a political revolution and the introduction of some form of eco-socialism? Or would it require grassroots movements to essentially do it themselves, building the new economy underneath the existing economy, without state assistance? My own view is that it would be unwise, at this stage, to commit unconditionally to any one strategy given the future is so uncertain.

I do think, however, that the Transition Movement (Hopkins, 2008), while not homogenous in its approach, currently has something of the right strategic balance here. Adopting what I would call 'participatory democracy', the movement basically accepts that change must be driven at the grassroots, community level, while at the same time being prepared to press on governments (mainly local governments) to assist in the transition whenever that seems to be a good use of limited energies. Furthermore, if the Transition Movement were ever to succeed in achieving its ambitious and diverse goals, I believe something resembling the sufficiency economy may well be the result. What is important is that the debate gets drawn away from the question of how to *maintain* the existing system, toward the urgent and necessary question of what new system should *replace* the existing system. In this sense the humble notion of a sufficiency economy can be seen as a revolutionary, but also necessary, project.

References

Alexander, S. 2011. 'Property beyond Growth: Toward a Politics of Voluntary Simplicity' (doctoral thesis, Melbourne Law School, University of Melbourne), http://papers.ssrn.com/sol3/papers.cfm?abstract_id=1941069 date accessed 5 May 2015.

Alexander, S. 2015a. *Sufficiency Economy: Enough, for Everyone, Forever.* Melbourne: Simplicity Institute.

Alexander, S. 2015b. *Prosperous Descent: Crisis as Opportunity in an Age of Limits.* Melbourne: Simplicity Institute.

Alexander, S. and McLeod, A. (eds). 2014. *Simple Living in History: Pioneers of the Deep Future.* Melbourne: Simplicity Institute.

Alexander, S. and Ussher, S. 2012. 'The Voluntary Simplicity Movement: A Multi-National Survey Analysis in Theoretical Context'. *Journal of Consumer Culture* 12(1), 66–88.

Astyk, S. 2012. *Making Home: Adapting Our Homes and Our Lives to Settle in Place.* Gabriola Island: New Society Publishers.

Brown, K. and Kasser, T. 2005. 'Are Psychological and Ecological Well-being Compatible? The Role of Values, Mindfulness, and Lifestyle'. *Social Indicators Research* 74, 349–368.

De Geus, M. 1999. *Ecological Utopias: Envisioning the Sustainable Society.* Utrecht: International Books.

Douglas, M. 1976. 'Relative Poverty – Relative Communication' in T. Jackson (ed.). 2006. *The Earthscan Reader in Sustainable Consumption.* London: Earthscan.

Gerland, P. et al. 2014. 'World Population Stabilization Unlikely This Century'. *Science* 18 September 2014: DOI: 10.1126/science.1257469.

Global Footprint Network. 2018. Reports available at: http://www.footprintnetwork.org/ date accessed at 31 March 2018.

Greer, J.M. 2008. *The Long Descent: A User's Guide to the End of Industrial Civilization.* Gabriola Island: New Society Publishers.

12. What would a sufficient economy look like?

Greer, J.M. 2009. *The Eco-Technic Future: Envisioning a Post-Peak World.* Gabriola Island: New Society Publishers.

Holmgren, D. 2002. *Permaculture: Principles and Pathways beyond Sustainability.* Hepburn Springs: Holmgren Design Services.

Holmgren, D. 2012. 'Retrofitting the Suburbs for the Energy Descent Future'. *Simplicity Institute Report* 12i, 1–8.

Hopkins, R. 2008. *The Transition Handbook: From Oil Dependency to Local Resilience.* Totnes, Devon: Green Books.

Intergovernmental Panel on Climate Change (IPCC). 2007. 'Climate Change 2007 – The Physical Science Basis'. http://www.ipcc.ch/publications_and_data/ publications_and_data_reports.shtml date accessed 29 June 2013.

Jackson, T. 2005. 'Live Better by Consuming Less? Is There a Double Dividend in Sustainable Consumption?' *Journal of Industrial Ecology,* 9, 19–36.

Jackson, T. 2009. *Prosperity without Growth: Economics for a Finite Planet.* London: Earthscan.

Jenkins, J. 2005. *The Humanure Handbook: A Guide to Composting Human Manure,* 3rd edn. White River Junction: Chelsea Green Publishing.

Kasser, T. 2002. *The High Price of Materialism.* Cambridge, Mass: MIT Press.

Lane, R. 2000. *The Loss of Happiness in Market Democracies.* New Haven: Yale University Press.

Latouche, S. 2009. *Farewell to Growth.* Cambridge, UK: Polity Press.

Ludlum, S. 2012. *Bike Vision: The Greens 2029 Perth Bike Plan.* http://scott-ludlam. greensmps.org.au/sites/default/files/bike_vision_greens_2029_perth_bike_plan_ small.pdf date accessed 15 June 2015.

MacRae, R. et al. 2010. 'Could Toronto Provide 105 of its Fresh Vegetable Requirements from within its own Boundaries? Matching Consumption Requirements with Growing Space'. *Journal of Agriculture, Food Systems, and Community Development* 1(2).

Meadows, D., Randers, J., and Meadows, D. 2004. *Limits to Growth: The 30-year Update.* White River Junction: Chelsea Green).

Miller, D. 2008. *The Comfort of Things.* Cambridge: Polity.

Moriarty, P. and Honnery, D. 2008. 'Low-Mobility: The Future of Transport'. *Futures* 40, 865–872.

Moriarty, P. and Honnery, D. 2012. 'Preparing for a Low-Energy Future'. *Futures* 44(10), 883–892.

Odum, E. and Odum, H. 2001. *A Prosperous Way Down: Principles and Policies.* Colorado: University Press of Colorado.

Pickett, K. and Wilkinson, R. 2010. *The Spirit Level: Why Greater Equality Makes Societies Stronger.* London: Penguin.

Princen, T. 2005. *The Logic of Sufficiency.* Cambridge, Mass.: MIT Press.

Purdey, S. 2010. *Economic Growth, the Environment, and International Relations: The Growth Paradigm.* New York: Routledge.

Rubin, J. 2009. *Why Your World is About to Get a Whole Lot Smaller.* London: Virgin.

Schumacher, E. 1973. *Small is Beautiful: Economics as if People Mattered.* London: Blond and Briggs.

Trainer, T. 2010. *The Transition to a Sustainable and Just World.* Sydney: Envirobook.

Trainer, T. 2011. 'The Radical Implications of Zero Growth Economy'. *Real World Economics Review* 57, 71–82.

Wiedmann, T. et al. 2015. 'The Material Footprint of Nations'. *Proceedings of the National Academy of Sciences in the United States of America* 112(20): 6271–6276. DOI: 10.1073/pnas.1220362110.

Woodward, D. and Simms, A. 2006. 'Growth Isn't Working: The Uneven Distribution of Benefits and Costs from Economic Growth'. http://www.neweconomics.org/ publications/entry/growth-isnt-working date accessed 28 August 2015.

Chapter 13

Suburban practices of energy descent[1]

Introduction

Cities are humanity's most intricate creations. They are the meta-formations within which other expressions of human creativity emerge and develop, and this complexity, like life itself, depends on energy for its sustenance and development (Smil, 2017). Energy is not just another resource or commodity: it is the key that unlocks access to all other resources and commodities, thereby giving shape to the physical boundaries within which human societies must take form. Responding to urban problems and pursuing societal goals almost always involve energy investment, yet the more problems that are faced or goals that are pursued, the more energy a society needs to maintain its way of life. This is how civilisations take form and evolve, both enabled and constrained by their energetic foundations (Tainter, 1988). Indeed, a society must be able to meet and afford *ongoing* energy requirements if its specific socio-economic form is to persist. If energy needs cannot be met or afforded, the society will transform or be transformed, voluntarily or otherwise.

Never has this energy dependency been truer than in the low-density urban landscapes of suburbia, predominantly comprised of stand-alone houses and generally inhabited by high-impact, energy-intensive households, which are both creatures and creators of the growth economy (Alexander and Gleeson, 2019). Suburban affluence is the defining image of the good life under globalised capitalism, often held up as a model to which all humanity should aspire. The dominant development model has seen the global consumer class expanding as more economies industrialise and urbanise. But every aspect of this industrial mode of existence has been shaped by the cheap and abundant fossil energy supplies that have become accessible in the last two centuries (Smil, 2017).

---

1 Originally published in *The American Journal of Economics and Sociology*, 79(3), 2020, pp 907–940, co-authored with Brendan Gleeson.

This dependency on fossil fuels has given rise to an energy crisis with two main dimensions (Moriarty and Honnery, 2011. First, fossil fuels are finite resources that are being consumed at extraordinary rates (IEA, 2018), such that their supply will one day peak and decline even as demand threatens to grow (Mohr et al., 2015). Second, the combustion of fossil fuels is also the leading driver of climate change (IPCC, 2018), meaning that humanity must decarbonise by choice even before we are forced to do so through geological depletion. Further to those challenges, it remains highly uncertain whether renewable energy technologies will be able to fully replace the energy services provided by fossil fuels in an energetically or financially affordable way (Moriarty and Honnery, 2016; Alexander and Floyd, 2018). Thus, the future will be defined by increased energy scarcity not energy abundance, which implies an 'energy descent future' with rising energy costs relative to today (Odum and Odum, 2001; Holmgren, 2012).

Rather than further diagnosing these problems, we assume the energy predicament outlined above and proceed on the basis that the cost of energy will rise in coming years and decades as the age of energy abundance comes to an end. We also take as given the close connection between energy and economic activity (Keen, Ayres, and Standish, 2019; Ayres and Warr, 2009). On that basis, we assume that declining energy availability and affordability will lead to economic contraction and reduced material affluence. In overconsuming and overdeveloped nations, such resource and energy 'degrowth' is desirable and necessary from a sustainability perspective, provided it is planned for and managed in ways consistent with basic principles of distributive equity. A large literature has emerged over the last decade defending and examining the various complex issues surrounding such planned degrowth (Weiss and Cattaneo, 2017; Kallis et al., 2018; Trainer, 2020). We are broadly sympathetic with that paradigm. It informs the analysis below. Of course, scarce and expensive energy may well arrive *without* sufficient planning and in inequitable ways. This means that societies may need to prepare for economic contraction which looks and is experienced more like recession, depression, or even collapse – an unplanned economic contraction. But whether economic contraction arrives through design or disaster – or some mixture – this profound turning point in industrial civilisation will be experienced very differently depending on context, including the vast array of suburban settings that now exist in the global urban age (Gleeson, 2014).

In this chapter, we examine how scarcer and more expensive energy may impact the suburban way of life and how households might prepare for this very plausible, but challenging, energy-descent future. While we acknowledge various structural challenges (especially access to land and the problem of carbon-dependent urban infrastructure), our analysis focuses primarily on the social or 'grassroots' responses that may be available within those existing structural constraints. In addressing this theme and context, we acknowledge a tradition of prior commentary on 'peak oil' adaptation (Heinberg, 2004; Greer, 2008; Hopkins, 2008; Holmgren, 2018). However, we do not fall into the catastrophism of some suburban analysts of energy descent (Kunstler, 2005). Our aim is to provide an up-to-date exploration of the energy challenges facing suburbanites in a carbon-constrained world. We also feel that our scholarly analysis and review of the issues are worthwhile contributions in an age where energy descent futures remain neglected and on the fringe of academic literature. We believe that scholarly neglect owes primarily to widely held techno-optimistic assumptions about renewable energy transitions. (For a critical review of those assumptions, see Alexander and Floyd, 2018.)

Our analysis involves an examination of energy demand management in suburbia and how the limited energy needed to provide for essential household services can best be secured in an era of expensive energy and climate instability. After reviewing various energy practices, we highlight the need for an ethos of sufficiency, moderation, and radical frugality, which we argue is essential for building resilience in the face of energy challenges. We begin, however, with an energy focus, and then explore the broader implications for urban material culture.

In order to delimit the scope of our analysis, we focus specifically on what we call 'new world' suburbia – the suburban contexts of the United States, Australia, and New Zealand, which share many cultural and geospatial characteristics. Often poorly designed in terms of energy efficiency, these extensive suburbs will not all be knocked down for them to be built again in 'greener' or more efficient ways. Built environments are highly fixed capital that evolve relatively slowly. Replacement rates occur at less than 5 per cent per annum in Australia (Gleeson, 2014; Dixon, Lannon, and Eames, 2018). Instead of rebuilding, we argue that the task is to *resettle* the suburbs according to a new imaginary (Alexander and Gleeson, 2019). We agree with permaculture theorist and practitioner David Holmgren (2018) and simplicity theorist Ted Trainer (2010) that when approached creatively, these low-density suburban landscapes show themselves to be a promising place to start a grassroots, transformative retrofit of the built environment in an age of rising energy costs and broader environmental crises. In what follows, we consider and outline the social practices and values needed to effect this deep suburban transformation, drawing on various literatures, including degrowth, permaculture, voluntary simplicity, urban studies, and critical energy analysis.

Unlearning abundance: Energy descent in the suburbs

What, then, might energy descent look like at the level of the suburban household? What does it mean for a household to plan for economic contraction and embrace a context of rising energy costs? Does this necessarily imply hardship, deprivation, and sacrifice? Or, if negotiated wisely, could such a managed descent give rise to an alternative, less materialistic form of prosperity? This raises practical questions about what suburban households can do to begin building a post-carbon economy within the shell of the old, but it also highlights the question of what role socio-cultural transformation needs to play in reclaiming the suburbs for a new era of energy scarcity.

Some of the practices and attitudes reviewed in this chapter will come as no surprise, such as retrofitting a house for increased energy efficiency; a material ethics of frugality and sharing; household investment in solar panels; mending and making things rather than always buying; radically reducing waste; cycling; relocalising food production via backyard gardening and urban agriculture; and connecting with local farmers and producers. Such 'old ideas' will not excite those who fetishise 'the new', but we argue that such practices deserve cursory restatement because they have a necessary and significant role to play creating the socio-cultural conditions needed for an energy-descent future to be managed well. If growth and consumerism cannot be maintained in a high-cost, energy-scarce future, it is important to understand what material and energy sufficiency would look like in suburban contexts that are currently so resource and energy dependent.

We also review other potential features of a retrofitted suburbia that have received far less attention in mainstream sustainability and resilience discourse, including domestic biogas production, disconnecting from fossil gas, composting toilets, solar ovens, peer-to-peer sharing, the gift economy, and re-commoning public and private space. Many of these practices are particularly suited – sometimes *only* suited – to the suburban landscape, in ways we will explain. We do not present such a brief survey as a universalisable or complete blueprint to be applied independent of context. By considering a range of such practices, and highlighting their underlying principles of motivation, it is hoped that we can begin to discern a new, post-carbon suburban imaginary that outlines a constructive and positive response to forthcoming energy descent.

Our underlying assumption is that sustainability in the suburbs (and more broadly) cannot be achieved merely through techno-efficiency improvements and the decarbonisation of consumer lifestyles (Hickel and Kallis, 2019). The extent of decoupling required is simply too great. Of course, all societies do need to exploit appropriate technologies and design innovations in order to produce and consume more efficiently. But to have any positive effect, efficiency must be grounded in an ethics, economics, and, ultimately, a politics of sufficiency and self-limitation (Alexander, 2015). In over-consuming and over-producing societies, that means a radical, but voluntary, demand-side reduction in energy and resource use. Efficiency without sufficiency is lost, as demonstrated by the increasing resource demands of growth capitalism over recent centuries (Kallis, 2017).

A demand-side reduction will involve the ethical renegotiation of our relationships with the material world, as well as a vast and growing politics of collective action to support and realise it (Read, Alexander, and Garrett, 2018). The rejection of materialistic values and practices is generally referred to as voluntary simplicity, otherwise known as 'downshifting' or just 'simple living' (Alexander, 2009). That means unlearning consumerist cultures of consumption which are so easily taken for granted and normalised in developed nations (Hamilton and Denniss, 2005). It also means relearning the lost arts of creative frugality which were commonsensical in previous eras of relative scarcity. But it also means creating the range of societal structures to support rather than inhibit post-consumerist, sufficiency-based ways of living. Even though it is currently out of intellectual and political fashion, we maintain that there is an utterly indispensable literature on sufficiency, moderation, self-limitation, and frugality that must inform any coherent sustainability-justice agenda, especially in anticipation of rising energy costs and climate instability (Westacott, 2016; Alexander and McLeod, 2014).

Recall that 'economy', according to Aristotle, meant the good management of the household, and, for him, the household was the foundation of the *polis*. In our age of governmental paralysis and failure of nerve, this Aristotelian perspective might again highlight the necessity of a social strategy that begins with the intentional transformation of daily life in the suburbs.

A necessary caveat: Energy descent for whom?

At once we need to highlight a critical tension raised by our approach to retrofitting suburbia – a tension that speaks to the complexity of any praxis and politics of suburban transformation. On the one hand, the new energy context of scarcity and higher prices that may soon dawn categorically entails a significant reduction in the energy and resource demands of the wealthiest societies, so it is important to grasp what such downscaling might look like in terms of lived experience. The forthcoming analysis considers that question in some detail. On the other hand, it is clear that there are many people, even in affluent societies like Australia (from where we write), who are in precarious financial situations, struggling simply to feed and clothe their families, and who certainly do not experience their consumption practices as being excessive and superfluous (Bauman, 2004). Degrowth and energy descent for whom, one might ask?

This raises structural and distributive issues concerning class, privilege, and property ownership. These issues entail a critique which has been levelled at the permaculture, ecovillage, sustainable consumption, and 'simple living' movements regularly (Frankel, 2018). Although the practices reviewed in this chapter will need to be a part of any post-carbon future, many (but not all) of the practices depend on the ownership of land or access to secure housing, which are privileges far from being universally provided.

Access to affordable land and housing is fundamental (Nelson and Schneider, 2018). This draws the analysis into radical and controversial territory, because broadening societal access to land and housing implies a revision of property rights and market structures which sit at the conceptual heart of capitalism. Options for radical 'top down' reform have been considered elsewhere, including the following: design new measures of growth to replace GDP, establish limits to resource use, reduce work hours, design public budgets for more public goods, invest in renewable energy, transform the financial system, and guarantee the right to housing (Alexander and Gleeson, 2019: 181–195). For now, the point is simply that some of the practices reviewed below are not easily embraced by those unable to secure ownership of, or secure access to, housing and land. As populations grow and put more pressure on cities, this problem of ownership and access to affordable housing threatens to intensify, unless there are some bold policy interventions aimed at broadening the distribution of wealth, power, and property in society (Nelson and Schneider, 2018).

Similarly, tenure is profoundly important. There are obvious reasons why people renting will not invest in solar panels or water tanks in a transient or insecure rental property. That is, renting implies what urban theorist Anitra Nelson (2018: 102) calls an 'unsettled temporariness'. Even digging up the lawn and growing food can depend on the permission of landlords. Furthermore, retrofitting a house can be expensive and many households may not have discretionary expenditure to invest in solar panels, efficient appliances, or water tanks, especially if trying to get into the housing market, which may imply oppressive mortgage obligations.

It would be naïve, therefore, to suggest that personal or household action alone can resolve the problems suburbanites face in an energy descent future. But the following programme of action still remains a necessary part of the picture of transformation. It just means that there are deep structural, financial, and cultural obstacles that lie in the way of such a grassroots transition scaling up.

Nevertheless, we also recognise the latent transformative potential of those who have the agency to downshift their material living standards (Holmgren, 2018). These relatively high-consumption suburbanites – relatively prosperous working and middle classes – may have to play a lead role creating the social conditions needed for a politics of energy descent to emerge. This chapter will focus predominately on that class capacity to act within existing structural constraints. But this focus on suburban homeowners can only be the start of any response to energy scarcity and rising energy costs, and ultimately this constituency must commit to and collaborate with broader social movements of solidarity, resistance, redistribution, and transition.

Suburban practices of energy descent

Our survey of household actions and attitudes begins by focusing on the central question of energy: how suburbanites can practice, and, in some instances, already practice energy descent (Holmgren, 2018). After reviewing these practices, we consider some broader homesteading activities consistent with an energy descent future, including the practice of voluntary simplicity, relocalising food production, and participation in alternative economies outside the market.

The necessity of demand reduction

The most important thing any household can do to decarbonise energy use and prepare for energy scarcity is simply to reduce energy demand. After all, a transition to 100 per cent renewables will be proportionately easier to achieve and more affordable if demand is significantly reduced. Since the Industrial Revolution, energy has been so cheap relative to its rewards that it has been easy to be wasteful and careless in energy use (Smil, 2017). That very wastefulness provides a source of grounded hope, however, because it means there are huge opportunities for demand reduction in ways that do not imply any reduction in wellbeing. In ways we will now outline, trimming superfluous energy use requires both behavioural changes and investments in household retrofitting activities for increased efficiency and self-provision (Sorrell, 2015).

In terms of behaviour change, households can practise a range of important but unexciting energy rituals, including: turning lights off when leaving the room; taking short showers; never using (or having) a clothes dryer; only judiciously using air-conditioning (more for health than comfort); washing clothes only when genuinely needed; closing curtains and windows on really hot days to keep the heat out; putting warm clothing on in cool temperatures before turning any heating on (and only heating the rooms being used); watching TV or online entertainment sparingly; unplugging appliances when not in use; and a long list of tiny other things too mundane to mention. One Australian study estimated that these types of behavioural responses could reduce average in-house energy use in a household by half (Alexander and Yacoumis, 2018. That study did not exhaust the range of practices available. Mainstream environmentalism has been on top of this behavioural advice for decades, and it should not be dismissed. But while such practices are necessary, they are far from enough to achieve sustainability, given the systemic embeddedness of consumption practices and the problem of structural 'lock in' (Trainer, 2012; Sanne, 2002). Nevertheless, they begin building household resilience, by anticipating reduced energy availability through voluntary energy demand reduction. In terms of retrofitting a house, options include:

- investing in efficient appliances (like a small fridge) and solar panels, and progressively electrifying all gas appliances;

- putting extra insulation in the walls and roof to minimise the need to heat and cool the house;

- closing gaps around doors and windows;

- planting a west-facing grapevine (in the Southern hemisphere) or deciduous tree that shades the house from afternoon heat with its foliage in summer, keeping it cool, but lets the sun hit the house in winter by dropping its leaves;

- installing thick curtains to keep heat in (or out) as needed; and

- other equally mundane but useful things of this nature.

A range of small and more significant changes can add up to surprisingly large demand-side energy reductions (Holmgren, 2018). All of them increase resilience in anticipation of energy becoming scarcer and more expensive. In short, if energy becomes increasingly unavailable or unaffordable in a context of energy descent and economic contraction (whether planned degrowth or unplanned recession), being able to manage with as little energy as possible becomes an essential household skill.

While there is obviously a privilege implied by owning a house – roughly 65 per cent of Australians own their home – frugal financial practices and minimising superfluous consumption can, to some extent, free up income to invest in a solar array, a biogas digester, heat-pump hot water system – all reviewed below – amongst other retrofitting investments. Within the permaculture (Holmgren, 2018), voluntary simplicity (Alexander and Ussher, 2012), and 'transition towns' (Hopkins, 2008) movements, households have been taking these types of actions and practising energy descent here and now, whilst governments have been relatively inactive. Alexander and Ussher (2012) conducted what remains the most extensive empirical examination of the downshifting movement, and conservatively concluded that as many as 200 million people in Western nations are practising voluntary simplicity, even if this subculture entails a wide range of practices, from light green consumerism to more radical expressions of simple living. Could this constituency yet radicalise, mobilise, and organise to become a social movement of transformative import? Journalist George Monbiot (2007: 42) famously declared that people never 'riot for austerity', but rioting for a new vision of frugal abundance no longer seems quite so implausible, even if this broad movement remains in its infancy as a political project.

While the systemic and structural challenges cannot be analysed in any depth in this chapter, the research and practices reviewed suggest that, in some suburban contexts, much can be done within existing structures to decarbonise the suburban household. Several suburban cases studies are reviewed in Holmgren (2018), with similarly promising and inspiring examples analysed in Nelson (2018). The structural problem of carbon 'lock in' is very real for some households (Sanne, 2002). Nevertheless, for many households, a significant portion of their carbon footprint is largely a *choice* or *habit* that could be modified. This highlights a cultural or normative challenge, which arguably can be best resolved incrementally through ongoing grassroots activities and the evolution of new cultural practices and norms 'from below'. To talk of 'incremental change' and 'evolution', however, should not be interpreted as downplaying the urgency of change that is needed.

The behavioural practices are free but involve the challenge of changing habits, which humans are not very good at without nudging or other incentives (De Young, 2014). The investments in efficiency or renewable energy production will cost money, and the challenge in that regard is about creating an ethos of sustainability that sees such investments as more important than other consumer commodities or experiences. That said, the economics of solar are becoming more attractive (Creutzig et al., 2017). Household solar is becoming less of a 'cost' and more of an 'investment', even though the upfront expense can still be a barrier. Expensive housing and rent will also make such investments difficult for many, although financial resources could become available for some households, if more frugal and mindful spending practices were adopted (Domingeuz and Robins, 1992). This is a point to which we will return.

Making the changes reviewed above obviously requires the *desire* or *incentive* to take energy demand reduction seriously, which is lacking in many affluent cultures today. This lack is primarily because the dominant paradigm of techno-optimism pushes the message that we can just 'green' supply rather than go to the trouble of reducing demand. Our counter-message is that significant demand reduction is achievable in many suburban households, and it is important that decarbonisation in the city begins with these changes wherever they are available. As more households take these small, but cumulatively transformative, steps, we contend new cultural norms would arise in relation to which current political and macroeconomic goals would be re-evaluated and, in time, potentially revised (Alexander, 2013). Without dedicated demand-side action, any transition to sustainable and more resilient energy systems will fail.

Some political economists, such as Frankel (2018), will be quick to dismiss such 'lifestyle' changes as being of little consequence, not recognising that the structural changes that are certainly needed will never arrive until there is progressive culture that demands them. Practising energy descent at the household level is an indispensable part of that cultural r/evolution, representing a prefigurative politics that is necessary to any post-carbon or post-growth transition (Alexander, 2013). The rest of the household actions reviewed below should be judged in that light also – not as direct, consumption-based 'solutions' to the problems of over-production, but as necessary groundwork for creating the new culture of sufficiency that will need to precede any new politics or macroeconomics of sufficiency.

Solar PV

On the path of household decarbonisation, the second-best thing to do – after significantly reducing demand – is to invest in solar photovoltaics (PV), a strategy most suitable for suburbanites with their typically low-density, stand-alone houses and private roof space. There is still academic controversy over the best ways to decarbonise economies (Jacobson et al., 2017; Heard et al., 2017; Alexander and Floyd, 2018; Heinberg and Fridley, 2016). Still, few deny that solar PV will need to play a greatly increased role in energy production. Most governments around the world (notably Australia and the USA) are failing to take the lead on a clean energy transition and initiate deep decarbonisation (IPCC, 2018). Therefore, by force of logic, there is an increased burden on households and communities to invest in their own renewable energy, even if this may not always be the most efficient way to do it (Borenstein, 2017). Household solar energy production is certainly more desirable than waiting, while governments do little or nothing. In any case, it is likely that a renewable energy future will be one that moves toward greater decentralisation of energy generation, especially if battery technology continues to advance (Liaros, 2019; Palmer and Floyd, 2020). The tide of household solar installations is strengthening this pattern, and grid architecture will need to evolve to adapt to changing patterns of generation and use.

Using the sun more directly through solar ovens is another practice highlighting the elegance of simplicity (Alexander and Yacoumis, 2018). This is obviously climate dependent. While unable to completely replace an inside oven, solar ovens can reduce electricity for cooking several days a week in the warmer months, while also teaching households important lessons about the art of living in accordance with solar energy flows.

An electric 'heat pump' hot water system

One of the key features of deep decarbonisation involves electrifying energy services previously provided by fossil energy. This presumes that electric appliances are powered by renewable electricity, since electric appliances running on coal-generated electricity can be more carbon-intensive than fossil gas appliances. Electric hot-water systems once cost much more than gas systems to operate, but developments in heat pump technology mean that electric systems are now up to 80 per cent more efficient than they used to be (Gehl et al., 2012). Without going into the technicalities, a heat pump absorbs heat from the air and transfers it to the water, minimising the need for further heating with electricity. This is a form of solar heating since the sun heats the air, and that heat gets transferred to the water, effective even in winter. Best of all, these heat pump units generally have a timer, which means that they can heat the water when the solar panels have maximum sun exposure. For this reason, heat pumps can be conceived of as a battery of sorts, with the sun and solar panels 'charging' the water when the sun is up and storing the energy in an extremely well-insulated tank. Residents can use the hot water in the mornings or in the evenings, when the sun is down. This minimises grid demand in ways that make a 100 per cent renewable energy transition more affordable and manageable.

Biogas in the suburbs

Most suburban blocks would have space for a domestic biogas digester, although this highly promising alternative technology is all but unknown in developed regions of the world. In this regard the so-called 'developing nations' have much to teach, with China having 27 million biogas digesters and India having 4 million (Bond and Templeton, 2011).

With irony, blindness, and paradox, the discourse of 'development' can barely conceive of the possibility that 'advanced' nations might have things to learn from the 'less developed' nations.

Biogas is produced when organic matter biodegrades under anaerobic conditions (without oxygen). The primary benefit of biogas is that it is a renewable energy source with net-zero emissions. Whereas the production of oil and other fossil fuels will eventually peak and decline, humans will always be able to make biogas so long as the sun is shining and plants can grow. Biogas has net-zero emissions because the carbon dioxide that is released into the atmosphere when the methane burns is no more than what was drawn down from the atmosphere when the organic matter was first grown (Alexander, Harris, and McCabe, 2019).

There are other benefits, too. The organic matter used in biogas digesters is typically a waste product. By producing biogas, households can reduce the amount of food waste and other organic materials being sent to landfills, which also means less methane in the atmosphere. Furthermore, biogas digesters produce a nutrient-rich sludge that can be watered down into a fertiliser for gardens, homesteads, or farms. All this helps develop increased energy independence, build resilience, and save money.

The level of food waste in affluent new world nations is alarming, around AU$8 billion worth in Australia alone each year (ABC, 2013). It makes sense to be diverting that waste from landfill to produce clean energy in the suburbs. Research by Reynolds et al. (2014) indicates that there would easily be enough food waste in Australia for all suburban households to cook on biogas without exhausting food waste streams, even if food waste were significantly reduced. New research on domestic biogas production suggests that putting approximately 1.5 kilogrammes of food waste per day in a domestic-scale biogas digester can produce on average 38 minutes of cooking per day, which is enough to cover most household cooking requirements (Alexander, Harris and McCabe, 2019). Coupled with a solar hot water system this can allow for complete disconnection from fossil gas and minimise electricity demand.

Biogas has the potential to be a disruptive alternative technology that could contribute to deep decarbonisation and increased energy security. We maintain that suburban households should exploit this innovation on the path to a post-carbon and resilient society. Although it can seem like an energy miracle – clean energy from food waste – biogas is really nothing other than an elegant example of permaculture: working with nature and natural processes, rather than fighting against them.

Post-carbon transport

Suburbia was built with cheap oil and designed primarily to be car dependent. Electric vehicles will inevitably play some role in the transformation of transport in the near- and longer-term future. We argue, however, that it is a mistake to think they can solve the problem of the carbon- and resource-intensity of private automobiles (Alexander and Gleeson, 2019: Ch 2). Any genuine transport solution will not involve electrifying the world's currently growing addiction to private motor vehicles but by finding ways to avoid the need for such vehicles altogether (Moriarty and Honnery, 2016). The alternatives are walking, cycling, and electrifying public transport, which have many environmental and health benefits (Higgins and Higgins, 2005).

Electric bikes are also likely to be of transformative significance, providing a kind of 'middle way' between electric cars and the human-powered bicycle. Electric bikes retain most of the benefits of the human-powered version, while extending ranges and load capacity to cope adaptively with settlements and economies structured to suit cars and trucks. By making cycling lower impact on the rider and much more accessible, electric bikes could be a lynchpin technology for managing energy descent and initiating a degrowth transition, at least as an enabler that gets many more people engaged with post-car transport and gives people their first taste of the personal benefits and freedoms available to the cyclist.

Walking or cycling will be non-viable in certain contexts, and even public transport is not always available. These structural problems are well known and not easily or swiftly resolvable, even if the solution is relatively clear: build more infrastructure to support these low-carbon or post-carbon alternatives. Nevertheless, there is also vast scope for replacing many car trips with alternative modes of transport that are less carbon-intensive, especially through a cultural embrace of cycling.

In Australia it has been estimated that three quarters of all personal car journeys are less than 10 kilometres, with half being less than 5 kilometres, and one third less than 3 kilometres (Alexander and Yacoumis, 2016). It is reasonable to assume that a significant proportion of those trips could be replaced with cycling without hardship, although disability, heavy freight, or other complexities would mean a full substitution would be difficult or impossible. Nevertheless, a study in the United States by Higgins and Higgins (2005) has shown that substituting walking and cycling for short car trips, based on recommended daily exercise, could reduce US domestic oil consumption by up to 34.9 per cent, while also having huge health benefits and leading to reduced healthcare costs. No doubt other oil-dependent nations could also achieve significant savings through this 'simple', low-tech strategy.

Recent research by Laskovsky and Taylor (2017) in Melbourne, Australia, also bears consideration: the vast amount of urban and suburban space dedicated to cars, roads, and parking is deeply wasteful, especially when it is understood how inefficiently that space is used in terms of irregular occupation. Reclaiming this land for other purposes is an exciting urban prospect, as it would open up vast tracts of land for an array of retrofitting activities limited only by our imaginations.

Low-meat diets and population issues

We close this section on energy with a brief consideration of decarbonising diets and family size. While not limited in relevance to the suburban context, these issues have significant implications for energy demands and thus deserve comment.

The production of animal products is hugely energy (and carbon) intensive and there is absolutely no way that average Western levels of meat consumption could possibly be globalised in a sustainable way (Poore and Nemecek, 2018). While there are some prospects for efficiency improvements in the production of animal products (which might come at the expense of animal welfare), the necessary but rarely acknowledged part of the equation is drastically reducing (or, for some, eliminating) meat and dairy consumption in diets (Hadjikakou, 2017; Hadjikakou and Wiedmann, 2017).

Nevertheless, this issue ought to be approached with the subtlety it deserves. Global averages can mislead, and a localised economy necessarily means shortening the chain between production and consumption in ways that demand context-dependent analysis (Holmgren, 2018). To provide an extreme example, it is no good asking the Inuit people to reduce meat consumption, given that eating sea mammals is their primary means of sustenance, and there are communities around the world similarly dependent on animal agriculture to survive. Much land is not suitable for cropping, in which case the distinction between grain-fed and pasture-fed animals is important. Reducing the former could certainly open up more land for lower-carbon, non-meat food production, which would be far more energy efficient on account of feeding that food to humans instead of feeding it to animals and then eating the animals. The role of grazing animals in landscape restoration and regeneration is also an important consideration, too often overlooked by those ignorant of land management and food production (Massy, 2017).

None of this changes the fact, however, that in many affluent societies significantly reducing meat and dairy consumption is one of the most impactful things people can do to decarbonise their lives (Wynes and Nicholas, 2017). Having small families is the other issue deserving of note, and, indeed, the growth paradigm treats population as a driver of growth and therefore presumptively a good thing. Yet both strategies (reduced meat consumption and lower fertility) get insufficient in mainstream environmental or political discourse. This wilful blindness is a major cultural obstacle to any post-carbon transition and one that is not easily overcome. The best that can be done is to show by example that low or no meat diets can be healthy, cheap, and delicious, and that small family size accrues many benefits (financial, increased free time, more sleep) aside from the environmental ones. Climate activist Bill McKibben (1999) suggested a good starting question for the next generation of parents-to-be: 'Maybe one?' As for diets, it is hard to improve upon the simple advice offered by food guru, Michael Pollan (2007): 'Eat [fresh, unprocessed] food. Not too much. Mostly plants.'

Toward a post-carbon suburban homestead: Reimagining the good life

Beyond direct energy considerations, the emergence of expensive energy and a contracting degrowth economy will require a revaluation of values and practices in other domains of life, too. Any consumerist culture is going to require a growth economy to meet its demands for ever-rising material living standards. The flip side of that coin is that a degrowth economy will depend on and require a material culture of sufficiency that embraces a post-consumerist existence of relative scarcity of energy and resources. The dual value of embracing this strategy is that it moves the culture of consumption in a more sustainable direction, but it also prepares the household for disruptive and unstable economic times in which reduced consumption is enforced rather than voluntarily chosen. That is, downshifting prepares the household for times of crisis or unplanned economic contraction, and thus increases resilience, even if the primary or initial motivating goal is sustainability.

By 'voluntary simplicity' we are talking about more than taking shorter showers, turning the lights off, and recycling. A degrowth culture of consumption in an energy descent context must assume a far more radical form of downshifting. According to the ecological footprint analysis, humanity would need four or five planets if the Australian or US way of life were globalised. If Australian living standards were attained by the projected global population of 2050, then humanity would need 10 planets (Trainer, 2012).

Few analysts of the global predicament seem to appreciate the magnitude of this challenge: it requires a 75–90 per cent reduction in ecological impacts compared to living standards in the wealthiest regions of the world, even if sustainable living will always be a context-dependent practice (Trainer, 2012; Trainer, 2020). As Hickel and Kallis (2019) have shown, efficiency, technology, and the decoupling strategy are failing to bring the global economy within sustainable bounds. It follows by force of logic and evidence that globalising Western-style material living standards is a recipe for catastrophe – both ecological and humanitarian. A just and sustainable world necessarily involves some radically transfigured practices of consumption and production compared to the ecocidal forms which have emerged in the West, and that means, among other things, embracing the all-but-forgotten wisdom of frugality, moderation, and sufficiency (Princen, 2005; Westacott, 2016).

Enlightened material restraint: The practice of sufficiency and self-limitation

What might this alternative suburban ethics of consumption look like in practice? As always, context is everything, but some broad comments may offer some general insight into how consumption practices may need to be transformed in and for an energy descent future. Above we addressed energy specifically, with the clear, but often complex, prescription being to radically reduce energy demand and invest in localised renewable energy production. In affluent societies of the 'developed' world, some of the funds for such investment could be found simply by reducing expenditure elsewhere. Voluntary simplicity or downshifting implies being extremely mindful with one's money and being aware that numerous small expenses (magazines, clothes, takeout food, that extra beer) over months and years can add up to considerable sums (Domingeuz and Robins, 1992). In a recessionary or depressed economy, of course, such downshifting may be enforced rather than voluntarily chosen, in which case it makes sense to anticipate the more austere material culture that lies ahead in an energy descent future. One thinks of the Depression-era slogan: 'Use it up, wear it out, make it do, or do without.'

This should not be presumed to imply hardship necessarily (Kasser, 2017; Lockyer, 2017). At least, how well an individual or household manages economic contraction is partly a function of the values and attitudes one brings to experience (Burch, 2012). Once sufficiency in material living standards is achieved (through basic provision of food, housing, clothing, energy), voluntary simplicity implies resisting the dominant cultural pressure to seek ever-higher incomes and instead seeking the good life in a range of non-materialistic sources of meaning and fulfilment (Alexander, 2009). This essential insight is supported by a vast body of social and psychological research showing that money and possessions have diminishing marginal returns; the richer people get, the less money contributes to quality of life (Lane, 2000; Kasser, 2002; Kasser, 2017).

In pursuit of voluntary simplicity, households will discover a number of practices that can reduce impact while also saving thousands of dollars every year:

• buying second-hand clothes;

• avoiding the lure of fancy possessions;

• growing a portion of household food;

• capturing water in tanks;

• making or mending rather than purchasing;

• developing cheap and low-impact leisure activities;

• sharing and borrowing;

- brewing one's own beverages; and

- minimising waste and avoiding packaging.

In these ways, creating a surplus can be directed into the clean energy revolution, or allow for reduced working hours which can open up more time to dedicate to community action, home-based production, or simply more time for family, friends, and private passions (Read, Alexander, and Garrett, 2018).

Of course, the usual proviso applies: many households even in affluent societies are living from paycheck to paycheck, with little room for voluntary downshifting. But in consumer cultures, there are many households that have normalised abundance with no conception of 'enough' (Hamilton and Denniss, 2005; Lane, 2000). In anticipation of an energy descent future, such a normalisation of abundance must be unlearned. The less people need to purchase to maintain their way of life, the less they are obliged to work to pay for that market consumption. By thus reimagining the good life beyond consumer culture, voluntary simplicity offers a path to maximising freedom and advancing genuine wellbeing, a transition that Soper (2008) calls 'alternative hedonism' and Raser-Rowland and Grubb (2016) refer to as 'frugal hedonism'. (This rightly implies that self-interest is an incentive beyond environmentalism or concern for the world's destitute, and empirical research verifies that voluntary simplicity offers this hedonic reward [Alexander and Ussher, 2012; Kasser, 2017].)

Even the most radically downshifted suburban households, however, are probably still overconsuming on a global scale, so the practice of sufficiency must remain an ongoing context-dependent process, not a static destination to arrive at or achieve once and for all (Princen, 2005). This again points to the systemic nature of global crises, since it can be very hard or even impossible to consume less within societal structures that have been created to promote limitless growth and unbounded consumerism (Sanne, 2002). Nevertheless, the structural transformation will never transpire until there is a post-consumerist culture that is prepared to embrace material sufficiency. Accordingly, new cultures of voluntary simplicity are required both to provide the social conditions needed for a degrowth economy to emerge systemically and to build resilience if economic contraction occurs through recession or depression rather than through planned design (Alexander, 2013).

The political significance of the Voluntary Simplicity Movement is most apparent in how it can carve out *more time for people to create the new (suburban) economy*. The politics of voluntary simplicity is typically conceived of in terms of 'political consumers' who express their values through what they buy and where they spend (Stolle and Micheletti, 2013). That is fine as far as it goes, but it misses the more significant matter of freedom and time. Building a new economy from the grassroots up in an energy descent future will take time, and currently most households are 'time poor', locked into the work-and-spend cycle (Robinson, 2009). By rethinking consumption levels, embracing frugality, and exchanging superfluous stuff for more free time, voluntary simplicity provides a pathway that can enable grassroots activism and suburban homesteading, while also being directly in line with the post-materialist values of degrowth and permaculture.

Eating the suburbs

We have been exploring some of the practices and values that may be needed in order to build suburban resilience in the face of an energy descent future and a contracting economy. Having reviewed direct energy considerations and the ethos of sufficiency that informs the voluntary simplicity and downshifting movements, we turn now to the relocalisation of food production and increased self-sufficiency through home-based production (Gaynor, 2006).

There is a flourishing 'local food movement' in many cities today (Norberg-Hodge, 2019). However, its full potential has not yet been fully realised (Trainer, 2019). Digging up backyards and front yards and planting fruit and vegetables, keeping chickens, and composting, are important practices, reconnecting people with the seasons, the soil, and the food on their plates. To borrow the phrase often spoken in Australian permaculture circles, we should 'eat the suburbs'.

There are lessons here from the Cuban experience in the early 1990s. When the USSR collapsed, Cuba quickly found itself having to manage with greatly decreased oil imports (Friedrichs, 2010). Despite this so-called 'special period' being a time of considerable hardship, a key strategy for dealing with energy descent in Cuba was to relocalise and decarbonise food production by scaling up organic food production in and near cities, deeply influenced by permaculture theory and practice (Viljoen et al., 2005: Ch. 17–18).

Furthermore, in an age characterised by what Louv (2008) has called 'nature deficit disorder', the rewards of home or community gardening go well beyond the environmental and physical health benefits of eating local, fresh food. Getting into the garden and out of our cars offers mental health rewards, too (Soga et al., 2017). There might be silver linings to more austere material futures where home-based production and cycling become necessary due to rising energy costs and tightening household budgets due to a contracting economy.

Recent scholarly analyses demonstrate the productive potential of suburban blocks. Ted Trainer has undertaken a detailed quantitative analysis of East Hills, an outer suburb of Sydney, Australia, where he lives. Trainer (2019: 25) demonstrates through quantitative analysis that urban and suburban agriculture has highly significant productive capacity, concluding that 'most, and possibly almost all food could come from within settlements, that is from home gardens, community gardens, neighbourhood commons, and very small farms.' Similarly, promising analyses have been published by the Melbourne-based Victorian Eco-Innovation Lab (VEIL, 2018; Trainer, Malik and Lenzen, 2019).

Nevertheless, few suburban households, if any, could be fully self-sufficient in fruit and vegetables, let alone in things like wheat, oats, and rice, as well as any number of other foodstuffs like salt, sugar, nuts, and milk. But producing as much as possible saves money, increases self-sufficiency, builds resilience, and, as noted, reconnects people with the land and soil. Trainer's analysis, just mentioned, also highlights the importance of moving beyond merely 'self-sufficiency' and working toward a 'collective sufficiency' wherever possible. This would involve reclaiming under-utilised public land, especially roads and car parks, and increased sharing of private land for food production (Laskovsky and Taylor, 2017).

In terms of creating soil, the suburban composting toilet may also have a place in a degrowth economy, as households stop exporting nutrient-rich waste in potable water and instead treat their own waste onsite. Michael Mobbs (2010) of Sydney is among the early adopters. A composting toilet helps close the nutrient cycle; it creates fertiliser for fruit trees; and it minimises or avoids the need to import fertilisers for the garden, saving money. Human waste needs to be respected for safety reasons but it need not be feared, as explained and scientifically justified by Joseph Jenkins (2005).

Home-based food production also offers a means of escaping the market, to some extent, thereby undermining the industrial food industry by withdrawing financial support for it, and redirecting that support, when necessary, toward local farmers markets (Norberg-Hodge, 2019). Over time we can imagine food production crossing beyond household boundaries too, re-commoning public space, and this is in fact already underway as people reclaim nature strips for food production, plant fruit trees in the neighborhood, establish community gardens, and cultivate unused land through 'guerrilla gardening'. Decarbonising food production generally means relocalising production – shortening the space between production and consumption. Urban agriculturalists are not waiting, and should not wait, for governments to lead this transition (Holmgren, 2018; Trainer, Malik and Lenzen, 2019).

Escaping the market: Sharing, gift, and the urban peasantry

We close this incomplete survey of energy descent resilience practices by highlighting the importance of sharing, gift, and home-based production, all of which have untapped prospects for decarbonisation, dematerialisation, and relocalisation. These are topics that also highlight how degrowth and energy descent involve an upscaling of informal, non-monetary, and 'post-capitalist' modes of economy, as well as increased economic localisation (Albert, 2004; De Young and Princen, 2012; Gibson-Graham, Cameron, and Healy, 2013; Holmgren, 2018).

By sharing more between households – facilitated by the internet or by traditional community engagement – less energy- and resource-intensive production needs to occur to meet society's needs. Indeed, even in a contracting economy (whether contraction is by design or by crisis), households can still secure access to the tools and other things they need, provided a culture of sharing emerges. This is the revolutionary reinterpretation of 'efficiency' implicit in the degrowth paradigm: produce less; share more; thrive. Nelson (2018) explores the potential of sharing land and housing as a promising means of overcoming some of the access barriers to this fundamental need.

On a similar note, degrowth also arguably implies an incremental re-emergence of the gift economy – to some extent, at least (Eisenstein, 2011). If living standards are forever expected to rise, long working hours required to support that ongoing material advance will generally leave people 'time poor', making it difficult for them to gift their skills and resources in the spirit of community and neighbourly support. By consuming less and carving out more time for practices outside the formal economy, downshifting can also enliven the informal gift economy.

As this culture of decommodification emerges, it becomes increasingly self-supporting: one household is liberated from the market economy to some extent by practising voluntary simplicity, allowing more time to gift skills and resources outside the market; but as other households do that too, the benefits and rewards of the gift economy return, reducing reliance on the market economy and making voluntary simplicity increasingly viable, which further supports the gift economy in a symbiotic loop of mutual support. Paradoxically, then, financial frugality enables generosity, solidarity, sharing, and redistribution (Gibson-Graham, Cameron, and Healy, 2013). Over time, a new economy could emerge from within the shell of the old economy.

Finally, degrowth and permaculture in the suburbs implies turning the household into a place of production, not merely consumption (Holmgren, 2018; Alexander and Gleeson, 2019; Trainer, 2019). On this point, some inspiration can be found in the past. Mullins and Kynaston (2000) assessed what they call the 'urban peasant thesis', and their review of the evidence shows that up until the middle of the 20th century, Australian urban households had operated a highly developed subsistence-based, domestic economy. This included the production of foodstuffs in suburban backyards, but extended to the manufacture of other household goods, including clothes, furniture, and even owner-built housing. Thus, the dwelling and the yard were seen primarily in utilitarian, rather than aesthetic, terms. This 'urban peasantry' declined, however, in the postwar boom, as the rise of mass consumer capitalism enabled households to purchase goods previously produced within the household. This suggests that any degrowth or energy descent future of reduced productive capacity in the formal economy may well see the re-emergence of an 'urban peasantry' in this sense, albeit one shaped by different times and concerns.

Conclusion

Some of the practices, attitudes, and approaches reviewed in this chapter are not new, and draw from modes of living that homesteaders, eco-villagers, permaculturists, hippies, and other counter-culturists have been doing for decades or more (Alexander and McLeod, 2014). We contend that the wider urban application of these practices is well justified in the face of a contracting economy and declining access to cheap energy, even if still often marginalised by dominant energy and consumption cultures. The social scientific evidence we have presented and reviewed is emerging to support these earlier exploratory and radical sustainability and resilience practices.

There are also a few new and emerging features, like domestic biogas and peer-to-peer sharing, facilitated by the internet, whose cultural potential is highly promising but remains largely untapped. Most of the practices are also enabled by the suburban context, such as solar PV, biogas, food production, solar-oven use, and water collection, which would be impossible, difficult, impractical, or at least significantly different in higher density urban contexts that deserve separate analysis.

These household practices and values are not a panacea to today's problems, but it is likely that managing an energy descent future is going to require more suburbanites embracing them, albeit in context and in household-dependent ways. Granted, things like second-hand clothes, biogas, composting toilets, home-based production, and sharing offer a humbler vision of the future than the eco-modernist visions defended today (Bastani, 2019). But we contend that our humbler vision is much more coherent when the challenges of climate change and peak oil are taken seriously and the limits of techno-optimism are understood (Hickel and Kallis, 2019). 'Greening' the supply of energy and resources is necessary but insufficient; high-impact, energy-intensive societies also need to radically reduce demand.

Promising and necessary though these practices of suburban downshifting are, things are not always or often as rosy or free from contradiction as they might first seem. We opened this chapter by acknowledging the deep structural obstacles of class, privilege, and property ownership that lie in the way of any degrowth transition. Although space has not permitted a 'top down' political analysis of energy descent planning in the national and/or international domains, there are myriad policy options available to assist with this transition, such as greater government funding of renewable energy, a strong price on carbon to quickly phase out fossil fuels, the development of broader networks of bike lanes, and exploration of distributive options (within and between nations) to ensure equity in a contracting economy (Alexander and Gleeson, 2019: Ch. 7). Without diminishing the importance of a 'top down' response, the regressive state of contemporary national and global politics prompted us to focus on the social or grassroots strategies available, which we hold up as the most promising spaces for transformative change in an age of widespread political paralysis.

We are also disconcertingly aware of how many of the efforts to transition beyond fossil fuels depend, to date at least, on the very fuels those efforts are trying to transcend, as well as the globally integrated supply chains that are enabled by fossil fuels (Alexander and Floyd, 2018). Solar panels, biogas digesters, heat pumps, and bicycles are currently a product of fossil fuels, and the same goes for nails, screws, steel sheet, and windows, as well as all the commodities that make households function, from pots and cutlery, to furniture and musical instruments. Indeed, even households with vast net surpluses of renewable energy production will, in the absence of expensive battery storage, still draw from and depend on the fossil energy grid at night to keep the fridge running and the lights on after dark.

These critical reflections should not be interpreted as undermining the strategy or importance of retrofitting suburban households in the manner and spirit outlined herein. It only points to the complexity of the predicament. Existing suburbanites can and should get to work building new, low-energy forms of life within existing structures, and, as we have argued, there is a huge amount that could be done in that space. The household may not be the world economy but changing the world will require changing the household. We contend that a resilient suburban future will embody many, if not all, of the values and practices reviewed.

References

Australian Broadcasting Corporation (ABC). 2013. 'Do Australians Waste $8 Billion Worth of Edible Food Each Year?'. *ABC* October 8. https://www.abc.net.au/news/2013-10-08/food-waste-value-australia/4993930

Albert, M. 2004. *Parecon: Life After Capitalism*. London: Verso.

Alexander, S. (ed.). 2009. *Voluntary Simplicity: The Poetic Alternative to Consumer Culture*. Whanganui: Stead and Daughters.

Alexander, S. 2015. *Sufficiency Economy: Enough, for Everyone, Forever*. Melbourne: Simplicity Institute.

_____. 2013. 'Voluntary Simplicity and the Social Reconstruction of Law: Degrowth from the Grassroots Up'. *Environmental Values* 22(2): 287–308.

Alexander, S. and Gleeson, B. 2019. *Degrowth in the Suburbs: A Radical Urban Imaginary.* Singapore: Palgrave Macmillan.

Alexander, S., Harris, P., and McCabe, B. 2019. 'Biogas in the Suburbs: An Untapped Source of Clean Energy?'. *Journal of Cleaner Production* 215: 1025–1035.

Alexander, S. and Floyd, J. 2018. *Carbon Civilisation and the Energy Descent Future.* Melbourne: Simplicity Institute.

Alexander, S. and McLeod, A. (eds). 2014. *Simple Living in History: Pioneers of the Deep Future.* Melbourne: Simplicity Institute.

Alexander, S. and Ussher, S. 2012. 'The Voluntary Simplicity Movement: A Multi-National Survey in Theoretical Context'. *Journal of Consumer Culture* 12(1): 66–88.

Alexander, S. and Yacoumis, P. 2018. 'Degrowth, Energy Descent, and "Low-Tech" Living: Potential Pathways for Increased Resilience in Times of Crisis'. *Journal of Cleaner Production* 197: 1840–1848.

Ayres, R. and Warr, B. 2009. *The Economic Growth Engine: How Energy and Work Drive Material Prosperity.* Cheltenham, UK: Edward Elgar.

Bastani, A. 2019. *Fully Automated Luxury Communism: A Manifesto.* London: Verso.

Bauman, Z. 2004. *Wasted Lives: Modernity and its Outcasts.* Cambridge, UK: Polity.

Bond, T. and Templeton, M. 2011. 'History and Future of Domestic Biogas Plants in the Developing World'. *Energy for Sustainable Development* 15(4): 347–354.

Borenstein, S. 2017. 'Private Net Benefits of Residential Solar PV: The Role of Electricity Tariffs, Tax Incentives, and Rebates'. *Journal of the Association of Environmental and Resource Economists* 4(S1): S85–S122. https://www.journals.uchicago.edu/doi/10.1086/691978 or https://pdfs.semanticscholar.org/2994/e6255314c3011f5ae90b8788af85e18d7777.pdf

Burch, M. 2012. *The Hidden Door: Mindful Sufficiency as an Alternative to Collapse.* Melbourne: Simplicity Institute.

Creutzig, F. et al. 2017. 'The Underestimated Potential of Solar Energy to Mitigate Climate Change'. *Nature Energy* 2. 17140. doi:10.1038/nenergy.2017.140

De Young, R. 2014. 'Some Behavioural Aspects of Energy Descent: How a Biophysical Psychology Might Help People Transition Through the Lean Times Ahead'. *Frontiers in Psychology* 5: 1255. doi: 10.3389/fpsyg.2014.01255

De Young, R. and Princen, T. (eds). 2012. *The Localization Reader: Adapting to the Coming Downshift.* Cambridge, MA: MIT Press.

Dixon, T., Lannon, S., and Eames, M. 2018. 'Reflections on Disruptive Energy Innovation: Methodology, Practice, and Policy'. *Energy Research and Social Science* 37: 255–259.

Domingeuz, J. and Robins, V. 1992. *Your Money or Your Life: Transforming Your Relationship with Money and Achieving Financial Independence.* London: Penguin.

Eisenstein, C. 2011. *Sacred Economics: Money, Gift, and Society in the Age of Transition.* Berkeley: North Atlantic Books.

Frankel, B. 2018. *Fictions of Sustainability: The Politics of Growth and Post-Capitalist Futures.* Melbourne: Greenmeadows.

Friedrichs, J.J. 2010. 'Global Energy Crunch: How Different Parts of the World Would React to a Peak Oil Scenario'. *Energy Policy* 38: 4562–4569.

Gaynor, A. 2006. *Harvest of the Suburbs: An Environmental History of Growing Food in Australian Cities.* Perth: University of Western Australia.

Gehl, A. et al. 2012. *Campbell Creek Research Homes: FY 2012 Annual Performance Report.* Oak Ridge, TN: Oak Ridge National Laboratory, U.S. Department of Energy. https://www.tva.gov/file_source/TVA/Site%20Content/Energy/Technology%20Innovation/CampbellCreekReport2012.pdf

Gibson-Graham, J.K., Cameron, J., and Healy, S. 2013. *Take Back the Economy: An Ethical Guide for Transforming our Communities.* Minneapolis: University of Minnesota Press.

Gleeson, B. 2014. *The Urban Condition.* London: Routledge.

Lane, R. 2000. *The Loss of Happiness in Market Democracies*. New Haven: Yale University Press.

Laskovsky, J. and Taylor, E. 2017. 'A Lot of Thought: The Space of Car Parks and Shopping Centres in Australian Cities'. In *Proceedings of Automotive Historians Australia, Vol. I: Driving Futures* (eds H. Edquist, M. Richardson and S. Lockrey), pp. 1–18. Melbourne, Victoria, Australia: Automotive Historians Australia, Inc. https://researchmgt.monash.edu/ws/portalfiles/portal/276977661/276977531.pdf

Liaros, S. 2019. 'Implementing a New Human Settlement Theory: Strategic Planning for a Network of Regenerative Ecovillages'. *Smart and Sustainable Built Environment*. https://doi.org/10.1108/SASBE-01-2019-0004

Lockyer, J. 2017. 'Community, Commons, and Degrowth at Dancing Rabbit Ecovillage'. *Journal of Political Ecology* 24(1): 519–542.

Louv, R. 2008. *Last Child in the Woods: Saving Our Children from Nature Deficit Disorder*. New York: Workman Publishing.

Massy, C. 2017. *Call of the Reed Warbler: A New Agriculture – A New Earth*. Brisbane: University of Queensland Press.

McKibben, B. 1999. *Maybe One? A Case for Smaller Families*. New York: Plume.

Mobbs, M. 2010. *Sustainable House*, 2nd edn. Sydney: New South Wales Press.

Mohr, S. et al. 2015. 'Projection of World Fossil Fuels by Country'. *Fuel* 141: 120–35.

Monbiot, G. 2007. *Heat: How to Stop the Planet from Burning*. London: Allen Lane.

Moriarty, P. and Honnery, D. 2008. 'Low-Mobility: The Future of Transport'. *Futures* 40: 865–872.

_____. 2011. *Rise and Fall of the Carbon Civilisation: Resolving Global Environmental and Resource Problems*. London: Springer.

_____. 2016. 'Global Transport Energy Consumption'. In: J. Lehr, J. Keely, T. Kingery. 2016. *Alternative Energy and Shale Gas Encyclopedia*. New Jersey: John Wiley and Sons.

Mullins, P. and Kynaston, C. 2000. 'The Household Production of Subsistence Goods: The Urban Peasant Thesis Reassessed'. In *A History of European Housing in Australia*, 9th edn. (ed. P. Troy), pp. 142–163. Cambridge, UK: Cambridge University Press.

Nelson, A. 2018. *Small is Necessary: Shared Living on a Shared Planet*. London: Pluto Press.

Nelson, A. and Schneider, F. 2018. *Housing for Degrowth: Principles, Models, Challenges, and Opportunities*. London: Routledge.

Norberg-Hodge, H. 2019. *Local is Our Future: Steps to an Economics of Happiness*. Byron Bay: Local Futures.

Odum, H. and Odum, E. 2001. *A Prosperous Way Down: Principles and Policies*. Colorado: University of Colorado Press.

Palmer, G. and Floyd, J. 2020. *Energy Storage and Civilization: A Systems Approach*. Singapore: Springer.

Piercy, E., Granger, C., and Goodier, R. 2010. 'Planning for Peak Oil: Learning from Cuba's "Special Period". *Urban Design and Planning* 163(4): 169–176.

Pollan, M. 2007. 'Unhappy Meals'. *New York Times Magazine* 28 January. https://www.nytimes.com/2007/01/28/magazine/28nutritionism.t.html

Poore, J. and Nemecek, J. 2018. 'Reducing Food's Environmental Impacts Through Producers and Consumers'. *Science* 360(6392): 987–992.

Princen, T. 2005. *The Logic of Sufficiency*. Cambridge, MA: MIT Press.

Raser-Rowland, A. and Grubb, A. 2016. *The Art of Frugal Hedonism: A Guide to Spending Less While Enjoying Everything More*. Hepburn Springs: Melliodora Publishing.

Read, R., Alexander, S., and Garrett, J. 2018. 'Voluntary Simplicity: Strongly Backed by All Three Main Ethical-Normative Traditions'. *Ethical Perspectives* 25: 87–116.

Reynolds, C. et al. 2014. 'Estimating Informal Food Waste in Developed Countries: The Case of Australia'. *Waste Management and Research* 32(12): 1245–1258.

Robinson, T. 2009. *Work, Leisure, and the Environment: The Vicious Circle of Overwork and Overconsumption*. Cheltenham: Edward Elgar Publishing.
Sanne, C. 2002. 'Willing Consumers – or Locked in? Policies for a Sustainable Consumption'. *Ecological Economics* 42(1): 273–287.
Smil, V. 2017. *Energy and Civilization: A History*. Cambridge, MA: MIT Press.
Soga, M., Gaston, K., and Yamaura, Y. 2017. 'Gardening is Beneficial for Health: A Meta Analysis'. *Preventative Medicine Reports* 5:92–99.
Soper, K. 2008. 'Alternative Hedonism, Cultural Theory and the Role of Aesthetic Revisioning'. *Cultural Studies* 22(5): 567–587.
Sorrell, S. 2015. 'Reducing Energy Demand: A Review of Issues, Challenges and Approaches'. *Renewable and Sustainable Energy Reviews* 47: 74–82.
Stolle, D. and Micheletti, M. 2013. *Political Consumerism*. New York: Cambridge University Press.
Tainter, J. 1988. *The Collapse of Complex Societies*. Cambridge, UK: Cambridge University Press.
Trainer, T. 2010. *The Transition to a Sustainable and Just World*. Sydney: Envirobook.
_____. 2012. 'Degrowth: Do you Realise What it Means?' *Futures* 44: 590–599.
_____. 2019. 'Remaking Settlements for Sustainability: The Simpler Way'. *Journal of Political Ecology* 26(1): 202–223.
_____. 2020. 'De-growth: Some Suggestions from the "Simpler Way" Perspective'. *Ecological Economics* 167 (forthcoming).
Trainer, T., Malik, A., and Lenzen, M. 2019. 'A Comparison Between the Monetary, Resource, and Energy Costs of the Conventional Industrial Supply Path and the "Simpler Way" Path for the Supply of Eggs'. *Biophysical Economics and Resource Quality* 4(3): 1–7.
Victorian Eco-Innovation Lab (VEIL). 2018. *Publications List*. https://veil.msd.unimelb.edu.au/#publications.
Viljoen, A., et al. eds. 2005. *CPULs: Continuous Productive Urban Landscapes*. Oxford: Architectural Press.
Weiss, M., and Cattaneo, C. 2017. 'Degrowth – Taking Stock and Reviewing an Emerging Academic Paradigm'. *Ecological Economics* 137: 220–230.
Westacott, E. 2016. *The Wisdom of Frugality: Why Less is More – More or Less*. Princeton: Princeton University Press.
Wynes, S. and Nicholas, K. 2017. 'The Climate Mitigation Gap: Education and Government Recommendations Miss the Most Effective Individual Actions'. *Environmental Research Letters* 12(7). https://iopscience.iop.org/article/10.1088/1748-9326/aa7541

Chapter 14

Degrowth as an 'aesthetics of existence'[1]

> Many of the great cultural shifts that prepare the way for political change are largely aesthetic.
>
> – J.G. Ballard

If once our species lived on a planet relatively 'empty' of human beings, today we live on a planet that is evidently 'full to overflowing'. The human population has grown exponentially to reach seven and a half billion people, trending toward 11 billion by the end of the century. As this expanding population continues to seek ever-rising material living standards by way of sustained economic growth, the global economy is being driven into gross ecological overshoot, dangerously crossing or threatening to cross a range of planetary boundaries with dire consequences that are already unfolding. Indeed, the metaphor of 'Earth as a Petri dish' has become worryingly apt, given that the dominant colony seems to be consuming all the available resources and is at risk of poisoning itself from its own wastes, raising questions about whether humanity can muster the intelligence to avoid the fate of common bacteria. Techno-optimists and free marketeers promise ecological salvation via continuous 'green growth', all the while the face of Gaia is vanishing as Empire marches resolutely on.

Lifting the poorest billions out of destitution is likely to place further burdens on an already overburdened ecosystem. This confluence of ecological and social justice imperatives calls radically into question the legitimacy of further economic expansion in the already high-impact, consumerist societies of the developed world. Unspeakable or even unthinkable in mainstream economic and political discourse, a compelling case can be made that responding to this context of ecological overshoot will need to entail *planned economic contraction* of the energy and resource demands of the most developed regions of the world, as well as a reconceptualisation of sustainable development in the Global South, beyond the conventional

---

1 Originally published as the introduction to Samuel Alexander, *Art Against Empire: Toward an Aesthetics of Degrowth*, 2017, Simplicity Institute, pp 1–30.

path of industrialisation. This 'limits to growth' position signifies an extremely complex, challenging, but arguably necessary paradigm shift in the dominant conception of human progress, one that is being explored boldly today within the nascent 'degrowth' movement.

Although the degrowth movement is diverse and defies singular definition, in general terms it seeks to initiate a transition beyond the existing order of globalised growth capitalism and in its place build a constellation of highly localised economies of sufficiency, based on renewable energy, appropriate technology, egalitarianism, participatory democracy, and non-affluent but sufficient material cultures of voluntary simplicity (Alexander, 2015a). Counter-intuitively, perhaps, the movement also contends that a degrowth transition of planned economic contraction can actually maintain or even increase quality of life, by reshaping cultures and societal structures to promote non-materialistic forms of meaning and wellbeing beyond consumerist conceptions of 'the good life'. Sometimes dismissed as utopian or naïve, the obvious rejoinder from advocates of degrowth is that nothing could be more fantastical than the current economic model that assumes the viability of limitless growth on a finite planet. In any case, in an era when it is commonly remarked that it is easier to imagine the end of the world than the end of capitalism, perhaps utopianism is not an indictment but a defence of radical movements today.

In recent decades the 'limits to growth' position has received a great deal of attention, mostly from economic and ecological perspectives. More recently, the degrowth movement has begun contributing an important range of new political and sociological analyses (D'Alisa, Demaria, and Kallis, 2014), offering deeper insight into the alternative paradigm, evaluating transition strategies, policies, and obstacles, while also continuing to update and refine the ecological critique of growth economics in response to those who continue to fetishise growth. The purpose of this essay, however, is neither to review these existing literatures nor offer another ecological critique of growth, but to extend and deepen the understanding of degrowth by examining the concept and the movement from a perspective that has yet to receive any sustained attention – namely, aesthetics.

Overview and justification

Defined further below, aesthetics can be understood as a domain of inquiry that examines not merely the meaning and function of art and the role of the artist in society, but broader considerations about taste, judgement, perception, imagination, and sensibility. In what follows I highlight and examine the aesthetic dimensions of degrowth, in the hope that this reveals new and worthwhile insights about the meaning and potential of this emerging sustainability movement. Might the degrowth imperative demand not just a radical political and economic engagement with the structures and goals of our growth-orientated civilisation, but also an engagement and transformation of our aesthetic sensibilities, capacities, and practices? And what is the relationship between the aesthetic dimensions of degrowth and the various ecological, economic, political, and cultural dimensions? These questions motivated and shaped the forthcoming analysis.

Admittedly, readers would be right to approach this aesthetic inquiry with a degree of scepticism. After all, in a world where ecocide, financial crisis, war, and creeping fascism loom ominously on the horizon like dark clouds gathering for a perfect storm – a situation that demands a radical political engagement in order to dissipate and transcend the various tragedies already taking form – a turn to aesthetics certainly needs justification. How could one look to poetry, literature, music, or the imagination in a world immiserated by violence, oppression, and unspeakable suffering? As critical theorist Herbert Marcuse noted as he began his own meditation on aesthetics: 'It would be senseless to deny the element of despair inherent in this concern: the retreat into a world of fiction where existing conditions are changed only in the realm of the imagination (Marcuse, 1978: 1).' At first instance, aesthetic considerations do seem like a petty indulgence or trivial distraction, reserved for the comfortable few who do not have to worry about the problems of the real world. Art, one might contend, is not a serious subject for the activist or theorist of political economy.

The following analysis deconstructs this dismissal of aesthetics by examining the distinction between art and political economy, in order to show that there is in fact an inherent aesthetic dimension to politics as well as a political or even revolutionary potential inherent to certain forms of art or aesthetic practice. In doing so the analysis is shaped by the emerging 'aesthetic turn' in politics and by various political interpretations of art and aesthetics, mixing and developing these substantive bodies of thought in the hope that this alchemy produces a deeper understanding of the blurry nexus that conjoins (as it attempts to separate) art and politics (Edelman, 1995; Ranciere, 2006; Bleiker, 2009; Kompridis, 2014).

To be clear, the premise of this essay is not that we *should* or *should not* infuse politics or economics with aesthetic considerations, but rather, as Jacque Ranciere states, that 'politics is aesthetic in principle' (Ranciere, 2006: 58) – an insight that extends to political economy more broadly in ways that will be explained. Moreover, it will be argued that only by acknowledging, appreciating, and operating within the aesthetic dimension can there be any hope for deep revision in the established politico-economic order in the direction and form of degrowth. After all, it is one thing to establish firm scientific, ethical, and philosophical foundations for degrowth, but if there is no *felt need* in society for such a transition then this can be understood in part as an aesthetic obstacle that demands an aesthetic intervention or series of interventions. A major prerequisite to deep societal transformation, as Marcuse implored, is 'the fact the need for radical change must be rooted in the subjectivity of individuals themselves, in their intelligence and their passions, their drives, and their goals.' (Marcuse, 1978: 3–4) Accordingly, the degrowth movement's neglect of the aesthetic realm arguably constitutes a failure that is hurting the movement for change.

After fleshing out the concept of aesthetics in the next section, the essay presents a brief but broad-ranging critique of the dominant consumerist and industrial aesthetics of advanced capitalism, in order to provide a background against which to contrast, in due course, an alternative aesthetics of degrowth. Critically examining aspects of the contemporary aesthetics of advanced capitalism will also function to show why the aesthetic dimension is not somehow separate or isolated from matters of political economy, but inextricably intertwined with them in ways that are important but not always obvious. The discussion attempts to emphasise the aesthetic challenges and opportunities presented by degrowth, as well as highlight the fact that the movement must not just engage the head but also the heart; which is to say, to be effective the degrowth movement must seek to change not only the way we think about the world but also the way we feel, perceive, judge, create, and, in the end, *exist* in the world. I argue that art – as well as broader aesthetic interventions in culture and politics – may well need to play a defining role prefiguring or provoking such *affective* changes in how we experience the world, thereby influencing how we act in it. Drawing on the aesthetic and cultural theories of Herbert Marcuse and extending the later work of Michel Foucault, this essay will introduce and ultimately defend the notion of degrowth as an 'aesthetics of existence'.

The aesthetic dimension

Narrowly defined, aesthetics refers to the philosophy of art, a domain of inquiry that seeks to understand the nature and meaning of art as well as how (or whether) judgements of beauty can be established or defended beyond appeals to subjective experience alone. However, aesthetics can also be understood to encompass a broader range of concerns and perspectives, examining aesthetic concepts like taste, form, creativity, perception, feeling, and sensibility to shed light on lived experience beyond the specific domain of 'art objects'. While questions of art and the role of the artist in society will be taken up in the final sections of this chapter, my analysis will be informed on the whole by this broader conception of aesthetics. The purpose of the current section is to unpack the meaning of the aesthetic dimension of experience in a little more detail, acknowledging from the outset that the discussion must be selective and very incomplete.

To begin at the most abstract level, the human condition has an inherently aesthetic dimension, insofar as lived experience is always shaped and mediated by language. That is, our linguistic concepts give order and form to our experience of the world and even to our conceptions of 'self'. This can be understood aesthetically in the sense that human beings have had to *create* those linguistic concepts and frameworks, and infuse them with meaning, for neither the concepts nor their meanings were given to us in advance. The concepts and their meanings could have been otherwise, have been otherwise, and in fact are always and everywhere changing due to the inherent semantic instability of language and the ever-changing contexts of human life within which language is used.

Furthermore, there is no way for us to step outside our linguistic constitutions and somehow perceive the world in an unmediated, pre-linguistic form; no way for us to shed the conceptual schemes through which we experience the world and see the world *as it really is*. Instead, reality is experienced through the lens of language, and the key point is that human beings *created* that lens. This is essentially all that is meant when philosophers talk of the linguistic or social 'construction of reality' (Berger and Luckman, 1966), even if explanations are usually dressed up in impenetrable, post-structuralist jargon.

There are various levels to this creative process of constructing reality through our linguistic practices. As children we are educated into a 'language game' that we did not ourselves create – first upon someone's knee, then through lessons ratified by wider society – but it is not as if this is a purely passive process. Humans both shape and are shaped by language, and this dialectical relationship is an ongoing process of co-creation and co-production. By inventing new concepts or vocabularies in response to a changing world, or creatively redefining the meanings given to existing concepts or vocabularies, human beings can literally reshape not just their *experience* of reality but, more fundamentally, *the reality* they experience, expanding the horizons of what can be thought, said, seen, and even felt.

This capacity to shape and reshape reality with the tool of language can be understood most clearly perhaps through the narratives we tell ourselves and each other about the world and our place in it. The universe, our histories, our relationships, and our lived experience all defy full and complete accounting by virtue of their infinite complexity. There is no way to tell The Whole Story, so to speak, for there is always more that could be said; other perspectives not yet considered; new events and situations that call into question previous interpretations or categorisations of the world, etc. Accordingly, when we find ourselves trying to make sense of the world, we are inevitably faced with the creative challenge of selecting which aspects of life to focus on and how to interpret or describe those limited aspects. In thus describing the world or our experience, we are effectively giving a narrative account of our lives – we are giving form to content – and in this sense we find ourselves in a position not dissimilar to the author tasked with telling a story (Nehamas, 1985).

If the meaning of life does not announce itself to us or lie 'out there' in external metaphysical reality waiting to be discovered, it follows that we must instead create as an aesthetic project the meaning of our own lives, as well as collectively shape as an aesthetic project the societies in which we live, just as that society inevitably shapes us. As Jean-Paul Sartre once noted: 'You can always make something out of what you've been made into' (Sartre, 1964: 101). The intention here is not to sound grandiose but simply to highlight the inherent aesthetic or creative dimension at the core of human existence – a point to which we will return.

Aesthetics also inquires less abstractly into our *sensuous* experience of the world. The traditional focus of analysis has been the experience of beauty: what is it about a particular painting, story, sonata, poem, or vista that stirs our soul and causes us to feel such uplifting yet mysterious emotions? Is beauty a 'property' of some objects and not others, capable of objective recognition by the discerning observer? Or is the experience of beauty a function of subjective tastes which we have been taught and internalised in culturally dependent ways? These are genuine aesthetic inquiries, but, as noted above, the aesthetic domain need not be limited to the study or analysis of art, beauty, and taste. More generally, our sensuous or aesthetic experience of the world also encompasses our passions, joys, hopes, sorrows, and fears, as well as our capacities for a range and depth of impressions, moods, feelings, and emotions. Additionally, aesthetic *practice* can be understood variously as forms and modes of creative activity, including artistic production, but extending more generally to the application of creativity and imagination to the broader realm of life, as we endeavour to give form and order to the world and our experience of it.

Having sketched this thin definitional boundary around the domain of aesthetics, I will now explore, specifically, the aesthetic dimensions of life within the consumer cultures of advanced, industrial nations. I will touch on the foundational 'story of progress' which lies at the heart of industrial development; review typical aesthetic features of postmodern urban life, with its ubiquitous advertising and consumerist messaging; highlight the dominant cultural modes of self-creation through consumption; outline the way all this impacts affectively or sensuously on our bodies and psyches; and, finally, I will address the question of 'taste' which drives and entrenches the industrial-consumerist aesthetic, and explain how this aesthetic underpins the political economies of growth capitalism. Albeit fleeting, this brief critical review will provide the necessary background against which to contrast, in later sections, the possibility and nature of an aesthetics of degrowth, while also exposing the blurry boundary between aesthetics and political economy.

The old story: A critique of industrial-consumerist aesthetics

Every individual and every society is an enactment of a story people tell themselves about the nature and purpose of their existence and of the world they live in (Berry, 1999; Quinn, 2017). Whether we conceive of ourselves as children of God, speaking apes, revolutionaries, artists, parents, bureaucrats, entrepreneurs, or consumers – perhaps all of these things or none of them – in the end we all give a narrative structure to our lives, or at least adopt the default narrative of the dominant culture, usually unconsciously. The myths and stories we tell ourselves situate us in space and time, shape our perceptions of the present, and guide us as we move into the future, influencing our interpretations of what is possible, proper, and important. As those individual narratives are woven together, the social fabric of a civilisation takes form.

Put simply, the Grand Narrative of industrial civilisation is a story of progress within which societies advance by way of continuous economic growth, rising affluence, and technological innovation. The very vocabulary of 'development' implies that some societies have reached maturity – the rich, developed nations of advanced capitalism – while the rest of the world is lacking the same degree of civilisation and therefore is in need of more growth, more industrialisation, and more capitalism in order to civilise, just as healthy children must grow to maturity in order to fulfil their potential. So convinced are the 'developed' nations of their linear story of progress that over the last three centuries they have been imposing this narrative on the rest of the world, seeking to establish a 'fully developed' world, created in their own image.

Although this mode of industrial development has brought with it many benefits, the dominant story of progress is not without its anomalies – anomalies so deep, one might argue, that today they are threatening the coherency of the paradigm itself. As noted in the introduction, environmental scientists have been demonstrating that the global growth economy is destroying the ecological foundations of life, while from a social justice perspective, the critique has been that the system has produced socially corrosive inequalities of wealth and left billions in conditions of poverty. These realities are often ignored or marginalised, but even when they are acknowledged the dominant political and economic response is simply to reassert 'sustained growth' as the only solution, (Monbiot, 2012) failing to recognise that growth may now be causing the very problems it claims it can solve.

What is most troubling of all, perhaps, is that even those individuals who have achieved the so-called 'consumerist ideal' – the house, the car, the gadgets, the clothes, the travel, etc. – all too often find themselves discontented despite their material abundance. In recent decades, this finding has been established consistently and independently by a litany of sociological and psychological studies (Lane, 2000; Kasser, 2002; Offer, 2006; Frank, 2009). Our civilisation's defining goal appears to be misconceived. There seems to be an emptiness to affluence that is never acknowledged in glossy advertisements, let alone discussed in schools or around the dinner table. It is perhaps the dominant culture's final, unspeakable taboo.

Needless to say, within mainstream discourse these criticisms are rarely considered fundamental flaws in the basic story of industrial development, but instead are treated as matters of detail in need of refinement, a little tweaking around the edges, nothing technology, market mechanisms, and more economic growth cannot manage or resolve. So dominant and uncompromising is this narrative that its contingency and historicity are easily missed, as if there were no other stories to tell, no other paths of progress. This 'myth of progress' has reified into an ideology, often shaping the consciousness of even those it oppresses, marginalises, and alienates.

Moving from the civilisational level to that of individual subjectivity, the narrative of industrial development is merely regurgitated in a personalised form. The dominant 'story of self' in consumer cultures today is one that treats material advancement as the clearest indicator of social success and the best means of acquiring self-esteem, social status, happiness, and respect. Anthropologists and sociologists have done considerable work studying and analysing the ways in which people communicate through their consumption; how they convey social messages – tell stories – about who they are through the symbolic content of commodities (Schor, 1998; Miller, 2010). It would seem that commodities are purchased not just for their functionality or use-value but also or primarily for what they signify about the people who possess them. By accumulating a certain body of commodities, individuals in consumer societies thereby shape their identities through consumption, defining themselves not by what they *do* but by what they *own*. This provides a basis to update Descartes' famous dictum in consumerist-existential terms: 'I shop, therefore I am.'

While this process of self-creation through the symbolic content of consumption can be considered an aesthetic process – albeit one of limited imagination within contextual constraints – it should be acknowledged that individuals do not simply shape, but are also shaped by, the dominant consumerist aesthetic to which they are exposed. Members of advanced capitalist societies (and increasingly all people around the globe) are bombarded, literally thousands of times every day, with advertisements, images, and other, more subtle, cultural and institutional messages insisting that 'more is better'. These cultural messages are devised by sophisticated marketers, highly skilled at manipulating people by preying on their deepest insecurities or emotional needs (Anon., 2017). It is no exaggeration to state that the implicit (sometimes explicit) message in every advertisement is: 'Your life is unsatisfactory as it is, but with this commodity you can attain happiness, beauty, meaning, love, respect, etc.' The rich and famous are glorified and celebrated at every turn, serving only to entrench the assumption that money means fame, success, and social admiration. There is barely a social space or even a private space today where one can find sanctuary from the onslaught of the consumerist aesthetic. We internalise the world 'out there' even as we produce and reproduce it. What we are exposed to, and what we give our attention to, we become.

The consumerist-industrial aesthetic is compromised further (or compromises *us* further) as people in highly developed societies today find themselves evermore disconnected from nature and often suffering a strange existential condition that some cultural theorists are calling 'affluenza' (Hamilton and Denniss, 2005). In urban and suburban contexts, the natural environment has been progressively covered with concrete or tarseal; skies are scarred with wires, power lines, and the contrails of aircraft; lives are lived mostly indoors under artificial lights, in front of computers or machines, disconnected from the changing seasons; the long, typically monotonous working day often begins and ends with a slow commute to or from work, in loud, heavy traffic, past the ubiquitous advertising billboards which impose themselves upon one's attention; only to be so tired upon the return home that there is no life-energy to do anything but sit in front of the television or computer, in 'nice clothes', eating a microwave meal and sedating oneself with alcohol or drugs in order to fight off the ennui. I am being polemical here, of course, and painting with too broad a brush, but the picture is accurate enough as far as it goes. Consumer culture seems to have failed to fulfil its promise of a meaningful and satisfying life, even as it destroys the planet. Is it any wonder that when Theodore Roszak looked into the eyes of modern consumers he saw only faces 'twisted with despair'? (Roszak, 1972).

The point is that consumerism is not just a relationship to material culture. It can also be understood as a mode of existence, an aesthetic state of being-in-the-world, one that seems to be generally coloured with a mood of disenchantment, disaffection, disconnection, and disillusionment.

14. Degrowth as an 'aesthetics of existence'

The real genius of consumerism, however, seems to be in how it seduces people into believing that, no matter how affluent they might become, the main things lacking from their lives are money and possessions. Thus the 'iron cage' of consumerism succeeds because it fails (Jackson, 2009: Ch 6), ensuring that the vicious circle of consumption continues. The spiritual malaise only deepens, for as the Parisian graffiti of 1968 stated: *Those who lack imagination cannot imagine what is lacking.*

To better understand the industrial-consumerist aesthetic and its implications on consumption practices, we could turn to the question of 'taste'. In the 20th century, French intellectual Pierre Bourdieu, in his seminal text *Distinction: A Social Critique of the Judgement of Taste*, took aesthetics beyond philosophy and into sociology, by demonstrating empirically that taste is closely related to class. What forms of clothing, music, literature, interior décor, leisure, etc. a person or household consumes is obviously a matter of taste, but in his research Bourdieu discovered that children are *taught* their tastes from an early age, and what they are taught is shaped along class lines. This aesthetic education becomes internalised, making taste seem natural or objective, yet this ends up serving an ideological function by entrenching certain cultures of consumption that demarcate class. At some intuitive level it seems this has long been understood, given that practices of 'conspicuous consumption' that deliberately show off certain levels of wealth to emphasise high status have been discussed at least since Thorstein Veblen's late-19th-century *The Theory of the Leisure Class*. Bourdieu argued that the acceptance of dominant forms of taste is a form of 'symbolic violence', because individuals in lower classes do not always have the economic or cultural means of accessing 'highbrow' cultures of consumption and are thus dominated by taste, forever trying to conform to the reigning aesthetic for fear of being socially ostracised by appearing crude, vulgar, or tasteless (Bourdieu, 1984: 358).

Anthropologist Mary Douglas offers further insight into how cultural tastes shape expectations about consumption, arguing that what is considered appropriate or necessary consumption is always culturally dependent. People do not merely consume to meet biophysical needs but also to meet social needs. In fact, Douglas argued that 'an individual's main object in consumption is to create the social universe and to find in it a creditable place' (Douglas, 2006: 243). This means that what are considered acceptable or appropriate practices of consumption in one society or social setting may be very different in an alternative social setting, such that even the notion of poverty can be understood as something that is culturally specific and not merely a biophysical universal. A particular level of consumption that is considered wealthy or prestigious in one society might be so low in another society as to be shameful; a particular object that is admired as tasteful or refined in one culture might be considered tasteless or uncouth in another. This can function to lock people into practices of consumption higher than they may feel necessary, not because they actually desire a certain level or manner of consumption but because they naturally desire social legitimation and acceptance, knowing that there are cultural expectations in this regard. Transcending consumerism therefore means overcoming aesthetic obstacles regarding taste.

One particularly pernicious aesthetic phenomenon in relation to consumption is the apparent need for *uniformity* in consumption practices, a phenomenon known by consumer researchers today as 'the Diderot effect'. Someone once gave the French enlightenment thinker Dennis Diderot a beautiful new scarlet robe, and without thinking he discarded his old one. But the next morning as he sat down to write he noticed that his old desk no longer did his robe justice. So he upgraded his desk. Then he realised that his chair, tapestries, and bookshelves looked dated against his new acquisitions, and slowly his entire material surroundings were upgraded. Juliet Schor describes this taste for uniformity in the following way:

> The purchase of a new home is the impetus for replacing old furniture; a new jacket makes little sense without the right skirt to match; an upgrade in china can't really be enjoyed without a corresponding upgrade in glassware. This need for unity and conformity in our lifestyle choices is part of what keeps the consumer escalator moving ever upward. And 'escalator' is the operative metaphor: when the acquisition of each item on a wish list adds another item, and more, to our 'must-have' list, the pressure to upgrade our stock of stuff is relentlessly unidirectional, always ascending (Schor, 1998: 145).

This highlights the insidious effect that 'taste' can have on our consumption practices, and how the growth economy more broadly is driven by (just as it produces) the seemingly insatiable desires of the modern consumer. Few people, it seems, have a taste for sufficiency. It should be noted, however, that Diderot eventually found himself sitting in the stylish formality of his new surroundings regretting the work of this 'impervious scarlet robe [that] forced everything else to conform with its own elegant tone'. Diderot had been master of his old robe but became slave of the new one. 'Opulence has its obstacles,' he concluded, a lesson we might learn from today (Diderot, 1769).

In this section I have attempted to provide some insight into various aesthetic dimensions of consumption practices in advanced industrial societies. The purpose has been to show that transcending consumerism and the growth economy will depend on first overcoming various aesthetic obstacles, practices, and tastes. These obstacles include the stories and myths we tell about ourselves and societies; the ways we shape our identities and communicate through consumption; the disaffection and alienation that evidently is widely experienced in consumer societies, even by those who have achieved the consumerist ideal; and the way dominant conceptions of taste and social legitimation with regard to material living standards entrench materialistic conceptions of the good life.

With the basic foundations laid, I will now outline Michel Foucault's notion of an 'aesthetics of existence' and then explore its relevance to consumerism, industrialisation, and the degrowth alternative. The thesis of this paper is that a transformation in our aesthetic relationships to the world and indeed to ourselves will need to precede any deep revision in the politico-economic order of growth capitalism in the direction of degrowth. In making this argument I begin by examining the aesthetic dimensions of human subjectivity and then offer some political and macroeconomic reflections.

Degrowth as an 'aesthetics of existence'

Throughout the Western philosophic tradition it has been argued, or simply assumed, that beneath the various historical manifestations of human subjectivity there lies an ahistorical or transcendental 'subject' or 'nature' that all human beings share. The notion of a 'universal form' of the subject is epitomised in the work of Immanuel Kant, who argued that human beings are endowed in common with rational faculties and that by correctly employing those faculties we can determine, on rational grounds, the universal moral rules that ought to govern human life. Michel Foucault rejected this universal notion of 'the subject' and the idea of a universalisable moral code that flowed from it. Just as Friedrich

Nietzsche had announced the 'Death of God' to signify the loss of faith in a transcendental basis for morality, Foucault famously anticipated the 'Death of Man' to signify the loss of faith in a basis for morality that was somehow grounded in a universal 'human nature' (Foucault, 2000; Foucault, 2002: 422).

If there is no universal form of *the subject* but rather only historically specific forms of *subjectivity*, what are the implications of this on how we understand the human situation? It is in response to this type of question or self-questioning that Foucault began developing his notion of ethics as 'an aesthetics of existence'. Rather than try to determine the moral code that universally deserves human obedience, Foucault's approach essentially was instead to ask: 'What sort of person should I become?' 'From the idea that the self is not given to us,' Foucault pronounced, 'I think that there is only one consequence, we have to create ourselves as a work of art' (Foucault, 2000: 262).

This aesthetic metaphor strikes many people as strange, for we are not generally accustomed to talking about life as a work of art. We might want to say, for example, that life is one thing, art is another, and that these distinct categories should not be conflated. But the distinction between art and life was precisely what Foucault was trying to question. In fact, it can be argued that Foucault was not actually using art as a 'metaphor' here at all. That is, he was not proposing that we are related to our own lives *like* the way the artist is related to his or her raw materials; instead, he was proposing that we are related to our lives *as* artists, whose raw material is life itself. As he once lamented in an interview:

> [I]n our society art has become something which is related to objects, and not to individuals, or to life. That art is something which is specialised or which is done by experts who are artists. But couldn't everyone's life become a work of art? Why should the lamp or the house be an art object, but not our life? (Foucault, 2000: 261).

Foucault's reasoning here is unusually straightforward: if the nature of 'the self' is not given to us in advance – that is, if there is no 'true self' to which we should be trying to interpret correctly or discover – then it follows, by default, that we must *create* ourselves. We are not, however, given a blank canvas to work with, so to speak; which is to say, we do not get to create ourselves from scratch, since our identities are by and large a *product* of linguistic, social, and institutional forces beyond our control or choosing. Nobody, for example, gets to choose the categories which structure their perception or interpretation of the world; rather, as noted above, we are all educated into – or subjected to – a form of life as we grow up, and through that process we find ourselves embedded within elaborate structures of power/knowledge that both enable and constrict our thoughts and actions. This education and those power/knowledge structures shape who we are as individuals and they define the nature of our subjectivity.

Nevertheless, Foucault argued we can also act upon ourselves, act upon our socially constructed subjectivities, through processes that he variously called 'self-fashioning', 'care of the self', 'techniques of the self', or 'arts of the self'. Foucault defined these Greek 'arts of existence' as: 'those intentional and voluntary actions by which men [sic] not only set themselves rules of conduct, but also seek to transform themselves, to change themselves in their singular being, and to make their life into an *oeuvre* that carries certain aesthetic values and meets certain stylistic criteria' (Foucault, 1990: 37). Through these processes, in which the self engages the self, human beings have the potential to transform their subjectivities in much the same way a sculptor transforms a given lump of clay. The subject, Foucault insisted, 'is not a substance... [i]t is a form', and what form that subject takes is up to us as individual agents, at least in part. This is the creative challenge – one might say the aesthetic challenge – with which we are all burdened. We must, as Foucault proposed, 'create ourselves as a work of art' (Foucault, 2000: 290; 262).

To be clear, Foucault's argument was not that we should try to make ourselves as beautiful as possible. Instead, *creativity* rather than *beauty* was the primary aesthetic value that defined his aesthetics of existence. He was not calling on us to be 'dandies' in the tradition of Oscar Wilde or Charles Baudelaire; rather, he was calling on us to avoid being merely products of our socialisation and to instead exercise our imaginations in response to the question, 'What sort of person should I become?'

How, then, is this related to the present focus on degrowth? In other writing I have explored in detail the notion of voluntary simplicity (or 'simple living') as an aesthetics of existence (Alexander, 2015b: Ch 11). I argued that because we are socially constructed beings, it should come as no surprise that our modes of subjectivity in advanced, industrial societies have been shaped by the dominant social and institutional forces that celebrate consumerism as a way of life, thereby marginalising consumption as a subject of ethical concern. Far from challenging us to explore lifestyles of reduced consumption in response to the ecological and social justice imperatives of our time, dominant forms of culture, economics, and politics call on us to consume as much as possible 'for the good of the economy'. Given that we will all have internalised these cultural narratives to some extent, often unconsciously, I argued that ethical activity today may require us to engage the self by the self for the purpose of *refusing who we are* – insofar as we are uncritical consumers – and creating new, post-consumerist forms of subjectivity.

The self-creation of these new forms of subjectivity is a necessary first step in any transition to degrowth society, for the simple reason that until there is a culture that embraces voluntary simplicity, the social underpinnings for degrowth will be absent (Alexander, 2013: 287–308). In other words, a politics or macroeconomics of degrowth will not be desired within consumerist cultures that seek and expect ever-rising material living standards, and politicians will never campaign for degrowth if it is clear there is no social support for it. So the emergence of a culture of voluntary simplicity seems to be a prerequisite to any degrowth transition, and the first step in this cultural shift involves transforming our subjectivities beyond the consumerist default setting. Among other things, this will involve taking seriously the question 'How much is enough?', and trying to reshape our relationships to material culture in line with the aesthetic values of balance and harmony.

Nevertheless, a re-fashioning of the self in line with voluntary simplicity will not be enough on its own to produce a degrowth society, owing to the fact that consumption practices take place within structural constraints. Within consumer capitalism it can be very difficult, at times even impossible, to consume in ways that accord with one's conception of justice and sustainability, because structural constraints can lock us into high-consumption, high-carbon modes of life. For these reasons, voluntary simplicity as an aesthetics of existence is a necessary though not sufficient response to existing crises. It lacks a systemic perspective, which is why I have been drawn to expand the analysis in terms of 'degrowth as an aesthetics of existence'. This is intended to highlight the fact that current crises are ultimately systemic crises that require a systemic response – not merely a cultural response – even if that systemic or political response begins with the aesthetic self-transformation of our given subjectivities; begins, as J.K. Gibson-Graham would put it, with a 'politics of the subject' (Gibson-Graham, 2006).

14. Degrowth as an 'aesthetics of existence'

A systemic analysis obviously requires a political and macroeconomic statement exploring new structures and systems suitable for a degrowth society. I have attempted such a statement elsewhere, which I will not attempt to summarise here (Alexander, 2016). Instead, I want to explore the *aesthetic foundations* of a politics or economics of degrowth, by extending Foucault's aesthetics of existence beyond the domain of the subject and propose a more holistic approach, based on Marcuse's work, that conceives of society, not merely the self, 'as a work of art' (Marcuse, 2007: Ch. 4).

Society as a work of art

What might it mean to speak of society as a work of art? Is it merely a degeneration into breezy, New Age theoretical nonsense? I ask the reader to resist such an interpretation and dare to take this perspective seriously. To begin with, a case has already been made that human experience in and of the world is socially constructed, mediated by linguistic categories and practices, the shaping and reshaping of which is an ongoing creative process. Indeed, cultures are, and have always been, founded upon stories, myths, and narratives that are always evolving, defining the contours of civilisation. We are both creatures and creators of this aesthetic process – both product and producer – and the present point is that when asking political and economic questions about how best to structure our societies, we inevitably offer answers shaped by the underlying stories of self and society. In short, I would argue that politics and economics are tools in the service of story. Crafting these stories is an aesthetic process of giving form to the content of our lives and societies, akin to a collaborative work of art.

It follows that a politics or macroeconomics of degrowth will depend upon an underlying and prior aesthetic revolution in our cultural stories of self and society. We need new visions of progress and prosperity. This suggests that before there can be systemic transformation in the existing societal structures there must be an imaginative redefinition of the meanings of many of our key concepts, categories, values, goals, and visions. After all, notions like freedom, justice, happiness, wealth, and progress will need to be transformed if degrowth is to make sense. I believe this is not so much a philosophical or scientific task about finding the 'essence' or 'truth' of such concepts and the relationships between them; it is better understood as a literary or aesthetic challenge, in the sense that the creative redescription of concepts and relationships need to be shown to make more sense within a New Story than within the Old Story.

In the Old Story, for example, a person might think they are free and happy because they have managed to acquire the largest house in the street; the thoughts, feelings, actions, and institutions of society all support this interpretation. In developing and prefiguring a New Story, however, another person might realise they are free and happy because they *don't need* a large house to live a full and meaningful life. Freedom and happiness mean very different things depending on the underlying stories of self and society, and if politics is partly about securing and maximising freedom, and economics is partly about advancing happiness, then obviously a restructuring of society will depend on a prior reimagining of how we understand fundamental terms like freedom and happiness. As more people develop new ways of seeing and understanding things, they begin to reimagine their lives, make different decisions, develop new hopes and dreams, engage people in new ways, and sooner or later the old ways die out; new thoughts, feelings, and actions begin to call into question the coherence of the Old Story, and pressure begins to mount on the laws and institutions of society. Over time, either incrementally or in bursts of discontinuity and rupture, society is remade according to the new vision or visions, limited only by the collective imagination in context.

Even when we accept that there are physical 'limits' to growth, this need not limit our lives, just as the limited number of keys on a piano has never limited the pianist. There will never come a time when all the beautiful sonatas have been written. Similarly, there are an infinite number of meaningful and fulfilling forms of life consistent with living a life of material sufficiency, which is to say, a life based on a certain material *content* can take any number of *forms*. To deny this, I would suggest, betrays a failure of imagination, even if the practice of material sufficiency in a growth-orientated society is deeply challenging: an ongoing creative process not a destination. Degrowth as an aesthetics of existence is about, first, imagining the various forms such a society of material sufficiency may take, and secondly, working toward creating such a society – individually, socially, economically, and politically – in order for the entire community of life to flourish within sustainable bounds. This raises questions not merely about what to do in order to create a degrowth society that is shaped by such aesthetic values as balance and harmony, but also questions about how our aesthetic experience of the world may change during the transition to such a society. For better or for worse, aesthetic matters are fundamental both to society and the individual.

There is much more to say about the notion of conceiving society as a work of art, both in defence and in response to potential criticisms.[2] Nevertheless, I would now like to bring the analysis down to Earth, so to speak, and explore in very practical terms – both individually and at a societal level – what an aesthetics of degrowth might look like or feel like in the real world, and how it might contrast with the dominant industrial-consumerist aesthetics already reviewed.

The new story: Toward an aesthetics of degrowth

In exploring an aesthetics of degrowth, we could begin with clothing, it being the domain of life where we express our personal aesthetics or 'style' most noticeably and immediately. The primary purpose of clothing is to keep us warm and its secondary function, at least in modern times, is to cover nakedness. That being said, those functions have been marginalised in consumer societies today, where clothing's purpose has evolved to be primarily about expressing one's identity or social status. There are powerful cultural expectations about looking a certain way depending on context, and since fashion changes so quickly, there is social pressure to constantly upgrade and expand one's stock of clothing. These aesthetic expectations drive consumerism and the growth economy at the expense of a healthy environment and create cultures overly focused on cosmetic concerns.

In a degrowth society, the social importance of high fashion could be drastically reduced or disappear, as people might come to see that clothing is really just a superficial shell – saying little or nothing about the depth of a person's character – and that always looking 'brand new' in an age of ecological overshoot is neither necessary nor cool. Of course, human beings have always expressed themselves through what they wear, so we should expect that 'style' would not so much disappear as evolve in a degrowth society. But this style would reflect the ethics of sufficiency and frugality that would shape material culture in all domains of life. People would probably have limited changes of clothing, buy secondhand whenever possible, mend the clothing they have, exchange items, perhaps even make their own, and wear their items in creative arrangements

---

2 See, e.g., Walter Benjamin's (2010 [1935]) concern about fascism being an aestheticisation of politics, which properly acknowledges that aesthetics is a two-edged sword, which can be used for good or evil, depending on the values and visions that drive its political and economic applications.

until they are worn out. This would require many people to rethink their 'image' in light of the new aesthetic – including their 'self-image', in ways that might require a deliberate reshaping of the self by the self.

Clothing would be functional first and foremost, comfortable and well-worn, so there would be no worry about lying down on the grass if the mood called for it, opening up new opportunities for a sensuous reconnection with nature. Neckties, high heels, and ostentatious displays of jewellery could slowly disappear as relics of a bygone era. A time would come, no doubt, when people wearing 'high fashion' would be the ones perceived as lacking style and taste, and, conversely, that the creative and eccentric clothing-makers and stylists would be the ones admired, esteemed, and sought-after – at which time it would be clear that a new, creative, post-fashion, and highly localised aesthetics of degrowth had emerged.

A similar aesthetic evolution might come to shape both our homes and how we furnish them. In contrast to the McMansions prevalent especially in the United States and Australia, housing in a degrowth society would come to reflect the 'small is beautiful' aesthetic (Schumacher, 1973). A small house minimises the materials and time needed for building, as well as shrinking the spatial footprint, thereby minimising pressure on urban sprawl. Most importantly, perhaps, a small house reduces the energy needed to heat and cool it, especially if well designed in terms of materials, orientation, window placement, and insulation. Less space inside also incentivises frugality and minimalism, as there would be little room for material clutter. There could be a widespread cultural embrace of William Morris's dictum: 'Have nothing in your houses that you do not know to be useful, or believe to be beautiful.'

Often furniture might be homemade (perhaps even the house itself); spaces would be dedicated to home production (e.g., arts and crafts) rather than merely consumption; renovations would rarely if ever be merely cosmetic; and the piano rather than the television might become the heart of the lounge. It should be clear, then, that nothing here suggests that homes in a degrowth society would be ugly, only that the sense of beauty and style would be very different, again reflecting a humble ethics of creative sufficiency rather than the slick uniformity of modernist chic. Scarcity begets creativity.

Continuing with basic material aspects of life, we could turn to food. One of the more perverse aspects of the industrial-consumerist aesthetic with respect to food is the bizarre expectation today for visually perfect, unblemished fruit and vegetables in supermarkets. Not only does this result in vast amounts of perfectly good food being thrown away or left to rot on account of it being aesthetically unacceptable to the contemporary consumer – highlighting the moral implications of aesthetics – but also the aesthetic demands for exterior perfection tend to impact negatively on the food's taste.

In a degrowth society, it would be considered utterly tasteless to throw away good food if even a single person went hungry, and cosmetic blemishes would not be considered flaws but merely the inevitable result of natural, organic production. Similarly, it would be considered bad taste to eat meat from factory farms and in general meat consumption would be greatly reduced or eliminated due to environmental, especially climate, impacts and the heightened sensibility with respect to animal welfare. Thus, the picture of an ordinary meal could begin to look very different from the highly processed, meat-heavy diets prevalent in the West and increasingly elsewhere, resulting in a new engagement with cooking styles, tastes, and recipes. Given that diets would probably be healthier on account of these changes, the very aesthetic of the human shape would likely transform in a degrowth society, with a reversal of the obesity epidemic. In terms of home production of food, the tidy but unproductive lawns and nature strips common today would be dug up and planted with fruit trees and vegetable gardens, transforming the 'look' of the suburbs and reminding people of the changing seasons. The productive garden or food forest might become new status symbols in the degrowth society.

This reference to status symbols provides a segue into a consideration of the aesthetics of transport and travel. In consumer societies today, the automobile sits alongside clothing and housing as an object of consumption that is often designed and desired in order to convey wealth, success, and status. But in a degrowth society, the Lamborghini or Porsche would be considered a bit tacky, extremely wasteful, destructive, and contrived – certainly not something considered beautiful or to be envied or admired. There would be far more interesting and important things to focus on, for, as Henry David Thoreau would say, 'Superfluous wealth can buy superfluities only' (Thoreau, 1983: 568).

A degrowth society would likely be a highly localised society, in which people's main forms of transport would be cycling or walking. Aside from the environmental benefits, this would be a positive aesthetic innovation because it would increase the human connection with nature, keep us fit, and expose us to the elements in ways that would enrich our sensuous experience of the world. 'Nature deficit disorder' would disappear (Louv, 2011). With good wet-weather gear and adequate lights, even cycling home at night in the rain would not concern members of a degrowth society, who would instead look forward to the soft exhilaration of an evening ride, as cyclists today already know. Rather than go on holiday in homogenous luxury resorts overseas, the practitioner of voluntary simplicity in a degrowth society would sooner take the family camping in the local national forest or beachside village, again transforming our aesthetic or sensuous experience of the world in ways that could enhance our lives, provided we had developed a 'taste' for simplicity, nature, and the outdoors. This could open the door to what is today called 'alternative hedonism' (Soper, 2008: 567) or 'frugal hedonism' (Raser-Rowland and Grubb, 2017).

It should be clear that this type of aesthetic revisioning could be extended to all domains of life, large and small. At the ecosystemic level, by creating a post-carbon way of life, members of a degrowth society might avoid experiencing in their day to day existence the worst climate impacts; the wind farm would be perceived as a vista of supreme beauty, enriching the landscape, not something aesthetically objectionable; at the household level, the impression of a 'good sized' family might tend toward one child; in matters of detail, not flushing urine in order to save water might raise aesthetic objections from within the consumer mindset but become the 'new normal' in a degrowth society; similarly, using a composting loo to create 'humanure' might offend the squeamish bourgeois sensibility and yet defecating in drinking-quality water might offend an alternative degrowth sensibility.

Furthermore, a degrowth society would likely produce vastly different urban and suburban landscapes, where advertising and cars were increasingly absent, de-polluting the visual, aural, and mental environments, allowing people to have thoughts of their own, liberated from the industrial-consumerist aesthetic. Even the arts themselves would doubtless evolve, with the corporate production of formulaic pop music, vapid television, and meaningless 'spectacles' of performance art losing hold on society and creating cultural space for a rebirth of authentic, local art, uninfluenced by the promise or seduction of the globalised market economy.

All this, of course, returns us to the question of 'story' – and its importance, both in terms of self and society. Mending one's clothes or growing one's own food within the Old Story might be considered by many to be a shameful requirement, symbolising an unsuccessful life of poverty. But within the New Stories being told by degrowth and related movements, such practices would be seen and experienced as a fulfilling exercise of creativity; an example of sensible frugality; and a small but meaningful act of ecological care that draws social admiration, and so forth. Each element in life looks very different depending on the underlying narrative that gives those elements context, and so Story can be understood as the meta-aesthetic issue that shapes the 'taste' we have for various aesthetic forms, values, and practices. A degrowth society therefore requires a story of self that transcends the consumerist story of self – requires a new aesthetics of existence, as I have argued, from which a 'taste' for degrowth aesthetics would emerge. Of course, the challenge here, to paraphrase the poet Samuel Coleridge, is to *create the taste by which we will be judged*.

How to do that is a question that leads nicely into our final subject of inquiry.

The role of art and the artist on the degrowth pathway

In these closing substantive sections I wish to reflect more directly, albeit briefly, on the role of art and the artist in the context of a degrowth movement. As noted from the outset, such an inquiry should be treated with some caution, for there is a risk that art merely signifies a pessimistic or even irresponsible retreat into the realm of the imagination at a time when the world needs committed and direct political and economic engagement, not merely beautiful pictures or creative stories. While a legitimate concern, I will maintain that art and aesthetic inventions in culture more broadly, far from merely representing an 'escape' from the real world, may be, in fact, necessary to provoke and drive the required societal transformations that the degrowth movement envisages. Here the work of Herbert Marcuse remains as relevant as ever. Marcuse held that 'art cannot change the world, but it can contribute to changing the consciousness and drives of the men and women who could change the world' (Marcuse, 1978: 32).

The foundational point – a negative one – lies in the realm of consciousness: currently there is little evidence within advanced, industrialised nations that people within the dominant culture think or feel that there is any need to transcend consumer capitalism. This is the reality of the situation and there is little use in denying it. The Marxian idea that the working classes would develop a revolutionary consciousness has not transpired and does not seem to be threatening to emerge. Indeed, within mainstream culture there does not seem to be any *felt need* to act for deep and urgent change, and without that cultural sensibility it is not clear how deep and deliberate change could ever eventuate. A radicalised consciousness seems to be a precondition for a successful degrowth movement, thus its absence should be a subject of critical concern.

I will offer two primary reasons (somewhat overlapping) for the broad cultural acceptance of the established reality of consumer capitalism. The first is related to the limits of human rationality; the second relates to the counter-revolutionary allure of affluence, which I argue limits the human imagination. Both of these issues reward an analysis through the lens of aesthetics and point to essential aesthetic responses.

The limits of rationality and the aesthetic implications

What is the nature of the human being? How do we make our decisions? The Enlightenment conception is, notoriously, a highly rationalistic one, assuming that our species shares a common nature by virtue of our rational faculties. The essential idea is that scientific progress and technological advancement are slowly lifting humankind out of the domain of historical ignorance and primitiveness, and by applying the scientific method we will continue to develop a broader range of knowledge and technologies with which we can better control and predict the workings of nature, thereby advancing human ends more effectively. The faith is that human beings are, by nature, rational – or capable of rational deliberation and reflection – and that increasingly we will shape how we act in the world according to the best scientific evidence we have at our disposal.

I am hardly the first to contend that human beings are far less rationalistic than this picture assumes (see the works of Nietzsche, Freud, Derrida, etc.). To take the ecological crisis as a case in point: arguably there was evidence enough in the 1970s or earlier to justify a fundamental transformation of our destructive modes of economic activity. If not historically, then certainly today. Climate change, deforestation, biodiversity loss, pollution, topsoil erosion, etc. etc. – at what point will there be 'enough' evidence to provoke change? I contend that perhaps it isn't 'better evidence' that is lacking.

Granted, there are vested interests at play which influence how democracies respond to the issues they face, but the fact is that culture broadly *knows* about the ecological crises that are unfolding yet people continue to vote for politicians that are essentially maintaining not subverting business-as-usual; little change seems to be coming from the personal or household domain either, even though marginalised counter-cultures are everywhere bubbling under the surface. Who, then, seriously thinks that yet another scientific report on the declining state of the environment is going to be the catalyst for transformative change?[3] It is important that evidence-based thinkers answer this question based on the evidence (Haidt, 2000: 814–34; Thibodeau and Boroditsky, 2011).

If humanity's social and environmental problems were just a result of an 'information deficit' or 'knowledge deficit', then perhaps a purely rationalistic approach to societal change would be justifiable. That is, the primary task would be simply to conduct the scientific research and publish the findings, and trust that human beings, as rational agents, will read and understand the evidence, change how they live, and vote for an appropriate political and economic response. It could be argued that this has been the defining faith of the environmental movement to date and perhaps points to its deepest failing.

I hasten to add that this is not in the slightest to denigrate the necessary and important work of environmental and social scientists. It is only to suggest that relying on 'the evidence' alone to do the hard work of societal transformation is naïve. Yes, it is critical to apply the scientific method rigorously to better understand the world; to pose and test hypotheses; to develop and apply appropriate technologies; to create cultures that think critically about the world; and to endeavour to be evidence-based decision makers at all levels of life. But it is just as important to recognise that it is not just *what* is communicated that matters, but also *how* it is communicated (Thibodeau and Boroditsky, 2011), and it could be that the environmental movement, and the degrowth movement in particular, has trusted too much in the provision of the evidence, neglecting the critical task of presenting the evidence in socially digestible forms. This

---

3 Disconcertingly, this critique seems to entail a meta-critique of itself: doesn't presenting a critique of the rationalistic conception of societal change, by relying on critique, still privilege a rationalistic conception of societal change?

is an aesthetic challenge because it highlights the importance of giving form to content. It follows, I contend, that the degrowth movement should be exploring ways of being more creative and engaging in its presentation of its own scientific and ethical foundations, in order to do those foundations justice. After all, it is not enough to be correct in one's diagnoses and prescriptions; one must also find a way to expand the audience beyond those already converted, and that points to a communications challenge.

On a related note, I would argue that the degrowth movement should be trying harder to appeal not merely to the head, but also – or especially – to the heart. Put otherwise, a persuasive case for degrowth must be made not just *intellectually* or *rationally* but also *affectively* or *emotionally* (Haidt, 2000; Amin and Thrift, 2013). No doubt there will be and are people who, when exposed to new evidence, reconsider their current thinking and adjust their worldview and actions to better reflect the facts. This is the rationalistic ideal and probably the self-image we all hold of ourselves. But most people would also probably accept that in many cases human beings fail to live up to this self-image, especially in this age increasingly called 'post-truth'. When confronted with evidence that challenges a cherished worldview (e.g., the growth paradigm), people can look away; assume the evidence is flawed; attack the authors rather than the evidence; blindly trust that markets or some new technology will solve the problem; go searching for evidence that validates (however dubiously) their current position or lifestyle; or undertake any number of other evasive strategies (see, for example, Hulme, 2008; Hamilton, 2010).

It is in these non-rational contexts where the artist arguably becomes a necessary agent of change, having the potential to provoke social change via different mechanisms of persuasion, making emotional, psychological, or even spiritual impacts on an audience at those times when science, logic, and argument have failed. The artist can conjure up new modes of perception, providing a feast of sensuous experience that anticipates, often explosively, a different way of living and being in the world, reshaping in some mysterious way not just the thoughts of individuals, but also their needs, feelings, hopes, and drives. As Marcuse pointed out long ago, art can communicate truths 'not communicable in any other language' (Marcuse, 1978: 10).

Beyond the work of art narrowly defined lies the potential of aesthetic interventions in culture and politics more broadly. The 'culture jamming' movement, for example, seeks to incite cultural and political change not through argument, evidence, and logic, but through provocative and jarring images that disrupt and unsettle our sense of normality, for the purpose of exposing the violence often hidden in our habits of thought and practice, and opening our minds to alternative ways of living and being. David Cox defines the practice of culture jamming as 'a vibrant counter-attack on the empire of signs' (Cox, 2010), and this counter-attack need not just be the production of images, but can include other acts or activity that function to disrupt people's ordinary experience and open new doorways of perception and understanding. Some refer to this as 'artivism' (see Jordan, 2016).

It is worth noting that the Canadian journal *Adbusters*, which is the global hub of the otherwise decentralised culture-jamming movement, was the institution that conceived of the Occupy Movement. This is the closest thing we have ever seen to a global uprising, but note that *Adbusters* did not create the discontent at the heart of the Occupy Movement. It merely gave imaginative form to content – created an ingenious 'branding' of that discontent – in ways that were able to mobilise and organise it for political and economic purposes. It fought the 'Society of the Spectacle' (Debord, 2000) on its own terms, and met with some success.[4] Culture-jamming is an oppositional aesthetic practice, I contend, that has yet to fulfil its potential.

The neo-pragmatist philosopher Richard Rorty has made a compelling case that art – the novel, in particular – is a far more effective means of provoking an expanded moral or ethical sensibility and reshaping social relations in the world than logic, science, or books of moral philosophy. Indeed, Rorty argues that paradigm shifts in human culture, science, and political economy rarely occur because a society has been rationally convinced, based on the evidence, of a new framework of understanding; instead, such revolutions are usually a result of creative interventions in the dominant story whereby many significant aspects of the old mode of understanding have been *redescribed* in new ways (Rorty, 1989). When a new generation grows up adopting and normalising these redescriptions, we find that the world has changed. This is perhaps why Percy Bysshe Shelley was prepared to declare that 'poets are the unacknowledged legislators of the world' (Shelley, 1890), suggesting that aesthetic revolutions often precede revolutions in political economy, sometimes in subtle ways. Perhaps the

---

4 Although failing in its greatest ambitions, I believe that, among other things, Occupy made it permissible again to talk about inequality in US politics, creating political space for the likes of Bernie Sanders, who was very close to being the Democratic candidate for the 2016 elections and some argue would have been a stronger opposition to Donald Trump.

ultimate lesson for the degrowth movement, then, is this: when all appeals to reason have failed, tell a new story (Burch, 2016).

The counter-revolutionary allure of affluence and the aesthetic implications

The reflections in the previous sub-section offered one take on why there is no broad cultural consciousness that seeks to transcend consumer capitalism. The argument was that the evidence in support has not been communicated sufficiently well and that the movements for change, including degrowth, have focused too much on an intellectual mode of persuasion, at the expense of emotional or affective modes of persuasion, which are arguably more effective in shaping or reshaping consciousness. It could even be the case that the very terminology of 'degrowth' is too confronting – is socially indigestible – in a civilisation where 'growth' is the defining metaphor of success. That is, degrowth invokes what it seeks to overcome, and therefore arguably reinforces the dominant metaphor. On the other hand, perhaps attacking the metaphorical foundations of civilisation is the only coherent means of achieving the types of changes required. I will not try to resolve that debate here, but note that it is far from being a merely cosmetic concern (Kallis, 2017; Thibodeau and Boroditsky, 2011).

In this closing sub-section I will briefly expand and extend this analysis by arguing that the promise (and to some extent the reality) of rising affluence in developed nations has functioned, in recent decades, to dissipate any large-scale social discontent or threat of social upheaval. The Grand Narrative of progress via economic growth has been widely internalised in consumer cultures, such that the working class – once the locus of the revolutionary sentiment – has found little need or desire to replace the 'economic base' of capitalism, even if little wealth has been trickling down. Even when ecological and social justice concerns are given attention by politicians or mass media, the social imaginary is so limited that resolutions to such problems are conceived of within the paradigm of growth and affluence, rarely if ever beyond it. People may shake their heads in concern when they hear of the latest warnings of climate scientists, or shake their heads in outrage when they hear that the richest eight men now own more than the poorest half of humanity, but when reflecting on what an alternative mode of existence might look like, the dominant culture shrugs its shoulders, unable to imagine anything other than green consumerism in a technocratic world. This is obviously a non-confronting 'response' to the crises we face because it does not question the growth paradigm, overpopulation, or consumerist conceptions of the good life.

The point I would like to make is that this inability to think beyond growth and consumerism is a troubling failure of imagination, and arguably one of the greatest obstacles in the way of transformative change in the direction of degrowth. It is all very well for scholars to present a range of devastating critiques of the existing order of neoliberal capitalism, but if people are unable to envision what a just, sustainable, and liberated world would actually look like, then the necessary task of mobilising communities for collective action will face insurmountable barriers. People will continue to seek meaning and advancement in the only ways the dominant culture permits: through consumption. Indeed, people may consume as a means of objecting to the dehumanising ways they have been treated under capitalism, not realising they are in fact being counter-productive.

Again, this is why art has a revolutionary or transformative potential and always threatens to perform a political function, albeit usually indirectly (Edelman, 1995). I would argue that one of the most important roles of the artist in society is not merely to make beautiful objects, images, stories, or songs, but to expand the conditions of possibility by breaking through the petrified social reality and unshackling the human imagination. Far from representing an 'escape' from reality, art and the artist can in fact expose the falseness and contingency of the established order, leaving the truth of alternative realities more accessible and perceivable. In the words of Marcuse:

> [T]he world formed by art is recognized as a reality which is suppressed and distorted in the given reality. This experience culminates in extreme situations (of love and death, guilt and failure, but also joy, happiness, and fulfilment) which explore the given reality in the name of a truth normally denied or even unheard. The inner logic of the work of art terminates in the emergence of another reason, another sensibility, which defy the rationality and sensibility incorporated in the dominant social institutions (Marcuse, 1978: 6–7).

With specific reference to degrowth, it would seem that the artist must help people see or feel more clearly, not merely the violence too often hidden in our cultural practices and economic and political institutions, but perhaps, most importantly, show that there are forms of flourishing and liberation that lie beyond consumer culture; forms of flourishing founded not upon affluence, growth, competition, and technology, but upon the visions and values of sufficiency, moderation, permaculture, community, cooperation, and self-governance. In short, an art for degrowth, first and foremost, must expand the collective imagination. The words of Gary Snyder speak to this approach with eloquent insight: 'It would be best to consider this an ongoing "revolution by consciousness" which will be won not by guns but by seizing the key images, myths, archetypes, eschatologies, and ecstasies so that life won't seem worth living unless one is on the transforming energy's side' (Snyder, 1970).

Such aesthetic interventions in the name or spirit of degrowth are beginning to emerge here and there (Jordan, 2016), but we are still waiting for the groundswell of creative activity that makes degrowth irresistible. We are still waiting for a new 'aesthetic education' (Schiller, 2004) that teaches us how to live in balance and harmony with nature; a new aesthetic education that re-enchants our lives in ways that make the status quo utterly unacceptable and the joys of defiant activism seem impossible to pass up. But now, at least, the challenge has been laid down – both to artists, in particular, and to artists-of-life more broadly.

We should, however, be cautiously pessimistic. If it turns out that neither art nor science can provoke the transformations needed to avoid the looming Apocalypse, then the role of the artist will only magnify further, as creative imaginations are tasked with interpreting and understanding civilisational descent in terms that give meaning to the inevitability of suffering; give sense to the pain we will feel (perhaps are already feeling) as global capitalism dies its inevitable death. At that stage, the therapeutic or even spiritual role of art will take precedence over its political function, a transition anticipated already by the Dark Mountain Movement (Dark Mountain, 2017). The very term Apocalypse has a dual meaning, not simply referring to the 'end of the world' but also signifying 'a great unveiling or disclosure' of knowledge. It will be the artist, not the scientist, I contend, who will contribute most to the human understanding of such a disclosure when, or if, it arrives. Rather than wallow helplessly as civilisation descends into barbarism, let us hope that our artists, novelists, poets, and filmmakers are up to the task of weaving narratives of human and ecological suffering into a meaningful web of solidarity and compassion – and thereby, perhaps, give birth to a new golden age of Grecian tragedy that offers both an education and cleansing of the emotions and passions in these turbulent times.

Perhaps that is the new dawn that lies beyond this dark hour.

References

Alexander, S. 2013. 'Voluntary Simplicity and the Social Reconstruction of Law: Degrowth from the Grassroots Up'. *Environmental Values* 22(2): 287–308.

Alexander, S. 2015a. *Sufficiency Economy: Enough, for Everyone, Forever.* Melbourne: Simplicity Institute.

Alexander, S. 2015b. *Prosperous Descent: Crisis as Opportunity in an Age of Limits.* Melbourne: Simplicity Institute.

Alexander, S. 2016. 'Policies for a Post-growth Economy'. (MSSI Issues Paper, No. 6, 2016).

Amin, A. and Thrift, N. 2013. *Arts of the Political: New Openings for the Left.* Durham: Duke University Press.

Anon. 2017. *Advertising Shits in Your Head.* London: Dog Section Press.

Benjamin, W. 2010 [1935]. *The Work of Art in an Age of Mechanical Reproduction.* New York: Prism Key Press.

Berger, P. and Luckman, T. 1966. *The Social Construction of Reality: A Treatise in the Sociology of Knowledge.* Garden City, NY: Doubleday.

Berry, T. 1999. *The Great Work: Our Way into the Future.* New York: Bell Tower.

Bleiker, R. 2009. *Aesthetics and World Politics.* London: Palgrave Macmillan.

Bourdieu, P. 1984. *Distinction: A Social Critique of the Judgement of Taste.* London: Routledge.

Burch, M. 2016. *Euterra Rising: The Last Utopia.* Winnipeg: Mark Burch.

Cox, D. 2010. *Sign Wars: The Culture Jammers Strike Back.* Melbourne: University of Melbourne Custom Book Centre.

D'Alisa, G., Demaria, F., and Kallis, G. 2014. *Degrowth: A Vocabulary for a New Era.* London: Routledge.

Dark Mountain. 2017. 'The Dark Mountain Project'. Available at: http://dark-mountain.net/ (accessed 20 May 2017).

Debord, G. 2000. *Society of the Spectacle.* Detroit: Black and Red.

Diderot, D. 1769. 'Regrets in Parting with My Old Dressing Gown'. Available at: https://www.marxists.org/reference/archive/diderot/1769/regrets.htm (accessed 20 May 2017).

Douglas, M. 2006 [1976]. 'Relative Poverty – Relative Communication', in T. Jackson (ed.). 2006. *The Earthscan Reader in Sustainable Consumption.* London: Earthscan.

Edelman, M. 1995. *From Art to Politics: How Artistic Creations Shape Political Consciousness.* Chicago: University of Chicago Press.

Foucault, M. 1977. *Power/Knowledge: Selected Interviews & Other Writings 1972–1977.* Edited by Colin Gordon. New York: Pantheon.

Foucault, M. 1990. *Michel Foucault: Politics, Philosophy, Culture – Interviews and Other Writings 1977–1984.* Edited by L. Kritzman. New York: Routledge.

Foucault, M. 2000. *Ethics: Essential Works Vol. I.* Edited by Paul Rabinow. London: Penguin.

Foucault, M. 2002. *The Order of Things.* London: Routledge.

Frank, R. 2009. *Luxury Fever: Why Money Fails to Satisfy in an Era of Excess.* New York: The Free Press.

Gibson-Graham, J.K. 2006. *A Post-capitalist Politics.* London: University of Minnesota Press.

Haidt, J. 2000. 'The Emotional Dog and its Rational Tail: A Social Intuitionist Approach to Moral Judgement'. *Psychological Review* 108: 814–34.

Hamilton, C. 2010. *Requiem for a Species: Why We Resist the Truth About Climate Change.* London: Earthscan.

Hamilton, C. and Denniss, R. 2005. *Affluenza: When Too Much is Never Enough*. Crows Nest, NSW: Allen & Unwin.

Hulme, M. 2008. *Why We Disagree About Climate Change: Understanding Controversy, Inaction, and Opportunity*. New York: Cambridge.

Jackson, T. 2009. *Prosperity without Growth: Economics for a Finite Planet*. London: Earthscan.

Jordan, J. 2016. 'Injecting Imagination into Degrowth', in *Degrowth in movements*. Available at: https://www.degrowth.de/en/dim/degrowth-in-movements/artivism/ (accessed 20 May 2017).

Kallis, G. 2017. 'You're Wrong Kate: Degrowth is a Compelling Word'. *Oxfam blogs*. Available at: http://oxfamblogs.org/fp2p/youre-wrong-kate-degrowth-is-a-compelling-word/ (accessed 20 May 2017).

Kasser, T. 2002. *The High Price of Materialism*. Cambridge, Mass: MIT Press.

Kompridis, N. 2014. *The Aesthetic Turn in Political Thought*. London: Bloomsbury.

Lane, R. 2000. *The Loss of Happiness in Market Democracies*. New Haven: Yale University Press.

Louv, R. 2011. *The Nature Principle: Human Restoration and the End of Nature-deficit Disorder*. New York: Algonquin Books.

Marcuse, H. 1978. *The Aesthetic Dimension: Toward a Critique of Marxist Aesthetics*. Boston: Beacon Press.

Marcuse, H. 2007. 'Society as a Work of Art', in D. Kellner (ed.). *Art and Liberation: Collected Essays of Herbert Marcuse (Volume Four)*. London: Routledge.

Miller, D. 2010. *Stuff*. Cambridge: Polity Press.

Monbiot, G. 2012. 'How "Sustainability" became "Sustained Growth"'. Available at: http://www.monbiot.com/2012/06/22/how-sustainability-became-sustained-growth/ (accessed 20 May 2017).

Nehamas, A. 1985. *Nietzsche: Life as Literature*. Cambridge: Harvard University Press.

Offer, A. 2006. *The Challenge of Affluence: Self-control and Well-being in the United States and Britain Since 1950*. New York: Oxford University Press.

Pickett, K. and Wilkinson, R. 2009. *The Spirit Level: Why Greater Equality Makes Societies Stronger*. London: Penguin.

Quinn, D. 2017. *Ishamel: A Novel*. New York: Bantam.

Ranciere, J. 2004. *The Politics of Aesthetics*. London: Continuum.

Ranciere, J. 2006. *Dis-agreement*. London: University of Minnesota Press.

Raser-Rowland, A. and Grubb, A. 2017. *The Art of Frugal Hedonism*. Hepburn Springs: Melliodora Publishing.

Rorty, R. 1989. *Contingency, Irony, and Solidarity*. New York: Cambridge University Press.

Roszak, T. 1972. *Where the Wasteland Ends: Politics and Transcendence in Postindustrial society*. New York: Doubleday Press.

Sartre, J-P. 1964. *Situations*. Paris: Gallimard.

Schiller, F. 2004. *On the Aesthetic Education of Man*. New York: Dover.

Schor, J. 1998. *The Overspent American: Upscaling, Downshifting, and the New Consumer*. New York: Basic Books.

Schumacher, E. 1973. *Small is Beautiful: Economics as if People Mattered*. London: Blond and Briggs.

Shelley, P.B. 1890. *A Defense of Poetry*. Boston: Ginn and Co.

Soper, K. 2008. 'Alternative Hedonism, Cultural Theory and the Role of Aesthetic Revisioning'. *Cultural Studies* 22(5): 567.

Snyder, G. 1970. 'Four Changes'. *Modern American Poetry*. Available at: http://www.english.illinois.edu/maps/poets/s_z/snyder/snyderessays.htm (accessed 20 May 2017).

Thibodeau, P. and Boroditsky, L. 2011. 'Metaphors We Think With: The role of Metaphor in Reasoning'. *PLOS ONE* 6(2): e16782.

Thoreau, H. 1983. *The Portable Thoreau*. Edited by Carl Bode. London: Penguin.

Veblen, T. 2009[1899]. *Theory of the Leisure Class*. Oxford: Oxford University Press.